Kaouther Karoui
Theorizing Justice in Contemporary Arabo-Islamic Philosophy

Philosophy

Kaouther Karoui, born in 1987, works as a research assistant within the cluster of excellence "Religion and Politics" at Westfälische Wilhelms-Universität Münster (WWU). Prior to this, she worked for the DFG-funded research project "Diversity, Power, and Justice: Transcultural Perspective" at Universität Kassel and at Universität Koblenz-Landau from 2016 to 2019. From 2019 to 2022 she worked as a research assistant at the Philosophy Department of WWU Münster.

Kaouther Karoui

Theorizing Justice
in Contemporary Arabo-Islamic Philosophy

A Transcultural Approach with Fatima Mernissi
and Mohammed Arkoun

This work has been accepted as a PhD in philosophy at the university of Münster.

Bibliographic information published by the Deutsche Nationalbibliothek
The Deutsche Nationalbibliothek lists this publication in the Deutsche Nationalbibliografie; detailed bibliographic data are available in the Internet at http://dnb.dnb.de

© 2024 transcript Verlag, Bielefeld

All rights reserved. No part of this book may be reprinted or reproduced or utilized in any form or by any electronic, mechanical, or other means, now known or hereafter invented, including photocopying and recording, or in any information storage or retrieval system, without permission in writing from the publisher.

Cover layout: Kordula Röckenhaus, Bielefeld
Printed by: Majuskel Medienproduktion GmbH, Wetzlar
https://doi.org/10.14361/9783839465516
Print-ISBN: 978-3-8376-6551-2
PDF-ISBN: 978-3-8394-6551-6
ISSN of series: 2702-900X
eISSN of series: 2702-9018

Printed on permanent acid-free text paper.

Contents

Acknowledgements 7

1. Introduction 9
1.1 The concept of justice in Arabo-Islamic and Western philosophy 12
1.2 The significance of postcolonial theory for the Maghrebian context 24

2. Background and methods in the thought of Fatima Mernissi 29
2.1 The concept of secular humanism: The necessity
of emancipating Islamic thought
from religious and nationalist conceptions 45
2.2 The concept of justice in the modern era: The entanglement
of descriptive and normative claims of justice theories 56
2.3 The rereading of ninth-century early Arabo-Islamic thought:
The theorization of notions of justice
through Mernissi's transcultural and humanistic approaches 77
2.4 Transdisciplinary approaches to establish gender justice
within the framework of Islamic feminism 96
2.5 The relevance of Mernissi's feminist thought
for a transcultural approach to feminism 138
2.6 Conclusion on the thought of Fatima Mernissi 151

3. Background and methods in the thought of Mohammed Arkoun 155
3.1 Mohammed Arkoun's rereading of the Islamic thought of Miskawayh
(d. 1030): A multifaceted concept of justice 165
3.2 The method of applied Islamology: A transcultural
and transdisciplinary key for the renewal of Islamic studies 189
3.3 Toward an emancipation from hegemonic constructions:
The critique of orthodoxy, Arab nationalism, and Euro-modernism 222
3.4 The concept of emerging reason:
A key for a democratic and cosmopolitan project 241
3.5 Conclusion on the thought of Mohammed Arkoun 254

4. Epilogue: Theorizing justice in contemporary Arabo-Islamic philosophy 261
4.1 The common approach to theorizing justice by Fatima Mernissi
and Mohammed Arkoun 262
4.2 On the relevance of a cosmopolitan theory of justice
based on a transcultural approach 266

Bibliography 275

Acknowledgements

First of all, I would like to express my deep gratitude to my supervisor, Prof. Dr. Franziska Dübgen. This book would not be what it is today without her assistance. In addition to her intellectual support, I would like to thank her for her moral support, for her encouragement and for believing in my intellectual capabilities despite all the challenges.

I would like to thank Prof. Dr. Ina Kerner for helping to shape and commenting on the first draft of this book during my stay in Koblenz. I am also indebted to my second supervisor, Prof. Dr. Syrinx von Hees, for her comments. I would like to thank the German Research Foundation for financing the project "Diversität, Macht und Gerechtigkeit: Transkulturelle Perspektiven" and for supporting the publication of my PhD thesis. In addition, I would like to thank the Cluster of Excellence "Religion and Politics" for financially supporting this publication.

I also thank Ms. Elizabeth Crawford for proofreading this book.

I would like to thank all my colleagues who have helped and supported me: my colleagues at the university of Kassel (April 2016–December 2017), the university of Koblenz (January 2018–September 2019), and the university of Münster (October 2019–May 2023). I would like to express my gratitude specifically to Victor Nweke and Iwona Kocjan, wherever you are now, for your help and support as well as for simply being nice friends and colleagues.

I certainly could not have completed this book without the support of my family in Tunisia. I would therefore like to thank Laila, my mother, for encouraging me to continue my academic career, despite all the difficulties we went through and overcame together. Thank you Maher, Mima, Hedia for being my family. Najat and Nabila rest in peace.

1. Introduction

Cosmopolitanism is based on the idea that people from a wide variety of cultures, belief systems and morals can interact with each other, have a right to justice and respect, and should be able to cooperate equally in the fields of culture, science, economics, and politics.[1] It is also important for people in a cosmopolitan world to be aware of the various forms of injustice that exist around the world. Hence, a central aim of this book is to demonstrate the necessity of developing a cosmopolitan theory of justice that integrates transcultural perspectives in order to promote the humanistic ideals of mutual respect and cooperation, solidarity, equality, and freedom.

First, in order to develop a cosmopolitan theory of justice, as the name implies, we need to outline the meaning of justice. It is crucial today to rethink justice from the perspective of the Global South in order to include all human beings in the debate on justice. For justice was and is an ethos that promotes moral equality and the democratization of institutions, supports human rights, and advances emancipation. In recent years, there have been protests in several Arab Muslim countries. In Tunisia, Egypt, Libya, and Syria, people mobilized in the streets to demand "an end to authoritarian rule and government corruption, as well as greater equality."[2] Thus, social and political movements have influenced and transformed the socio-political system in North Africa. Islamic-oriented political governments have emerged that promise justice and use Islam in the political agenda as a means to bring it about. However, these Islamic political regimes will not last longer than previous dictatorial regimes, if they fail to deliver justice as promised and to put an end to corruption.

The pursuit of justice must therefore be examined with regard to the religious, cultural, and socio-political contexts in order to develop a philosophical approach that promotes more context-sensitive notions of political democracy, freedom, emancipation of thought vis-à-vis orthodoxy and fundamentalism, human rights and justice in the face of discrimination and racism.

Second, it is important to conceptualize a cosmopolitan theory of justice from a transcultural perspective that facilitates dialogue between the Global South and the

---

1   Kleingeld and Brown 2006.
2   Esposito, John L., Tamara Sonn and John O. Voll 2016: 21.

Global North. The social and political developments in the Global South have implications for the transnational socio-political context. One of these effects is the increasing migration, which leads to the encounter of people with different cultural, ethical, and religious backgrounds. This requires that everyone be open to the recognition of others. Based on the idea of making the globe a place of peaceful coexistence, we need to cultivate the attitudes of openness, diversity, and pluralism rather than indifference, egocentrism and selfishness.

Another reason for a transcultural approach is that the debate about justice has been dominated by European and Anglo-Saxon philosophy in recent decades. The dominance in the justice debate by the Western tradition of thought leads to a narrow focus of what justice consists of. This discourse considers itself as superior and seeks to instruct the Global South on what justice is and what it requires, while the readers in the Global South are relegated to the position as listeners and are supposed to apply what has been theorized in the Global North.

Thus, the construction of the debate in Western tradition leads to a hegemonic conception of justice. Conversely, justice from a transcultural approach, means avoiding hierarchies within the debate between the Global North and the Global South. It demands engaging in a more cooperative and reciprocal debate about justice.

In this context, theorizing justice from a transcultural approach challenges the idea of universality of provincially developed justice theory for the entire globe. The justice discourse as developed in the Western discourse cannot be universal, because it does not take into account the notions of justice prevalent in the Global South, which are informed by different cultural and socio-political experiences: These include the absence of women's rights in many countries, social injustices political dictatorships, a strong religious tradition, patriarchy, and a poor educational system, as well as the economic exploitation by the Global North. In this sense, a transcultural concept of justice allows for a transnational understanding of the different types of injustices that occur in the Global South and the actions needed to achieve a debate on justice by considering socio-cultural differences.

In addition, gender justice has largely been theorized with regards to the experiences and living-conditions within the Global North, disregarding transcultural perspectives. In this regard, a transcultural approach helps to avoid the stereotypes, misinterpretations, and misrepresentations that have been developed about other thoughts and cultural traditions. It challenges the stereotype that women from the Global South cannot claim their rights and accept their socially inferior position to men. A transcultural dialogue on gender justice is essential for the enforcement of women's rights by bringing women from the Global South and the Global North closer together to assert their rights. To put it simply, a one-sided perspective on justice may lead to the construction of a hegemonic discourse of justice that continues to allow the Global North to dominate the Global South. This hegemonic justice debate, as it has developed, is being challenged in the current debates on justice. Hence, recent research adresses the concept of justice from a transcultural approach that incorporates intellectual debates from both the Global South and the Global North.³

Consequently, a transcultural dialogue on justice is needed, directed against identitarian trends, such as the emerging nationalism, and religious fundamentalism, all of which lead to a deadlock.⁴ Additionally, the debate on justice based on a transcultural approach rail against "a domestic, statist or nationalist notion of justice."⁵ Justice in the domestic sphere is conceived of as independent from the transnational concerns of humanity and their struggle against the different forms of injustice and discrimination of our present time, such as climate change, poverty, violence, sexism, neo-colonialism, racism, Islamophobia, and antisemitism (to cite only a few). Domestic justice is rather concerned with national institutions of one country, one nation, and one society. Essentially, theorizing on domestic justice, which is only focused on national issues, can generate a philosophy of greed, selfishness, and materialism, as every nation is concerned with its economic and political privileges over other nations. This runs the risk of strengthening power relations between humans, nations, and cultures rather than challenging these transnational injustices, and leads to the Global North always having the primacy to theorize about justice, to influence and represent the ideals of human rights, democracy, and civilization, and to dominate the entire world.⁶

What one needs in this present time of emerging pandemic hate is to rethink our normative perceptions and thought. One needs to expound more on diversity, tolerance, and humanism. Theorizing on justice based on a transcultural approach between the Global North and the Global South requires a strategy of philosophical and cultural dialogue in order to overcome our centrism manifest in our thought – and to experience, explore, and understand other, different approaches of thought.

This research explores such a transcultural approach to justice in order to bring together different philosophical traditions and provide insight into alternative notions of justice. It connects different schools of thought and different disciplines. The research foregrounds and examines different approaches to justice in the context of Arabo-Islamic thought. It aims to promote a humanistic ethos for the transnational sphere of human interaction. This is to fulfill the cosmopolitan promise of peaceful cooperation and solidarity as well as tolerance and justice between humans around the globe.

---

3   Dhouib and Dübgen 2016; Dhouib (ed.) 2016; Dübgen 2020.
4   Dübgen 2020: 893.
5   Flikschuh 2013.
6   Forst 2013: 43.

1.1 The concept of justice in Arabo-Islamic and Western philosophy

Justice is an indisputably important concept. The history of different traditions of philosophy shows that philosophers in diverse cultures have always reflected on justice. As part of the tradition of Western philosophy, Greek antiquity provided a significant concept of justice both in the abstract, namely the world of subjectivity (man and his soul), as well as in the concrete, namely the world of intersubjectivity (human interactions).

According to Plato, justice is the quality of the soul, and based on the purification of the soul, through which humans put aside their irrational desires. Plato argued that justice results from the harmonization of the three faculties of the soul. Since reason supervises the rational faculty, it produces virtuous acts. Thus, when the faculty of reason directs the soul to knowledge, it will act correctly and virtuously. For Plato, justice is a master virtue because when the soul performs justice, it is realised in the realm of human interaction.[7] Aristotle considered the social nature of human beings in his work, *Politics*, where he stated that any humans who are unable to live in a society or who have no need of the society because they are self-sufficient "must be either a beast or a god."[8] In this sense, Aristotle gave a notion of justice based on human social interaction. His notion of distributive and corrective justice aims at restoring a fair relationship between individuals.[9]

In Western contemporary scholarship, justice has been aptly described as the "first virtue of social institutions,"[10] and "the highest political-moral virtue by which legal, political, and social conditions as a whole – the basic structure of society – can be measured."[11] John Rawls played a significant role in how the debate on justice has developed in the liberal context.[12] Rawls's liberal theory of justice intends to have a universal outreach.[13] However, Thomas Pogge, among many other scholars, has raised the question of whether the principles of liberal justice set forth by Rawls can be applied on a global scale. Pogge refers to Rawls's analysis of economic justice as an example to illustrate how economic justice in Rawls's thought still shapes and reshapes a national economic order.[14]

One could argue that Pogge's critique of Rawls's liberal theory of justice opens up the possibility of philosophizing about justice on a global scale. This is an important

---

7   Plato 2009.
8   Aristotle 1946: 4.
9   Aristotle 1975.
10 Rawls 1971–1999: 3.
11 Forst 2002: xi.
12 Forst 2013: 42.
13 Flikschuh 2013: 41.
14 Pogge (ed.) 2001; Pogge 2001:16.

shift in the history of justice theory. Since that time, philosophers and political theorists have tried to develop a more transnational notion of justice. They have become interested in discovering different injustices that occurred in different societies and cultures, and question whether Western theories of justice are applicable on a global scale. As a result, interesting studies have emerged in academia in recent years, as I mentioned earlier, dealing with a more transcultural notion of justice, involving philosophers and political theorists from the Global North (Germany) and the Global South (North Africa). Their ideas are closely related to the themes of identity, historical justice, and cultural belonging. The complex structure of their ideas suggests an openness to other philosophies about justice and calls for an examination of justice within a transcultural approach.

Writing from the perspective of Arabo-Islamic philosophy, the concept of justice in Islamic thought is based on the notion of divine justice and in relation to the purification of the soul. Divine justice is the foundation for acquiring happiness and achieving human justice. The spiritual meaning of Islam demands to promote justice. In Islam, a purification of the soul is highly recommended as the following Qur'anic verses state: "The one who purifies his soul succeeds and the one who corrupts it fails."[15] Islamic thought does not limit the notion of justice solely to divine justice. Due to their openness to Greek philosophy, early Muslim philosophers have reflected on other forms of justice related to the political, economic, and social spheres.

In this sense, early Muslim philosophers integrated Islamic religious ethics and Greek philosophy to develop their concept of justice. This reflects their humanistic inclination and shows an early dialogue developed between ancient Greek (Western) philosophy and early Islamic thought. Such a dialogue points to an intellectual atmosphere of transcultural thinking between these two different schools of thought that met and enriched one another.

The integration of Greek thought in Islamic ethics contradicts Western Eurocentric discourse, which assumes that Islamic thought can have no connection to philosophy. In contrast to this assertion, early Muslim scholars show that Islamic thought never was a stranger to philosophical and rational thought, and that philosophical tools are fundamental to the interpretation of Islamic discourse.

In the history of Arabo-Islamic philosophical scholarship, two works are particularly worthy of attention on the concept of justice: one by Majid Khadduri (d. 2007), *The Islamic Conception of Justice* (1984) and the other by Majid Fakhry (d. 2021), *Ethical Theories in Islam* (1991). Both authors offer a systematic and analytical study of the concept of justice. Khadduri classified the concept of justice into various realms, such as legal, divine, and human justice. The concept of justice has been explained in the light of the various schools of thought and philosophers who have contributed

---

15   The Qur'ān, Chapter 91, The Sun, Verses 10–11.

to its theory. Fakhry's work focuses on the ethics of Islam in relation to the spiritual, religious, philosophical, and theological realms. According to Fakhry, Islamic ethics is based primarily on the concept of justice. Khadduri and Fakhry emphasize the transculturality between Greek and Islamic thoughts. Additionally, they discuss the impact of Persian and Indian literatures on the development of Islamic philosophy and science. It is interesting to note that both studies refer to controversial schools of thought that contributed to the development of Islamic thought: the Mu'tazila school of theology, the Jabarites school of theology, and the Islamic doctrine of Voluntarism (see chapter 2.3; chapter 3.1). Their work cultivates the diversity of thought that characterizes Islamic thought.

In the context of postcolonial thought, North African intellectuals from the Maghreb have determined how justice must be thought of from a transcultural approach, specifically considering the postcolonial debate on human rights and individual liberation that has taken place in most Muslim societies, developing their thinking from the perspective of a critical reading of traditional Arabo-Islamic discourse.

Thus, this research presents the concept of justice by two contemporary thinkers from North Africa. It focuses on the works of the Moroccan feminist thinker Fatima Mernissi (1940–2015) and the Algerian philosopher Mohammed Arkoun (1928–2010). Mernissi is one of the most prominent feminist thinkers in Arabo-Islamic philosophy, while Arkoun is one of the most prominent modern philosophers in contemporary Arabo-Islamic thought.[16]

This research explores their thoughts on the concept of justice in the postcolonial Maghreb. Mernissi and Arkoun share an interest in defending the concept of justice through socio-political, religious, historical, and feminist approaches. Mernissi's and Arkoun's contemporary conception of justice is based on a renewed interpretation of religious discourse in order to theorize justice. For example, Mernissi invokes the interpretation of the Islamic heritage to launch a concept of gender justice. Arkoun's contemporary intellectual project, known for rethinking Islamic thought, implicitly seeks a social and egalitarian conception of justice based on a humanistic ethos. The approach I take in this study is to carve out their notion of justice based on their reinterpretations of Islamic discourse.

My aim is to point out Mernissi's and Arkoun's contributions to a cosmopolitan theory of justice based on a transcultural approach. Mernissi introduces Sufi concepts, which fit within the context of cosmopolitan thought and transcultural dialogue between cultures. The Sufi tradition is alluded to in Mernissi's novel *Scheherazade Goes West: Different Cultures, Different Harems* (2001). For example, the Sufi practice of travel (*safar*) allows one to explore other cultures and transcend the boundaries of cultural and traditional constraints (see chapter 2.5).

---

16   Dübgen 2020 : 896.

Humanism was the subject of Arkoun's dissertation (1970), which deals with Arab humanism from the 3rd/9th to the 4th/10th centuries and considers Miskawayh (d. 1030) as one of the most important humanist intellectuals in early Islamic thought. Based on Miskawayh's combination of Islamic ethics and the Greek thought of Plato and Aristotle to create his own concept of justice. Arkoun emphasizes a transcultural humanism that promotes dialogue between different cultures and different schools of thought and is guided by a rational method of thinking, which also plays a role in Miskawayh's early thought (see chapter 3.1). In this way, Arkoun speaks of a "humanistic critique" and a "non-isolated humanism"[17] as Edward Said suggested in the introduction of *Orientalism* (2003).

Next to his reconsideration of philosophical humanism in particular and the concept of justice in general in the work of Miskawayh, Arkoun also explores the transdisciplinary, comparative, and rational approaches established in the thought of the Muslim theologian and philosopher Al-Amri (d. 992). Arkoun thereby urges contemporary Muslims to reconcile with the rational Islamic heritage, to "rethink" and "liberate" Islamic traditional thought from orthodox ideas.[18] Aside from this, Arkoun points to the humanist heritage of Islamic thought, in order to correct Western misconceptions and simplifications of the rich Islamic intellectual heritage.[19]

As a feminist thinker, Mernissi presents the normative thought concerning justice, power, and law in early Islamic thought by examining the concept of legal justice in the work of the Muslim jurist Malik Ibn Anas (d. 795), divine justice in the work of the Sufi al-Hallaj (d. 922); and rational justice according to the Mu'tazila, a rationalist school of Islamic theology (8th–10th century). In this way, Mernissi intends to challenge what is actually a reductive interpretation of Islamic law (Shari'a). Specifically, patriarchal constructions deprive women in Islam of their modern political, legal, and social rights. Mernissi uses the rational heritage of early Islamic thought to reshape contemporary discourse on gender justice and democratic values.

Mernissi and Arkoun revive the early humanist thought of Islamic philosophy, while also incorporating Western Enlightenment thought and the notion of modernity. In her early works that characterize her secular thought, Mernissi turns to modernist narratives on women's rights, the United Nations Organization (UN) and the Universal Declaration of Human Rights (UDHR), to advocate political justice based on the concept of representative democracy; a combination of legal, social, and epistemic justice that she relates to this modern and secular framework with the goal of achieving women's rights. In her last work, which establishes her Islamic feminist thought, Mernissi states that secular thought fails to demand and assert women's rights in the field of religious discourse, which is still dominated by men.

---

17   Said 2003: xvii.
18   Karoui 2021: 322.
19   Karoui 2020: 915.

Mernissi's approach to Islamic feminism is progressive and liberal, aiming at an innovative interpretation of Islamic discourse in order to achieve gender equality within Islam. She does this by applying different methods of thinking that combine hermeneutical, historical, and linguistic analyses of some verses of the Qur'anic and some Hadith (sayings of the Prophet Muhammad).

In addition, Mernissi criticizes Orientalist discourses that develop a stereotypical image of Muslim women. Mernissi's contribution to both approaches, secular and Islamic feminism, makes her thought an innovation in the field of feminism as she adopts a transdisciplinary approach that considers several fields of study – secular modernity and religion – in order to realize the emancipation of Muslim women.

In the same line of thought, Arkoun advances an ambivalent understanding of the concepts of modernity and secularism. On the one hand, Arkoun defends modern and secular thought and considers it the basis for promoting freedom of thought, freedom of religious beliefs, and democratic ideas in most Muslim societies. On the other hand, he disapproves of a notion of modernity based on capitalist systems and a notion of secularism based on a total rejection of religion. Arkoun considers religion an essential socio-cultural element of societies that cannot simply be discarded. Rather, religion as a field of study must be examined and critically rethought in order to disentangle it from fundamentalism.

By combining secular, modern Western thought and Islamic thought, Mernissi and Arkoun call for human rights and transcultural justice. They both propose a rational reinterpretation of Islamic discourse and an opening of Islamic intellectual discourse to dialogue with other cultural traditions. In this sense, their contemporary critical thought challenges *religious fundamentalism*, *French neo-colonialism*, *Arab nationalism*, *Eurocentrism*, and *Orientalism*:

1. In the works of Mernissi and Arkoun, both *Eurocentrism* and *Orientalism* appear as an object of critique. Both discourses construct Western representations of other cultures. On the one hand, Eurocentrism undervalues and excludes other cultures' achievements in both cultural and philosophical terms. Western achievements are considered the most significant accomplishments according to Eurocentrism.[20] As outlined above, Mernissi's and Arkoun's rereading of early Islamic thought undermines Eurocentric superiority, its closed mentality, and its judgment of other cultures. Both scholars intend to remind Eurocentric scholars that a rational concept of justice has been central to Arabo-Islamic philosophy. Orientalism, on the other hand, pertains to the study of the language, the history, and the culture of the 'Orient' and Muslim societies by Western scholars .[21] Mernissi and Arkoun seek to extricate Islamic culture from Orientalist clichés.

---

20   Amin 2009.
21   Said 1994a; Ahmad 1994.

As a feminist thinker, Mernissi criticizes the subservient image that some Orientalists portraits of women in Muslim culture, such as "veiled" woman, "naked" woman in a bath, "servant" woman. According to a stereotypical Orientalist's representation, women in most Arab countries are excluded from the public sphere of human interaction. They exist in the enclosed sphere of the harem, e.g. the house of the husband, the "sultans," or the male relative. It is through her deconstructivist approach that Mernissi challenges the Orientalist stereotypical representations and Western clichés about women in Islam. For Mernissi, the harem is not only the sphere of seduction and sexual desire, where women have to serve sex and food.

As a child born in a traditional harem in Fez in the 1940s, Mernissi's autobiographical work *Dreams of Trespass: Tales of a Harem Girlhood* (1994), which has been translated into several languages, posits the harem also as a locus of women's emancipation. Despite her mother being illiterate and living under her husband's domination, she instructed her daughter (Mernissi) to be independent. She sent her to school, and let her interact with her male cousins. During that time of conflict between the colonial powers, it was difficult for women in Morocco to encourage their daughters to take the first steps towards emancipation. Embracing feminist thinking within Arabo-Islamic tradition meant removing oneself from local traditional culture and social restrictions, as well as from Western clichés. As a feminist thinker, Mernissi engages in the deconstruction of both local and Western discourses.

In the same line of thought, Arkoun criticizes the traditional method of some Orientalist historians who define Islam as a body of constructed beliefs. Indeed, their representation of Islam is based on the Qur'an and the Tradition (sayings and actions of the prophet) without submitting these corpuses to critical analysis. Moreover, some Orientalist historians are not familiar with connecting the field of Islamic studies with Islamic philosophy. Arkoun has a broad education in diverse disciplines, having studied Arabic literature, history, law, and philosophy. This transdisciplinary background helps him to integrate several disciplines into the field of Islamic studies in order to realize his project of rethinking Islam.

The Oxford Encyclopedia of the Islamic World published an article (2009) that critically reviews Orientalism and its relationship with Islamic studies. Arkoun is presented in this article as one of the few thinkers belonging to contemporary Arabo-Islamic philosophy who has attempted to enunciate an overall vision of Islamic studies and its agenda. Arkoun discusses the implicit and explicit tenets of Islamic thought. The work of Arkoun is considered as an audacious project in expressing certain methodological approaches that he considers to be inseparable from epistemological theories in order to integrate Islam and Muslim cultures into a global critical theory of knowledge and values. Arkoun's critique of the Orientalist method is therefore essential in dislocating Islamic thought from a monolithic approach of thinking. His critical thought is also important for opening up the field of Islamic studies to various approaches and fields of research, such as comparative studies, linguistic studies, and poststructuralist approaches.

2. *Arab Nationalism* argues that all Arabs are one nation, characterized by a strong sense of shared identity, by their language, culture, history, ethnicity, geography, and politics that unites all Arabs.[22] This poses the following questions: Can it generally and validly be argued that Arabs share the same identity, culture, and ethnicity? What about the 'minority' groups with diverse ethnicity, religion and culture who are living in the Arab world? Are they part of this shared culture?

Mernissi asserts that Arab nationalism is ambivalent. In several passages of her book *Islam and Democracy Fear of the Modern World* (2002), Mernissi applies a historical approach to emphasize the great heritage of Arabo-Islamic civilization. For her, Arabs have made great strides in a variety of fields. She highlights the knowledge and scientific developments that characterized the earlier period of the Abbasid empire (750–1517). During that time, Muslim Arabs, Arab Jews, and Arab Christians worked together for the advancement of philosophy and science. Greek philosophy played a prominent role in their advancement of knowledge. 'Arab' intellectuals "transport,"[23] interpret and integrate Islamic and Western ideas. By translating Greek thinking of antiquity, they opened themselves up to other traditions of thought, and bridged the gap between different religious and philosophical perspectives. During that time of the Arab empire, there was a sense of diversity and a willingness to embrace other philosophical traditions. Mernissi evokes the complex heterogeneity within Islamic civilization to challenge the contemporary notion of Arab nationalism that conflates politics with religious faith and focuses on the notion of Islamic statehood.

Arkoun also criticizes Arab nationalism, which claims that all Arabs have the same tradition, share the same religion, culture, language, and ethnicity. He demands the reformation of Islamic thought on both the socio-religious and political level.

On the socio-religious level, he defends the rights of ethnic and religious minority groups such as the Berber community in North Africa, which was severely discriminated against during the colonial and post-colonial era in Algeria. (I examine this in chapter 3.3). In his writing, Arkoun further considers the diversity and plurality within Muslim communities, such as Shi'i, Sunni, and Khariji Islam. Arkoun's work in many ways draws to the linguistic and cultural diversity of the Maghreb. He argues throughout his career for a pluralist Islamology, i.e., a comparative, interdisciplinary study of Islam, and against definitive interpretations, which he considers to be surrogates for political authoritarianism.[24] On the political level, Arkoun

---

22   Dawisha 2016.
23   Mas 2021: 338.
24   Dobie 2020 : 254.

calls for reconsidering the conditions for the establishment of fundamentalist organizations that have contributed to the development of extremist Islamic thought. In particular, he refers obliquely to the Algerian civil war between the Algerian government and various Islamist rebel groups from December 1991 to February 2002. In this way, "Arkoun sought the reform of Islamic thought along secular and philosophical lines as the means to solve the enduring violence in Algeria and in other parts of the Islamic world." [25]

3. The critique of *French neo-colonialism* is presented in the thought of Mernissi and Arkoun through the demystification of the promises of modernization and civilization that the French protectorate in Morocco (1912–1956) and the French colonization of Algeria (1830–1962) came to promote.

Mernissi critiques the colonial system that reinforces the discrimination between native Moroccan and French women. The myth that "France is a modernizing force is mere colonial fantasy," [26] claimed Mernissi. Modernity, which defends education as a means of emancipating women from tradition, was not supported by colonial France in Morocco. The aim of Mernissi is to demystify the narrative that the emancipation of native women was the outcome of the modernization project undertaken by the French protectorate. She makes it clear, , that the colonial administration did not support the education of native women, even if they belonged to the urban upper classes of Morocco like herself. [27]

Arkoun presents a controversial argument against French colonialism, and especially against the ideas of Enlightenment and modernity, which are criticized within the framework of postcolonial theory. Arkoun belongs to the first generation of colonized subjects to be educated in French colonial schools. This French education paved the way to exploring the effects of colonialism on the division between Berber and Arab Maghrebian. [28] In fact, "when Europeans colonized North Africa,

---

25   Mas 2021 : 339.
26   Mernissi 2003: 7.
27   Rhouni 2010: 48–49.
28   Muslim Arab conquerors used the term 'Berber' to refer to the people who lived in what they called 'the West' (al-maghrib). Before the Muslim-Arab conquest, the inhabitants of northwest Africa belonged to the same landmass and formed a unique entity. After World War II, the response to the ravages of nationalism and racism did not extend to the category of Berber. The national independence of Morocco and Algeria, but not Berberia, located Berber identity both on the infranational level and as counter-nationalism. The point is not to distinguish between Arabs and Berbers in the Maghreb and to question the origin of its inhabitants, because the Maghreb is part of the Mediterranean and consists of a variety of inhabitants with different religious, cultural and ethnic backgrounds that contribute to its civilizational wealth. Rather, the aim is to shed light on the social discrimination of the Berbers during European colonization and after independence, caused by the rise of Arab nationalism and Islamization. See: Ramzi Rouighi, (2019 b): *Inventing the Berbers History and Ideology in the Maghrib*: University of Pennsylvania Press. Introduction (pp.1-12).

they imposed their preoccupation with race onto its diverse peoples and deep past".[29] Arkoun, by contrast, developed an interest in Arabic literature and eventually became a leading scholar of Islam.[30] "It was the renowned French Orientalist Louis Massignon that encouraged Arkoun to pursue his postgraduate studies in La Sorbonne".[31] Hence, one might argue that this turn to the Arab language was a form of resistance in order to denounce the powerful culture of the Francophonie. The French government sought to disrupt the pluralism of Algeria as a country with Arab and Berber languages. However, after independence in 1962, Arkoun left Algeria to teach in France and never returned to Algeria. During his intellectual career, he did not publish any of his work in Arabic, although it is a language that he admired. During his lifetime, Arkoun's thought was more welcome in Tunisia and Morocco. Indeed, like many other Algerian intellectuals of his generation, Arkoun criticized the increasingly military authority in post-independence Algeria. Moreover, in the 1980s, he came into conflict with another group of critics – the Islamists. In the 1990s, as Algeria traversed a period of violent conflict between the state and Islamist militias, Arkoun grew closer to Morocco. He was ultimately buried in Casablanca with full honors of the Moroccan state.[32]

During his intellectual exile in France, Arkoun was the defender of a progressive and liberal Islam. His thought was enthusiastically received in French academia, as his thinking was situated in the tradition of the Enlightenment, of which the French were proud. Despite his questioning of Western reason, labeling it hegemonic reason,[33] Arkoun found in the Western tradition of 'intellectual modernity' (inspired by the post-modern thought of Jürgen Habermas) and the notion of 'post-secularity,' groundbreaking intellectual ideas for the emancipation of Islamic thought from religious dogmatism and political authority. Arkoun mainly defended a notion of multicultural-humanistic secularity against the French tradition of laicism. His aim was to defend the notion of religious diversity in France, always remembering French civilization in terms of its promise of tolerance and human rights. During his stay in France, Arkoun was a vehement critic of the Islamophobia and discrimination, which is faced by the Muslim community in France up until this day.

Arkoun's biography is significant in locating his thought in an ambivalent position towards modern thought. Despite his critique of French colonialism, he had respect for 'les Père Blancs.' These missionaries, according to colonial thought, came to modernize and civilize the native people of Algeria (and the Maghreb region). Despite his criticism of the methods used by some Orientalist historians to study

---

29 Rouighi 2019 a.
30 Dobie 2020: 255.
31 Hashas 2015.
32 Dobie 2020: 255.
33 Arkoun 1995.

Islamic thought, Arkoun was aware that Orientalist thinkers helped to convey the richness of Islamic culture to Western readers. It has been argued that Arkoun would not have become one of the most important pioneers of Islamic philosophy without the help of the Orientalist Louis Massignon.[34]

4. As a last inquiry into Arkoun's and Mernissi's critical thought in this introduction, I provide an overview of their critique of *religious fundamentalism* in Islam. From a postcolonial angle, I would like to point out that Islamism is embedded in global political powers relations. Neo-imperialist political and economic structures create injustices on the transnational level. The result of this has been an expansion of corruption and the establishment of authoritarian regimes in most Arab countries, which in turn affects the economic and social wellbeing of many Muslim citizens. Thus, Islamic fundamentalism is partly the result of the socio-economic injustice that most Muslim are experiencing in their countries.

Furthermore, Islamic fundamentalism is the result of racial and religious discrimination which affects most Muslims. In this sense, the socio-political movements that emerged in 2011 in most Arab-Muslim countries were a hope for national and transnational socio-political and economic justice and a quest for human rights and democratic prospects. However, these emancipatory aspirations were not achieved. As a result, the world witnessed emigration movements and the displacement of several ethnic and religious minorities in Arab countries. Meanwhile, terrorism increased on a transnational level with new fundamentalist organizations such as the Islamic State (*Daesh*). The world also witnessed a wave of terrorist attacks (Tunisia: Sousse and Bardo 2015, Paris 2015, Berlin 2016, Nice 2016). Indeed, terrorism not only affects the Global South, but has also taken root in the Global North and has become a transnational phenomenon.

In addition to the political and socio-economic developments that have already been mentioned as sources as well as consequences of fundamentalism, one could also argue that the rise of Islamic fundamentalism has its foundations in the Islamic discourse itself, which is constrained by the traditional method of conformity (*taqlid*) advocated by some Muslim jurists and Muslim intellectuals.

In contrast to the fundamentalist agenda, Mernissi and Arkoun aim at a rational interpretation of Islamic scriptures. They hence deserve to be studied in order to challenge the phenomenon of fundamentalism, because both thinkers call for *ijtihad*, the free and open intellectual method of the struggle of thought, against the *jihad*, the terrorist struggle. Their approach to Islam echoes the pioneering thinking of the early Muslim rationalist and humanist thinkers.

Hence, this book examines some philosophical approaches in the interest of revolting against Islamic fundamentalism and defending the concept of justice from a transcultural perspective, in search of political freedom and gender equality. As

---

34 Günther 2019.

a feminist scholar, Mernissi criticizes the system of patriarchy in Moroccan society. Mernissi's defense of gender justice is relevant not only to Morocco and the Maghreb countries in general, but it is further significant to all countries, where there is a reliance on a patriarchal interpretation of Islamic law (*Shari'a*) as source of legislation. According to a patriarchal interpretation of Islamic law, man is constructed as superior to woman, since God privileges men over women. This patriarchal system of thought is the basis of discriminatory discourse against woman in most Islamic countries. It cannot foster a society, in which women and men are treated equally in the political, social, and legal realms. In what follows, I focus on the legal realm of personal status law (family law) as an important locus of gender discrimination.

As an example, I shall focus on the debate on women's rights that occurred in postcolonial and post-revolutionary Tunisia. In recent years, women in Tunisia have been increasingly affected by violence and social discrimination. The emergence of Islamic parties restricted various rights Tunisian women have gained under the state's gender policy. The first Code of Personal Status (CPS), or family law, in Maghreb originated in Tunisia in 1956. After independence, Tunisia elaborated the CPS, which is a set of progressive Tunisian laws aimed at gender equality. Under the regime of Bourguiba (the first president of Tunisia, in office from 1957–1987), several reforms were carried out. The most successful reform has been the emancipation of Tunisian women. The CPS banned polygamy, granted equal rights in divorce, and established a minimum age for marriage and mutual consent. It granted women the right to work, move, open bank accounts, and start businesses. Bourguiba insisted on upholding women's rights through social institutions .[35]

Tunisian women's rights have been improved through policies by the state , (although so-called state feminism has also been criticized).[36] However, little attention has been paid to the remnants of decades of state feminist regimes since the second half of the 20th century. After Tunisia's independence, for example, the nationalist modern regime introduced certain rights (only) for certain women. The policy of state feminism was followed without significantly changing gender relations and processes of racialization. The mostly male government officials followed a state nationalist agenda presented as feminist and sought to stabilize state power rather than implement intersectional feminism. The agenda of state feminism in post-independent Tunisia is primarily aimed at projecting a modern image of Tunisian women that shows mainly unveiled women participating in social life; this is done by oppressing veiled women and women with religious backgrounds. In addition, state feminism failed to address discrimination against Tunisian women of color and women from rural and subaltern classes. In addition, state feminism in Tunisia

---

35   Charrad 1997; 2007; Grami 2018; Moghadam 2018.
36   Badran 2009; Hobuß, Khiari-Loch and Maataoui, (eds.) 2019.

did not engage in a national debate on the commitment to human rights, the establishment of social justice, and the realization of democratic ideals based primarily on the right to pluralism. It has, however, focused on the symbolic politics of giving a voice to modernized, urban women.

Thus, Mernissi's thoughts on gender justice are crucial for today's Muslim societies to protest against various forms of discrimination and fundamentalism as well as against patriarchal structures. As a feminist thinker, she considers women as equal to men. Mernissi defends full participation of women in the public sphere of human interaction. She urges women from all classes and levels of education to become free and emancipated subjects, and to participate equally with men in the improvement of their countries. Mernissi revolts against the discourse "of sending women back to the kitchen,"[37] precisely what the patriarchal ideologies would like to revive. Mernissi uses multiple disciplinary approaches to deconstruct patriarchal discourse, such as using the approach of Islamic feminism to provide a new feminist interpretation of the Islamic heritage and limit the male hegemony in Islamic discourse. Mernissi is one of the founders of this critical approach (see chapter 2.4).

In his critique of fundamentalism, Arkoun challenges the orthodox discourse. He opposes the monolithic interpretation of Islamic scriptures as introduced in the Sunni and Shi'i traditions. Orthodoxy merely repeats the linear chronological account of the historical spread of Islam and reaffirms the theological-legal articulation framework of Islam as a belief system justified by what are considered to be God's words. It is an established and dominant discourse, excluding other opinions and perceptions about Islam. Moreover, orthodoxy considers different opinions as heretical. It represents reason as a threat to a fixed religious dogma, established a priori by orthodoxy (see chapter 3.3). Consequently, orthodoxy influences the development of fundamentalist thought because orthodoxy prevents Islamic discourse from being critically analyzed.

Hence, Arkoun calls for an emancipation of Islamic thought from orthodox or fundamentalist belief systems. To this end, he analyzes various socio-historical events and conceptual notions involved in the establishment of orthodoxy. Arkoun deconstructs the so-called 'logocentric enclosure' of Islamic reason and discourse, pointing to the ruptures in Islamic intellectual history dating back to the fourth/tenth or fifth/eleventh centuries. For him, Islamic thought experiences its decadence and the establishment of orthodoxy starting from these centuries. In this regard, 'logocentrism' corresponds to the creation of the closed realm of the thinkable – the closure of the *ijtihad* in Islam – by some orthodox Muslim religious scholars. Importantly, Arkoun's concept of the Islamic fact/event describes how Islam was transformed from a spiritual and religious faith into an ideological and

---

37   Mernissi 2002: 165.

political tool used by orthodox scholars to legitimize and maintain power (see chapter 3.3).

Thus, Arkoun's critique of orthodoxy in our time serves to "open the gate of *ijtihad*"[38], a concept in Islamic legal theory that denotes the creation of norms based on independent reasoning. It represents the effort of making one's own judgments. The purpose of *ijtihad*, defined as independent and rational effort to understand and interpret the religious Islamic sources, is to seek the optimal legislation within the Islamic legacy that promotes the common good (*maslaha*) of Muslims in our contemporary times. Arkoun considers philosophical rational methods as the first basis for the liberation of Islamic reason from orthodoxy. The *ijtihad* that Arkoun promotes is inspired modern and postmodern philosophical theories. In this sense, philosophy offers an analytical ability, the capacity for reflective thinking, and openness to critique in order to overcome the constraints of any cognitive system.[39]

Mernissi's and Arkoun's critical thinking is important in exposing the various forms of discrimination and fundamentalism in our times. In addition, their intellectual oeuvre paves the way for situating postcolonial theory in the Maghrebian context and for developing a concept of justice in Arabo-Islamic philosophy that starts from the deconstruction of the hegemony involved in the formation of Islamic discourse.

1.2 The significance of postcolonial theory for the Maghrebian context

Most Maghrebian universities rarely engage with postcolonial thought, in contrast to Western universities, which are becoming increasingly interested in postcolonial studies. One might argue that Maghrebian academia should engage in the debate on postcolonial thought, since the Maghrebian countries have been colonized. In addition, postcolonial studies can be related to Maghrebian thought, since poststructuralist methods form the basis of postcolonial theory and poststructuralist thought has been also used by Maghrebian scholars to critique hegemonic, orthodox, and patriarchal Islamic discourses. Furthermore, postcolonial thought also serves to critique the neo-colonialism and the nationalism which, as noted above, are challenged in the works of Mernissi and Arkoun. There are several realms in most Maghrebian societies that continue to be influenced and controlled by neo-colonialism, even though the Maghrebian countries are formally independent. As a case in point, French remains the language of culture in most Maghrebian countries, the language of the intellectuals and the bourgeoisie. Their administrative bureaucracy still reflects the system of French colonialism. Because of France's neo-

---

38 Hallaq : 1984.
39 Günther 2019.

colonial influences, most academics in the Maghreb are interested in the Western tradition of thought.

Nevertheless, advocating against neo-colonial rules that continue to influence the current global does not mean that in this research I follow an approach of *decolonial thinking* in the sense of the Latin American thinker Mignolo (2011).[40] For decolonial thought demands a strict departure from Western modernity and enlightenment in order to fully attain independence from a neo-colonial and dominant system of thought. As outlined above, this research rather aims at building an intellectual bridge between Western and Maghrebian thought. Thus, a transcultural approach is required and should be based on a mutual intellectual dialogue between both traditions.

In this sense, the concept of double critique from the Moroccan scholar Abdelkebir Khatibi (d. 2009) is crucial in locating a postcolonial approach of thinking. Double critique challenges and disrupts all sorts of binary definitions of Self and Other, East and West. As its name implies, double critique analyses together philosophical lines of influence that come both from the East and the West. Through his works, Khatibi tries to liberate the field of humanities and social sciences in most Maghreb academia from colonial boundaries. In addition, his critique addressed a notion of "the unity of Arab" that participates in the marginalization of "(Berber, Coptic, Kurdish ... and the feminine)."[41] His ethical aim is to promote the thought of difference by which the Maghrebian identities could recognize themselves. Khatibi considers the critique of the West by the West, by which I mean the poststructuralist critique of Western modernity, as a starting point for his intellectual project.

In his book *Plural Maghreb* (2019) (French original: *Maghreb Pluriel* (1983)), Khatibi seeks to communicate with and integrate 'the thought of difference' of Maurice Blanchot and Jacques Derrida in order to apply their critical methods to Maghrebian thought; to deconstruct it from the rigidity of nationalism and traditionalism.[42] He claims that one could take from them not only their style of thinking, but also their strategy and mainly their 'war machine',[43] in order to place them at the disposition of the Maghrebian thought for an effective decolonization.[44] The decolonization of Maghrebian philosophy as suggested by Khatibi, in this sense, calls for plurality and

---

40 See: Mignolo, Walter. D. (2011): *The Darker Side of Western Modernity: Global Futures, Decolonial Options*. Durham, London: Duke University Press.
41 Khatibi 2019: 19.
42 Khatibi 2019: 19.
43 Khatibi borrows this concept from the French poststructuralist thinker Gilles Deleuze. In its basic meaning, the concept serves to name and theorize artistic and political dissidence and creativity. See: Deleuze, Gilles and Felix Guattari (1986): *Nomadology: The War Machine (Semiotext(e) / Foreign Agents)*, transl. by Brian Massumi. Los Angeles, USA: Semiotext(e).
44 Khatibi 2019: 20 .

diversity. Khatibi demands that Maghrebian thinking should open up to the experience of difference and move beyond its ideal of (Arab) unity. In this research, I argue that Mernissi and Arkoun participate in developing postcolonial thought in the Maghrebian context in line with Khatibi.

Hence, I argue that it is possible to situate the thought of Mernissi and Arkoun as 'postcolonial theory.' According to Achille Mbembe (2008), postcolonial thought was essentially developed based on the work of poststructuralist thinkers. In addition, it has been influenced by the critique of Orientalist discourse developed by Edward Said.[45] Therefore I emphasize that postcolonial theory emerged around the time when Edward Said published his book entitled *Orientalism* in 1978. Mbembe declares:

> It was Edward Said, a stateless Palestinian, who laid the first foundations for what was gradually to become "postcolonial theory," in the sense this time of an alternative form of knowledge about modernity and a separate academic discipline.[46]

Thus, this implies that the poststructuralist critique of the constraints of knowledge, the Marxist critique of capitalism, and the critique of the discourse of the 'intellectual hegemony' of grand narratives are important critical theories that underpin postcolonial thought.[47] For example, Edward Said invokes Michel Foucault, one of the most influential exponents of poststructuralist thought, to critique Orientalist discourse. Said argues that Orientalist discourse embodies a discourse of power that represents the colonial agenda by representing a demeaning, negative, and stereotypical image of 'the Orient.' Another figure of poststructuralist thought, as just outlined, is Jacques Derrida, whose concept of deconstruction dislocates and transforms the normativity that continues to influence the discourses of neo-colonialism, nationalism, and religious orthodoxy. Derrida's concept of deconstruction will be briefly discussed in order to situate Mernissi's and Arkoun's contemporary intellectual project within the field of postcolonial studies, particularly because Arkoun is heavily influenced by Foucault and Derrida's critical methods.

Indeed, the work of Derrida describes and transforms the ways in which one thinks about life and death, culture, philosophy, literature, and politics. Derrida's work is specific because it transforms terminologies by providing other possible meanings. Derrida's thought is transformative. The method of deconstruction challenges the dominant interpretations of texts. This means that deconstruction destabilizes traditional approaches of thinking. It is about shaking up, dislocating,

---

45 Mbembe 2008: 5–6.
46 Mbembe 2008: 5–6.
47 Williams and Chrisman 1994: 2-5-13.

and transforming the verbal, conceptual, psychological, textual, esthetic, historical, ethical, social, political, and religious landscape. Its concern is to disrupt ad de-sediment, and its desire to transform discourses, actions, and institutions. Such a transformation n has to do with language *and* with "more than language."[48]

In the same line of thought, Mernissi returns to the origin, myth, and foundations of Islamic discourse in order to deconstruct it from patriarchal constructions. In her book entitled *The Veil and the Male Elite: A Feminist Interpretation of Women's Rights in Islam* (1991), in which she develops her approach of Islamic feminism, Mernissi breaks with both misogynist and fundamentalist traditions related to Islam. Mernissi applies historical and linguistic approaches to religious texts, examining the socio-historical contexts of some Qur'anic verses and some Hadith (sayings of the Prophet Muhammad). She concludes that the patriarchal, misogynistic, and fundamentalist assessments of the holy scriptures that represent Islam today are the result of a political abuse of religion. As a result, most Muslim scholars use these backward fundamentalist and patriarchal assessments in order to deny women their rights in Islam. In this way, Mernissi attempts to offer new plausible interpretations of Islamic discourse in order to rid it of misogyny and fundamentalism.

Arkoun draws, as mentioned already, on poststructuralist approaches such as Foucault's concepts of 'discourse' and 'épistème,' *The Order of Things* (2001), (French original: *Les Mots et Les Choses* (1966)); *The Archaeology of Knowledge* (1982), (French original: *L'Archéologie du Savoir*, (1969)). In addition, he is interested in Derrida's 'deconstruction,' *Of Grammatology* (2016) (French original: *De la Grammatologie*, (1967)) and Deleuze's concept of 'difference,' *Difference and Repetition* (1994) (French original: *Différence et Répétition*, (1968)). His writings are also inspired by the applied anthropology of the ethnographer Roger Bastide, an expert on African-Brazilian religions.[49] These various poststructuralist approaches and different disciplines contributed to the establishment of 'Applied Islamology' Applied Islamology aims to reform and rethink Islamic discourse, to open the horizon of Islamic discourse to plural meanings and to transfer the religious texts from the framework of historical studies to the field a critical analysis. Applied Islamology is a rigorous criticism and moves beyond any ideological agenda.[50] It expresses Arkoun's cosmopolitan ethos, which is manifest also in his other philosophical concepts, such as the concepts of 'exhaustive tradition' and 'emerging reason.'

Arkoun's concept of exhaustive tradition brings to light the hidden, repressed, and marginalized cultural traditions of Islam as opposed to the dominance of one religious tradition and theological school. The concept of emerging reason is in line

---

48 Royle 2003: 21.
49 Kersten 2019: 37.
50 Kersten 2019: 37–38-39.

with the idea of transcultural dialogue between different cultures and systems of thought. In addition, emerging reason calls for interreligious dialogue, which is crucial today to resolve religious and political conflicts and to create an atmosphere of tolerance and religious plurality for peaceful human coexistence.

This study, therefore, presents the works of Fatima Mernissi and Mohammed Arkoun by examining their different concepts and approaches as forms of initiating a transcultural debate on justice from an Arabo-Islamic perspective. The study has two main parts: The first is devoted to Mernissi's works and consists of five chapters that analyze her valuable feminist project which combines secular and Islamic feminism. The second part focuses on Arkoun's oeuvre and is divided into four chapters. Each chapter offers an examination of his various concepts, from his rethinking of early Arabo-Islamic philosophy to his implementation of his own various critical concepts. The research ends with an epilogue that recapitulates Mernissi's and Arkoun's contributions to theorizing justice in Arabo-Islamic thought. The epilogue also calls for a cosmopolitan debate on justice, based on a transcultural approach that helps to liberate the debate on justice from Western hegemony.

2. Background and methods in the thought of Fatima Mernissi

There are a number of approaches to academic philosophy. Not all of them become important fields of study. Feminist philosophy is one of those approaches that has not had a central place in academic philosophy. In response to the current radical changes in academia, however, the question of which approaches are of most interest may be shifting. Indeed feminist philosophy has been gradually gaining acceptance. For this reason, it is one of the focal points in this study. Feminist philosophy plays an important role in transforming traditional philosophical problems and concepts in the mainstream of academic philosophical debate. It critically analyzes the ways in which traditional philosophy reflects and perpetuates bias against women. Feminist philosophy defends philosophical concepts and theories that assume women have the same rights as men.[1]

In the first part of this study, I introduce the concept of gender justice as a feminist philosophical concept. The aim is to shed light on a different aspect of feminism than the discourses that have developed in the context of Western feminism tend to focus on. Feminist and gender discourses are culturally and socially constructed and rooted in different contexts. They vary from place to place, time to time, language to language, and ideology to ideology. Therefore it is fair to say that today, debates about gender equality, about women's political, legal, and socioeconomic rights, must be transcultural. In this sense, the task is to rethink the issue of women's rights in the Global South and the Global North by considering the various social contexts such as class, race, ethnicity, and faith. Accordingly, this research addresses academic debates that develop and expand theories of feminism that are confined within sociocultural boundaries, norms, and stereotypes. It explores an alternative discourse on feminism in Islam by analyzing the contemporary thought project of Fatima Mernissi, whom I have selected because she is a Maghrebian thinker. Before I begin to situate the structure of this research, I give an overview of Mernissi's thought. The ideas I briefly introduce here are helpful in situating her thinking on gender justice and postcolonial theory. The subsequent chapters will analyze her

---

1   Hall and Ásta 2021.

concepts and theories in more detail in terms of their intellectual development and change.

Fatima Mernissi (1940–2015) received her PhD in sociology from Brandeis American University in 1974 with a dissertation entitled *The Impact of Modernization on Male-Female Dynamics in a Muslim Society: Morocco*. Her dissertation was published in a book entitled *Beyond the Veil: Male-Female Dynamics in Modern Muslim Society* (1975). This book became one of the classic texts in cultural studies in the United States and was reprinted several times and translated into French under the title *Sexe, idéologie, Islam*. In 1975, Mernissi returned to Morocco and became a professor of sociology at the University Mohammed V in Rabat. Through her academic writings and her numerous activities in the civil and educational fields, Mernissi became known as a defender of women's rights in Morocco and in Muslim countries. One civil society project that was close to Mernissi was Synergie Civique, a project that ran from 1997 to 2004. Mernissi arranged with selected NGO leaders for an exchange of ideas between their intellectual members (musicians, intellectuals, artists, poets, and writers). The members of two of these NGOs helped Mernissi with her research and formed a bridge between the people of rural and urban Morocco. She helped the NGOs and groups write and publish collaborative books. She also organized writing workshops in Tunis that led to the publication of the anthology *Tunisiennes en devenir*.[2] Moha Ennaji (2020) argues that Mernissi's activism in civil society plays a prominent role in her shift from a secular to an Islamic feminist approach to defending women's rights. He writes:

> Her contact with women from different socio-economic and cultural backgrounds helped her get into grips with the reality of Moroccan women on the ground. This action had a strong impact on the evolution of her writings and perspective on women and society and on the pragmatic approach and practical ways leading to their empowerment.[3]

This biography shows that Mernissi is a theoretical scholar who has drafted academic books to convey her thoughts on feminism. At the same time, she is also an empirical researcher interested in practical work. Mernissi bridges the theoretical and empirical realms of research. Her shift from secular to Islamic theories of feminism is the result of her diverse intellectual education. Her goal was to empower Moroccan women and Muslim women in general. Thanks to her meticulous work on the cultural history of Arabo-Islamic heritage and the presentation of an alternative image of women, Mernissi is considered one of the most prominent figures in

---

2   Talahite and Ennaifar 2017: 68.
3   Ennaji 2020: 6.

feminist thought not only in the Maghreb but also in the wider Muslim world and beyond.[4]

During the Arab revolution of 2011, there was a demand for justice. The issue of women's rights continues to be a subject of debate between modern and traditional adherents. In most Muslim countries, women are eager to defend their rights and resist the assumptions of traditionalists. Today, it is imperative to revisit the issue of feminism in Islam in order to challenge the fundamentalist interpretation of Islamic heritage. For this reason, Mernissi's thought is helpful because she rethinks the Islamic heritage to address women's rights. Moreover, Mernissi's thought actively engages with contemporary debates about freedom, individualism, and freedom of thought, which are current issues in most Arabo-Islamic societies.

An article dedicated to Mernissi asks the question, "Le concept de 'Réflexivité' est-il connoté culturellement ? (Qu'en est-il en particulier dans le monde 'arabo-musulman' ?" (2004). In this article, Wolfs and el-Boudamoussi not only target Mernissi as a feminist thinker, but they also portray her as a reformist Muslim thinker. They attempt to reveal the perspective from which most Muslim culture prescribes the meaning of autonomy, freedom of thought, and freedom of expression, defined as modern secular ideas. Hence they refer to Mernissi's book *Islam and Democracy Fear of the Modern World* (1992- 2002) and confirm that the concepts of autonomy, freedom of thought, and freedom of expression reactivate a feeling of fear. According to Mernissi, this fear is based on three historical aspects of the history of Islam : first, the pre-Islamic era, in which these terms are etymologically linked to the notions of egoism and arrogance, which were considered the personal character of humanity before the spread of Islam. Mernissi would argue that the fear of autonomy and freedom of thought and expression in the collective memory of most Muslims is activated because these precepts are reminiscent of chaos and violence, and of the polytheism that prevailed in Mecca in the pre-Islamic era. Second, in the collective memory of most Muslims, the concepts of autonomy, freedom of thought, and freedom of expression recall the history of Islam after the death of the Prophet Muhammad, when the Kharijite sect attempted to establish political justice by killing the despotic leader. In other words, autonomy, freedom of thought, and freedom of expression are associated by most Muslims with the violence and disorder of the Kharijites. Third, most of Muslim culture teaches that one should feel a sense of social solidarity with and loyalty to the ummah, the community of Muslims. In this sense, autonomy and freedom of thought and expression could endanger the unity of the Muslim community.[5]

Following a similar line of thought, Mernissi revives Al-Hallaj's (d. 922) philosophical stance by defending the concept of self-direction (freedom). Wolf and

---

4   Talahite and Ennaifar 2017: 68.
5   Wolfs and El-Boudamoussi 2004 : 23.

Boudamoussi argue that the fear that most Muslims have of the concepts of autonomy, freedom of thought, and freedom of expression cannot obscure the fact that there were Muslim thinkers in the 9th century who fought to assert these ideas. Al-Hallaj was among the Muslim intellectuals who defied political authorities because the ideas of autonomy, freedom, and freedom of thought that he defended threatened the leader's despotic regime.[6]

That article shows two contradictory understandings of the concept of autonomy, freedom, and freedom of thought. On the one hand, these terms remind most Muslims of the disorder and tyranny in the pre-Islamic period and after the death of the Prophet Muhammad. They remember the chaos, the assassination, and they see the contradiction with the idea of the community of Islam. For these reasons, fear of these ideas usually prevails in most Muslim culture. On the other hand, these ideas were the intellectual argument of some earlier Muslim intellectuals who were against the political despotism of their time. In modern times, autonomy, freedom, and freedom of thought are demanded by several Muslim individuals who seek their rights and protest against their dictator. Thus, one could conclude that Mernissi gives these terms the connotation of fear to describe the psychological feeling that most Muslims feel towards modern secular ideas. This fear is related to Islam's past socio-cultural history. Mernissi addresses Muslim individuals to correct the thinking that leads to this fear. She wants to state that in our modern times, autonomy, freedom, and freedom of thought are the basic rights of human emancipation.

It is instructive to look into this article dedicated to Mernissi, because it presents Mernissi as a revolutionary feminist thinker. She revisits the concepts of autonomy, freedom, and freedom of thought held by many Muslim citizens today expressing their opposition to their dictatorial rulers, especially during the Arab Revolution of 2011. This makes Mernissi's thoughts a challenge for our times. In what follows, the aim is to understand according to which philosophical feminist theories Mernissi advocates gender justice. The question must be asked: What are the fundamental problems of modern Muslim societies that Mernissi intends to examine as part of her revival of the Islamic heritage?

Situating Mernissi's feminist thought: Her contributions both to secular and Islamic feminism

In Mernissi's work, I am particularly interested in her defense of women's rights, which she conceptualizes in two ways: Mernissi defends Muslim women's rights within both the secular feminist approach and the Islamic feminist approach. In what follows, I briefly present her contribution to these feminist theories.

---

6   Wolfs and El-Boudamoussi 2004: 23.

On the one hand, one could argue that Mernissi is interested in the approach of secular feminism because it improves democracy and grants civil rights to women. I refer here to secular feminism as elaborated by Western feminists and by which Mernissi herself was influenced at the beginning of her intellectual career. Secular feminism emerged in the mid-1850s with a liberal stance that sought women's rights to political activism, to full citizenship including universal suffrage, to self-determination, and to higher education.[7]

Mernissi defends the same rights as secular feminists in her early writings. An example of these rights would include a woman's right to participate in political decision-making, her family law rights, and her social and economic rights. To realize these rights, Mernissi sees the secular modern regime as guaranteeing the rights of all women, including Muslim women, as it renounces the patriarchal interpretation of Islamic tradition by creating a modern legal system. In other words, the secular regime is based on the separation of the state and religion, thus, preventing the interference of religion and its use in the public affairs of the state. According to Mernissi, Muslim women should be able to demand political, social and legal justice without being restricted by fundamentalist religious groups.

To shed light on the connection between secular insight and the demand for political, legal, and social rights within feminist discourse in the Arabo-Islamic world, it should be noted that the first feminist movement in the Arab world emerged in Egypt in the early twentieth century.[8] The goal of Muslim secular feminists was initially to open up public space for women as citizens so that they could freely participate in political and social life. In other words, Muslim secular feminists believed that equality between men and women should be realized primarily in the form of political and social equality. This meant that women, as members of society, should participate in public life on an equal footing with men. Secondly, they believed that it should be realized in the religious sphere, that is, in the private sphere of family law, as far as legislation in Islam is concerned. In fact, the Muslim secular feminists called for legislative and legal reform where, for example, the woman can legally go through the divorce process while the man should fulfill his family responsibilities. However, Muslim secular feminists have failed to call for a complete reform of Islamic legislation. As a result, Islamic legislation based on Shari'a law continues to be constrained today by religious interpretations that conform to patriarchal ideas. This is the case even though the understanding of Shari'a law varies across Muslim countries, depending on their cultural and social background.[9]

One could argue that Muslim feminists have recognized that a comprehensive demand for women's rights in countries that apply Shari'a law requires the devel-

---

7   Hawthorne 2007: 539.
8   Badran 2009: 243.
9   Badran 2010 a: 27–28.

opment of Shari'a-based legislation. It is true that secular feminism has fulfilled its historical role in most Muslim countries by paving the way for women's entry into politics and society.[10] However, since the Arab revolution, we have seen the rise of a phenomenon called political Islam. Muslim women are still affected by the domination of men over religious discourse.

On the other hand, Mernissi's shift from secular to Islamic feminism indicates her recognition that women cannot exercise their rights without the improvement of Islamic laws. Therefore, Mernissi's defense of Muslim women's rights focuses on Islamic feminist theory. Indeed, she attempts to reveal the egalitarian rights of women within the Islamic heritage. Mernissi does this within the framework of interpreting the established texts of Islam. In doing so, she attempts to expose the falsity of many Hadith (sayings of the Prophet Muhammad) and to point out the patriarchal and misogynistic interpretation of some verses. In this context, I would like to define the theory of Islamic feminism in order to better situate Mernissi's thinking within this feminist theory.

"Islamic feminism has been a widely discussed phenomenon since the emergence of the term in 1990s".[11] Islamic feminist discourse is, thus, represented by (Arab) Muslim feminist scholars who challenge the patriarchal readings of the Qur'an and the Hadith. They point out that it is not the texts themselves, but their interpretation which has enabled the patriarchal traditions in Islamic culture. Indeed, Islamic feminists argue that the Qur'an contains principles of gender equality and broader issues of gender justice.[12] Islamic feminism seeks to discover a hidden meaning of Islam that promotes social justice and equality. For example, Islamic feminists re-read Islamic sources to show that the inequalities enshrined in Islamic jurisprudence (*fiqh*) do not represent Islamic heritage or an irredeemably backward social system, but are constructions of patriarchal interpretations.[13]

The movement of Islamic feminism involved not only Muslim women; feminists of different beliefs have been able to contribute to this movement.[14] For example, women who have converted to Islam, women who are not Muslims, and even secular (Muslim) women could contribute to Islamic feminism.[15]

As a working method, Islamic feminist scholars apply hermeneutic interpretation (*tafsir*) of the Qur'an and Hadith, as this methodology is vouched for in the tradition of Islamic legacy. In other words, they rely on the time-tested right of intellectual struggle (*ijtihad*), alongside the use of linguistic, historical, sociological, and

---

10   Mir-Hosseini 2006: 644.
11   Kynsilehto 9: 2008.
12   Kynsilehto 9: 2008.
13   Mir Hosseini 2006: 642.
14   Cooke 1999: 95.
15   Badran 2009: 247.

anthropological tools,[16] to reveal the egalitarian message of the Qur'an and Hadith. Indeed, they value the full potential of Islam, which they believe provides social justice, including gender equality.[17]

Islamic feminists believe that Islam upholds equality between men and women. They see Islam's message as different from and even contrary to the assumptions of patriarchal Islamists and official religious scholars who seek to impose their narrow view of Islam on Muslim women.[18] While the ideals of Islam originally called for human equality, patriarchal beliefs have been replaced over time with theological, legal, and social theories that place Muslim women in an inferior position.[19]

Islam has been reframed to mean that "Women are created of men and for men; women are inferior to men; women need to be protected; men are guardians and protectors of women; also female sexuality differs, and is dangerous to the social order."[20]

According to Mir-Hosseini and Ennaji, most opponents of Islamic feminist discourse fall into three broad categories: Muslim traditionalists, Islamic fundamentalists, and secular fundamentalists. First, Muslim traditionalists reject Islamic feminism because it challenges their eternal, valid, and dogmatic interpretation of Shari'a law. Second, Islamic fundamentalism developed in the Middle East and North Africa. It is in an increasingly open power struggle with the ruling state elite in the Arab world. Islamic fundamentalists are against Islamic feminism because they do not accept progress within Islamic thought and practices, but want to return to an earlier, 'purer' version of Islam.[21] Third, secular fundamentalists are Western and non-Western advocates who argue that religion should be abandoned so that Muslim women can achieve their emancipation and liberation.[22] Secular fundamentalists believe that Islamic feminism threatens their project, because Islamic feminism represents a renewal and reinterpretation of Islam based on equality between the sexes. This is in contrast to the stereotypical picture they try to paint of Islamic culture, in which they claim that Islam, at its core, has nothing in common with justice and equality. These opponents of Islamic feminism have one thing in common: an essentialist and non-historical understanding of Islam and Islamic law.[23]

Having outlined secular and Islamic feminism as the basic insights of Mernissi's feminist thought, I must point out that there are scholars who claim that secular and

---

16 Badran 2009: 247.
17 Badran 2001: 50.
18 Badran 2001: 50.
19 Mir-Hosseini 2006: 642–643.
20 Mir-Hosseini 2006: 642–643.
21 Mir-Hosseini 2006: 642–643.
22 Ennaji 2020: 4.
23 Mir-Hosseini 2006: 644.

Islamic feminism diverge. They argue that secular feminism, and even the idea of feminism itself, "has strong associations with political modernity [and] is similarly a construct associated with European modernity."[24] Therefore, feminism is considered to result from a Western secular feminist approach, which is based on the tradition of modernity and criticizes all religious beliefs. In contrast, Islamic feminism is grounded in Islam as a religion that takes for granted "strict rules and norms about existence and behavior."[25]

To respond to these claims, one could argue that there are points of convergence between secular and Islamic feminist discourse. One could argue that both discourses share the goal of emancipating women from the patriarchal cultural structures of their societies in order to realize their political, social, and legal rights. Indeed, women's rights and feminism are the common theme that both secular and Islamic discourses seek to defend.[26] Moreover, Islamic feminism demands the right of everyone to speak about women and Islam. In this way, Islamic feminists work against Islamist orthodoxies and Western prejudices about Islam. Through their work, they encourage debate between Muslim and non-Muslim scholars, which could also help establish a dialogue between different approaches to feminism.[27] From this perspective, Margot Badran affirms:

> Islamic feminism is a global phenomenon. It is not product of East or West. Indeed, it transcends East and West. As already hinted, Islamic feminism is being produced at diverse sites around the world by women inside their own countries, whether they be from countries with Muslim majorities or from old established minority communities. Islamic feminism is also growing in Muslim Diaspora and convert communities in the West.[28]

Islamic feminism is a global and transcultural feminist movement. It unites women from different cultures to defend the cause of women's rights. It rejects the conventional interpretation of the Qur'an and Hadith, which perpetuates the subjugation of women. It opposes male domination in religious discourse. It gives woman the right to prove her equality with man in Islam. In this sense, Islamic feminism accomplishes what secular feminism does not; that is, the reform of religious discourse.[29]

---

24 Seedat 2013: 30.
25 Moghadam 2007.
26 Badran 2009: 246–247.
27 Pepicelli 2008: 99.
28 Badran 2002: 4.
29 My presentation of the thought of Mernissi in workshops in Tunisia and in Germany was consistently met with two intellectual confrontations. a) Some claim that Mernissi is a purely secular Western scholar who erases Islamic heritage and identity in her writings. I counter that those who claim this are not well informed; Mernissi turns to Islamic feminism to pro-

In the following, I would like to clarify that by applying the poststructuralist method of Islamic feminist hermeneutics to the interpretation of Islamic legacy, I am able to situate Mernissi as a postcolonial thinker. Indeed, my purpose is to emphasize the similarities between Islamic feminism and postcolonial theory.

Islamic feminist hermeneutics as an entry to the field of postcolonial study

Is Mernissi a postcolonial thinker? As I mentioned above, Mernissi, like other Muslim feminist scholars, is concerned with the rewriting of Islamic history and the reinterpretation of Islamic texts. Thus, she is interested in the scholarship of religious hermeneutics and historiography.[30] In my definition of Islamic feminism, I present the hermeneutic approach as the main method used by Islamic feminists with the aim of interpreting a different reading of the basic sources of Islam—the Qur'an and the Hadith.

It is important to clarify that hermeneutics was first used in theology as biblical hermeneutics, which deals with the general principles for the proper interpretation of the Bible. More recently, hermeneutics has been further developed as a research tool in a number of disciplines, including feminism. The adaptation of the hermeneutic method in feminist theory results from the influence of poststructuralists and postcolonial theories on Western secular feminist movements in 1990;[31] Islamic feminism also experienced the same influences.

---

tect Islamic heritage from Western stereotypes and misunderstandings and to denounce male patriarchy. b) Others argue that Mernissi never claimed to be an Islamic feminist. Scholars who claim this are afraid of the label of Islam. For them, Islamic feminism is synonymous with the approach of traditional and fundamentalist Islamism. They do not realize that Islamic feminism serves to emancipate Islamic thought from patriarchal and fundamentalist interpretations.

30   Cooke 1999: 95.
31   Hawthorne 2007: 540.

In this sense, the hermeneutics applied is Islamic feminist hermeneutics [32] incorporating three approaches that operate together in order to introduce a renewed interpretation of the Islamic heritage that contradicts the patriarchal constructions: First, within the framework of the hermeneutic method, Islamic feminists propose rethinking the Qur'anic verses and Hadith in order to correct patriarchal interpretations that have become common among Muslims; for example, the assumption that women are inferior to men. Second, Islamic feminists cite Qur'anic verses that clearly proclaim equality between men and women. Third, they deconstruct verses that purportedly illustrate and justify male supremacy.[33] In this way, Islamic feminists re-contextualize Qur'anic verses and sayings of the Prophet in relation to the modern era of human existence. This connects their use of hermeneutics and their renewed interpretation of Islamic heritage to the socio-cultural circumstances in which Muslims live and experience today. As part of their hermeneutical method, they employ important tools such as etymology and the genealogy of concepts. As I will show, Mernissi uses the Islamic feminist hermeneutics in conjunction with linguistic and socio-historical approaches to deconstruct traditional metaphysical premises about Islam.

In this context, one could further argue that Mernissi's thought opens the way to a revision of religious knowledge. She attempts to deconstruct the monolithic composition of Islamic texts and thereby reform their rigid historical and cultural understanding. In this way, Islamic feminist thought itself is at the center of the postcolonial approach. When it comes to feminism, the word Islam does not stand for a particular identity or faith, but for a constantly renewing discourse dedicated to deconstructing, reinterpreting, and reforming cultural and historical Islamic knowledge. Similarly, postcolonial thought aims to expose the falsification of various interpretations in relation to religious, cultural, and historical knowledge. In fact, postcolonial thought seeks to reevaluate and reconstruct a renewed understanding of this knowl-

---

32   I use the expression "Islamic feminist hermeneutics" with reference to Raja Rhouni. In her article entitled "Rethinking 'Islamic Feminist Hermeneutics': The case of Fatima Mernissi," Rhouni employs the same expression with reference to the Islamic thinker Nasr Hamid Abu Zeid, who she says describes the work of Islamic feminist scholars as "feminist hermeneutics of the Qur'ān." Furthermore, the term hermeneutics is used by Asma Barlas in her book "Qur'ānic Hermeuneutics and Women's Liberation," wherein she highlights that the concept of hermeneutics is represented as a Western concept and alien to Islam. In contrast, Margot Badran affirms that hermeneutics is intrinsic to the Qur'ān; she defines hermeneutics as an interpretative methodology, and affirms that the Qur'ān provides interpretations, and thus employs hermeneutics. See Rhouni, Raja (2008): "Rethinking 'Islamic Feminist Hermeneutics': The case of Fatima Mernissi". In: Anitta Kynsilehto (ed.) *Islamic Feminism Current Perspective*. Finland: University of Tampere Finland, fn. 1.

33   Badran 2009: 248.

edge.[34] The work of postcolonial scholars often consists of other readings of established texts and provokes new and refreshing investigations of canonized knowledge. They read the canon more skeptically, curiously, and exploratively.[35]

In the same line of thought, Islamic feminism aims to deconstruct the patriarchal construction of the masculine in Islam by using the approaches of postcolonial thought as poststructuralist methods of thinking, including hermeneutics. Islamic feminism liberates Islam from male domination. It proposes a different reading of the Islamic canon. In this context, Mernissi opposes the monolithic constitution of Islam introduced in the obscurantism of the "Grand Récit"[36], based on a narrow ideological system of historical explanations that illustrates knowledge without examining the past, present, and future horizons.[37] Mernissi proposes a fragmentary and deconstructive re-reading of religious texts.[38] A fragmentary approach involves a rational reading of the Qur'an and the Hadith within a pluralistic interpretation of the text. Her method is based on interrogating, reorganizing, reconstituting, and interpreting the cultural and historical circumstances of Islamic knowledge with the aim of presenting a new way of thinking about Islam.[39]

One might add that Islamic feminism makes similar intellectual inquiries as postcolonial feminism. For example, Islamic feminism develops its theory not from the experiences of women in Western culture or in former colonies, but from the conditions of Muslim women living with the social and cultural challenges of their societies.

The idea of justice in Mernissi's work: A multi-dimensional approach

As noted above, the concept of justice is discussed in Mernissi's work on women's rights, and indeed feminist thought is one of the main themes in her work generally. However, justice is not a limited concept but rather has various characteristics. Majid Khadduri, for example, analyzes various aspects of justice in his book *The Islamic conception of justice* (1984). He does not, however, address gender justice.

In most of the earlier writings on justice in Arabo-Islamic thought, gender justice was not considered an area of interest. In this study, I shall elaborate on the concept of gender justice as presented in Mernissi's work through my own interpretation of her political, legal, epistemic, and social conception of justice, as these concepts are revealed through profound interpretation of her thought. Accordingly,

---

34   Moura 1999: 149–150.
35   Said 1994 b: 78.
36   Benalil 2010: 20.
37   Angenot 2001: 61–62.
38   Benalil 2010: 20.
39   Benalil 2010: 20.

Mernissi understands political justice within the framework of the establishment of democracy in Muslim societies, namely as a representative democracy that gives all citizens an equal right to participate in political decision-making.

With this understanding, Mernissi advocates a normative definition of representative democracy which assures all citizens the right to freely express their opinions by choosing their representatives in elections. Furthermore, I argue that Mernissi advocates legal justice by emphasizing the modern constitutional contract of the Universal Declaration of Human Rights (UDHR), which is the foundation of humanist ideas. In doing so, she contradicts the traditional Islamic contracts of legislation, for example regarding the personal status law (*Mudawana*), also known as the family code, in Moroccan law. The Mudawana is based on Shari'a law, which, according to a patriarchal interpretation, makes most Muslim women second-class citizens.

I argue that Mernissi demands social justice by exposing the situation of workers, especially Moroccan women; indeed she demands social protections, and in fact calls for favorable working conditions in the first place. Finally, Mernissi highlights the problem of education in Morocco and its relationship to class structure, where she argues for epistemic justice to create an egalitarian education system that serves both the working class and the wealthy.

Following my interpretation of Mernissi's concept of political, legal, social, and epistemic justice, I conclude that there is an interrelationship between these different areas of justice. Political justice is based on the principle of participation, on the idea of fair representation of citizens, and demands equality among individuals. By granting all individuals the right to express their political opinions, political justice is related to legal justice. The legal contract of the UDHR is based on the secular, modern, humanistic values that protect human rights by assuring individuals their freedom of thought and expression, which is also considered the foundation of democracy. Finally, political and legal justice provide good conditions for the creation of social justice. So the question arises: where might I place the issue of gender justice, introduced as a major theme in Mernissi's thought, among the areas of political, legal, social, and epistemic justice?

Based on the idea of moral egalitarianism, which assumes the equality of all human beings, a Muslim woman has the right, as a human being, to participate in political life; she also has the right to be equal to man in the field of legislation and in the private and public spheres of human interaction. In addition, most Muslim women have the right to education and work, among other social rights. In this regard, gender equity should be realized in most Muslim societies through political, social, and legal reforms.

In addition, Mernissi's reference to early Arabo-Islamic philosophy is discussed in this study in terms of its theoretical significance. The so-called "golden age" of Islam (c. 8th to 13th centuries) is an important source of reference for many contemporary Arabo-Islamic intellectuals through which to interrogate and reinterpret their civilizational heritage. Her reactivation of early Islamic thought of the 9th century of Islamic civilization has a constructive significance, as it shows an enrichment of the philosophical tradition at that time which promoted a transcultural openness to other schools of thought. In this way, the research elaborates the symbolic dimension of the transculturality of early Arabo-Islamic philosophy and interprets this dimension as partly responsible for the affirmative reference to this heritage by contemporary thinkers such as Mernissi.

In the Mu'tazilites of the 9th century, Mernissi focuses on a rationalist school in the history of Islam that distinguishes between human and divine justice. According to this school, humans must use their own reason to provide justice on earth. Moreover, the Mu'tazila problematized the relationship between rulers and ruled, and advocated popular participation in decision-making processes. On this basis, Mernissi criticizes blind obedience to religious authorities—such as the imam—and argues for more political participation rights. This is relevant for contemporary Muslim societies when it comes to the demand for political justice in the sense of democracy.

Shifting themes and methods in the work of Mernissi

Nouzha Guessous (2016), one of the commentators of Mernissi's work, divides that work into three periods. The first of these was from 1973 to 1985, and is characterized by the boldness of her revolutionary thinking. During this period, Mernissi aims to deconstruct the historical arguments used to justify and maintain the segregation of most Muslim women in the name of Islam. Her book *La femme dans l'inconscient musulman* (1982), published under the pseudonym Fatna Ait Sabbah, was evidence of her revolutionary stance. The second period was 1985–1990 with publications such as *Beyond the Veil Male-Female Dynamics in Modern Muslim Society* (1975–2003), *Le harem politique: le Prophète et les femmes* (1989) (English translation: *The Veil and the Male Elite: A Feminist Interpretation Of Women's Rights In Islam* (1991), and *La Peur-modernité: Conflit Islam et démocratie* (1992) (English translation: *Islam and Democracy Fear of the Modern World* (2002). Mernissi addresses Western readers. She criticizes and relativizes their interpretation of Islam with the aim of changing their stereotypical image of most Muslim women. The third period extended from the last years of the 1990s until her death in December 2015. It is characterized by the diversity of topics and methods of her research. For example, Mernissi conducted action research by giving prominent voice to women and men from different areas to improve their living conditions.[40]

Moha Ennaji (2020) interprets Mernissi's intellectual career similarly. He too emphasizes the change and development of her thinking over three periods of time.

---

40   Guessous 2016.

He asserts that "at the beginning of her career, her work and approach were overtly secularist. [Mernissi] criticized the different institutions that subjugate women and discussed the strategies of resistance they embrace in their daily fight for survival and dignity."[41]

This was the first phase of her career, which is known for its secular feminist approach. The second phase of her career consists of her activism in civil society, which she had previously introduced through her work in civil society and with civil organizations such as the NGO. She established links between rural and urban society in Morocco. She organized academic workshops. She also helped women from villages in the rural Rif areas to exhibit and display their crafts and art in national and international galleries.[42] Mernissi's goal was to empower Moroccan women and allow them to participate independently in the economic and social spheres of society. In this study, I do not address her activism in civil society, as my research focuses more on her theoretical work. I use current data to find out how the position of Maghrebian women has improved over the recent decades.

The third phase of her career includes her involvement in the field of Islamic feminism. In this vein, Ennaji argues:

> Mernissi's book *The Veil and the Male Elite* displays a drastic shift from her earlier secular feminist approach to Islamic feminism. It attempts to reinstate the initial egalitarian dimension of Islam by means of a progressive re-reading of some scriptures, in the Qur'an and the *Hadith*, which purportedly show women's inferior social status in the religion. The book is a fascinating 'revision of a few misogynous *Hadiths* that are believed to be sound but that she sees as incongruous with the egalitarian politics of Prophet Muhammad.'[43]

Hence, Mernissi allows for a progressive interpretation of Islam by opening a space for most Muslim feminist scholars to claim their rights within their Islamic tradition and heritage. In this way, scholars prominent in the field of Islamic feminism today, such as African American scholar Amina Wadud, consider Mernissi not only a follower of Islamic feminism, but the mother of Islamic feminism. Wadud has called her 'one of our greatest foremothers.' Others see her as the one who gave confidence to the idea of Islamic feminism and its struggle for human dignity, equality, and social justice at a time when Western feminism was still Eurocentric, anti-religious, and not Third World enough.[44]

Mernissi, thus, draws on different approaches and methods (i.e. secular and Islamic) to defend women's rights. This shows her transculturality and her openness

---

41 Ennaji 2020: 3.
42 Boutni 2017: 30–37.
43 Ennaji 2020: 7.
44 Kynsilehto: 2008 9–14.

to Western theories of feminism. Mernissi is aware that the universal thoughts on gender justice are to protect women from male domination. Thus, the defense of gender equality is a global issue.

Method and structure of the research

My working method in this study is reconstructive, analytical and argumentative. Therefore I cannot deal with Mernissi's contemporary intellectual project without presenting her rich and detailed work. Mernissi's project is highly descriptive, as is her reactivation of 9th century Muslim rationalist thought, pre-Islamic female deities, and Muslim rebels in earlier Islam.

Thus, in the context of Mernissi's historical description, I show what her goal is in her return to and revisionism of Islamic heritage. However, my critical approach also includes her descriptive account. I refer to her normative claims, which I attempt to examine in the context of this research.

Following this, I present the most important of the books that I focus on in this research. From among her many works, I have chosen Mernissi's scholarly book entitled *Islam and Democracy: Fear of the Modern World* (2002) specifically because by examining it I can show the extent to which Mernissi is both a secular feminist and an Islamic feminist thinker. As mentioned earlier, I consider Mernissi a secular feminist because she introduces modern secular humanism, which she considers a principle that drives the spread of humanist ideas such as freedom, freedom of belief, and autonomy in Muslim societies. Moreover, I consider Mernissi's insight into secularism, namely by emphasizing the idea of separation between religion and the state. In focusing on the aforementioned book, I conceptualize Mernissi as an Islamic feminist thinker by examining her historical investigation and reactivation of the rational thought of the Islamic tradition, which she does by referring to several scholars from the pre-Islamic period to the 9th century.

To shed light on the question of insight into Islamic feminism in Mernissi's work, I refer to other of her writings to highlight her interest in interpreting religious texts such as Hadith (sayings of the Prophet Muhammad) and Qur'an. Among these writings, I have selected *The Veil and the Male Elite* (1991), in which Mernissi discusses the issue of the veil in Islamic legacy. I also present her scholarly book entitled *The Forgotten Queens of Islam* (1993) (original title: *Sultanes Oubliées* (1990), not to introduce the queens of Islam whom Mernissi introduces historically, but to point out the implicit message that Mernissi wanted to convey to the reader when she authored this book. These three scientific texts form what is called "the trilogy of Mernissi." After this scientific trilogy, Mernissi "shifted her interest from scientific books to fiction."[45]

---

45 Rhouni 2010: 9.

As for Mernissi's books of fiction, I focus on two of her novels in this study: the first is an autobiographical novel entitled *Dreams of Trespass: Tales of A Harem Girlhood* (1994); the second is a novel entitled *Scheherazade Goes West: Different Cultures, Different Harems* (2001). The purpose is to examine Mernissi's feminism from a transcultural perspective. Mernissi's deconstructive reading of several myths related to Islamic culture and women in Islam are outlined. As an example, I discuss how she deconstructs the myths of an essentialist Arabo-Islamic identity, the myth of a subordinate Muslim woman, and the myth of the harem. Mernissi does this by arguing that there are multiple identities and ethnicities in Muslim world. She also dispels the Orientalist stereotype that portrays women in Islam as subordinate and lacking intellectual capacity by challenging it as a sexist view of Scheherazade.

Furthermore, Mernissi deconstructs the myth of the harem as a place of sexual desire, where women appear naked and seductive to satisfy the desires of men, by introducing the harem of Fez where she grew up and where the uneducated women refuse to accept their subordinate status. In addition, Mernissi points out that the West also has its harem, which means that the harem culture is not limited to Islamic culture, but also reaches the West, albeit with different ideas and symbols.

The last part of this study focuses on Mernissi's article, "Palace Fundamentalism and Liberal Democracy: Oil, Arms, and Irrationality" (1996) and her interview, "The New Arab Mass Media: Vehicle of Democracy" (2006). With these two works, Mernissi returns to the Islamic heritage of Sufism and introduces two concepts: adab—the art of dialogue and communication—and movement—specifically, the crossing of boundaries. These concepts are used to deconstruct the myth of boundaries (*hudud*), which stands for cultural boundaries that prevent cultural communication on a transcultural level. The purpose is to explore Mernissi's vision of a transcultural world where cultures can engage in dialogue regardless of borders. In her view, transcultural dialogue should be promoted with a strong notion of pluralistic democracy and global justice.

The thematic outline of this research is as follows: The first chapter introduces Mernissi's concept of secular humanism. The second chapter addresses her concept of justice and explains her political, legal, social, and epistemic conceptions of justice. The third chapter introduces Mernissi's reactivation of Islamic heritage from the 9th century. In the fourth I examine Mernissi's transdisciplinary approach to establishing her concept of gender justice in Islam. In the fifth chapter, the research situates Mernissi's contemporary intellectual project within the perspective of transcultural feminism. Finally, I evaluate Mernissi's thinking according to my personal point of view.

2.1 The concept of secular humanism: The necessity of emancipating Islamic thought from religious and nationalist conceptions

This chapter explores Mernissi's concept of modern secular humanism and examines the reasons for the failure of the modern secular concept in most Muslim countries. It presents the various positions of nineteenth-century Arab Muslim reformists, to show that most Arab Muslim reformists did not take a clear position on the concept of secularity. Mernissi uses linguistic and social historical approaches to try to explain why most Islamic cultures rejected concepts such as freedom and individualism. She believes that freedom and individualism are not implemented in most Muslim cultures due to the social history of the pre-Islamic era, when these terms were associated with disorder and perception of arrogance, traits that Islam forbids. The chapter ends with an examination of Mernissi's reinterpretation of Arabo-Islamic humanist thought, which aims to reveal an Islamic social contract that is based on notions of equilibrium and equality.

It is important to begin by examining the modern history of secular humanist thought in its Western tradition to identify the perspective from which Mernissi views this concept. It was in the late fifteenth or early sixteenth century that the term 'humanism' emerged, in the work of the Italian humanist Giovianni Pico della Mirandola entitled *On the dignity of Man* (1486). Pico used the term to emphasize the value of human achievements: as the faculty of reason permitted human beings to understand natural laws, they had a responsibility to detach themselves from their desires and cultivate their genius in the understanding of existence by studying rhetoric, grammar, poetry, history, and ethical philosophy. Indeed, this humanistic knowledge remained intricately linked to the influence of the Christian Church.[46]

In the early nineteenth century, the term 'humanism' came to be linked more closely with the rejection of religious beliefs and detached from the authority of the church. The renewal of the term 'humanism' during the Renaissance was advanced through the work of the German historian and philosopher Jacob Burckhardt entitled *Die Kultur der Renaissance in Italien* (1860), and also by the English poet and literary critic John Addington Symonds in his book, *The Renaissance in Italy, the Revival of learning*, (1877). Both thinkers see a division between the Church and humanistic knowledge.[47] Consequently, the liberation of human beings from orthodox religious belief guides us toward what came to be called modern secular humanism, a school of thought which was more readily embraced by French enlightenment philosophers, who shared an outright rejection of orthodox religious belief. Scholars of the enlightenment appealed to reason and experience to go against orthodoxy and

---

46 Noram 2012: 8–9.
47 Noram 2012: 8–9.

tradition, to criticize prejudice and superstition, as well as to reject the tyranny of religion.[48] In the early nineteenth century, scholars and intellectuals from France, Germany, and Britain no longer used the terms 'humanist' and 'humanism' to describe themselves, instead preferring to use such labels as 'freethinker,' 'secularist,' or 'rationalist.'[49]

This brief historical sketch aims to distinguish between diverse kinds of humanism. First of all, humanism emerged under firm religious domination. Renaissance humanism emphasized the rejection of orthodox religious belief and the liberation of human beings from the domination of the church. Lastly, modern secular humanism focused on human reason and criticized religious and political tyranny. Its proponents expounded humanistic notions of freedom of thought, freedom of belief, and tolerance.

Mernissi's concept of modern secular humanism

Mernissi's definition of secular humanism is in line with that of James Davison Hunter. She focuses on his book entitled *Culture Wars: The struggle to control the Family, Art, Education, Law, and Politics in America* (1992), published in the same year as her *Islam and Democracy* (1992–2002). Hunter's book describes 'culture wars' as a proxy for the conflict between the sacred and the secular, and argues for the necessity of religious pluralism in American democracy. Nevertheless, one could argue that this view of secularism, which protects religious pluralism, ignores the complexity of secularism in our day. Secularism has become a dispute about the language and limits of acceptable religious pluralism; about where and how and on what terms the boundaries of tolerable diversity should be drawn.

Mernissi develops her notion of secularity by stressing its conflict with the contemporary religious monarchies in many Arabo-Islamic countries. Her interest is to emphasize the privileges that secularity provides to human beings. Thus, she argues:

> Secular humanism, as defined by the American sociologist James Davison Hunter, is one of the things taught by American public schools: "Public school curricula tend to reflect an emphasis on the individual as the measure of all things and on personal autonomy, feelings, personal needs, and subjectively derived values—all of which are independent of the transcendent standards implied in traditional theism." American secular humanism was developed not so much against religion as against state interference in religion and especially manipulation of it.[50]

---

48   Noram 2012: 8–9.
49   Noram 2012: 8–9.
50   Mernissi 2002: 45.

Thus, secular humanism is not an attack on God, but on the officials who used religion as an authority to sustain their despotism. Furthermore, secular humanism was established within the preaching of humanistic ideas, which Mernissi describes as follows:

> By this I mean the secular humanism that has allowed the flowering of civil society in the West. Humanistic ideas—freedom of thought, the sovereignty of the individual, the right to freedom of action, tolerance—were propagated in the West through secular schools.[51]

It is clear that Mernissi emphasizes the humanistic values of a secularity that ensures the freedom of women in Muslim countries. In this sense, modern secular notions protect women's rights against religious authority.

According to a postcolonial perspective, secular humanism traces its roots back to the Western Enlightenment. This would make modern secular humanism Eurocentric in nature. According to postcolonial theorists, the Enlightenment expresses secular humanism in its explicit discourse by staking out universalistic and transcendental principles and linking them to the conquest of non-European humankind, viewed as inferior to Europeans. Indeed, the European existence was felt to be qualitatively superior to other forms of human life.[52] In line with the postcolonial criticism, Mernissi declares:

> To tell the truth, moving from one institution to another had no bad effect on me. Perhaps it was because the spirit of Descartes and Enlightenment philosophy, reflected through the mirror of a French colonial lycée and taught by Catholic teachers, didn't succeed in shining through. In any case, no one ever taught me tolerance, and I never saw it practiced during my long period of schooling. I learned it not from my teachers but in chance encounters with humble people in the shops, alleys, and neglected areas of the Fez medina.[53]

This statement by Mernissi shows her resilience against colonization. Mernissi is aware of the failure of French colonization to spread the universal values of the Enlightenment in her colonies. From a different perspective, Mernissi presents modernity in terms of the basis of the secular humanist concept of freedom. One could argue that Mernissi defines the concept of modernity in its ideal form. However, modernity as a category is much more contradictory and dialectical. It also contains colonial and totalitarian political constructs, from secular to religious authoritar-

---

51   Mernissi 2002: 42.
52   Serequeberhan 1996: 333.
53   Mernissi 2002: 179 fn.15.

ian forms.⁵⁴ It will soon become clear that Mernissi not only revives the tradition of Western humanism, but also rereads the tradition of Islamic humanism. In the following, I shall first explain Mernissi's theory of modern secular humanism, and then highlight the reasons she provides to explain why the secular process failed in most Muslim countries.

The Arab reformists and nationalists against a modern secular notion

Mernissi refers to Arab intellectual history from the nineteenth century to explain the ban on secular rule in most Arab Muslim countries. In this context, she argues:

> On the contrary, individualism always held a rather ambiguous place among the "reformers" of the nineteenth-century nationalist movement. This movement, focused on the struggle against colonization and therefore viscerally anti-Western, was obliged to root itself more deeply than ever in Islam.⁵⁵

Facing the "militaristic, imperialistic" power of the West, the Arab reformers chose to take shelter in their past by reactivating the tradition of Islam based on the tradition of obedience, *ta'a*.⁵⁶

The concept of individualism is one of the cornerstones of secular thought. This concept is seen as contradictory to the tradition of obedience, *ta'a*, rooted in the Islamic tradition, because it implies that people are free and can make their own decisions as individuals. Most post-independence Muslim societies prefer to preserve their traditional heritage by reviving the Islamic tradition based on obedience—obedience to the leader—rather than adopting the Western concept of individualism, in which they see a threat to their conventional understanding of the Islamic religion. Their goal is to use the obedience-based religion to protect their political despotism.

Looking at the term 'obedience' from the perspective of a feminist register, one might assume that Mernissi means women's obedience to men. Mernissi highlights this concept because it implies the diminishment of a woman's personality in order to make her passive and dependent on a man. On the political level, the concept of obedience implies that citizens should obey the leader.

Mernissi does not say exactly who the reformists of the nineteenth century were. In this respect, she could be accused of generalization and inaccuracy with regard to her reactivation of Arab intellectual history. Indeed, to shed light on this sociohistorical context of the nineteenth century in Arab Muslim countries, one needs to understand that the most famous of the Arab reformists were both important

---

54 Mirsepassi 2014a: 180.
55 Mernissi 2002: 42.
56 Mernissi 2002: 42.

thinkers and political agitators, namely Jamal al-Din Al Afghani (1839–1897) and his pupil Muhamed 'Abdu (1849–1905).[57] In fact, Afghani and Abdu are considered the founders of pan-Arab nationalism for their advocacy of the concept of the Islamic community at the expense of building Arab national states. In their understanding, the Muslim community encompasses all Muslims, regardless of their countries of origin, cultures, nationalities, and languages, insisting on their justification that all of them belong to Islam. Thus, they argue that the purpose of Islam is to unite Muslims of all countries and to obliterate all traces of race. Consequently, and ultimately to defend their claim for Arab nationalism, most Islamic reformists proclaim that it was Western foreigners who touted the conception of secularism to fight Arab nationalism. They maintain that the defenders of secularism are the allies of the West because they would like to expound Western secular ideas in order to divide the Islamic ummah (community of Muslims).[58] The Arab reformists and nationalists reject the idea of secularity in this colonial context because it contradicts their interpretation of Islam and their desire to unite all Muslims politically. They realize that Western promotion of secularism is a form of colonial aggression.

Hence, it is incorrect to suggest that the slogan of secularism is not prevalent in the Arab World, and therefore that the Arab does not embrace secularism. In the Arab World, secularity was used by Syrian Christian intellectuals during the Ottoman Empire's rule of Arab countries in the East, and when the Ottoman sultan promoted himself as caliph and protector of all Muslims. In fact, the secular ideology was developed by Syrian Christians who wanted to oppose the Turkish rulers who used religion—Islam—to expand their political power. Syrian Christian intellectuals advocated an Arab nationalism that would uphold Arab unity, independence, and the concept of secularity. However, secular Arab nationalism is no longer maintained when Islamist politicians and intellectuals proclaim that the separation of state from religion, one of the secular principles of Western thought, calls into question the Islamic religion.[59] This historical context of the history of Arab nationalism and its relationship to secularity and colonialism of the nineteenth century highlights the division between Arab Muslim nationalists who wanted to build a Muslim community in line with the Islamic tradition, and Arab non-Muslim nationalists who pushed for secular rule to be advocated in Arab countries.

One might object that Mernissi does not comment on her attitude of humanist secularity toward religious minorities, the Christian and Jewish communities, even though they have a long tradition in the Arab world, and the Maghreb region is known for its religious and cultural diversity. It is important to highlight this observation because secular humanism in its Western tradition advocates freedom of be-

---

57 Dawisha 2016: 18–19.
58 Dawisha 2016: 20–21.
59 Dawisha 2016: 27.

lief in order to protect the notion of religious diversity and pluralism. Consequently, Christian nationalists in Arab countries realized that secularism means respecting their religious freedom in a country dominated by Muslims.

To support Mernissi's idea that religion and politics must be separated in order to establish secular rules, I refer to the Moroccan philosopher Mohammed Abed al-Jabri (1935–2010) who advocates secularity along the same lines as Mernissi. Thus, Al-Jabri argues:

> What a Muslim society needs, in the absence of a religious organization, is to separate religion from politics, namely, to avoid the exploitation of religion for political purposes, as religion represents what is constant and absolute, while politics represents what is relative and changeable. Politics is motivated by personal or group interests, while religion must be above all this; otherwise, it will lose its essence and spirit.[60]

Al-Jabri evokes the notion of religious organizations, a connotation to describe religious fundamentalism and modern Islamist politics (political Islam). This refers to an earlier tradition of Islam with a claim to the past based on historical authenticity. It is a dangerous enemy to rational Islamic thought. An example of modern religious organizations are the Muslim brotherhoods.

In Islamic thought, the concept of a civil state/government (dawla madaniyya) to refer to the separation of religion and state is used as a reference to secularism. Yet Mernissi does not explain this idea in her book (2002). A year before she died, she stated in an *al-Jazeera* Arabic documentary that she uses the term 'civil state' or 'government' (dawla madaniyya) to explain the Islamic approach to the separation of religion and politics.[61]

The next section discusses Mernissi's combining of socio-historical with linguistic approaches. Here I explore how modern secular principles of freedom and individualism were interpreted and received within most Islamic tradition, from the perspective of Mernissi's reactivation of Islamic humanist thinking.

The connotation of freedom in Arabic etymology: A sense of social discrimination

The notion of freedom is the foundation of modern secularity. Freedom is equated with individual freedom, freedom of belief, and freedom of thought. In her book *The forgotten Queens of Islam* (1993), Mernissi argues that etymologically, in the Arabic

---

60   Al-Jabiri 2009: 57.
61   See the link to this documentary: https://www.aljazeera.net/programs/almashaa/2014/7/10 /والسندباد-فاطمة-الرباط/ (last accessed August 16, 2021).

language the words free (*hurr*) and freedom (*hurriyya*) have the sense of the opposite of slavery, and therefore they have nothing to do with that sense described in the first article of the UDHR, "All human beings are born free and equal in dignity and rights".[62] Consequently, Mernissi explains, when French children say *"liberté,"* associations come to their minds of the people's demonstrations and struggles in the streets of Paris in 1789 to fight for their rights and to demand freedom. In contrast, when Arab children say freedom (*hurriyya*), the images that come to their minds are of the dichotomy of slaves and aristocrats, wherein the etymological sense of free (*hurr*) describes the master, the aristocrat, the free man, and (*al- hurra*) describes the free woman—both of aristocratic descent—as opposed to slaves.[63] To put simply, the Arabic etymology of the word 'freedom' does not refer to a political claim or a matter of constitutional rights, but rather remains, in the consciousness of most people socialized in Arabic, correlated with the narrow sense of a person of aristocratic descent.

One could argue that the etymological significance of the link between freedom and aristocracy has other implications in most Arabo-Islamic societies. In the same line of thought, the veil in the Islamic tradition was a sign of the free, aristocratic woman. This creates a social hierarchy between the veiled aristocratic free woman and the unveiled slave woman. It can be seen that the practice of veiling has a religious foundation based on ideas of honor and virtue.[64] These ideas were reflected in most Muslim societies across time, with veiled aristocratic nobles and unveiled marginalized women. The collective memory of Arabs also associates the notion of being free with aristocracy. This interpretation demonstrates social discrimination.

Is there a contradiction between Islamic tradition and the notion of freedom of belief?

Through etymological, genealogical, and socio-historical analyses, Mernissi clarifies the reasons behind Islam's probation of freedom of thought and belief. She first explains the notion of freedom of thought and its relationship to Islam. She argues that

> the word *islam* refers to a relationship: submission. The Arabic linguistic root *istislam* means "to surrender"—to lay down weapons ending a state of war (*harb*). Istislam and *tasallum* (to receive) result in a truce halting hostility; *salam* is one of the words for prisoner of war.[65]

---

62 Mernissi 1993: 14.
63 Mernissi 1993: 14.
64 Youssef 2012: 28.
65 Mernissi 2002: 85.

Mernissi emphasizes the etymology of Islam, which implies that Islam spreads peace between individuals to eliminate war and violence. Before the advent of Islam, freedom of thought led to diversity of opinion and plurality of opinions, which contribute to divergence and disagreement among Muslim communities. In this sense, Islam bans the notion of freedom of thought in order to spread peace (*salam*).

Mernissi then underlines the connection of the polytheism of the Pre-Islamic era and the notion of freedom of belief declared in the modern legacy of UDHR. She writes:

> *Shirk* is the most appropriate word for translating the word "freedom" in Article 18 of the Universal Declaration of Human Rights, which is posed as an ideal to be attained: "Everyone has the right to freedom of thought, conscience and religion; this right includes freedom to change his religion...." This article is the very definition of the *jahiliyya*, the chaotic pagan world before Islam ... It is in that brief Article 18 and the concept of *shirk* that the conflict between Islam and democracy lies.[66]

In other words, in the collective memory of most Arab Muslim individuals, the modern concept of freedom of belief, which admits of the possibility of heresy, poses a major challenge to the principle of Islam that affirms the belief in one God.

To support her argument Mernissi refers to a famous statement attributed to the prophet Muhammed, indicating the rejection of polytheism and freedom of religious practices in Mecca with the phrase "even if you succeed in capturing the sun and bringing it and placing it in the palm of my hand, I will never change my mind".[67] This Hadith relates to the socio-historical circumstances prevalent when the prophet was spreading Islam in Mecca. During that time, the Quraysh tribe said to the prophet Muhammed that they would not convert to Islam and yet would demand the possibility to live together with the Muslims in Mecca. The citation above, quoted by Mernissi, was the prophet's reaffirmation of his answer to the Quraysh tribe, which was his refusal to allow them the freedom to practice their religion. There could be other interpretations of the story revealed by Mernissi. One could argue that the idea of religious diversity and, thus, pluralism, which is thought of as a modern secular concept, was discussed in the early days of the rise of Islam.

Huff notes that Mernissi's analysis of the matter of freedom in the linguistic realm was interpreted as her most radical work, because she associates the freedom of belief with *shirk*, which means disorder and confusion. In this regard, Huff argues

---

66 Mernissi 2002: 87.
67 Mernissi 2002: 99.

that Mernissi employs a provocative argument in which she links the freedom of belief, as a principle of modern human rights, to the Arabic substantive *shirk*, which means polytheism and, in its evident meaning, atheism.[68]

Contrary to Huff's assertion, one might suggest that Mernissi's message is not to explain the incompatibility of Islam with the modern principle of freedom and liberty of thought and religion, but to emphasize that Islam rejects the idea of polytheism (*shirk*, belief in multiple gods) due to the historical context of the pre-Islamic era when religious freedom led to disorder and violence. Mernissi makes this argument to show how this context still shapes contemporary understanding of the secular concept of freedom of belief in many Muslim societies. In doing so, she deconstructs this contradiction by historicizing it.

The social contract of Islam: From freedom to a strong notion of equilibrium

Besides reviving Western secular humanism, Mernissi revives the humanistic heritage of Islamic thought. Her interpretation of *rahma* combines several humanistic meanings, including love, forgiveness, and tenderness. The spread of these notions leads to the spreading of unity among Muslims. Accordingly, she argues:

> *Rahma* is a rich concept with multiple facets: sensitiveness (*al-riqa*), tenderness (*al-ta'attuf*), and also forgiveness (*al-maghfira*). It is everything that is sweet and tender, nourishing and safe, like a womb. ... The *umma*, the mythic Muslim community, is overflowing with *rahma*, as is the relationship of love that links the members of a family and makes each one concerned about the fate of the others.[69]

Like Mernissi, one could interpret the Islamic humanist concept of *rahma* (care of each other) as an ethical value in Islam that should be achieved through the sharing of the rational soul between Muslims and the worship of divine power. Among other concepts that connect humanity in Islam are perfection (*kamal*), friendship (*mahabba*), affection (*tawaddud*), compassion (*tahannun*), and friendliness (*ra'fa*).[70]

In this context, Mernissi maintains that the Islamic humanist value of *rahma* can be established only through the sacrifice of *ahwa*, which means desire and passion. She writes:

> *Hawa* means both "desire" and "passion," but it can also signify "personal opinion." It is the unbridled individual interest of a person who forgets the existence of others in thinking only of his own advantage. Desire, which is individual by

---

68   Huff 1995: 514.
69   Mernissi 2002: 88.
70   Daiber 2013: 300.

definition, is the opposite of *rahma*, which is an intense sensitivity for the other, for all the others, for the group.[71]

In other words, the sharing of rationality and rational conduct among Muslims are the principles upon which to establish the ethical value of *rahma* and renounce individualism, seen as the pursuit of individual interests (*ahwa'*). Moreover, we note that Mernissi maintains that desire, *hawa*, can also signify personal opinion. Thus, desire is the uncontrolled individual interest of a person who thinks only of his own advantage and interest.

Mernissi further clarifies that the aim of Islam should not be understood as rejecting desire. On the contrary, the proposal of Islam is to deal with the negative and positive poles of human conduct. According to Mernissi, the ideal of Islam is equilibrium. She writes:

> But—and this is the genius of Islam—*hawa* is not to be excluded or eradicated; it must rather be managed in such a fashion that it will not exceed the *hudud*, the sacred limits. Islam doesn't reject anything; it manages all things. Its ideal schema is ... equilibrium which does not put the security of the group in danger.[72]

Mirsepassi comments on Mernissi's reactivation of the Islamic humanist ethics. He perceives Mernissi acting on her conviction that "the macro-institutional counterpart to the 'task of memory' in revitalizing traditional Islamic humanist concepts such as ... *ra'y* (personal opinion), and *rahma* (care for others), is open public debate intended to resolve inherited discursive ambiguities over power and public life."[73]

Is there a contradiction between Islamic thought and the notion of individualism?

Mernissi follows her linguistic approach to clarify the role of individualism in the history of Islam. She affirms that the substantive 'individual,' in Arabic etymology, describes the characteristics of a *taghiya*, who was "a man such as a tribal chief, a king, or an aristocrat who held earthly power through the cult of personality and despotic ambition."[74] She points out that in the Qur'an, "*taghiya* means 'tyrant,' a holder of power that knows no limits." The word *taghiya* is used to describe "the leader who is contemptuous toward everything, including the divine." [75]

---

71 Mernissi 2002: 89.
72 Mernissi 2002: 90.
73 Mirsepassi 2014 a: 189.
74 Mernissi 2002: 105.
75 Mernissi 2002: 105.

Referring to the socio-historical context of pre-Islamic Mecca, Mernissi explains that the call for individualism was conceived of as the characteristic of an arrogant and aristocratic Arab in pre-Islamic times. According to her, Islam is against arrogant individualism and boundless self-confidence; hence the prophet Muhammed demanded that Arabs give up their striving for individualism, which implies arrogance and self-confidence, and submit their destiny to God.[76] In contrast to individualism, Islam promotes equality among individuals.

The submission to one God: from individualism to a strong notion of equality

In what follows I reconstruct and discuss Mernissi's argument concerning the idea of equality in the tradition of Islamic humanism as exchange to individualism. Mernissi declares "it is the absolute equality of all, men and women, masters and slaves, Arabs and non-Arabs, which Islam guarantees, in exchange for the surrender of individualism."[77]

To support her argument Mernissi quotes the Qur'anic verse 13 of chapter 49: "O mankind! We have created you male and female and have made you nations and tribes that ye may know one another."[78] This verse, as Mernissi explains, articulates two messages: first, that the ummah, the community of Muslims, is formed of equals, making no difference between the male and female. The second is the message of solidarity between nations and tribes despite borders and cultures.[79]

One might argue that the submission to one God promotes the egalitarian notion of justice. Equality in this sense comes to establish equal relations between individuals. All humans are equal in front of God; equality refutes the arrogance of individualism. Hence Islam comes to establish an egalitarian community, where there is no difference between an aristocratic Arab and others.

In line with Mernissi's thought, in his book entitled *The Islamic conception of justice* (1984), Khadduri emphasizes the notion of equality that Islam comes to foster. He claims the prophet Muhammad found widespread inequity and oppression in the society in which he had grown up and sought to establish order and harmony within which a distinct standard of social justice would be applied. As a prophet, he naturally stressed religious values, but he was also a social reformer. The idea of justice was of particular interest to him. The prophet noticed the discrimination and inhuman acts in his society and in fact he acted to improve the status of women, end slavery, and prohibit infanticide and other unjust acts and practices.[80]

---

76 Mernissi 2002: 110.
77 Mernissi 2002: 110.
78 The Qur'ān: chapter 49: The Private Rooms, Verse 13.
79 Mernissi 2002: 110.
80 Khadduri 1984: 8–9.

In summary, this chapter examined Mernissi's position on secularity. Secularism allows for the separation of state and religion. As a feminist, Mernissi's call for secularity makes sense because it promises equal rights for women. Thus, in a secular state, women's rights are protected without being compromised by male interpretations of religious legacy. Mernissi seeks to understand why most Muslims reject the concept of freedom and individualism, the fundamental concepts of secular thought. She notes that the socio-historical context of pre-Islamic culture, which reminds most Muslims of disorder and atheism, is behind this rejection. Her *Islam and Democracy* was referred to as "ethnography rather than a philosophical or historical work."[81] Since she uncovers the socio-historical context of the pre-Islamic period within a limited systematic study of individual culture, her examination cannot generalize to all Muslim societies.

Last but not least, Mernissi puts forward the notions of tenderness and equality as virtuous ideas of Islamic ethics. Critics contend that Mernissi's use of Arabic etymology to explain several words (*rahma, ahwa', taghiya*) is a limited approach. There exist Muslims who cannot understand the role the implication of these notions in the history of the Islamic thought. Therefore, one might argue that Mernissi "does injustice to the plurality and richness of the Muslim world"[82] in that her account is addressed to Muslims who are familiar with the Arabic language.

2.2 The concept of justice in the modern era: The entanglement of descriptive and normative claims of justice theories

This chapter examines justice as defined by Mernissi. It speculates on the notions of political justice, legal justice, social justice, and epistemic justice which one could interpret from Mernissi's thought. The first section examines a notion of political justice which is interpreted from Mernissi's claim about the concept of representative democracy, in which she asserts that individuals must have equal participation in political decision-making. Using a model of Western political tradition, Mernissi also clarifies Islam's relationship to democracy. Mernissi maintains that a plausible newer reading of Islamic thought may lead to an accordance between Islam and the concept of democracy.

The second section analyzes a notion of legal justice which is established based on Mernissi's call for egalitarian access to laws by every individual. I outline her reference to modern treaties concerning human rights such as the Universal Declaration of Human Rights (UDHR), which she compares with the Universal Islamic Declaration of Human Rights (UIDHR). Her argument is that the UIDHR remains

---

81 Mirsepassi 2014a: 178.
82 Mirsepassi 2014a:179.

based on an injustice between men and women perpetuated by Islamic law. The third section discusses a notion of social justice derived from Mernissi's assertion of the right of every individual to enjoy social rights. My analysis will center on her empirical research about the struggle of the exploited proletarian women in Morocco.

The last section of the chapter explains another aspect of Mernissi's notion of justice: epistemic injustice. A notion of epistemic justice is obtained from her strong appeal to the importance of education. For her, education is the basis for emancipating women from male domination. Indeed, education will enable women to assert their rights in the public sphere and establish themselves within society. In this context, one could affirm that Mernissi argues for an implicit notion of epistemic justice by exploring the unequal access to knowledge formation and cultural resources among children of the poor and children of the rich in most Arab Muslim countries.

Political justice as equal participation in political decision making

One can derive from Mernissi's writing an appeal for political justice. In her writings, political justice implies that citizens are to participate equally in the political decision making. For this reason, she recognizes that democracy is a pillar on which to establish a notion of political justice. She argues for "democracy—that is, insistence on the sovereignty of the individual rather than of an arbitrary leader."[83] As a model of democracy, Mernissi highlights representative democracy and clearly affirms:

> This produced a virtual cutoff of the Third World from the advances of humanism in the last centuries in both its aspects: the scientific aspect (promoting the use of government resources to invest in scientific research and encourage freedom to explore and invent), and the political aspect (*establishing representative democracy*, with citizens' exercise of the right to vote and to participate in political decision making) [emphasis added].[84]

One could argue, in agreement with Mernissi, that democracy stands for direct rule by the people. The word 'representation'refers to giving another person the right to represent a person in order to defend, claim, or protect that person's rights. In political science, representative democracy is currently understood in terms of four main characteristics:

> (a) the sovereignty of the people expressed in the electoral appointment of the representatives; (b) representation as a free mandate relation; (c) electoral mechanisms to ensure some measure of responsiveness to the people by represen-

---
83   Mernissi 2002: 16.
84   Mernissi 2002: 46.

tatives who speak and act in their name; and (d) the universal franchise, which grounds representation on an important element of political equality.[85]

Thus, representative democracy is the cornerstone for creating an egalitarian notion of political justice. Representative democracy gives citizens (men and women) the right to be represented by others, whom they themselves have chosen, to gain or limit political power. Most importantly, representative democracy makes citizens active in the political world, thereby strengthening the authority of citizens.

One might argue that Mernissi is developing an elementary notion of democracy. In doing so, she stresses the benefits of democracy. Mernissi presents only the positive side of the concept of democracy. Her normative concept of democracy explains why it is morally desirable. Her aim is to emphasize the beneficial instrument that democracy provides to citizens as a guarantee of their sovereignty and participation in political decision making. In this sense, Mernissi classifies the various privileges that democracy provides to individuals. She declares:

> The term [democracy] covers an impressive array of freedoms and privileges, of rights to exercise and taxes to pay, from the right to eat pork or drink wine or read censored works; to the right to fall in love, have a platonic friendship or embark on an affair, marry one's partner or not, have children or not; to the right to demand a wage at least equal to the legal minimum wage, and appeal to a union if unjustly treated; to the right to elect a prime minister, and then to protest when the government-run television station gives him prime airtime at taxpayers' expense.[86]

Mernissi considers the rights and duties to which citizens are entitled in a democratic state. Citizens enjoy several rights but also have some duties, such as paying taxes. Mernissi highlights the rights that democracy provides. She mentions subjective rights that are in strict contradiction to what most Muslim culture generally proscribes, such as the right to drink wine, eat pork, or choose not to marry a partner. She, thus, claims very modern privileges of democracy that are forbidden in the cultural tradition of most Muslim societies. In this sense, Mernissi rises against the socio-cultural tradition of several Muslim societies.

Mirsepassi considers that Mernissi's idea of democracy comes from the definition of democratic enlightenment.[87] In this sense, democracy tends to make people decide for themselves and make collective decisions. In democratic societies, individuals are encouraged to be more autonomous. Democracy gives citizens some control over the political decision-making process. Democracy educates citizens to

---

85 Urbinati 2012: 23.
86 Mernissi 2002: 50–51.
87 Mirsepassi 2014a: 187.

be active and productive individuals rather than passive citizens. Democracy makes people think carefully and rationally because what they do or do not affect political outcomes. Democracy strengthens the moral qualities of citizens. When they participate in decision-making, they must listen to others, they must justify themselves to others, and they are forced to think partly in terms of the interests of others. Some have argued that people who find themselves in such a situation can be expected to think genuinely in terms of the common good and justice. Democratic processes tend to promote autonomy, rationality, activity, and morality among participants. Because these positive effects are seen as intrinsically valuable, they argue in favor of democracy and against other forms of rule.[88]

This Enlightenment tradition of democracy emphasizes the universal privileges of democracy, which must be recognized by all citizens and shared by all nations. Democracy, thus, affirms autonomy and responsibility and provides the common good of citizens. It must be asked: What if not all citizens are aware of the privileges of democracy? What if a particular cultural tradition of a particular country does not accept democracy? This leads us to think about a notion of relative democracy, rather than a universal notion of democracy.

In this context, Mernissi shows how individuals from different social classes, as well as Arab and non-Arab Islamic regimes, perceive democracy. First, she sees that there are individuals who defend democracy, such as the intellectual and middle-class citizens of Muslim societies who believe that democracy protects their political and social rights. She writes

> Some groups of people think that [democracy] can promote their interests, especially those who know foreign languages, who have access to Western knowledge and culture (including such amenities as bank credit, social security, paid vacations, and so on). This is generally the case with bourgeois city dwellers, both men and women, who operate in the fields of finance and business. It is also the case with university professors, artists, and intellectuals, all of whom are involved in the creation and manipulation of knowledge, both traditional and modern.[89]

By contrast, lower-class citizens conceive that democracy contradicts the values of Islamic legacy. Mernissi argues:

> Others feel their interests to be terribly threatened by that *dimuqratiyya*. Considering the intensity of the opposition to democracy, which sometimes results in violence, they must believe that their very survival is in danger. This is apparently the situation of all those excluded from the good things mentioned above.

---

88   Tom and Bajaj 2021.
89   Mernissi 2002: 53.

Can it be that that what they perceive of democracy is so distorted that its corollaries, personal and political initiative, seem threatening to them? Can it be that the most dispossessed in our societies cling to Islam because they fear being forgotten by their own people ... ?[90]

Mernissi's argument can be interpreted as elitist reasoning to affirm why we should educate and enlighten people about the necessity to establish democracy. In an interpretative stance, Mernissi suggests that illiterate citizens without access to the benefits of modernity might make an unwise decision when voting. They might not choose their representatives wisely. This is because some political representatives' resort to populist discourse to manipulate the emotions of the electorate; for example, by using religious and idealistic discourses to attract citizens. This assumption relates to critical theories on the concept of representative democracy.[91] Following this train of thought:

> Most people do not have the kinds of intellectual talents that enable them to think well about the difficult issues that politics involves. But to win office or get a piece of legislation passed, politicians must appeal to these people's sense of what is right or not right. Hence, the state will be guided by very poorly worked out ideas that experts in manipulation and mass appeal use to help themselves win office.[92]

Representative democracy would not be possible in a low-education country. Occasionally, citizens without political engagement and without any idea of how to claim their political rights are manipulated by their representatives' ideas. Thus, an educational approach to enlighten citizens about democracy is necessary to shape rational citizens who will participate in political decision-making. Political justice is hence dependent on epistemic justice, understood as equal access to education.

Second, there are Muslim countries that claim the law of Shari'a as the basis of legislation. They therefore reject democracy as contradictory to their interpretation of Islamic rules. In contrast, there are regimes that present themselves as secular modern regimes, but without truly maintaining the privileges of democracy. Mernissi argues:

> But what is still more astonishing is that what goes for individual goes for governments too. Some have more need of Islam, more need to find their identity

---

90 Mernissi 2002: 53.
91 Von Beyme 2012.
92 Tom and Bajaj 2021.

in religion, than others. There are two kinds of governments: those that reject democracy as contrary to their identity, and those that embrace it.[93]

Mernissi directs her criticism at regimes that profess modern and secular rules but reject democracy. In this sense, citing the example of President Habib Bourguiba of Tunisia (president of Tunisia from 1956–1987), Mernissi argues:

> President Bourguiba, whom we all admire for his past as a nationalist leader, would certainly have had a shorter presidency if he had not put government funds into publicity for himself as the *mujahid akbar* (Great Warrior). If I mention President Bourguiba, it is because Tunisia is one of the rare Arab states that have declared themselves modern ...
> ... The regime of President Bourguiba monopolized the mass media and the schools to tell citizens that they must modernize and renounce tradition while refusing to grant them the essence of modernity: freedom of thought and participation in decision making.[94]

One could argue that Mernissi does not highlight the example of Bourguiba's regime for nothing, as Tunisia is known for its modern and secular political achievements, especially for granting several rights to women. Mernissi's interpretation of the socio-political facts in Tunisia under Bourguiba's regime is shared by several contemporary scholars. On the one hand, it is correct to assert, like Mernissi, that "Bourguiba prioritized education and made it his mission to liberate the Tunisian people from the remnants of their past; this included the emancipation of women."[95] On the other hand, one can agree with Mernissi that Bourguiba did not promote democratic rules in Tunisia. Under Bourguiba's regime Tunisia was a one-party state dictatorship. In other words, there were no democratic rules and no diversity of political parties. There was no pluralism nor different political opinions in the political world. There was only one political party that ruled the country. Hence, "To consolidate its rule, Bourguiba's regime relied on a party militia, whose existence was not formally recognized, and a secret police force, a component of the Department of State Security that specialized in propping up the regime."[96] Mernissi's overview of the socio-political facts of post-independent Tunisia illustrates Tunisia's political process from a post-colonial dictatorial state to a post-revolutionary democratic state and shows that Mernissi's concept of representative democracy works in post-revolutionary Tunisia.

---

93   Mernissi 2002: 53.
94   Mernissi 2002: 64–65.
95   Jebnoun 2014: 108.
96   Jebnoun 2014: 107.

The rule of a dictatorial political party in Tunisia has lasted for eighty-five years. Democracy and the modern tools of freedom of thought, the press, and expression have been completely absent for decades. In 2011, citizens were protesting the continued dictatorship in postcolonial times. The protest aimed to support a new democratic system. This demand resonates with Mernissi's concept of representative democracy, developed already in the 20th century.

The new constitution of 2014 makes Tunisia an open and democratic state. Various independent political representatives and parties were elected and represent most Tunisian citizens who participated in the drafting of the new 2014 constitution. Subsequently, the Assembly of People's Representatives was elected by citizens (men and women) in numerous sessions, most recently in 2019, who participate in political decision-making through their elected representatives. In line with Mernissi's promise of democracy, this socio-political fact of Tunisia's post-revolutionary modern history confirms that a notion of democracy could only be achieved by starting a revolution. Thus, "Mernissi's work, on the political front, courageously confronts the twentieth-century legacy of dogmatic totalitarianism linked to the one-party nation-state, or revolutionary statism in its various incarnations."[97] Mernissi's notion of representative democracy was realized at the latest after several social and political struggles in Tunisia.

Previously we learned about Mernissi's attitude towards a modern notion of representative democracy. Mernissi not only examines democracy by setting out its privileges, but she also invites us to reflect on the following question that has preoccupied scholars: Is Islam compatible with democracy?.[98] In doing so, Mernissi shifts her field of research from a socio-political study of modern times to an etymological and genealogical study. She analyzes the etymological connotation of the term democracy in the Arabic language and through a reinterpretation of the socio-historical context of the pre-Islamic period. Mernissi's examination of the concept of democracy is valuable because she methodologically establishes a link between Western and modern political thought and the tradition of Islamic thinking. In this sense, Mernissi writes

> The debate turns on six key words that constitute its two poles. On one end is the pole of allegiance to the leader, confounded with faithfulness to God; it inseparably links together three words: *din* (religion), *i'tiqad* (belief), and *ta'a* (obedience). At the other end are grouped together three words that are just as strategic and that all affirm individual responsibility: *ra'y* (personal opinion), *ihdath* (innovation, modernization), and *ibda'* (creation).[99]

---

97   Mirsepassi 2014 a: 180.
98   Esposito and Voll 1996; Bayat 2007; Esposito, John L., Tamara Sonn and John O. Voll 2016.
99   Mernissi 2002: 40.

In this statement, Mernissi highlights two contradictory concepts: the concept of personal opinion as opposed to the concept of allegiance. Personal opinion refers to the fact that an individual is innovative, creative, and productive. These are the characteristics of a free individual. Thus, democracy ensures the right to have one's own opinion. It is one of the fundamental pillars of democracy. In contrast, allegiance refers to the characteristic of an obedient and submissive individual. Importantly, Mernissi links the concept of allegiance to the leader, which has a political connotation, with the concept of allegiance to God, which has a religious meaning. In what follows, Mernissi examines how the attributes of the concept of personal opinion are constructed in the collective memory of Muslims. She highlights the concept of arrogance as set forth in the Qur'an. She argues: "Arrogance is condemned in the Koran: "Allah loveth not such as are proud and boastful!.""[100] Thus, not only was the attribute of arrogance forbidden, but also the meaning of imagination, which was associated with the notion of creation, innovation, and production. As Mernissi states:

> Khayal (the imagination) and ikhtiyal (arrogance) come from the same linguistic root. Imagining is full of risks for society because it is the power to create and think in images—that is, to create a different reality.[101]

In Lisan al-'Arab, a dictionary of the Arabic language, Mernissi points out that the verb 'to imagine' is takhala, which means to imagine God or to create an image of God. The definition in Lisan al-'Arab takes us back to a pre-Islamic period when the Arabs created idols in the form of sacred scripture, which incarnate their gods or the gods of their tribe; for this reason Islam forbids the production of images. She writes:

> To imagine something," says the Lisan al'-Arab, "is to create an image of it." Creating an image is what was slapped with a ban, because the images that the pre-Islamic Arabs created were those of idols. They were the reproduction of their personal gods, or the gods of their tribes, each of which might contain only a few families.[102]

Huff speculates accordingly about the argument that asserts Islam and democracy are at odds. Consequently, a traditional interpretation of Islamic heritage may conclude that Islam is based on submission to one God, in contrast to democracy, which is based on individual opinion, innovation, and plurality.[103] Additionally, he argues that Islam is in opposition to the Christian religion, which promotes the freedom

---

100   Mernissi 2002: 94; The Qur'ān, chapter 4, Women, Verse, 36.
101   Mernissi 2002: 94.
102   Mernissi 2002: 94.
103   Huff 1995: 505.

of thought of individuals.[104] In this regard, the New Testament declares, "You will know the truth and the truth will make you free."[105]

Mernissi, however, does not fall into the trap of following this mainstream reading of Islam, which sets up a strict dichotomy between true Islam and democracy. Mernissi proposes a different reading of the relationship between Islam and notions of democracy. One could argue that Mernissi does not claim that Islam forbids the idea of democracy. Rather, she returns to the socio-historical context of the pre-Islamic era to clarify that Islamic culture dictates that personal opinion, which has led to the idea of innovation, creation, and production in the modern era, was prohibited in the circumstantial context of the pre-Islamic era. In fact, she clarifies that Islam prohibited personal opinion as a pillar of democracy in this exclusive historical context of the pre-Islamic era because at that time violence and disorder prevailed in the tribal society of Arabia before the spread of Islam. For this reason, Islam comes to expound monotheism and prohibit polytheism. However, this historical stance does not mean that Islam prohibits personal opinion and a pluralistic society. Thus, it was pragmatic political reasons that led to the prohibition of personal opinion. Moreover, the problem of lack of access to democratic rules in most Islamic societies is an example of how Islamic leaders in more recent centuries use the argument of banning opinion to deny citizens access to their political rights. Mernissi wants to point out that Islamic leaders confuse the tradition of obedience to a leader with obedience to God to maintain their despotism.

Mernissi "unveils the historical conditions and power relations that underlie the democratic deficit and unachieved democratic potentials of Muslim/Arab societies."[106] In this way, she turns the question of Islam and its compatibility with democracy around, claiming that the problem lies in how the traditional interpretation of Islamic culture explains the contradiction between Islam and democracy. One could argue that Mernissi does not provide a decisive answer to the question of the compatibility of Islam and democracy. However, we could implicitly claim that Mernissi's aim is to find a plausible justification to develop a democratic concept of Islam beyond traditional interpretations, but her thoughts on this topic remain unspoken, and an open space for varied interpretations.

To further develop Mernissi's argument for a notion of democracy that fits Muslim societies, there are liberal and democratic Muslim scholars who claim that there are concepts in the Qur'an that point to a form of democracy. These concepts include *shura* (consultation), *ijma'* (consensus), *al-hurriya* (freedom), and *al-huqquq al shar'iyya* (legitimate rights). The Qur'anic chapters of The Family of 'Imran (*Al-'Im-*

---

104 Huff 1995: 505.
105 The Bible: John 8: 32.
106 Mirsepassi 2014a: 178.

ran)¹⁰⁷ and of the chapter Consultation (Ash-Shura)¹⁰⁸ talk about electing leaders to represent the community and rule on its behalf.

In our present time, we must find a way to tackle a hermeneutical project so that it can be re-appropriated without being corrupted. Since the concepts of *ijma'* إجماع and *shura* شورى do not in themselves provide a fully satisfactory framework for elaborating a model of Islamic democracy, a more convincing approach would be to use both concepts as the basis for legitimizing a reappropriation of a tradition and a culture that are not democratic in themselves, and see how we may explore the possibility of an enlarged democratic understanding of them without corrupting their essence.¹⁰⁹ Moreover, a new interpretation of Islamic thought should refute the traditional interpretation of Islamic fundamentalists.

In sum, Mernissi's concept of political justice is based on an egalitarian notion of representative democracy. Mernissi focuses on a normative definition of what democratic rule should serve for, namely granting fundamental subjective rights to all citizens. She places the concept of democracy in the tradition of Enlightenment thought. Similarly, Mernissi provides a reinterpretation of traditional Islamic thought by historically situating the prohibition of personal opinion in pre-Islamic times. Mernissi explains that a traditional interpretation of Islamic thought is responsible for the assertion of a contradiction between Islam and democracy. One can argue that Mernissi's study cannot provide a definitive answer to the question of the compatibility between Islam and democracy. This question remains the subject of several contemporary studies in the field of Arabo-Islamic philosophy. In the next section, I derive from Mernissi's writing an appeal for legal justice.

Legal justice as equal protection under law

In Mernissi's view, everyone should be able to access the legal system. In this sense, legal justice requires that there be no discrimination between men and women in terms of laws. Mernissi is interested in the concept of legal justice because the legal realm is the important issue to promote justice in societies and to guarantee equal access to right and equal treatment under law. Woman can guarantee her equal status with man only when she enjoys the same rights as man. This emphasis on rights resonates with her arguments for political justice as mainly providing and protecting subjective rights. In our modern time there are universal organizations and treaties such as the United Nations (UN) and the Universal Declaration of Human Rights (UDHR) that prescribe important decrees to realize human rights. Mernissi turns to these universal treaties to show their importance for maintaining

---

107   The Qur'ān, chapter 3, The family of 'Imran, Verse, 159.
108   The Qur'ān, chapter 42, Consultation, Verse, 38.
109   Mestiri 2010: 7.

a universal notion of human rights. Mernissi shows how several Islamic countries, despite signing on to these contracts, do not practically apply their laws within their own boundaries. In the following section, I discuss Mernissi's thoughts on the reasons why several Islamic countries do not apply the rule of the universal contracts, and their justification for doing so. Mernissi refers to the UN, and highlights the universality of its constitutional charter. She argues:

> The United Nations Charter has the effect of law … It is impossible to imagine one more forceful, for it claims to be superior to all local laws, the ideal that will reform and transform them. It is the supreme model: a higher law than those of the states' constitutions themselves. [110]

In his article entitled "Human Rights, Democracy, and Development," Donnelly emphasizes the universality, power, and legitimacy of the UDHR, which Mernissi also refers to in her work defending a universal concept of human rights and secular rule—as I will explain below. Donnelly argues that the UDHR has an international legitimacy; it links the regimes that foster prosperity and political rights to a universal realm. Whatever the specificity and particularity of the states, the states' leaders that have signed on this covenant should respect the universality and the internationality of its laws.[111] Mernissi and Donnelly are not far apart. Both agree that the universal treaties of UN and the UDHR are universal and legitimate treaties. Therefore Mernissi believes that democracy should be contextual, but rights are universal. Mernissi aims to undermine the ideological and political systems that silence and oppress most Muslims in many Muslim societies and deny them access to these universal rights. As a socio-political thinker, Mernissi aims to show the reasons why most Arab countries do not apply the rules of these treaties in their countries, although they have signed them. Do most Muslim leaders refuse to submit to the rules of these treaties because they promote strong notions of democratic rules that conflict with a sense of obedience, *ta'a*, to authority figures?

In this context, Mernissi argues that the Arab and non-Arab Muslim countries such as Iran, Turkey, Lebanon, Syria, and Saudi Arabia have signed on to the charter of San Francisco on June 26, 1945. Afterwards, they sent their diplomats to confirm their desire to become members of the UN on November 21, 1947. They also signed the United Declaration of Human Rights (UDHR) adopted by the General Assembly of Human Rights on December 10, 1948, which obliges all member nations to promote the respect of human rights.[112]

---

110   Mernissi 2002: 62.
111   Donnelly 1999: 609.
112   Mernissi 2002: 62–63.

However, most of the Muslim countries that signed on to UDHR do not agree with Article 18. This article asserts the principle values of democracy and secular states as the right of individuals to participate in political decision-making, and the freedom of religious beliefs. These emancipatory rights contradict dictatorship rule, which is based on obedience to the leader. In this regard, Mernissi writes:

> The states that were signatories of the charter and the international conventions had a choice between two possible approaches: they could seize the opportunity of the adoption of these new universal laws to open up a full public debate on the nature of power and explain to the people the mechanisms of participatory democracy; or they could hide these laws away, sequestering them like clandestine courtesans who are an embarrassment when one wants to play the role of imam and demand ta'a. It was the second option that was chosen (...). Mobilizing the media and millions of teachers to explain Article 18 would have meant explaining the philosophical basis of the secular state.[113]

In the context of this debate, it is worth mentioning the Universal Islamic Declaration of Human Rights (UIDHR), adopted in September 1981, which also takes up an important concept of human rights; but we might wonder whether these human rights have been adopted and under what legal tradition the drafting of this treaty took place.

The UIDHR recognizes the religious and cultural specificity of most Muslim countries. In fact, most Muslim countries took part in drafting this document. The charter declares the right of freedom, the right of justice, as well as the right to freedom of religion by stressing that "Every person has the right to freedom of conscience and worship in accordance with his religious beliefs."[114] Furthermore, human rights are fostered in the Cairo Declaration on Human Rights in Islam (CDHRI) adopted in August 1990, but with some restriction. Indeed, it stresses in the two last articles that "All the rights and freedoms stipulated in this Declaration are subject to the Islamic Shari'ah".[115] Moreover, it points out that "the Islamic Shari'ah is the only source of reference for the explanation or clarification to any of the articles of this Declaration."[116] Thus, despite the modern treaties of UIDHR, as well as the CDHRI, both of which assured to Muslim individuals fundamental legal rights, these treaties remain restricted in comparison with the Universal Declaration of Human Rights, due to the law of Shari'a, meaning a strict interpretation of the religious text of the Qur'an and Tradition used for guiding Islamic legislation. (I will explore this issue in a later section.)

---

113 Mernissi 2002:64.
114 UIDHR, 1981, Article XIII.
115 CDHRI, 1990, Article 24.
116 CDHRI, 1990, Article 25.

Thus, it makes sense that Mernissi places more emphasis on the UDHR adopted by the UN than on the Islamic Declaration of Human Rights mentioned above to establish her respective notion of legal justice. In this manner, Mernissi's critique of Article 20 of UIDHR underlines how the notion of law is used with an ambiguous and at the same time significant meaning. The article asserts "Rights of Married Women" in situations of marriage and divorce. It emphasizes that a woman has the right to seek divorce through the court of law. Mernissi argues that the rights asserted by the UIDHR in favor of women should not threaten the law of Shari'a. She declares: "What do we understand from reading the text of this reservation? Not much, since the equality ensured in Article 16 in no way "prejudices" the *shari'a* if that is interpreted to guarantee a 'just balance.'"[117]

Mernissi recognizes that the concept of Shari'a law is implicitly used in this article to violate women's rights. In fact, returning to Article 20 of UIDHR, it is worth noting that the conception of law was introduced twice; "Every married woman is entitled to seek and obtain dissolution of marriage (*Khul'a*) in accordance with the terms of the Law", "Every married woman is entitled to inherit from her husband, her parents, her children, and other relatives according to the Law."[118] However, one could observe that the notion of law is not clarified in this article. In other words, which type of law must woman pursue to demand her rights; the civil laws or the traditional law of Shari'a restricted by religious and patriarchal interpretations? This is crucial when we consider certain areas of law, such as family law.

There are several Muslim feminist scholars from different Islamic cultural traditions who agree with Mernissi on the necessity of a reinterpretation of the Shari'a to guarantee legal rights for women.[119] Mir-Hosseini asks: In a state that claims to be guided by the Shari'a, why are justice and equality not reflected in the laws that regulate gender relations and the rights of men and women? Why do Islamic jurisprudence texts—which define the terms of the Shari'a—treat women as second-class citizens and place them under men's domination?.[120] To put it simply, considering that justice and equality are intrinsic values and cardinal principles in Islam and Shari'a, why is a woman unequally treated? One might affirm that the inequality between man and woman in the terms of legal texts of Islamic legislation is present in different realms. In this regard, I refer to the rules for the marriage contracts and the rules for the dissolution of marriage according to Islamic legacy, to follow Mernissi's argumentation on this example. The aim is to further illustrate the injustice between men and women in order to understand why Mernissi is fighting against a patriar-

---

117 Mernissi 2002: 67.
118 UIDHR, article XX.
119 Sadiqi 2006–2009; Mir Hosseini 2006; Charrad 2007; Eddouada 2008; Badran 2009.
120 Mir-Hosseini 2006: 629.

chal interpretation of Islamic law, and appealing for an egalitarian interpretation of law in line with the UN Declaration of Human Rights.

Hence, a woman in Islam, according to the traditional interpretation of the Shari'a law, has not the right to express her refusal to marry. She does not even need to be present at the contract of marriage. The "matrimonial guardian," who is usually her father or, in his absence, another male member of her family, can speak and decide in her name. In cases of disagreement between the woman and her father over the choice of a spouse, the right of decision is legally granted to the father or legal guardian. Furthermore, the Islamic legislation of Shari'a law accords to woman only fragile rights concerning divorce. In this way, the law of Shari'a facilities the termination of marriage by offering three procedures to end the marriage: the first is a unilateral repudiation of the wife by the husband, the second is a repudiation negotiated between the spouses and the last is a judicial dissolution of the marriage through appeal to a religious judge. Hence, the first one represents the strictest form of divorce; when the husband has the right to end the marriage by simply pronouncing the formula "I repudiate thee" three times, which mean that the husband has ended the marriage without recourse to the judicial authorities.[121] The idea conveyed in this statement is that women are second-class citizens. Women are deprived of their right to freely choose their spouse and to obtain a divorce under patriarchal interpretations of Islam. Hence this interpretation of Islamic law does not grant each human being equal rights and violates any egalitarian understanding of justice.

Mernissi's concept of legal justice, conversely, is strongly based on the notion of the equality of men and women in relation to laws. Mernissi recognizes that modern human rights treaties are important in elaborating gender equality, in contrast to Islamic human rights declarations that are based on male dominance over the Shari'a law. Mernissi rejects the patriarchal interpretation of Islamic laws that make women second-class citizens.

Despite Mernissi's understanding of the UDHR as an important source of legal justice for the advancement of women's rights at the time of her writing of this book (1992), the UDHR is currently the subject of critical debate in contemporary feminist scholarship. Feminist critiques of human rights seek to destroy some of the hierarchies embedded in the human rights regime. Criticizing the basic assumptions of human rights as they were formulated in 1945–48, feminist have demonstrated that these assumptions are inadequate, that men and women have different relationships with the state, and that rights are not fixed and unchanging. They are, in fact, historically, socially, culturally, and economically contingent.[122]

---

121 Charrad 2001: 33–35.
122 Parisi 2017.

Social justice as access to social rights

Mernissi's vision of social justice is also based on a strong notion of egalitarianism. Mernissi emphasizes the social rights that state institutions should ensure to citizens. Mernissi's concept of social justice entails equal access to social rights by everyone. Her empirical research in this regard focuses on women from the subaltern class in post-independent Moroccan society. I refer here to "her original training as a sociologist and her scholarly production that strives to present the history of laywomen. Mernissi's avowed agenda is to make audible to state planners subaltern women's voices that speak about or reveal real issues—illiteracy, minimum wage, and social security, for instance."[123] In this regard, I would like to emphasize that after the independence of Morocco in 1956, Moroccan scholars and political activists aspired to establish a notion of social justice. They argued that state policies had created unequal social development in post-independent Moroccan society. In doing so, the political activists of the leftist parties fought for the interests of the popular masses of the lower class.[124]

One might consider that Mernissi as a feminist thinker and activist in civil society belongs to this social reformist movement, in that she defends the right of Moroccan woman from the sub-class to have access to social rights. Indeed, it was in an interview with "Mina," a Moroccan carpet weaver, that Mernissi depicted the typical situation of a Moroccan woman who has no access to such social rights as health insurance. The woman in the interview knows that the employer she seeks to get a job from does not offer her health insurance. Mernissi argues:

> An interview I had with Mina, a Moroccan carpet weaver who was hospitalized with a broken wrist incurred in an on-the-job accident, perfectly summarizes the democratic, cultural, and linguistic handicaps suffered by people like her. As a result of her accident, and despite ten years' seniority, Mina had been fired by the factory where she worked, which offered her no medical coverage or compensation.[125]

This story describes one of the normative issues of social justice, which states that every worker should have access to social insurance. Mernissi comments that the woman interviewed is aware that to not be insured at work is unjust. She also notes that the woman in the interview does not realize that there is a law which can protect her social rights.[126] In this line of ideas, one might assume that the law Mernissi indicates is the International Covenant on Economic, Social and Cultural Rights (ICE-

---

123 Rhouni 2010: 44.
124 Rachik and Bouriqa 2011: 7.
125 Mernissi 2002: 57.
126 Mernissi 2002: 57.

SCR). This international covenant was adopted in 1966 by the UN in accordance with the UDHR. It asserts normative claims of social justice in the sense of basic social rights. In addition, social justice requires legal justice, in the sense of equal access to law by every citizen.

Contrary to this, Mernissi asserts that Arab businessmen are afraid to see their workers as responsible individuals who claim their social rights.[127] Mernissi means by social rights "the right of everyone to the enjoyment of just and favorable conditions of work" (ICESR Part III, Article 7). Article 9 of the ICESCR, moreover, recognizes the right of everyone to "social security, including social insurance". In this context, she speculates on the reasons for unemployment among young university graduates. She affirms:

> One of the reasons for unemployment among young university graduates in Morocco is that the factory owner fears letting in among his workers "educated" people who have participated in demonstrations on their campuses.[128]

To put it simply, a young intellectual might be able to request their rights because they know of the international conventions that protect human rights. Therefore most employers do not hire educated young employees. Mernissi's speculation is based on empirical investigation done in 1987 in Moroccan manufacturing. It could not be generalized to all Arab countries. Mernissi continues her investigation to examine the role of women in the textile industry. She argues that "many workers testified that it was much easier to be hired if one wore a traditional djellaba."[129] In Maghreb countries like Morocco and Tunisia, the traditional djellaba is an exceedingly popular dress for women. Women from the lower classes usually wear it. This attire is a symbol of a societal divide between women who dress in a modern way, wearing jeans and t-shirts from modern stores, and women who wear traditional clothes, such as a djellaba from a Souk store. As a covering for the female body, it might be argued that the djellaba has an Islamic religious as well as socio-economic symbolism.

Raja Rhouni claims that Mernissi critically focuses on the traditional and poor Moroccan woman who is unaware of her social rights; that Mernissi wants the proletariat woman to have a "class consciousness" in order to be aware of the conflict with the bourgeois class, and to make the decision to fight for liberation from capitalism through organized structure.[130] Hence, according to this analysis, there can be no

---

127 Mernissi 2002: 58.
128 Mernissi 2002: 59.
129 Mernissi 2002: 59.
130 Rhouni 2010: 78.

gender justice without social justice. In this sense, one could argue that Mernissi exhibits a Marxist approach. Her pursuit of social justice reveals the conflict between proletariat and bourgeois classes.

It must be noted here that the League of Arab States also adopted the Arab Charter on Human Rights (ACHR) on September 1994 in Cairo, which affirmed several social rights to the workers; it affirms in Article 30 that the state guarantees every citizen the right to work and to social security.[131] Moreover, Article 32 of ACHR maintains that "[t]he State shall ensure that its citizens enjoy equality of opportunity in regard to work, as well as a fair wage and equal remuneration for work of equal value."[132] Thus, there are legal texts that protect human rights in the socio-economic sphere in most Arabo-Muslim societies, but they are not implemented in practice.

As I mentioned above, Mernissi's research dates to 1987, so one might question whether the empirical results she gathered are still relevant for examining social policy in the Arab world today. A more recent empirical study (2014) examines the social policy and the development of social rights in the Middle East and North Africa region after the 2011 Arab revolutions. An emphasis is placed on Tunisia post-revolution. It shows that while Tunisia achieved political success, its impact on social policies remains limited. Karshenas, Moghadam and Alami (2014) argue that an integrated social policy regime linking education, health, labor markets, and women's participation is imperative. Specifically, the authors favor the participation of unions, employer organizations, women's rights groups, and other horizontal civil society organizations in the development of social policy that can realize the social and economic rights of citizens.[133] The lack of social rights that Mernissi outlined in her time is, thus, still relevant today, according to social scientists. In this regard, Raja Rhouni argues:

> Mernissi is one of the first Moroccan sociologists to attempt to bring poor rural and urban working women to the sphere of representation, against the grain of official economic and political discourses that ignore their existence. ... Combining a Marxist and feminist approach, she is the first sociologist to draw attention to female labor in Morocco and to declare the existence of a Moroccan female proletariat.[134]

Thus, Mernissi's thoughts relate to postcolonial theory, which is concerned with the defense of subaltern women. Mernissi takes a critical look at the social politics of post-independence Morocco. She explores the social injustices that affect most Moroccan women workers. Her purpose is to bring the voices of the subaltern to

---

131 ACHR, 1994, Article 30.
132 ACHR, 1994, Article 32.
133 Karshenas, Massoud, Valentine Moghadam and Randa Alami 2014: 737.
134 Rhouni 2010: 86–87.

the forefront. Social injustice disproportionately affects lower class and illiterate women. In this sense, Mernissi believes that equal access to education is necessary to protect women from legal and social injustice.

Epistemic justice as equal access to knowledge formation and cultural products

Mernissi compares two systems of education to reveal the inequality of access to knowledge formation. Her focus is on Muslim societies, especially Maghreb societies. Based on her egalitarian stance, one might point out her sense of injustice in this regard and call it epistemic injustice, in the sense of domination in and by the sphere of knowledge formation. According to her normative stance, epistemic justice entails equal access to knowledge formation, as well as equal access to cultural products. In this sense, she writes: "It is in the types of knowledge available in each institution that we find the inequalities that today divide the Arab world and create an intense animosity between classes."[135]

In order to point out the inequality in educational systems she compares the traditional system of the Qur'anic school and the modern system of the kindergarten. Mernissi affirms that most children who join the Qur'anic schools belong to the poor classes.[136] Hence, in the context of Mernissi's analysis, epistemic injustice goes hand in hand with social injustice. She declares that children of the poor are excluded from early training in modern learning, especially mathematics and modern educational games; also, they are not getting access to the foreign languages. The system of education is limited to the recitation of Qur'anic verses and the learning of the Arabic language without any openness to other foreign languages and without the experience of modern knowledge.[137] By contrast, in the English-style kindergartens or French-style *maternelles* in Maghrebian countries, children of the rich learn to read and write by reading "Snow White" and "Alice in Wonderland" in foreign languages and devote only a few hours to the Arabic language and religious education.[138]

In Mernissi's view, social injustice is at the root of people's inability to achieve good quality of education. For Mernissi the unequal access to knowledge among children in most Arab Islamic countries in matters of learning foreign languages and gaining access to modern knowledge would affect their capabilities for intercultural exchanges and openness to Western countries, and their future careers. In this regard, she explains:

---

135 Mernissi 2002: 80.
136 Mernissi 2002: 80.
137 Mernissi 2002: 80.
138 Mernissi 2002: 80.

This difference in the cultural universe of Muslim children, depending on their social class and parents' income, is probably responsible for the xenophobia and rejection of the West in those who were deprived early in life of access to modern education. Chances of finding employment are in turn dependent on mastery of modern knowledge.[139]

Another point Mernissi makes is that individuals in most Muslim societies do not have access to cultural resources. She affirms:

When I visit a Muslim country ... I see bitterness over blocked ambition, over frustrated desires for consumption—of clothes, commodities, and gadgets, but also of cultural products like books and equality films and performances which give meaning to life and reconcile the individual with his environment and his century.[140]

In line with Mernissi's earlier arguments, the international covenant on human rights can be invoked to emphasize the need for equal distribution of knowledge, education, and cultural resources to all, which is a universal right alongside the right to respect for human dignity. Indeed, the International Covenant on Economic, Social and Cultural Rights (ICESCR) states that everyone has the right to freely participate in the different systems of education, which should be promoted equally for everyone. For example, "primary education shall be compulsory and available free to all" and "The development of a system of schools at all levels shall be actively pursued, an adequate fellowship system shall be established, and the material conditions of teaching staff shall be continuously improved".[141] Moreover, it is important to recall that the treaty assures that everyone has the right to take part in cultural life and that the state should encourage cultural performances. [142]

Mernissi argues in line with theorists on the concept of epistemic justice who defend an account of distributive epistemic justice in the production of scientific knowledge.[143] They realize that science should produce the knowledge citizens need to reason about the common good, their individual good, and pursuit thereof. Science should produce the knowledge those serving the public need to pursue justice effectively. Finally, science should be organized in such a way that it does not aid the willful manufacturing of ignorance. From the same perspective, Mernissi realizes that education is a fundamental right and enables people to acknowledge and request their social and legal rights. The right to educate oneself is essential to a

---

139 Mernissi 2002: 80–81.
140 Mernissi 2002: 56.
141 ICESCR, Part III, Article 13, Sections 2a and 2e.
142 ICESCR, Part III, Article 15.
143 Kurtulmus and Irzik 2021.

woman's empowerment. Contrary to Kurtulmus and Irzik, Mernissi focuses more on an elementary notion of education than on a high view of science and higher education.

Mernissi's aim is to reveal the societal poverty, discrimination, and injustice in most Muslim societies. According to her, social injustice is correlated with epistemic injustice in the Global South. Her work marks a change in basic assumptions in the discourse on epistemic justice, pointing to unequal power relations between the Global North and the Global South.[144] Mernissi defines epistemic justice within the context of the Global South. Her interest lies in Muslim societies.

The concept of justice that Mernissi focuses her work on is not studied to defend the rights of the proletariat and rural women, as some critics of Mernissi's concept of justice claim. In this sense, Anouar Majid states that Mernissi defends a capitalist model of economics and politics, arguing : "The prominent feminist sociologist Fatima Mernissi, however, has accepted the capitalist models of human relations."[145] Furthermore, he notes that Mernissi agrees with the bourgeois notion of democracy and individual liberties by holding up the UN definition of human rights and democracy.[146]

In response to this criticism, I argue that Mernissi seems to refer exclusively to Western constitutional treaties when describing democracy, human rights, and social development, while she does not refer to Islamic treaties because Islamic treaties still reflect misogynistic interpretations of Islam. For this reason, her feminist project calls for (re)interpreting the Islamic heritage in order to fulfill the rights of Muslim women. Moreover, Mernissi emphasizes the role of education in the emancipation of women to condemn misogynist and patriarchal advocates who see women's education as a threat to Islamic legacy. In her book entitled *Beyond the Veil : Male-Female Dynamics in Modern Muslim Society* (2003), Mernissi quotes Qasim Amin[147] as follows : "Many people still believe that it is not necessary to educate women. They even go so far as to think that to teach women how to read and write is against the *shari'a* and a violation of the divine order."[148]

Mernissi's main critique is directed at the male and patriarchal interpretation of Islam, which she sees as responsible for the exclusion of women from the political, legal, social, and educational spheres. Her focus in articulating this critique is the subaltern woman in Islam who is under man's dominance. Mernissi is against

---

144 Dübgen 2020.
145 Majid 1998: 328.
146 Majid 1998: 329.
147 Qasim Amin (1863–1908) was an Egyptian philosopher, reformer, and judge. Amin is considered one of the "first feminists" of the Arab world. His advocacy for more rights for women sparked a debate on women's issues in the Arab world. He criticized the veiling, early marriage and lack of education of Muslim women.
148 Mernissi 2003: 14

an untamed capitalist system because she obviously defends the rights of the laboring class, for example of women who work in domestic services and such economic sectors as crafts and agriculture. Mernissi criticizes development policies and global capitalism, and their impact on subaltern woman.[149]

In some ways, I argue, Mernissi's ideas on justice are in the middle of a controversy between communitarian and liberal perspectives. Raja Rhouni, for instance, considers Mernissi a communitarian feminist thinker since she defends proletarian women. According to Anouar Majid, Mernissi is a liberal thinker because she links liberal politics with capital and economic development. According to another interpretation, Mernissi's views on development are understood as related to those of Amartya Sen and Micheline Ishay in the context of the capability approach, as "she insists upon the crucial link between economic development and public freedom" in the sense of political and social rights, and on "the self-reliance that includes a respect for certain existential questions of dignity."[150]

In the case of Mernissi's study of the concept of justice and human rights, she rejects the discourse that accuses Western thought of being hegemonic. Consequently, she views human rights and justice as universal rather than a Western achievement. Mernissi is concerned with individual rights. When she wrote *Islam and Democracy* (2002), she believed that justice and human rights were well developed in the West. A common problem in many nations which Mernissi wants to solve is that of power relations. On issues of human dignity and women's emancipation, she advocates openness to other ways of thinking, including Western ones.

This chapter has explained Mernissi's stance on the concepts of justice based on her critical empirical research in most Muslim societies. Mernissi presents justice in terms of the universal treaties of human rights and criticizes the patriarchal interpretation of the legal system within the Islamic heritage that denies women access to their rights. In the next chapter of this part of the study, I examine Mernissi's concept of justice through her revision of 9th century Arabo-classical Islamic thought. The aim is to show that Mernissi offers a new perspective on the concept of justice and human rights. In doing so, she identifies the concept of justice simultaneously with two traditions: first, with the modern tradition of Western thought—as explained above in chapter two—and second, with the historical tradition of classical Islamic thought.

---

149   Rhouni 2010: 1.
150   Mirsepassi 2014a: 181.

2.3 The rereading of ninth-century early Arabo-Islamic thought: The theorization of notions of justice through Mernissi's transcultural and humanistic approaches[151]

In this chapter, I discuss Mernissi's reinterpretation of ninth-century Arabo-Islamic thought. First, the purpose is to show Mernissi's interest in questions of divine justice, legal justice, and political justice as derived from her account of the thought of the jurist Malik Ibn Anas, the Sufi Al-Hallaj, and the Mu'tazila theological school. This chapter presents the main normative ideas on justice, power, and right in early Arabo-Islamic thought to inspire contemporary discourses on gender justice and democratic rules. Second, the chapter highlights the reception of rational Arabo-Islamic thought in ninth-century Islam. The aim is to show the influence of this rational thought on the development of a transcultural and humanistic approach that shaped early Arabo-Islamic thought. The chapter ends with the argument that reinterpreting early Arabo-Islamic thought is a crucial task because it challenges conventional interpretations within the Islamic heritage and corrects Western misunderstandings and simplifications of the rich intellectual heritage of Arabo-Islamic thought.

Legal justice as the right of interpretation (*ijtihad*)

One can argue that in the context of Islamic feminism, Mernissi focuses on the right of interpretation (*ijtihad*) to find the meaning of justice and promote legal rights for women. Here, in her reinterpretation of early Islamic thought, Mernissi turns to the Muslim jurist Malik Ibn Anas, whom she portrays as an intellectual who advocates justice.[152]

Mernissi uses a transcultural and comparative approach, pointing to early Arabo-Islamic thought and invoking the Western modern tradition of human rights. She affirms that the Western treaty of the UDHR does not frighten the Arab masses because it declares that "the will of the people shall be the basis of the authority of government" and that "everyone has the right to take part in the government of his country."[153] However, the UDHR frightens Arab leaders because it brings back memories of the earlier Muslim intellectuals and philosophers who promoted thoughts of justice, freedom, and autonomy.[154] Among these Muslim

---

151 This chapter is quoted from: Karoui, Kaouther (2020): "Relektüren des Klassisch-islamischen Erbes für eine Gerechtigkeitsgrammatik der Gegenwart". In: Transkulturelle Perspektiven auf Gerechtigkeit, Special Issue for: Deutsche Zeitschrift für Philosophie, (Vol. 68, No.6, pp. 915–927) Berlin: De Gruyter.
152 Mernissi 2002: 19.
153 Mernissi 2002: 19–20.
154 Mernissi 2002: 19–20.

intellectuals and philosophers, Mernissi introduces Imam Malik Ibn Anas, the founder of the Malikite school.

> The West compels Muslims to remember Imam Malik Ibn Anas, the founder of the Malikite school, which we adhere in North Africa. [He died as a result of] torture ordered by the caliph ... [because Ibn Anas] refused to take back his words ... [which] expressed his opinion, which was different from the caliph's.[155]

Mernissi does not give us any further information about Ibn Anas' intellectual role, especially in developing an assertive conception of jurisprudence. I would therefore like to discuss Ibn Anas's conception of juridical justice as interpreted in modern academic texts dealing with the question of justice in Islam. In this way, I would like to illustrate the idea of justice that lies behind Mernissi's unveiling of Ibn Anas' thought. Before I do this, I define the concept of legal justice in Islam in the following.

In Islamic vocabulary the substantive 'legal justice' is the core of the Islamic law of Shari'a, which consists of a declaration of rights and wrongs called permissions and prohibitions. However, Islamic law does not specify categories of permissions and prohibitions. The question is: What is the measure which distinguishes the just from the unjust, the right from the wrong? Muslim jurists propose to distinguish between just and unjust acts by pointing out the ultimate goals or the purposes of what Islamic law ought to be.[156]

In this sense, Ibn Anas explains the principles of legal justice based on the principle of interpretation (*ijtihad*) as a method of legal thinking that aims to find and protect the common good or the public interest. Ibn Anas was reputed to be the first Muslim jurist in Islamic history to use the concept of public interest (*maslaha*) as a basis for legal decisions.[157] First, the principle of public interest (*maslaha*) is implied in the Qur'an. Ibn Anas maintains that Islamic law is derived from the Qur'an, and, thus, it could not guide man to the path of evil because God does not desire evil to befall man, and as a result Islamic law is designed to protect the public interest.[158] Yet one should consider that the Qur'an declares that a man is not always aware of what is good for him: "Fighting is ordained for you, though you dislike it. You may dislike something although it is good for you, or like something although it is bad for you: God knows, and you do not".[159] This Qur'anic verse could be interpreted as a request for various interpretations, to understand how to do the good and how to avert the evil, because human beings cannot realize what is good for them. To avoid

---

155 Mernissi 2002: 19.
156 Khadduri 1984: 136; Kamali 1989: 216–217.
157 Khadduri 1984: 137.
158 Khadduri 1984: 137.
159 The Qur'ān, Chapter 2, The Cow, Verse 216.

this quarrel, Ibn Anas insisted on the principle of the understanding of the ultimate goals (*maqasid al- shari'a*) based on the intellectual struggle *ijtihad* to achieve legal justice.

Second, the concept of public interest is indicated in the Tradition (sayings and actions of the prophet Muhammed). The Tradition asserts different issues on how to do what is just. For example, it asserts that injury should neither be imposed nor inflicted on human beings. Indeed, only the public interest (*maslaha*) should be implemented in Muslim societies because no God and no prophets wish evil upon humankind.[160] It is important to note that in modern-day Tunisia, a Sunni country that adheres to the Maliki school of legislation, the public interest is a source of legislation used by Muhammad bin 'Ashur,[161] the former rector of the notable Zaytuna Mosque. Ibn 'Ashur asserted that the public interest should be the basis of all legal decisions.[162]

One could speculate about the reasons behind Ibn Anas's torture, as outlined by Mernissi above. According to Ibn Anas, Islamic legislation must interpret intellectually. Ibn Anas sought to foster a sense of justice among all Muslims through interpreting the Qur'an and Tradition. His aim was to search for the interest of Muslims. Therefore his conception of legal justice challenged the politics of his time, just as it could also challenge the politics of most Muslim countries today that use Islamic law as a tool to maintain power and close interpretation gaps.

One could argue that due to the influence of Ibn Anas on Mernissi in her role as an Islamic feminist scholar, Mernissi provides a challenging interpretation of the sources of Islamic Shari'a law: the Qur'an and Tradition to establish a search for the interest of Muslims, especially women in contemporary societies. This will be clarified below. In fact, Mernissi discusses the issue of the revelation of the Qur'an and the transmission of the Tradition of the Prophet Muhammad in two of her books, *The Veil and the Male Elite: A Feminist Interpretation of Women's Rights in Islam* (1991) and *Islam and Democracy: Fear of the Modern World* (2002).

First, I refer to her thoughts regarding the Qur'an to point out her doubts about the circumstances of its revelation to the prophet Muhammad. According to Mernissi, the Qur'an was transmitted to the prophet Muhammed orally. The prophet controls neither the time nor the length of the chapters of the Qur'an. According to her, the order of the written Qur'an that Muslims have today is different from

---

160 Khadduri 1984:137.
161 Muhammad bin 'Ashur was born in Tunisia in 1879 and died in 1973. He was one of the great Islamic scholars. He was a prolific writer and author about reforming the education and jurisprudence of Islam. See Nafi, Basheer M,(2005), Tahir ibn 'Ashur: The Career and Thought of a Modern Reformist *'alim*, with Special Reference to His Work of *tafsir*, in the Journal of Qur'anic Studies, Volume 7 Issue 1, pp.1-32.
162 Khadduri 1984:138.

the order of the revelations of the Qur'anic chapters as exposed to the prophet. For example, there are chapters revealed at Mecca that set forth dogma and the duties of Muslims, and there are chapters revealed at Medina that are related to problems that the Prophet faced and to the questions asked him by the first Muslims.[163] Hence Mernissi's statement about the revelation of the Qur'an puts forward two problems: on the one hand, the Qur'an revealed to the prophet Muhammed orally. On the other hand, the prophet does not control the length and the order of the Qur'anic chapters. Mernissi wants to argue beyond this statement that an understanding of the Qur'an, which is the most important text in the development of legal claims in Islam, should be based on a clarification of the circumstances of the revelation of each chapter in order to understand the goals and the message that each Qur'anic chapter intends to convey.

Second, according to Mernissi, the Tradition is divided into two grounds: The sayings of the prophet, called *Hadith*, and the acts of the prophet, called *Sunnah*. She argues that the content of the Tradition is important in drawing ethical duties for most Muslim communities. Mernissi declares that most Muslims, since the prophet's death, seek to follow his ideals, which were illustrated by his Tradition.[164] In Mernissi's view, Tradition was not illustrated by God or the Prophet Muhammad, but was formulated after the Prophet's death, when the succession issue developed and it became necessary to replace the Prophet in both his political and legislative roles.[165] Consequently, Mernissi presents a rereading of the Qur'an and the Tradition that looks for a notion of legal justice in Islamic law and promote the needs and interests of women. In this regard, she argues in her book, *Scheherazade Goes West: Different Culture, Different Harems* (2001):

> What is debated is whether *Shari'a*, the law inspired by the Koran, can or cannot be changed. The debate is therefore reduced to "who" made the law. If it is men who made it, then the text can be reinterpreted; reform is possible. But extremists who oppose the democratization of the laws claim that *Shari'a* is as divine as the Koran and therefore unchangeable.[166]

This affirms that Islamic law can be reformed because it is man-made and not divine in nature, thus, it can be reinterpreted according to the times and conditions of societies. As just outlined, one might affirm that Mernissi refers to Ibn Anas's notion of *ijtihad* to preserve her right as an intellectual Muslim woman to participate in

---

163   Mernissi 2002: 75–77.
164   Mernissi 1991: 25–48.
165   Mernissi 1991: 25–48.
166   Mernissi 2001: 22–23.

the interpretation of the religious corpora. In this context, Mernissi portrays the social segregation between men and women in her Moroccan society.[167] She challenges "religious authorities" and "functionaries of the Ministry of Justice" in Morocco who, after independence, signed the Personal Status Code—*Mudawana*—depriving Moroccan women of their rights.[168] Thus, the first code of personal status, instituted in 1957 in Morocco, called the *Mudawana*, was masterminded by men only. It was presented as Islamic law to make it 'sacred' and not open to public debate. Its key features consist in asserting women as minors and distancing them from the public sphere.[169]

As discussed earlier (see 2), today and in most Muslim countries, scholars within Islamic feminism discourse continue to engage in the task of interpretating Islamic law (*Shari'a*), to claim gender justice in Islam. They demonstrate how it is not the religious scriptures themselves but their interpretation that allows for the construction of patriarchal traditions within Islamic legacy. Moha Ennaji (2020) argued that Mernissi is one of the prominent founders of Islamic feminism. Mernissi sought to reclaim the ideological discourse on women from the monopoly of patriarchy. She critically analyzes the traditional corpus of religious-juristic texts, including the Hadith, and reinterprets them from a feminist standpoint. She argues that the perceived Muslim ideal of the 'obedient woman' has nothing to do with the genuine message of Islam. Rather, it is a production of the *ulama*,' the male jurist-theologians, who manipulated and interpreted the Islamic texts to defend the patriarchal system.[170] Thus, Mernissi uses Ibn Anas' concept of *ijtihad* to claim her right to interpret Islamic law to challenge today's patriarchy and masculine interpretations.

Divine justice as the principle of self-direction (*freedom*)

Sufism[171] constituted the core of spiritual belief in the tradition of Islam. However, certain misconceptions and prejudices were proclaimed against this Islamic doctrine. These prejudgments were most often due to ignorance of Sufism or because

---

167 Mernissi 2003: 138.
168 Mernissi 2003: 149.
169 Sadiqi and Ennaji 2006: 20.
170 Ennaji 2020: 20.
171 Sufism is a belief and practice in which Muslims seek to find the truth of divine love and knowledge through direct personal experience of God. Sufism consists of a variety of mystical paths to achieve union with God: Purifying the soul, knowing God, union with God, or extinguishing oneself in him, and dying oneself and living again through him. About the doctrine of Sufism in Islam see: Schimmel, Annemarie, *Mystische Dimensionen des Islam. Die Geschichte des Sufismus* (Frankfurt am Main, 1995); *Le Soufisme ou les dimensions mystiques de L'Islam* (Paris, 1996); *Mystical Dimensions of Islam* (Chapel Hill, 1975).

rulers perceived in Sufism a menace to their authority.[172] Thus, one can predict that Mernissi presents the thought of the Sufi al-Hallaj[173] as a good critique of contemporary political authorities who contribute to denying Muslims their democratic rights to freedom and autonomy.

Mernissi introduces al-Hallaj's thought in two of her books, *Islam and Democracy: Fear of the Modern World* (2002) and *Scheherazade Goes West: Different Cultures, Different Harems* (2001). Mernissi declares at the beginning of her presentation of the Sufi doctrine of al-Hallaj that "the Sufis' thirsting for freedom"[174] was in contrast with the caliphs and their *Shari'a* interpretation of divine law, which was very authoritarian.[175] Always based on her transcultural and comparative methods of early Arabo-Islamic thought and the modern Western tradition of human rights, Mernissi argues that:

> The West, which constantly talks about democracy via its satellites and media networks, is frightening to some because it awakens the memory of forgotten greats of the past ... the defenders of that little thing, so fragile, so vulnerable, called *karama*, 'dignity.'[176]

In other words, Mernissi suggests al-Hallaj's concept of freedom is comparable to our contemporary conceptions of autonomy, self-determination, and freedom of thought. In this sense, al-Hallaj's thought has been associated with the modern notion of freedom of thought and opinion.[177] Thus, Mernissi reminds the Muslims of today of their humanistic past, and the West that in the heritage of Islam there was already a claim to sovereignty of the individual before the Western declaration of human rights. She argues that there was al-Hallaj the Sufi who insisted that human

---

172 Geoffroy 2010: 30.
173 Al-Hallaj was born in 858 in Persia and died in 922 in Baghdad. He was a controversial writer and teacher of Sufism. Al-Hallaj was attracted to Sufism as a way of life at an early age. He was not satisfied in learning the Qur'ān by heart; he wanted to understand the deeper meaning of it. During his childhood and when Sufism was in its formative period, al-Hallaj began to seek individuals who were able to instruct him in the Sufi way. The French orientalist Louis Massignon looks at the Sufi thought of Al-Hallaj. See: La passion de Hallaj, martyr mystique de l'Islam, 4 vols. (Paris, Gallimard.,1975); trans. Mason; Herbert, The Death of Al-Halla j: A Dramatic Narrative (Notre Dame Press, ed., 1991). The German orientalist Annemarie-Schimmel, too, wrote extensively on the thought of Al-Hallaj. See: *al-Halladsch, Martyrer der Gottesliebe; Leben und Legende* (Köln, 1968).
174 Mernissi 2002: 19.
175 Mernissi 2002: 19.
176 Mernissi 2002: 19.
177 Wolfs and El-Boudamoussi 2004: 23.

beings are the depository of *haqq*, 'truth,' and that each person should be necessarily sovereign.[178]

According to Mernissi, the question evoked by al-Hallaj is how human beings who possess the truth and incorporate the divine beauty of God are condemned to obey to the authority of the Imam. Al-Hallaj insisted on the idea that human beings are the creatures of God, indeed, they are capable of self-direction. Mernissi continues by affirming that al-Hallaj's ideas challenge the political authority of his time because he simply declared that human beings should be independent from the authority of the rulers. Mernissi assumes that the ideas of al-Hallaj were received by the Muslim masses and discussed in the streets and bazaars of Baghdad; as a result, and for fear of its anti-authoritarian content, the caliph ordered his execution.[179] Putting it simply, the spiritual thought of al-Hallj consists of distorting the boundaries between human beings and God that the imam or the caliph (the leader in Islam) wished to establish. In the core of Islamic religion there is no intermediary between God and the individual. "Al-Hallaj believed that if you concentrate on loving God, without intermediaries, a blurring of the boundaries with the divine becomes possible."[180] Mernissi quotes from Ibn Khallikan's description of the painful death of Al-Hallaj: " 'He received a thousand blows and didn't utter a word ... The executioner cut off his hands and feet, cut off his head, which he kept aside, and then burned the body. When it was nothing but ashes, he threw it into the Tigris and planted the head on Baghdad's bridge.'"[181]

As outlined earlier, the concept of divine justice introduced by al-Hallaj has been associated with modern notions of self-direction and freedom. To better understand Mernissi's purpose behind her reference to this school of Islamic tradition, I discuss divine justice as it appears in secondary literature.

Al-Hallaj's notion of divine justice was described as a manifestation of spiritual experience gained directly from the union with God and not from ordinary human actions. Hence, it consists in highly abstract and poetic symbols like Light, Beauty, and Love. The goal of the Sufi is to achieve the apprehension of truth (*al-haqq*), but this truth is deeper, it is in the soul. Indeed, to achieve perfection and to gain the truth, human beings should exercise their soul to become isolated from everything foreign to the truth. It means to keep the soul out of all that is not divine. When the soul is finally united with the divine, the Sufi transformed from the state of extinction, (*al-fana*), the reality of existence, to the state of (*al-haqq*), the ultimate reality or the reality of union with the divine.[182] Al-Hallaj declared to have achieved union

---

178   Mernissi 2002: 20.
179   Mernissi 2002: 19–20.
180   Mernissi 2001: 3.
181   Mernissi 2002: 20.
182   Khadduri 1984: 70–71.

with God, and he used to say, "I am the Truth." For this declaration he was accused of heresy and brought to trial. He was condemned to death, and was executed by beheading and crucifixion. [183]

To sum up, al-Hallaj asserts that human beings are the sole repositories of truth. He thereby promoted the idea of self-guidance. It means human beings should not surrender to the ruler's power and determinations. In this way, to achieve divine justice, human beings should get rid of the earthly restrictions and manipulations to unite with God. The phrase *I am the truth* declared by al-Hallaj was to express that he had achieved the peak of Sufism, meaning his unification with God and the mingling of his soul with the Divine. The Divine is God, and God is the Just, therefore the Sufi who achieved incarnation with God incarnates divine justice. It means God incarnates, reflects, and reproduces in him His Justice. *I am the truth* means *I am the just*. As a result, one can understand that Mernissi refers to al-Hallaj and particularly his idea of self-direction, i.e. freedom, thus, arguing that Muslims have the right to self-determination through democratic means in contemporary Muslim societies.

Political justice in the tradition of Islam: A tangle of rational and fundamentalist arguments

In most Muslim societies today, citizens claim their political rights. In most cases, they assert their rights through rational or fundamentalist arguments. Based on this fact, Mernissi uses the history of the Arabo-Islamic thought to argue that fundamentalism is inappropriate for claiming political rights in contemporary societies. She focuses on two traditions within the history of Islam: first, the Kharijites[184] who used violence to demand political rights, which led to fundamentalism. Second, the Mu'tazila[185] who fought for political rights based on rational values. I discuss this in the following section.

---

183 Khadduri 1984:72.
184 The Kharijites were the first identifiable sect of Islam. The specific context for the emergence of the Kharijites was the struggle for leadership of the Muslim community following to Uthman the third caliph after the prophet's death. The community leaders choose Ali ibn Abi Talib as the successor of Uthman. However, Mu'awiya, the governor of Damascus, was against the election of Ali as leader. The supporters of Mu'awiya are the Kharijites who assassinated Ali in 661. The Kharijites sect has been revived in the context of late 20th century by few Muslim groups. In this context: See; Jeffrey, Kenney. Muslim Rebels: Kharijites and the Politics of Extremism in Egypt. Oxford: Oxford Univ. Press, 2006.
185 Al-Mu'tazila is a rationalist school of Islamic theology, which flourished in the cities of Basra and Baghdad both now in Iraq, during the 8th and the 10th centuries. It is an important school of Islamic theology. It is mentioned as the first school of speculative theology. And it is often argued that the thought of Islamic theology developed from it. Al-Mu'tazila are not just theologians, but they also discussed philosophical problems concerning psychology and physics. It is evident that the thought of Al-Mu'tazila inspired most contemporary Muslim thinkers.

Political justice as the entanglement of political fundamentalism

Mernissi introduces the idea that the Kharijite sects claim political rights by force, which could be interpreted as violence, terrorism, and fundamentalism today. Mernissi explains, "In theory, it is the Muslim's duty to revolt against an imam who makes unjust decisions".[186] According to Mernissi, the Kharijites thought that by rebelling against the imam and killing him, they could establish justice. In fact, they ask the question: Why do you have to obey the imam if he does not protect your rights? The Kharijites' answer is this: You are not obligated to obey the Imam. You can detach yourself from obeying the imam because you only have to obey God.[187]

Mernissi also clarifies that the Kharijite not only go out from obedience to the imam, but they also adopt his murder as a solution for defending their rights. Hence, they sustain the use of terrorism as an answer to revolt against the injustice of the imam or the caliph. In this context, Mernissi draws on a list compiled by Ibn Hazm of those caliphs who were assassinated by the Kharijite during the eighth and ninth centuries of Islam. Among them she points out the caliph, 'Umar Ibn al-Khattab, who was the second caliph to govern after the death of the Prophet Muhammed. She argues that 'Umar Ibn al-Khattab was the figure with the greatest reputation for justice; he was one of the supporters of *ra'y*, individual judgement, as the source of decision-making.[188] One might argue that Mernissi uses the Kharijite conflict with Muslim leaders by demanding political rights to express her disagreement with, disdain for, and rejection of terrorist and fundamentalist thought.

Moreover, Mernissi uncovers the history of Arabo-Islamic thought on fundamentalism to argue that it is still prevalent in today most Arab Muslim societies. As evidence, she cites the fundamentalist attack on Egyptian President Anwar Sadat (1970–1981), who was killed in October 1981. Mernissi mentions the killings of "hundreds of imams and Muslim leaders, the last of whom was President Anwar Sadat of Egypt. Political dissidence is expressed in Islam as condemnation of the leader. It is this rebel tradition that links dissidence with terrorism".[189] Notwithstanding Mernissi's claim that Anwar Sadat was the last Muslim ruler to be assassinated, I would like to add that there are other Muslim leaders who have been assassinated in recent times, such as Saddam Hussein (he was president of Iraq from 1979 to 2003) and Muammer Gaddafi (he was president of Libya from 1979 to 2011), both of whom

---

See: Arnaldez, Roger: « l'analyse des sept arguments mu'tazilites » in *Les sciences coraniques: Grammaire, droit, théologie et mystique*. Paris Vrin, 2005, p.130-132.
186 Mernissi 2002: 27.
187 Mernissi 2002: 27.
188 Mernissi 2002: 28–29.
189 Mernissi 2002: 27–28.

were killed and tortured under different circumstances because of their positions as despotic and unjust Muslim leaders.

In her account of the Kharijite sect and its adherence to a notion of righteousness within the framework of fundamentalism, Mernissi fails to tell us in more detail that the Kharijite sect was divided into two groups: the radical group she highlights and another, less radical group. Indeed, in his book, *The Islamic Conception of Justice* (1984), Majid Khadduri states that the less radical Kharijite sect favored social justice in the broadest sense of the word and therefore kept a simple lifestyle and resisted the worldly ways and lax habits of urban life. They are adamant about defending freedom and equality.[190] If one examines early Arabo-Islamic thought more closely, one can avoid generalizations by making more nuanced judgments than Mernissi suggests. Indeed, it is necessary to consider other schools of Islamic thought that flourished during the ninth century, which sought justice through more moderate and logical frameworks. I have mentioned the less radical Kharijite sect as an example.

Mernissi chooses to discuss the Mu'tazila, an Islamic school of theology which, she argues, promotes the idea of political rights through reason. In this context, I examine the Mu'tazila's claim to political justice, which I understand from Mernissi's account.

Political justice based on reason and free will: A philosophical approach to morality in Islam

The Mu'tazila and the Kharijites favor political transformation, but the Mu'tazila dispute with the Kharijites on one point. They disagree with the Kharijites on the issue of killing a leader and using violence and terrorism. The Mu'tazila did not believe that by the usage of weapons political rights and political change can be attained. They believed in reason as a philosophical tool for the achievement of political rights.

The Mu'tazila are a school of Islamic theology that flourished in Baghdad at the beginning of the ninth century. Along with their speculations on the relationship between the ruler and the ruled, the Mu'tazila also put reason as the basis of understanding Islamic law. Therefore their views on Islamic theology also disagree with other theological schools of their time, such as the Jabarites.[191] The following section goes into more detail about this. My purpose is to develop from Mernissi's ex-

---

190 Khadduri 1984: 22.
191 The Jabarites theological school is often associated with the traditionalist school of Salafism that based their argumentation on the textual sources of Qur'an and Tradition by affirming that human actions are predestined by God, without taking into consideration other texts which on the contrary affirm the responsibility of man. See: Bouamrane, Chikh: Le Problème De La Liberté Humaine Dans La Pensée Musulmane (Solution Mu'tazilites), Section 2 Les Sources Doctrinale: Les Début de la Doctrine Jabrites. Paris. J. Vrin pp. 34–42.

planation of "the rationalist tradition of the Mu'tazila"[192] a notion of political justice founded on reason as a philosophical principle. In this sense, Mernissi argues:

> The Mu'tazila moved the problem [of the relationships between the ruler and the ruled] to the philosophical level, asking, What is the purpose of our existence on earth, and to what use should we put *'aql* [reason], that marvelous gift from heaven? If God has created us intelligent, it is to carry out a plan. ... By introducing reason into the political theater, the Mu'tazila forced Islam to imagine new relationships between ruler and ruled, *giving all the faithful an active part to play alongside the palace.* [emphasis added][193]

Indeed, according to Mernissi, the Mu'tazila questioned the ruler-ruled relationship and argued for the participation of the ruled in decision-making processes. With this in mind, Mernissi criticizes blind obedience to religious authorities and argues for greater political rights. This leads me to argue that it is of current importance to re-read the Islamic philosophy of the Mu'tazila because it establishes the basic principle of the modern concept of democracy, namely the ability of the people to choose their ruler. The importance of the Mu'tazila, then, for Mernissi, was political. Mernissi draws out the Khariji/Mu'tazili contrast, as outlined earlier, as a theme of Islamic political history and as a basis for understanding the fear Islamic fundamentalists have, as she claims, of rationalism and democracy.[194]

Some further explanation is needed regarding the philosophical approach of the Mu'tazila school of Islamic theology in rethinking Islamic legislation to make it more compatible with their political philosophy. One could argue that there is a sense in which theology and politics are correlated, because when Islamic law is interpreted based on reason, justice will prevail in the political sphere. Theological justice is in accordance with the doctrines laid down by the theologians concerning the attributes of God (the will and power) and the essence of god (the essence and perfection), that make up divine justice. Indeed, theologians of Islam like the Jabarites agreed that justice is divine, and God is the source of justice, by directing their argument at the textual sources (Qur'an and Tradition) and at the principle of predestination. The question then must be: How could this divine justice, attributed to God, be realized on Earth? Here the theologians are divided into two schools: The school of Revelation based on the texts, which is the Jabarites School, and the school of Reason, the Mu'tazila, who are the followers of reason in calling themselves the partisans of justice and Oneness.[195]

---

192 Mernissi 2002: 32.
193 Mernissi 2002: 32–33.
194 Martin, Richard C., Mark. R. Woodward and Dwi S. Atmaja 1997: 208.
195 Khadduri 1984: 40–41.

The Mu'tazila conceive the existence of two levels of justice: divine and human. The former is laid down by God and the latter, determined by reason. Indeed, they argue that divine justice is based on the essence of God and not on the attributes of God. They conceive that God can do only what is salutary for man. Therefore, how can man realize this divine justice of God on earth? The Mu'tazila maintain that only by reason can man endeavor to achieve justice on earth. It means that God predicts the just and the salutary, and man can realize the determinations of God through his (man's) reason and free will (choice, *ikhtiyar*).[196] In this regard, Mernissi explains,

> One of the questions the Mu'tazila debated, and which drew crowds, was the question of *qadar*, "predestination": are we free (*qadir*) to act and thus responsible for our fate, or is our destiny already fixed by God? One branch of the Mu'tazila, the Qadiriyya, made this its central concern. Its adherents, the Qadiri, were "believers in free destiny, who thought that the human being was free to decide his own acts and so was responsible for everything he did, for evil as well as good."[197]

Following from this, the Mu'tazila argue that a man is obliged to establish justice according to his faculty of reason. Hence they understand that the achievement of justice on earth depends on the free will (choice) of man, who decides to realize justice or not; in fact, man is responsible for whether his acts are just or unjust. The Mu'tazila undertake three principles to determine that justice is based on reason:

1) The principle of reason: that justice is determined by reason.
2) The principle of voluntarism: that the acts of man are the product of his free will.
3) The principle of responsibility: that individuals should assume their choice, knowing that they could be punished in accordance with their choice of justice or injustice.

Furthermore, the Mu'tazila undertake the principle of *the metaphorical method of interpretation (al-ta'wil)* to avoid the conflicting meanings of the revelation's texts (Qur'an and Tradition). They argue that the foundation of legal justice requires that *the rational judgement* should be made in accordance with the judgement made by the theologians who refer to the Revelation.[198]

Hence, the Mu'tazila correlates with considerable aspects of justice, such as theological, divine, and legal. These concepts of justice have already been discussed above, including Ibn Anas's notion of legal justice and Al-Hallaj's notion of divine

---

196   Khadduri 1984: 40–41.
197   Mernissi 2002: 34–35.
198   Khadduri 1984: 41–44.

2. Background and methods in the thought of Fatima Mernissi   89

justice. The main characteristic of Mu'tazila thought is that they attach foremost importance to reason as a tool of philosophy. They recognize human beings as the owner and possessor of reason. Human beings are responsible for their actions and choices; they can make decisions based on their own free will. In this way, they are self-determined and are not predetermined. In addition, Mu'tazila argues that the Qur'an and Tradition must be interpreted rationally. In this sense, the Mu'tazila thought relates to the notion of legal justice of Ibn Anas based on the right of interpretation, and to the notion of divine justice of al-Hallaj based on self-determination.

Furthermore, Mu'tazila's thought is relevant in that it enables reason to be a part of the political framework. In their view, humans are rational beings capable of choosing and making political decisions. As outlined earlier, "The importance of the Mu'tazila, according to Mernissi, is that they asked philosophically: 'What is the purpose of our existence on earth, and to what use should we put *'aql*, that marvelous gift from heaven?.'"[199] Moreover, one could affirm that the Mu'tazila assert a notion of political justice by arguing that the ruled should participate in political decision-making. I mentioned this above. They argue that the ruler and the ruled are equal. This suggests an important level of equality between humans. Thus, their political philosophy conflicts with Islamic political tradition—by which I mean the Shi'a political tradition—which asserts that the imam, the ruler, is infallible. Mernissi declares, "Islam is based on an absolute prohibition against confusing God with man, so the obedience owed to the imam must in no way be considered equal to that owed to God."[200] Mernissi uses this interpretation to criticize blind obedience to religious authorities and to argue for more political rights in our contemporary societies. From a feminist perspective, one could argue that Mernissi radicalizes this idea by stressing the right of a Muslim woman to political participation. She stresses the principle of the equality between *all citizens*, men and women, to practice their political rights, and underlines the sovereignty of humankind, who freely select their representative (see 2.2).

Mernissi not only sheds light on the function of reason in enforcing political rights and, thus, political justice, but also on another concept of the Mu'tazila, namely the concept of neutrality. In this context, she argues:

> The entry of the Mu'tazila onto the political scene transformed and intellectualized it by bringing in new concepts: for example, *i'tizal*, that is, taking a middle position, weighing the pros and cons. This issue was important because it brought

---

199   Martin, Richard C., Mark. R. Woodward and Dwi S. Atmaja 1997: 208.
200   Mernissi 2002: 33.

up the question of tolerance. What should be done with a Muslim who commits a sin? The Mu'tazila chose the second option—neutrality, and thus, tolerance.[201]

According to Mernissi, neutrality corresponds to the modern notion of tolerance. One could not take for granted that being neutral is the equivalent of being tolerant. The concept of neutrality could be differently interpreted. Being neutral means not expressing individual opinions. Thus, personal morals engage in neutrality. Tolerance, however, has more to do with the public interest. The concept of tolerance affirms the acceptance of different religious beliefs, political opinions, and differing cultures to achieve the common good and to maintain a peaceful society.

Importantly, the Mu'tazila support the importance of reason, which Mernissi stresses throughout her exposition of the Mu'tazila's thought. Reason is therefore alleging that one should reflect before taking a decision. As Mernissi declares, "One cannot condemn someone without mature reflection on his conduct."[202] Hence, reason cultivates in human beings the moral conduct of (*at-tarayyuth*); this means to examine or to reflect to learn whether something is correct. Furthermore, reason nurtures the philosophical conduct of (*at-ta'aqqul*). This Arabic word comes from the Arabic verb (*ta'aqqala*) . It means being rational and reasonable; one should listen to reason—be careful; be cautious; be discerning; be discrete; be judicious; be rational in taking decisions.

Through reactivating early Islamic thought on Mu'tazila's rationalism, Mernissi sheds light on contemporary Arab philosophers and thinkers who, as she asserts, embody the rational and humanistic ideas of Mu'tazila in our time. In this regard, she declares:

> In face of this convergence, Arab intellectuals, mostly philosophers, are defending the opening to all humanistic thought, whether ancient or modern. (...). Contemporary philosophers and ideologues like Muhammad 'Amara, Husayn Mruwa[203] (who was killed a few years ago in Beirut), and Muhammed al-Jabiri

---

201 Mernissi 2002: 35.
202 Mernissi 2002: 35.
203 Mernissi has a list of rational, modernist Arab intellectuals suffering from malign neglect on the part of Europe, such as Muhammad 'Amara Husayn Mruwa, Muhammad al-Jabiri, Taha Husayn. Only Taha appears in a European language in the Berkeley catalog, and then the only work is his autobiography. Mruwa does not appear at all. I argue that Mernissi had not discovered al-Jabri's translations at the time when she wrote this declaration. "The work of al-Jabiri and the others are not translated, and their authors are not interviewed by Western television networks" (Mernissi 2002: 38). A-Jabri's books have been translated into French, English, and German. English translations: Al-Jabri, Muhammad Abed (January 1999). *Arab-Islamic Philosophy: A Contemporary Critique*. Translated by Abbassi, Aziz. Center for Middle Eastern Studies; University of Texas Press. (2008). *Democracy, Human Rights and Law in Islamic Thought*. I. B. Tauris. (2010). *The Formation of Arab Reason: Text, Tradition, and the Construction*

(one of today's most important thinkers) have become more well known in the Arab world than hit singers and often more popular than the heads of state who try to repress them. The Moroccan al-Jabiri is the philosopher most red by Arab youth, if I can judge by the remarks of students in conference debates and informal discussions.[204]

Mruwa and al-Jabri, according to Mernissi, are claiming the openness toward other cultures and philosophies. They thereby defend reason and humanism as the Mu'tazila did in the ninth century of Islam. In a book entitled *Defenders of Reason in Islam* (1997), Mernissi is considered alongside contemporary thinkers like Mohammed Arkoun, Fazlur Rahman, and Hassan Hanafi who were influenced by Mu'tazila's rational philosophy and transmit their humanistic ideas in the contemporary time. Thus, Mernissi, one of the thinkers cited, sees the rationalism and free thinking of the Mu'tazila as symbolic of the ability of Muslims to stand up to external challenges in order to enforce a rethinking and reform of the Islamic legacy.[205] The Mu'tazila's view of rationalism, then, deserves to be explored for our contemporary times in seeking to demand more political rights and, thus, give meaning to political justice. Following Mernissi, I would further elaborate on the reception of the rational heritage of the Mu'tazila in the ninth century of Islamic civilization. This historical detail is presented by Mernissi by highlighting the transcultural and humanistic approaches that characterized early Arabo-Islamic thought. The transcultural approach is crucial to my research in showing how Arabo-Islamic thought and the various philosophical schools interacted. The humanistic approach is also important to show how intellectuals of different religions and identities lived together and participated in the development of knowledge under the rule of an Islamic empire.

The reception of the rational heritage of the Mu'tazila in the ninth-century of Islamic civilization

Mernissi emphasizes the reception of the rational heritage of Arabo-Islamic thought of the Mu'tazila and its influence on changing the dictatorial political rules of their time. According to her, "The ... Mu'tazila triumphed and succeed in burying a corrupt

---

of Modernity in the Arab World. I. B. Tauris. French translations: *La Pensée de Ibn Khaldoun: la Assabiya et l'État. Grandes lignes d'une théorie Khaldounienne de l'histoire musulmane*. Paris: Édima, 1971. *Pour une Vision Progressiste de nos Difficultés Intellectuelles et Éducatives*. Paris: Édima, 1977. *Nous et Notre Passé (Al-Marqaz al-taqafi al-arabi). Lecture contemporaine de notre patrimoine philosophique*, 1980. *Critique de la Raison Arabe* - 3 volumes, Beyrouth, 1982. German translation: *Kritik der arabischen Vernunft, Naqd al-'aql al-'arabi, Die Einführung*, Perlen Verlag, Berlin 2009.
204 Mernissi 2002: 38.
205 Martin, Richard C., Mark. R. Woodward and Dwi S. Atmaja 1997: 207.

dynasty, the Umayyads, through the insistence on the preeminence of '*aql*.'[206] Indeed, one could understand that the Mu'tazila's demand for political rights achieved in the ninth century a revolution against the corrupt and despotic regime.

Moreover, she asserts that the Mu'tazila's rational thought was encouraged by the Abbasid dynasty (750–1258) during the ninth-century. She declares, "Unlikely as it seems, the Abbasids came to power riding the fiery steed of triumphant reason, which the Mu'tazila proposed to a fantastic medieval Islam."[207] Mernissi equally highlights that during the reign of the Abbasids there was encouragement of translation and of cultural openness toward other schools of thought.

> The Abbasids adopted the Mu'tazila philosophy as their official doctrine for a least a century, the century of openness. Openness meant embracing all human knowledge, including the scientific treaties and Greek philosophy now translated into Arabic.[208]

Thus, according to Mernissi, the translation of the Greek humanistic heritage into Arabic started out as a government project. As she declares, "Hunayn Ibn Ishaq,[209] a Christian (d. 873), founded a school of translators which recruited its staff from among the most brilliant intellectuals of Baghdad and the whole empire".[210] As one can see, Mernissi mentions an important detail in her account about Hunayn Ibn Ishaq: that Ibn Ishaq was a Christian Arab. The purpose of this statement is to demonstrate the religious tolerance that prevailed during the time of the Abbasid empire. To put simply, Mernissi's declaration shows that, even though Ibn Ishaq was not a Muslim, he was intellectually active during a time when an Islamic dynasty ruled.

Furthermore, in her book entitled *Scheherazade Goes West: Different Cultures, Different Harems* (2001), Mernissi highlights the interconnectedness of different ethnic groups, religions, and cultures during the ruling time of the Abbasid empire. She argues:

---

206 Mernissi 2002: 33.
207 Mernissi 2002: 33.
208 Mernissi 2002: 35.
209 Hunayn ibn Ishaq (809–873) was an Arab Christian doctor. He was known for his translations from Greek to Syriac, the language of his community, and his translations into Arabic. He was nicknamed "master of translators." See: Micheau, Francoise, Mécènes et médecins à Bagdad au III e /IX e siècle: Les commentaires des traductions de Galien par Hunayn ibn Ishaq, in: Les Voies de la Science Grecques: Etude sur la transmission des textes de l'Antiquité au dix-neuvième siècle, publiées sous la direction de Danielle Jaquert, (1997) pp.147.
210 Mernissi 2002: 36.

To be a foreigner in the Abbasid court was not really a drawback, however, since the culture encouraged diversity and rewarded people for speaking many languages and bringing the richness of their own backgrounds into their performances. In fact, during the Abbasid dynasty, "scholars, artists, and *littérateurs* came from a variety of ethnic backgrounds (speaking Aramaic, Arabic, Persian, and Turkish), colors (white, black, and mulatto), and creeds (Muslim, Christian, Jew, Sabian, and Magian). It was this cosmopolitanism and multiculturalism of Baghdad that made for its enduring strength as great center of culture."[211]

One can affirm that Mernissi describes the acceptance and tolerance of religious diversity, interdependence between Muslims and Christians, and the absence of racial discrimination. Mernissi wants to indicate that the intellectuals who participated in the flourishing of science and culture came from different ethnicities. Hence, not only were Arabo-Muslims, Arabo-Christians, or Arabo-Jews responsible for the prosperity of sciences, but also intellectuals from Europe, Asia and the Persian Empire. This illustrates the harmony between various religions and ethnic identities, thus, illustrating the humanist atmosphere that reigned in an Islamic empire. In this way, "the basis of the relationship between Christians, Muslims, Jews, Mazdeans, Zoroastriens, etc. is human reason. We are dealing here with a humanistic universal discourse, a non-sectarian discourse" [translation mine].[212]

Mernissi uncovers another important detail about the reception of Greek heritage. She argues that the scholars of that time not only translated Greek heritage, but "they also turned to Iran and India to collect, translate, and synthesize everything that the genius of other cultures had accumulated."[213] This assumption by Mernissi deconstructs, as she explains, "the Western stereotype"[214] that claims Arab scholars only translated the Hellenic heritage. Moreover, Mernissi affirms that the period of the ninth century was that of intellectual flourishing and emancipation of the mind, thereby the foundation of new rational science called *falsafa* (philosophy). In this sense, she declares "This importation and translation of foreign learning was enriched by original scholarship, producing the flowering of Muslim thought, which come to be known as *falsafa* (philosophy)."[215]

On the same lines as Mernissi, I wish to draw attention to this crucial event, which occurred in the ninth century of the Islamic Empire and marked the birth of philosophy. In Baghdad, schools of philosophy began to be established at the beginning of the tenth century. Philosophy was transmitted by teachers to students in or around Syriac monasteries. It was Al-Farabi (870–950) who founded what is

---

211 Mernissi 2001: 124.
212 Samir 2013: 28.
213 Mernissi 2002: 36.
214 Mernissi 2002: 36.
215 Mernissi 2002: 36.

known as the "Aristotelian School of Baghdad". There were disciples of different religions at this school. Miskawayh (d. 1030) and al-Tawhidi (d. 1023) are among the Muslim philosophers who frequented this school, and Ibn Zur'ah (d. 1108) is among the Christian philosophers. The philosophers of this school continue to translate and comment on Greek philosophical works. There is a commentary on Aristotle that has endured for generations. This text is now preserved in Paris in a large manuscript from the middle of the 11th century.[216]

In her re-reading of the Arabo-Islamic intellectual history, Mernissi wants to unearth and recover a transcultural and humanist tradition within the Arabo- Islamic thought of the ninth century. The aim is to show that disciples from different religions were participating in the flourishing of the science of philosophy, in order to give insight into their openness to different traditions of thought.

However, the intellectual openness that characterized the Arabo-Islamic world in that time does not persist. In this regard, Mernissi declares, "Alas, very quickly the Abbasids fell into despotism."[217] According to her, the result was that the opening to reason, individual opinion, and the cult of private initiative was condemned as a foreign enterprise. Philosophers (*falasifa*) were hunted down, and freethinkers condemned as infidels and atheists. She declares that the Abbasid rulers invoked the tradition of Islamic Shari'a law, based on obedience, *ta'a*, against the freedom of thought.[218] Recent research on Islamic philosophy can show that Mernissi's interpretation of the end of rationalism and the revaluation of obedience with the end of Abbasid rule is not tenable.[219] Indeed, because of her aim to criticize the dispotic legal systems of several Arabo-Islamic states, Mernissi adopts this Orientalist perspective.

She explains,today, the end of rational intellectual property still affects most Muslim societies, because in such societies it is difficult to access other thoughts that might contradict conventional beliefs. This prevents the improvement of democracy,

---

216 Samir 2013: 6.
217 Mernissi 2002: 33.
218 Mernissi 2002: 36–37.
219 Among the numerous research dealing with the history of Arabo-Islamic culture in its postclassical era, aiming to refute the notion that the end of rationalism in Islamic culture occurred during the classical period and especially with the end of Abbasid rule, I would like to highlight the intellectual work of Sabine Schmidtke, who has played a central role in researching previously unedited and unknown theological and philosophical writings. Her work focuses on the history of Islamic thought in the post-classical period (thirteenth to nineteenth centuries), with an emphasis on reconstructing the textual heritage and intellectual significance of the Islamic intellectual world. See: Sabine Schmidkte (2000): *Theologie, Philosophie und Mystik im zwölferschiitischen Islam des 9./15. Jahrhunderts Die Gedankenwelten des Ibn Abī Ğumhūr al-Aḥsāʾī (um 838/1434/35 – nach 906/1501)*. Brill, Leiden, Boston, Köln.

2. Background and methods in the thought of Fatima Mernissi   95

which includes the concept of pluralism and the acceptance of differences. To protect their interests, Muslim rulers adhere to man-made interpretations of Shari'a law, thereby overriding the principle of rational thought. In this context, she says:

> This tradition is called the *shari'a*, creating the confusion that today blocks the democratic process by linking our blind obedience to the leader with our respect for religion. All calls for a rational relationship between the imam and his followers as well as any criticism of the leader are discredited as a rejection of Islam and a lack of respect for its principles and ideals. [220]

Still in accordance with Mernissi's investigation of the early Arabo-Islamic heritage, I would like to highlight one idea: that despite the despotism, which was spread by the caliphs in the ninth century of Islam, there was encouragement for the scientific and economic achievements. In this sense, Mernissi argues that Harun al-Rashid (786 - 809), one of the Abbasid caliphs, who was the architect of a most successful despotism, "used the decision-making power he took from the people to carry out great scientific and economic projects".[221] On the same lines as Mernissi, one could argue that the Period of Harun al-Rashid and his successors, the Abbasids, represents the period of scientific achievement across a wide range of scientific domains. Dmitri Gutas, one of the experts in Medieval Islamic philosophy has also confirmed this idea:

> A truly epoch-making stage, by any standard, in the course of human history. It is equal in significance to, and belongs to the same narrative as, ... that of Pericles' Athens, the Italian Renaissance, or the scientific revolution of the sixteenth and seventeenth centuries, and it deserves so to be recognized and embedded in our historical consciousness.[222]

Moreover, Mernissi uses the socio-historical context of the ninth century of Islamic heritage to compare early despotism with contemporary despotism in most Muslim societies. She finds that modern despotism does not aim to promote scientific development, but rather is involved in intellectual, political, and economic decadence and dependence on the West. In this regard, she declares "modern despotism takes decision-making power from the people to buy Kabir watches from the Japanese."[223]

Consequently, despite the Abbasid despotism, rational thought played a crucial role in the progress of philosophy and other disciplines. Moreover, Abbasid rule offers a glimpse into the transcultural and humanistic atmosphere of the Arab world in

---

220   Mernissi 2002: 37.
221   Mernissi 2002: 143.
222   Gutas 1998: 8.
223   Mernissi 2002: 143.

the ninth century, achieved by fostering a commitment to philosophy and the development of the humanities. Nevertheless, most Muslim societies today are still concerned about political despotism because they continue to adhere to traditionalism to protect their political interests, which poses a threat to the philosophical legacy of rationalism.

Hence Mernissi's rereading of ninth-century Arabo-Islamic thought offers a crucial insight into the rational heritage embodied by the Muslim jurist Ibn Anas, the Sufi Al-Hallaj, and the Mu'tazila philosophers. They advocate the right to interpretation (*ijtihad*), self-determination, and rationality as imperatives for human progress and the flourishing of Islamic thought. From this, an appeal for issues of legal justice can be derived by emphasizing the right to interpretation (*ijtihad*) as a method of finding rights via Islamic law. It was also argued that divine justice is expressed in the notion that human beings make their own decisions and are responsible for their destiny. Moreover, political justice was derived from the underlying principle of equality between ruler and ruled, with the latter having the right to participate in decision making. In addition, Mernissi introduces the rational, transcultural, and humanistic tradition of the early Arabo-Islamic heritage to remind contemporary Muslims that a notion of democracy and justice is not foreign to Islamic thought, but that it is truncated due to political interests when despotic leaders cultivate the tradition of obedience instead of autonomy and freedom of thought, to protect their regimes. Mernissi also addresses the West by pointing to the rational and humanistic thinking of the Islamic heritage to counter the fundamentalist interpretive stereotypes with which Arabo-Islamic culture is presented today.

2.4 Transdisciplinary approaches to establish gender justice within the framework of Islamic feminism

One of the goals of my research is to examine the transdisciplinary approaches Mernissi uses to enforce gender justice in Islam. The first section of the following chapter focuses on her return to the pre-Islamic era, to show how Mernissi revives the story of female deities who occupied the political and religious spheres. With the advent of Islam and for religious and political reasons, the symbolic role of these female deities was hollowed out by creating a false interpretation about their mythical and symbolic existence. Mernissi attempts to provide an alternative interpretation of their existence. In her study of the pre-Islamic period, she argues that women, even as deities, were subject to patriarchal judgments.

The second section examines Mernissi's historiography of women at the time of the Prophet Muhammad and after his death. It examines her depicting of the economic, intellectual, and leadership roles played by the Prophet's wives. Mernissi shows how the emancipatory image of women in an earlier period of Islam was suppressed due to a misogynistic interpretation of the Tradition, with the intention of displacing and dismissing women from the religious and political spheres.

The third section presents Mernissi's socio-historical and linguistic interpretive methods for the Qur'anic verse about the veil. This is done by describing and analyzing the complex network of thoughts about the veil—which even Mernissi did not consider—that might be applied to advocate for the recognition of veiled women in our contemporary society.

The fourth section discusses the socio-economic situation and legal rights of most women in Maghreb countries in the political context of the first Iraq war (1991) as a commentary on the liberation of women through their participation in protest. An important goal is to explain that many rights of women in Maghreb countries have still not been obtained. In most Maghreb countries, women still face economic and legal discrimination. Patriarchal systems of power use religious persecution as a means to eliminate and exclude women from the public sphere and the labor market. By comparing the 2011 uprising in the Maghreb with Mernissi's 1991 study, I show the relevance of Mernissi's study to the struggle of Maghrebian women today.

More or less detailed critical comments are made at the end of this study, first on Mernissi's secular feminist approach as a radical feminist agenda and second on the reception of her Islamic feminist approach as reformist. The aim is to demonstrate the potential of using transdisciplinary approaches—secular and Islamic—to demand Muslim women's rights; a method that Mernissi shares with other researchers who contribute to the growing framework of Islamic feminism.

Female deities in the pre-Islamic era: Symbols of divinity and power

In a passage from the book of Ibn Sa'd, entitled *Tabaqat*, Mernissi explains the arrival of the prophet Muhammed in Mecca with the aim of spreading monotheism, and therefore renouncing the worship of gods. She explains that when the prophet Muhammed made the ritual circuits around the temple and around the Ka'ba, while saying that the truth had come and falsehood has vanished, the gods slid from their pedestal. Mernissi declares that among the gods that slid down were feminine deities.[224] However, she declares "these goddesses did not have the facial expression of the tenderness (*rahma*) associated with the nurturing mother, for they wallowed in the bloodbaths of the sacrifices that they demanded."[225] In many cultural traditions, women are considered sensitive and delicate creatures. Accordingly, women were limited to the role of a mother. The goddesses of the pre-Islamic period are

---

224 Mernissi 2002: 86.
225 Mernissi 2002: 86.

the opposite of this image of women, as they exist in the public sphere of the sacred and powerful.

In this regard, Mernissi turns to chapter 53 of the Qur'an, in verses 19 and 20, where the names of the three most important goddesses are mentioned. "[Disbelievers], consider al-Lat and al-'Uzza, and the third one, Manat."[226] Mernissi explains the meaning of the names of every deity. She says, they are *al-'Uzza*, which means 'power' in the military sense of the word, *Manat*, which comes from the same root as *maniyya* (death), and *al-Lat*, which is the contraction of *ilahat* (goddesses).[227] One could argue that Mernissi refers to these female deities in pre-Islamic times to criticize the position of women in many Muslim societies today. Mernissi points out that female deities held important positions in both the sacred and political spheres. However, their position was misinterpreted after the spread of Islam (see below). As in modern times, Islamic law—as interpreted by men—prohibits women from participating in religious and political activities.

Mernissi highlights that the most powerful goddess is *al-'Uzza*; the etymological root of which comes from the Arabic *'izz* (power), as outlined above, and *quwwa* (physical force). Mernissi adds that al-'Uzza was considered the most powerful goddess because she has multiple symbols used in worship. For example, she was worshiped in the form of a tree, and was represented by an idol, and a temple was dedicated to her.[228] According to Mernissi, the deity *al-'Uzza* reigned not only on earth but also in the stars, as Venus, *Zahra*, is one of the names attributed to this deity.[229]

However, the spiritual symbol of al-'Uzza has a certain frightening aspect. It is this frightening aspect of the gods that has led to the denial of women's participation in the sacred sphere, when it was claimed that the gods require a sacrifice. Therefore, Mernissi claims that according to historians, burial of baby girls (*al-wa'd*) was considered a sacrifice offered to al-'Uzza.[230] Mernissi adds that "some verses directly link *al-wa'd* to the demands of the deities, which would make it human sacrifice".[231] One example is seen in verse 138 of chapter 6, which confirms that the burial was inspired by the divinities. The verse asserts

> ****In the same way, their idols have induced many of the pagans to kill their own children, a bringing them ruin and confusion in their faith: if God had willed

---

226 The Qur'ān, Chapter 53, The Star; Verses 19–20.
227 Mernissi 2002: 116.
228 Mernissi 2002: 118.
229 Mernissi 2002: 122.
230 Mernissi 2002: 119.
231 Mernissi 2002: 119.

2. Background and methods in the thought of Fatima Mernissi 99

otherwise they would not have done this, so [Prophet] leave them to their own devices.[232]

Mernissi refutes this Qur'anic theory that claims that the deities demand the killing of newborn girls. She argues:

> The idea of a deity who demanded the killing of children was inconceivable. To my mind, it is this phobia that explains the horror about the *jahiliyya* that up to the present day blocks scholarly research on that period. Before year of 1 of the Hejira (A. D 622), humanity had no history. There was nothing but darkness—only a zero.[233]

Mernissi argues that most Muslims do not know enough about the pre-Islamic era, which constituted the historical past, and the cultural heritage. She admonishes Muslims to "explore everything that has contributed to Islamic civilization" (meaning before and after the dawn of Islam). They should explore the "past with all its historical and mythical component parts, with its 'truth' and its 'lies,' its 'high points' and its 'low points.'"[234]

From this we might conclude that the history of Islamic civilization before the advent of Islam was shaped by the idea that goddesses demanded the death of female infants and, thus, engaged in immoral practices. This reminds us of the reasons for the fear of democracy and autonomy as symbols of the chaos (see 2.1) that led Muslims to ignore and reject their past. Thus, the period before Islam is perceived as a time of ignorance. In Arabic, this ignorance is called Jahiliyyah. "The word 'Jahiliyyah' comes from 'jahl' or ignorance. Thus, the age of Jahiliyyah refers to an age of ignorance existing in the pre-Islamic Arab peninsula. It is unclear what time span is covered by that age. Sometimes it covers all pre-Islamic Arab history, but more often it refers only to the last century before Islam."[235] By referring to the pre-Islamic period, Mernissi wants to correct false assumptions about the female deities of the pre-Islamic period to clarify that these assumptions were used for political reasons after the spread of Islam, to deny women participation in the sacred realm.

Like Mernissi, Azizah al-Hibri, in her article entitled "A study of Islamic herstory: or how did we ever get into this mess?" (1982), uncovers the historical past and the role of female deities in pre-Islamic times. In this context, al-Hibri argues:

> The northern people of Jahiliyyah built shrines for goddesses. The most famous among them were: al-Laat, al-Uzzah and Manat. They were referred to as *God's*

---

232 The Qur'ān, Chapter 6, Livestock; Verse 138.
233 Mernissi 2002: 120
234 Mernissi 2002: 122.
235 Al-Hibri 1982: 208.

daughters. [emphasis added] However, these and other gods were part of a hierarchy topped by one major God. They were not worshipped, since only God was. Their role was to advise and intercede with God on behalf of their followers. They were so influential in that role that they were mentioned both in the Qur'an and by the prophet.[236]

Accordingly, Mernissi ignores the historical fact revealed by al-Hibri that these goddesses were considered the daughters of one major God. Based on this discovery it is possible to assume that in the pre-Islamic period there was the belief in the idea of one major God. This would have been a preform monotheistic belief.

Like Mernissi, al-Hibri opposes the theory that killing female infants was a demand from the goddesses, as it is stated in the Qur'an as noted above. Al-Hibri provides the following interpretation, which is also shared and asserted by Mernissi. Al-Hibri and Mernissi argue that the parents killed their female infants because of poverty, when the female children are considered an economic burden, or because of the fear of shame, as the daughters could be captured during a raid and turned into sex slaves by their captors.[237]

Another fact about the pre-Islamic era revealed by al-Hibri is that women who were not goddesses preoccupied a particularly important role in the political, socio-economic, and cultural spheres. One of these women is Khadija, the first wife of the prophet Muhammed, whose prominent position at the time of the prophet Muhammed I will explore later. In this regard, al-Hibri argues:

> Among the famous women warriors [was] … Hind Bint Rabi'ah who fought against [the prophet Muhammed]. Among the famous women poets are al-Khansa,' and Um-Jandab. But the most famous businesswoman was Khadijah Bint Khuwailed, who gave the prophet his first job, sending him to trade in Damascus when he was only twelve. (She later proposed to him in marriage, and he accepted.) And finally, among the wise women we know of Suhum Bint Lukman and Jum'a Bint Habis al-Ayadi. Taken out of context, these facts could lead to the erroneous conclusion that women were possessed of their rights in pre-Islamic Jahiliyyah.[238]

Hence, in the pre-Islamic era women had a great deal of self-determination. They performed poetry, served in the military, and conducted business. These contributions made them active in their societies. In addition, a woman had the right to express her emotions and to choose her husband. The practice of this cultural tradition

---

236   Al-Hibri 1982: 208.
237   Mernissi 2002: 119–120; Al-Hibri 1982: 209.
238   Al-Hibri 1982: 209.

is uncommon even in most modern Muslim societies, when controlling female emotions is considered as necessary. Thus, the revealing of the roles of female goddesses and female mortals in pre-Islamic Arabia is important, for it reminds us that there were women before the dawn of Islam who occupied important positions in their societies, and we learn that women were free from those misogynist traditions that now forbid them such positions.

As a result, in her historical rereading of the pre-Islamic era, Mernissi stresses more the role of goddesses who reigned in Arabia before the dawn of Islam. Yet the reign of these goddesses is negatively represented, when it was claimed that these female goddesses demanded the killing of infant girls. Therefore one should consider the reasons behind this claim. One interpretation is given by Mernissi herself. She affirms that "the monotheistic order required that the feminine should be barred from the sphere of power, which coincided with the sacred."[239] Indeed, the dismissal of pre-Islamic goddesses from sacred and reigning spheres would have an impact on the role of women, particularly after Islam became a political power and, thus, was used as a means of controlling women. In this way, in most Islamic traditions, women inhabited the harem. They were not allowed to cross the boundaries of the private sphere and lived under the leadership of men. In this regard, Mernissi argues:

> Woman would be the equal of man in all domains in Islam, since she was also a believer and endowed with reason and will; but she was henceforward to be invisible in the political sphere. In the palace of the caliph she had her place— ... in the harem—the "forbidden space."[240]

Along the same lines as Mernissi, Laila Ahmed (1982) asserts that the harem has a deplorable connotation in the imaginary of most Arab and non-Arab Muslim women. Harem reminds women of the Turkish harem of the Ottoman Empire, where women were chosen for their beauty and destined for the pleasure and service of the sultan. Women were classified in pyramidal form, where the most beautiful and talented were given the opportunity to share the bed of the sultan, thus, becoming the favorite companion of the sultan, as opposed to the less beautiful and talented women, who were kept out of the group.[241]

Thus, Mernissi and Ahmed agree that the harem is a derogatory institution for women. Ahmed emphasizes the sexual and hierarchical dimensions of the harem, while Mernissi underlines the spatial aspect. Mernissi considers the harem as the

---

239 Mernissi 2002: 126.
240 Mernissi 2002: 126.
241 Ahmed 1982: 154

forbidden sphere where foreign men could not enter, and women could not escape. She considers the harem as a place of confinement, and thus, denial of spatial freedom.

In her autobiographical novel *Dreams of Trespass: Tales of a Harem Childhood* (1994), Mernissi tells of her childhood growing up in a harem in Fez, 1940. She recounts:

> I was born in a harem in 1940 in Fez, a ninth-century Moroccan city some five thousand kilometers west of Mecca, and one thousand kilometers south of Madrid, one of the dangerous capitals of the Christians.[242]

Mernissi provides an innovative conception of the harem. As such, the harem remains the place of the forbidden, but it is also the place where women seek to escape confinement. She describes how being in the harem with illiterate women inspired her to acquire literacy and develop a strong female identity. Despite living in a harem, Mernissi explores the ability to cross spatial boundaries and to fulfil her dreams. She affirms:

> Aunt Habiba was certain that we all had magic inside, woven into our dreams. "When you happen to be trapped powerless behind the walls, stuck in a dead-end harem," she would say, "you dream of escape. And magic flourishes when you spell out that dream and make the frontiers vanish. Dreams can change your life, and eventually the world. Liberation starts with images dancing in your little head, and you can translate those images to words."[243]

Indeed, the patriarchal system of the harem ironically empowers women in specific ways. Nausheen Ishaque (2019) argues that Mernissi provides a new conception of the harem which challenges Western orientalist assumptions in relation to the female inhabitants of harem, who are historically believed to be passive receivers of traditional patriarchy.[244] At the end of this study, I will elaborate on Mernissi's innovative conception of harem (2.5).

Mernissi's reinterpretation of pre-Islamic Arab civilization is essential. She demonstrates the significant roles that female deities occupied in both the sacred and ruling realms. However, the Qur'an states that their role was associated with immoral functions. This allows most Muslims to obscure and ignore the history of female deities. Therefore, in her historical review, Mernissi attempts to identify the reasons for women's exclusion from the religious and political spheres in most Muslim societies and during the period when only men ruled Islam. She identifies

---

242 Mernissi 1994: 1.
243 Mernissi 1994: 113–114.
244 Ishaque 2019.

the symbolic pushing down of female deities from their pedestals as one of the factors that contributed to the confinement of most women in Islam to the forbidden space, the harem.

Women rebels in the time of the prophet Muhammed: Religious and political roles

In *The Veil and the Male Elite: A Feminist Interpretation of Women's Rights in Islam* (1991), Mernissi looks at historical sources in order to uncover the significant role that the prophet's wives played in his time and after his death. The prophet Muhammad's first wife, Khadija, played a crucial role in his life as the first woman with whom he shared his first revelation. Moreover, Aisha was also regarded by most Sunni Muslims as a source of the Tradition (sayings and actions of the prophet) and was viewed as rebellious against patriarchal rules. Mernissi reveals the story of the Prophet's wife to assert that women played an important role in the Prophet's time. They were the confidants of the Prophet and participated in both the religious and political spheres. This is to refute false assumptions that, first, women cannot be the provenance of transmission of religious sources and, second, that they do not participate in politics.

Khadija Bint Khuwaylid

Mernissi argues that Mecca was one of the most important towns of Arabia in Muhammed's time (even before he received the revelation). Mecca had become indispensable for the security of the great international trade routes. Muhammed, as a member of the clan of Quraysh, the most powerful clan in Mecca, was destined to become a merchant. He went into business with a businesswoman named Khadija Bint Khuwaylid.[245] Mernissi provides the following information about the personage of Khadija:

According to Mernissi, Khadija was a widow, who like Muhammed, belonged to the tribe of Quraysh and who had inherited a large fortune from her late husband. Khadija was so happy with her cooperation with Muhammed and so surprised by his rectitude (which must have been a rare quality) that she proposed marriage to him. He accepted. He was twenty-five years old, and she was over forty. It was his first marriage. Although Khadija could not know that fifteen years later the man she married would become the prophet of a new religion, she was nevertheless convinced that he was no ordinary husband, and she had complete confidence in him. The first revelations were distressing to him, and, terrified by the voice he had heard, he went and described them to Khadija. He was assailed by self-doubt: "O Khadija, I fear I am

---

245   Mernissi 1991: 27.

going mad." She reassured him, convincing him that what had happened was marvelous and unique. Khadija celebrated the event by converting to the new religion of her husband; she was Islam's first adherent.[246]

These historical details about Khadija, as narrated by Mernissi, can help us realize that a woman at the time of the Prophet was a trustee, a self-confident and economically independent person. Moreover, it is important to know that the first person to convert to Islam was a woman. This challenges the patriarchal claims about most Muslim women as well as the dominant role of men over Islamic heritage. It likewise challenges the assertion that man can be the sole representatives of Islam and must forbid women's participation in the interpretation of Islamic law and in the performance of religious functions such as leading prayers.

In a similar vein, Miriam Cooke explores the personage of Khadija in her article entitled "Feminist Transgressions in the Postcolonial Arab World"(1999). Like Mernissi, Cooke describes Khadija as a successful businesswoman who proposed marriage to her employee, even though she was older than him. Also like Mernissi, Cooke asserts that Khadija was the first who believed her husband after he reported his revelation and was the first who converted to Islam. She argues that "when she died in 619, the prophet Muhammed lost one of his most influential supporters."[247]

One could argue that Cooke emphasized the historical personage of Khadija to highlight one of the approaches used by Islamic feminist scholars to achieve women's rights in Islam by looking to an equitable understanding of the Islamic legacy as interpreted by women. In this context, Cooke affirms that "some Islamic feminists are interrogating the historiography at the time of Muhammed, finding there a goldmine of information about women."[248]

Mernissi is undoubtedly one of the most important Islamic feminist scholars whose work Cooke presents in her article mentioned above. Cooke shows how Mernissi challenged false assumptions about Islamic legacy and criticized misogynistic Traditiona that are commonly attributed to the prophet. Cooke argues that Mernissi "dared to question the unquestionable, namely the reliability of a 'sound' Tradition or saying attributed to the prophet."[249] For Cooke, Mernissi requested a proper understanding of a Tradition that has been introduced to Muslims as sound. In Arabic, sound is (*sahih*). This term implies that a Tradition is attributed to the prophet and, thus, is not subject to questioning or refuting by Muslims. Cooke underscores that "Mernissi notes that the source of the misogynist Tradition is the key to its authority."[250] Following on from this, in accordance with Mernissi, I present

---

246   Mernissi 1991: 28.
247   Cooke 1999: 97.
248   Cooke 1999: 97.
249   Cooke 1999: 89.
250   Cooke 1999: 100.

an example of a misogynist Tradition that has been attributed to the prophet. The purpose is to show how it remains an argument used against women to exclude them from the sphere of political guidance.

Aisha bint Abī Bakr

Mernissi declares that Muhammed is close to four men: Abu Bakr al-Siddiq, Umar Ibn al- Khattab, ʿAlī ibn Abī Tālib, and ʿUthman Ibn ʿAffan.[251] As explained by Mernissi, the first and the second of these are the prophet's fathers-in-law. Muhammed married Aisha, the daughter of Abu Bakr, and Hafsa, Umar's daughter.[252] The third and fourth men are the prophet's sons-in-law: ʿAli married Fatima, the prophet's eldest daughter, and ʿUthman married Ruqayya, who is also one of the prophet's daughters.[253]

Likewise Mernissi, Cooke argues that these four men were remarkably close to Muhammed. She further explains that these men were to be the next to succeed the prophet after his death.[254] In other words, these men were the caliphs of the prophet. The word caliph comes from the Arabic verb (*khalafa*) meaning 'to succeed.' In the *Sunni* Islamic legacy, the theory of succession is known as the Islamic caliphate (*al-khilafa al-Islamiyya*). The caliphate (*al-khilafa*), according to Sunni Islamic tradition, is a system of government that is based on the succession of a Muslim leader (caliph) to assume the leadership of a community of Muslims. It is called the caliphate because the caliph is the one who succeeds the prophet Muhammed.

Mernissi provides valuable historical details about the biography of Aisha, the daughter of Abu Bakr and the youngest wife of Muhammed. One could speculate that Mernissi does this because Aisha was considered, after the death of the prophet Muhammed and by most Sunni Muslims, as the mother of the faithful, and her life became a role model for most Sunni Muslim women. Indeed, "after Muhammed's death, Aisha was long considered the chief source of Traditions as well as a respected interpreter of the Qur'an."[255]

Indeed, Mernissi tells us the following: "It was year 36 of the Hejira (AD 656), and public opinion was divided: should one obey an "unjust" caliph (who did not punish the killers of ʿUthman), or should one rebel against him and support Aisha, even if that rebellion led to civil disorder?."[256] Thus, one can deduce that Aisha guided a battle against ʿAli because he did not punish the killers of ʿUthman, his prior caliph.

---

251   Mernissi 1991: 33.
252   Mernissi 1991: 33.
253   Mernissi 1991: 33.
254   Cooke 1999: 97.
255   Cooke 1999: 98
256   Mernissi 1991: 54–55

Hence, according to Mernissi, Aisha decides to go to Basra—a city in the south of Iraq—to accuse 'Ali. She chose Basra because there were people in this town who did not like 'Ali, and therefore would most probably support her.[257]

Mernissi describes the procedures Aisha adopted before she led war against Ali. An essential detail which Mernissi mentions is that Aisha usually accompanied the prophet Muhammad, before his death, on his military expeditions. She therefore pursued similar strategies before waging war. For example, she informed the Muslim community about her choice to conduct war, asked people for their opinions and negotiated with those who disagreed with her. Mernissi explains accordingly:

> Aisha, who often used to accompany the Prophet on military expeditions, knew the procedure for the negotiations that took place before the military occupation of a city and had conducted matters correctly. Before besieging the city, she had sent messengers with letters to all the notables of the city, explaining to them the reasons that had impelled her to rebel against 'Ali, her intentions, and the objectives that she wanted to attain, and finally inviting them to support her.[258]

This historical narrative about Aisha demonstrates her strong personality as a rebel woman who established herself as a war leader among males. However, according to Mernissi, Abu Bakra, one of the prophet's companions, and a member of the notable of Basra, negatively responded to the demand of Aisha, by evoking a Tradition—which he remembered twenty-five years after the prophet's death. The Tradition stated, "Never will succeed such a nation as lets their affairs carried out by a woman."[259]

One could think that the Tradition recalled by Abu Bakra might be a reason for the defeat of Aisha. However, Mernissi asserts that Abu Bakra remembered this Tradition attributed to the prophet, and especially in this political context, only for the purpose of denying Aisha the right to wage war against Ali. Mernissi argues, "Abu Bakra had a truly astonishing memory for politically opportune Hadith which curiously – and most effectively – fitted into the stream of history."[260]

Mernissi claims her right as a Muslim woman to examine misogynist Tradition, like the Tradition quoted above. She argues:

> So nothing bans me, as a Muslim woman, from making a double investigation – historical and methodological – of this Hadith and its author, and especially of

---

257   Mernissi 1991: 50.
258   Mernissi 1991: 54.
259   Mernissi 1991: 56–57.
260   Mernissi 1991: 58.

the conditions in which it was first put to use. Who uttered this Hadith, where, when, why, and to whom?[261]

Accordingly, Mernissi demonstrates her intellectual role as an Islamic feminist scholar to examine misogynist Tradition attributed to the prophet, in order to remind contemporary Muslims about the right of interpretation and the search of the common good (*maslaha*) established by Imam Malik Ibn Anas in the eighth century of Islam (see 2.3). In this sense, Ibn Anas, according to Mernissi, considered "this religion as a science."[262] Therefore, religious claims should be verified through logical and scientific methods of interpretation. Mernissi quotes Ibn Anas as follows:

> "This religion is a science, so pay attention to those from whom you learn it. I had the good fortune to be born [in Medina] at a time when 70 persons [Companions] who could recite Hadith were still alive. They used to go to the mosque and start speaking: The Prophet said so and so. I did not collect any of the Hadith that they recounted, not because these people were not trustworthy, but because I saw that they were dealing in matters for which they were not qualified."[263]

Thus, if one considers Ibn Anas' assessment, Abu Bakra is unqualified to recount the Tradition. By means of Ibn Anas' critique, Mernissi shows that misogynist Traditions are wrongly attributed to the prophet. Therefore, for her, a historical and methodological analysis is necessary to examine the Islamic legacy. Later on, I will discuss Mernissi's methodological analysis of one of the Qur'anic verses to provide alternative interpretations of the meaning of 'veil' in Islamic legacy. First I shall explore how Mernissi sees the Tradition, which was recited by Abu-Bakra, as a continuing challenge for women today who aspire to be political leaders.

In her book *The Forgotten Queens of Islam* (1993), Mernissi asks: "Was Benazir Bhutto the First?"[264]. Mernissi provides historical and political details about the personage of Bhutto. She recounts that Benazir Bhutto became Prime Minister of Pakistan after winning the elections of 16 November 1988. According to Mernissi, all who monopolized the right to speak in the name of Islam, and clearly who lost the democratic election in Pakistan, appealed to the past and Tradition. Indeed, they evoked the same famous Tradition recited by Abu Bakra in 656, which is also employed by the opponents of Bhutto with the aim to eliminate her from participation in political life, claiming that "the political decision-making among our ancestors,

---

261 Mernissi 1991: 49.
262 Mernissi 1991: 59.
263 Mernissi 1991: 59.
264 Mernissi 1993: 2.

they said, was always a men's affair".[265] Thus, Mernissi explores how political adversaries of Bhutto obstructed her democratic right to be a political leader. Mernissi reveals that this political event took place in Pakistan in 1988, to inform us how the same Tradition used against Aisha to dismiss her from leadership in the past was reactivated to dismiss Bhutto as well.

To counteract this misogynist Tradition which claims women cannot hold leadership positions, Mernissi applies the method of historical investigation in order to introduce Arab and non-Arab Muslim queens who achieved power and attained leadership positions. In this context, she asserts:

> Just as in a fairy-tale, queens, malikas, and khatuns emerged little by little from the soft crackle of yellowed pages in old books. One by one they paraded through the silent rooms of the libraries in an interminable procession of intrigues and mysteries. Sometimes they appeared in twos or threes, passing the throne from mother to daughter in the faraway isles of Asiatic Islam. They were called Malika 'Arwa, 'Alam al-Hurra, Sultana Radiyya, Shajarat al-Durr, Turkan Khatun, or, more modestly, Taj al-'Alam (Crown of the universe) and Nur al-'Alam (Light of the universe). Some received the reins of power by inheritance; others had to kill the heirs in order to take power. Many themselves led battles, inflicted defeats, concluded armistices. Some had confidence in competent viziers, while others counted only on themselves. Each had her own way of treating the people, of rendering justice, and of administering taxes. Some managed to stay a long time on the throne, while others scarcely had time to settle down. Many died in the manner of the caliphs (either orthodox, Umayyad, or Abbasid) – that is, poisoned or stabbed. Rare were those who died peacefully in their beds.[266]

It is interesting to note that Mernissi highlights the importance of women in early Islamic history. Mernissi presents women who engaged in politics and war as queens and warriors. Her work is a basic historic-cultural analysis. She returns to historical sources to delve into women's visibility in Islamic history. By doing so, she highlights the political involvement of Muslim women. Besides the historical context, Mernissi aspires to demystify the error of believing that Muslim women did not play a role in politics. Therefore, she challenges patriarchal beliefs that seek to conceal the past activism of women in Islam.

The previous sections contained a historical and socio-cultural analysis of the position of women in the pre-Islamic period and at the beginning of Islam. The goal was to show the significant role that women have played in Islamic history. As we have seen, patriarchal views and interpretations contributed to the distortion of the Tradition by aiming to exclude women from the political and religious spheres. In

---

265 Mernissi 1993: 2.
266 Mernissi 1993: 3.

what follows, I present Mernissi's deconstructionist socio-historical and linguistic approach to interpreting a Qur'anic verse. In addition to Mernissi's historical analysis of the Tradition, as presented above, I will also consider her methodological analysis of one of the most challenging Islamic legacies for Muslim women today: the concept of the veil in the Qur'an.

The question of the veil in Islamic heritage: Mernissi's deconstructionist socio-historical and linguistic approaches

In her book entitled *The Veil and the Male Elite: A Feminist Interpretation of Women's Rights in Islam* (1991), Mernissi interprets verse 53 of chapter 33 of the Qur'an, entitled *The Joint Forces (Al-Ahzab)*. There are other verses in the Qur'an that deal with the issue of the veil. Mernissi has chosen to focus her interest on this one, which discusses the veil in Islam as follows:

> Believers, do not enter the Prophet's apartments for a meal unless you are given permission to do so; do not linger until [a meal] is ready. When you are invited, go in; then, when you have taken your meal, leave. Do not stay on and talk, for that would offend the Prophet, though he would shrink from asking you to leave. God does not shrink from the truth. When you ask his wives for something, do so from behind a screen: this is purer both for your hearts and for theirs.[267]

The word for 'screen' in Arabic, the original language of the Qur'ān, is 'hijab,' حجاب. The word 'hijab' is interpreted by Muslim jurists to mean veil: the veil that a woman puts on her head to cover herself from the gaze of men. In this context, I explore the methods applied by Mernissi in the socio-historical investigation as well as linguistic studies to reinterpret the above-cited Qur'anic verse. The purpose is to provide an alternative interpretation of the notion of the veil in Islamic legacy, to challenge the traditional understanding of it. In addition, I aim to show Mernissi's crucial contribution to Islamic feminism in her use of transdisciplinary methods including socio-historical, and cultural forms of analysis. I argue that Mernissi's application of different methods and approaches throughout her career has made her a major contributor to Islamic feminism.

It is important first to clarify that the purpose of this deconstructivist study of the notion of the veil is not to go through the controversial debates on veiling or not veiling, which may sometimes lead to social or political discrimination against women. Indeed, I agree with Tunisian scholar Soumaya Mestiri, who maintains that "there is no difference at all between a woman who is naked in public and a veiled woman, both of whom are obsessed with their bodies. The struggle for unveiling,

---

267 The Qur'ān, Chapter 33, The Joint Forces; Verse 53.

then, seems to be a false struggle: if we must speak of unveiling, it is rather that of the mind"[translation mine].[268] Indeed, the fight of a woman is not just about sensual and corporal veiling or non-veiling; her challenge is more important intellectually and spiritually. A woman in Islam must free her mind from dogmatic and traditional barriers in order to discover the Islamic heritage and hold her rights without being reliant on men's prescriptions.

According to Mernissi, verse 53 of chapter 33 of the Qur'an, cited above, is regarded by experts in the science of jurisprudence as the basis of the institution of the veil.[269] Their interpretation was based on the testimony of Malik Ibn Anas (see 2.3) which was reported by al-Tabari, who was bent on the explanation of the Qur'ānic verses.[270] Below, I provide Mernissi's reference to the explanation of Al-Tabari.

Mernissi recounts that the prophet had married, and Ibn Anas was charged with inviting people to the prophet's wedding supper. Many people came and ate; then they dispersed. Only a small group of tactless guests remained, lost in conversation. The prophet, who had good manners, wanted to be alone with his wife. But he was irritated because the groups of men did not leave his home. Afterwards, upon their departure, God revealed the verse on the veil to the prophet; the prophet drew a curtain between himself and Ibn Anas, who was the witness, while the prophet recited chapter 33, verse 53.[271] Mernissi quotes from al-Tabari's report of what Ibn Anas said: "It was in this position that he let fall a *sitr* [curtain] between himself and me, and the verse of the *hijab* descended at that moment."[272]

However, as Mernissi asserts, this narration of Al-Tabari's about the veil lacks the socio-historical context in which the verse descended.[273] In this context, I present Mernissi's explanation of the socio-historical circumstances of the descent of the verse of the veil. As Mernissi tells us, year 5, the year of the descent of chapter 33 of the Qur'an, was a particularly disastrous year after the military defeat in several battles dating from the year 2 until the spring of year 8, when the prophet won a decisive victory.[274] Indeed, Mernissi claims that we need to pay attention to the following: On the one hand, this verse arrived in a difficult time filled with doubts and military defeats. That might explain the rapidity of the revelation of this verse which split the Muslim community in two. On the other hand, this verse came to further strengthen the morals of the companions of the prophet. Thus, it was revealed to promote moral values that the companions of the prophet seemed to lack, such as not entering a

---

268 Mestiri 2016: 8 fn. 5.
269 Mernissi 1991: 85.
270 Mernissi 1991: 93.
271 Mernissi 1991: 87.
272 Mernissi 1991: 87.
273 Mernissi 1991: 87.
274 Mernissi 1991: 89.

dwelling without asking permission, and to forbid Muslims to marry the prophet's wives after his death.[275] In this sense, the verse declares,

> It is not right for you to offend God's Messenger, just as you should never marry his wives after him: that would be grievous in God's eyes.[276]

Having begun by illustrating, according to Mernissi's investigation, the sociohistorical circumstances in which the Qur'anic verse of the veil is exposed, I demonstrate the linguistic method used by Mernissi to uncover the various meanings, which the term 'veil' entails. In this line of thoughts Mernissi distinguishes between the linguistic dimension and the anatomical meaning of the word 'veil.'

a) The linguistic dimensions of the word 'veil'

According to Mernissi, the word 'veil' is three-dimensional, and these three dimensions often blend into one another. The first dimension is a visual one : to hide something from sight. The root of the verb *hajaba* means to hide. The second dismension is spatial : to separate, to mark a border, to establish a threshold. On this basis, the veil is used to divide two spaces. And finally, the third dimension is ethical : it belongs to the realm of the forbidden.[277] In this sense, Mernissi introduces the veil of a prince, to clarify the three dimensions of the word veil. The prince, who was the most powerful man in the Muslim community, had recourse to the veil. The veil of the prince was used to escape the gaze of his entourage and further to divide two places : the place of the prince and that of the members of the court. Hence, the veil of the prince was used to forbid the member of the court to gain access to the prince's palace.[278]

b) The anatomical use of the word 'veil'

The anatomical use designates the positive and negative connotation of the term 'veil.' I start with the positive connotation which the word 'veil' implies. Referring to the field of linguistics, Mernissi explains that the veil in the Arabic language means *hijab* and, literally, the curtain which is used as a protection, such as the eyebrows, *al-hajiban*, which protect the eye from the sun's rays. Another example that Mernissi

---

275 Mernissi 1991: 89–92.
276 The Qur'ān, Chapter 33, The Joint Forces; Verse 53
277 Mernissi 1991: 93
278 Mernissi 1991: 94.

adds in this context is the diaphragm of the stomach, *hijab al-jawf*, and the hymen of virginity, *hijab al-bukuriyya*.[279]

As opposed to this, Mernissi points out the Sufi's conception about veiling and other verses from the Qur'an to explore a negative connotation of the word 'veil.' In the Sufi tradition, one calls veiled, *mahjub*, the person whose consciousness is determined by sensual or mental passion and who as a result does not perceive the divine light, because he is 'covered.' Likewise, in other references in the Qur'an, the word 'veil' has a negative significance, as when it describes the inability of certain individuals to perceive God. An example is in verse 5 of chapter 41, entitled *Made Distinct*, which asserts:

> They say, 'Our hearts are encased against [the faith] you call us to; our ears are heavy; there is a barrier between us and you. So you do whatever you want, and so shall we.'[280]

In this verse the same Arabic word is used, namely hijab, while it is (always) interpreted and translated as "barrier", never as "veil".[281]

Thanks to her deconstructionist linguistic and socio-historical approaches, Mernissi uncovers that the veil does not necessarily signify the clothing that shrouds Muslim women, limiting their access to human interaction in public spaces.

Mernissi provides a multi-layered analysis of the different meanings of the veil. Here, the term 'veil' does not refer to the covering that women wear to protect themselves from male gaze. In addition, Mernissi offers an examination of the socio-historical circumstances under which the Qur'anic verse was revealed. In doing so, she clarifies the causes of the revelation (*asbab al-nuzul*). Thus, Mernissi provides a new reinterpretation of the hijab, the veil, as part of the Islamic heritage.

Along with her methodological examination of the veil's connotations, I would like to draw attention to Mernissi's autobiographical novel, *Dreams of Trespass: Tales of a Harem Girlhood* (1994), to further clarify her critical stance towards the veil. Mernissi's conception of the veil is connected to her childhood memories. As she writes about them, Mernissi perceives the veil as a representation of women's oppression, subjugation, and exclusion to the extent that the veil defines spatial and intellectual boundaries (*hudud*). Mernissi refers to her mother as a way of rebelling against the veil. Although she lives in a harem under the control of men, her mother does not want her daughter (Mernissi) to cover herself. As Mernissi attributes the following words to her mother:

---

279   Mernissi 1991: 96.
280   The Qur'ān, Chapter 41, Made Distinct; Verse 5.
281   Mernissi 1991: 96–97.

"Covering your head and hiding will not help. Hiding does not solve a woman's problems. It just identifies her as an easy victim. Your Grandmother and I have suffered enough of this head-covering business. We know it does not work. I want my daughters to stand up with their heads erect and walk on Allah's planet with their eyes on the stars." [282]

In her book entitled *Rethinking Muslim Women and The Veil: Challenging Historical & Modern Stereotypes* (2010), Katharine Bullock states that Mernissi's notion of "veil" is widely adopted in the West. According to Bullock, Mernissi views the veil as "a symbol of unjust male authority over women."[283] Bullock refers to Mernissi's autobiographical novel (1994), which is cited above to show the reasons behind Mernissi's refutation of the veil. Bullock describes Mernissi's tale that during the Second World War II, when Mernissi was almost nine years old, out of fear of Adolf Hitler, who according to Mernissi hated dark-haired people, Mernissi—as a child—concluded that she needed to protect herself by covering her head.[284] In this context, Mernissi recounts, "Hi-Hitler – that was the name of the king of the Allemane – hated dark hair and dark eyes and was throwing bombs from planes wherever a dark-haired population was spotted".[285] Bullock argues that Mernissi's mother refused to allow her daughter—Mernissi—to cover her head.[286] In this regard, Mernissi affirms:

That night, Samir begged his mother to promise to put henna in his hair, in order to redden it, the next time we went to the hammam (public bath), and I ran around with one of my mother's scarves securely tied around my head, until she noticed it and forced me to take it off. [287]

Bullock argues that Mernissi investigated the veil because of her traumatized childhood memories. She contends that Mernissi's whole work on the veil issue is a search for the source of her pain. Bullock apparently sees Mernissi as supporting "the negative stereotype that hijab is a symbol of Islam's oppression of women."[288] In addition, Bullock asserts that Mernissi's examination of the reasons for covering is restricted to the societal system of her Moroccan society.[289] In this regard, Mernissi asserts:

---

282 Mernissi 1994: 100.
283 Bullock 2010: 14.
284 Bullock 2010: 14.
285 Mernissi 1994: 99.
286 Bullock 2010: 14.
287 Mernissi 1994: 100.
288 Bullock 2010: 15.
289 Bullock 2010: 15.

While upper-and middle-class women threw away the veil, the newly migrant peasant women who came to Fez after independence would wear one to proclaim their "urbanity," to show that they belonged to the city and were no longer part of the countryside where the veil was never, throughout North Africa, worn by women. Even today, the highly political Islamic *hijab*, which is a distinct headdress, is an urban, middle-class, educated phenomenon in Morocco. Peasant and working-class women do not join in that fashion.[290]

Following on from this, I argue that Mernissi highlights the socio-cultural significance of wearing the veil by pointing to its function as a discriminatory practice between upper middle-class women and peasants in Morocco. In the same manner, in post-independence Tunisia, middle- and upper-class urban women refuse to wear the veil to resist traditional dress and express their modernization. Conversely, migrant women who come from rural areas to work in the city often wear the veil as a sign that they are urbanites, as the veil is not traditionally worn in many rural areas of Tunisia.

If we turn to the history of independence in Algeria, we could understand that Frantz Fanon gives a revolutionary meaning to the veil. He explains the cultural significance of the veil in his book *A Dying Colonialism* (1965). Fanon, a psychiatrist who deals with postcolonial studies, gives Algerian women's veil a revolutionary meaning. Algerian women wore the veil in colonial Algeria as a form of cultural resistance against French attempts to unveil Algerian women during the Algerian struggle for independence in 1950. Fanon argues:

Removed and reassumed again and again, the veil has been manipulated, transformed into a technique of camouflage, into a means of struggle. The virtually taboo character assumed by the veil in the colonial situation disappeared almost entirely in the course of the liberating struggle.[291]

Indeed the veil was used in a variety of socio-cultural settings and was not always associated with religion. According to some interpretations, the veil does not necessarily represent oppression or backwardness, and is not meant to exclude women from the mainstream of public life and social interaction. In this context, Bullock criticizes Mernissi for failing to recognize the cultural and historical significance of the veil, and that different people have enacted Islam differently at different times and places. Bullock believes that Mernissi's explanation of the veil is reductive because she ignores the multiplicity of discourses that surround it.[292]

---

290 Mernissi 1994: 120 fn. 2.
291 Fanon 1965: 61.
292 Bullock 2010: 15.

Presently, most Muslim migrant women living in Europe wear different types of veils to self-identify as Muslims. In addition to expressing religious tradition, wearing the hijab has been argued to be a manifestation of resistance to racism and Islamophobia, particularly in the context of French laicization.

> Within the secular French Republic, which constantly redefines its secularism in terms of a racial order of appearances, where it is not so much the manifestations of the religious as of Islam that are considered repugnant, the veil acts as a phobogenic object, cluttering the nation's ordinary field of vision. [translation mine] [293]

Despite the criticism directed at Mernissi, her work on the concept of the veil deserves attention. This has been proven by exploring her deconstructionist socio-historical and linguistic approach to provide an alternative interpretation of one of the verses about the veil in Islamic heritage. Nevertheless, her assumptions about the veil presented in her autobiographical novel (1994) could be critically questioned. On this basis, one could argue that veiled women are not always subject to male dominance, or that a woman wearing a veil is automatically subordinate to a man. In fact, the veil represents the right of choosing one's own dress, as its wearer does not impose it on other women by allowing intrusive religious discourse.

It is possible to interpret Mernissi's position on the veil differently: For example, one could argue that Mernissi does not condemn the veil as an Islamic religious garment, but she does condemn it when it is used to control women's social interactions in public spaces and when it is imposed by men. Here, Mernissi gives the concept of the veil a spatial connotation. In this context, Mernissi links the concept of the veil to the concept of the harem to specify spatial boundaries. In this line of thought Mernissi declares, "in the palace of the caliph she [woman] had her place—behind the *hijab* [the veil], in the harem—the 'forbidden space'".[294]

Nevertheless, it is not the fate of women to remain confined in harems behind the veil. In modern times, the socio-political and cultural situation of most Muslim societies has changed drastically. Since the independence of several Muslim countries, nationalist politics has promoted emancipation for women and has defended their rights—although the emancipation of women from patriarchal rule has not always been fully realized.

Socio-economic, and political challenges continue to impact the situation of women. Taking this into account, the section below explores Mernissi's examination of socio-political events that took place in Maghreb countries after independence. Indeed, she focuses on earlier events that followed the end of the Gulf War of

---

293   Benthouhami 2017: 272.
294   Mernissi 2002: 126.

August 1990. She describes the protest of most Maghrebian women in February 3, 1991, against the first Iraq War (1990–1991). The protests of women are important, for Mernissi, because they have a noticeable effect on women's lives. Hence, the entrance of women into the public sphere and their decision to leave the male dominated boundaries by appealing to their opinion is a feminist uprising. However, the Gulf War had a detrimental effect on the socio-economic situation in the Maghreb, affecting women the most.

Following on from this, I would like to present Mernissi's empirical and socio-political investigation into Maghrebian women's demonstrations after the Gulf War. To do this, I apply a comparative method to examine the socio-political circumstances of the Maghrebian Revolution of 2011 and of the Gulf War of 1991. Indeed, in 2011, Maghrebian women demonstrated against dictatorship regimes and demand political and social rights. In this way, I explore the commitment of Mernissi's feminist thought which is relevant and vibrant for today's women's socio-economic and political struggles.

The situation of women in contemporary times: From freedom to social, economic, and political crisis

In *Islam and Democracy: Fear of the Modern World* (2002), Mernissi devotes several pages to the post-Gulf War political context.[295] By examining this political situation, Mernissi addresses the socio-political consequences of the appearance of Maghrebian women in the public sphere denouncing the first Iraq War (1990–1991) and calling for peace. Mernissi examines the socio-political and economic impact of this in Maghreb countries, focusing, particularly on Morocco. She notes:

> The most desperate outcry against the war was from women throughout the world, and especially from Arab women. A perhaps unnoticed detail, which nevertheless constitutes a historical breakthrough, is that during this conflict women, veiled or not, took the initiative in calling for peace—without waiting, as tradition demanded, for authorization from the political leaders, inevitably male. In Tunis, Rabat, and Algiers, women shouted out their fear louder than all the others; they were often the first to improvise sit-ins and marches, while the men could decide to do something only after drawn-out negotiations between various powers and minipowers.[296]

Mernissi describes this as illustrative of the solidarity felt between the veiled and unveiled women. As one can observe here, Mernissi changes her mind about veiled women, claiming that even veiled women are leaving the private sphere of men's

---

295 Mernissi 2002: 1–9; 14–15; 149–151.
296 Mernissi 2002: 2.

2. Background and methods in the thought of Fatima Mernissi 117

control, and they participate in the protest alongside unveiled women. This means that women from traditional and modern backgrounds are standing side by side, united in their opposition to the war in Iraq and their rejection of male control. In fact, for Mernissi:

> What is certain is that women have decided to listen no longer to *khutaba* (sermons) they have not had a hand in writing. They are ready for takeoff. They have always known that the future rests on the abolition of boundaries, that the individual is born to be respected, that difference is enriching. [297]

Thus, Mernissi emphasizes that Maghrebian women, with their different cultures and ideologies (veiled or unveiled), are entitled to their individual rights, such as protest rights and the right to express their opinions. Therefore, women are emerging into the public sphere, leaving the confines, the spatial boundaries of the harem.

In *Beyond the Veil: Male-Female Dynamics in Modern Muslim Society* (2003), Mernissi provides a substantial definition explaining her notion of the division of the public and the domestic spaces. She declares:

> Strict space boundaries divide Muslim society into two sub-universes: the universe of men (the *umma*, the world of religion and power) and the universe of women, the domestic world of sexuality and the family. The spatial division according to sex reflects the division between those who hold authority and those who do not, those who hold spiritual powers and those who do not. The division is based on the physical separation of the *umma* (the public sphere) from the domestic universe. These two universes of social interaction are regulated by antithetical concepts of human relations, one based on community, the other on conflict.[298]

According to Mernissi, Muslim society is strictly divided "into two hierarchical spaces"[299], the public space and the domestic space. Hence, in "the public sphere" (by definition, "male spaces")[300]"only one sex manages politics and monopolizes decision making." [301] Boundaries separate these spaces to prevent intersex interaction. Moreover, Mernissi believes that men occupy both public and domestic spaces, but women occupy only the domestic one.[302] The purpose of this is to illustrate the unequal relationship between the two sexes, where men occupy two

---

297 Mernissi 2002: 152.
298 Mernissi 2003: 138
299 Mernissi 2002: 156.
300 Mernissi 2003: 138.
301 Mernissi 2002: 156.
302 Mernissi 2003: 138.

spaces while women occupy only one. Additionally, Mernissi asserts that women are subordinated to men in the domestic sphere. In this regard, she states:

> The duty of the Muslim women is to obey... The separation of the two groups, the hierarchy that subordinates the one to the other, is expressed in institutions that discourage, and even prohibit, any communication between the sexes. [303]

My intention here is to identify Mernissi's concept of the division of the domestic and public spaces as an important aspect of her thought. For Mernissi, the domestic space is a place of subordination and segregation for women, which she must escape to be free of male dominance. I turn now to Mernissi's book, *Islam and Democracy: Fear of the Modern World* (2002), in which she describes the Maghrebian women's protests in 1991 and their effect on transforming both religion and politics levels.

On the religious level, according to Mernissi, the entry of women into the public space challenges the religious order which is manipulated by men. Hence, she argues that

> the imams, who have proclaimed for centuries that marital *ta'a* (obedience) is a duty, are fuming. Obeying the husband means obeying God. The word *ta'a*, which appears in contemporary civil codes, reproduces in the harem blind obedience to the caliph.[304]

Mernissi refers here to the religious-political monarchies, which have been installed in many Islamic countries and in which the imam (religious leader) rules. Mernissi uses this argument to show her opposition to religion interfering in politics, thus, showing her support for secular humanist ideas (see 2.1).

On the political level, women's obedience to their male counterparts has always been regarded as one of the key pillars that has legitimized the power of political rulers. Indeed, she affirms "if domestic *ta'a* is challenged by weak women, how can men be expected to lower their eyes in deference to the leader?."[305] In other words: If a woman does not obey her husband in the domestic sphere, the man will feel inclined not to a revolt against the political leadership. Conversely, women's withdrawal from the domestic sphere triggers men's revolt against their leaders. One could argue that Mernissi's feminist stance is not radical in this regard. To put it simply, men are not excluded from Mernissi's advocacy of women's rights. In her view, both men and women play a key role in changing society.

---

303 Mernissi 2003: 138.
304 Mernissi 2002: 152–153.
305 Mernissi 2002: 153.

A as result, the regime seeks to oppress this male-female revolution. Therefore, religious-political authoritarian procedures will be employed to distract the citizens from revolt. Thus, Mernissi declares:

> A Muslim sovereign ... has recourse to the traditional measures of destroying the stores of wine and placing a ban on women leaving their homes, and especially on their using the same means of transportation as men ... Wine and women—here we have the Gordian knot of the crisis. *Tathir*, the ritual purification of the social body, requires the destruction of the first and the confinement of the second.[306]

In other words, both women and wine are considered as impurities. The public sphere, therefore, should only be accessible to men; women should be excluded. This confirms with the religious practice of cleanliness (*Tathir*), which is a tenet of Islam. *Tathir* refers to women's exclusion from public arenas. We can speculate about the humiliation women experience when they are branded impurities. The question that must be asked is the following: Which social strata of woman are repressed? To answer this question, Mernissi describes two types of women:

1. The first is a proletarian woman. As Mernissi describes her, she wears the traditional *djellaba* (see 2.2). She is worn out by long bus trips to and from work, and she is underpaid and without union protection.[307]
2. The second is a middle-class woman. As described by Mernissi, she has had access to education and valorizing salaried jobs. She enjoys and exercises all the visible privileges of modernity. She is bareheaded, with windblown hair, she drives a car, and she has identity papers and a passport in her own name in her handbag. This woman, from the height of her new academic *minbar* (mosque pulpit), preaches, writes, educates, and protests.[308]

Thus, Mernissi suggests that women who enjoy the benefits of modernity are the main targets of religious fundamentalists and political dictatorships.[309] In other words, a woman who can stand up for her legal, economic, and political rights. Mernissi, a woman who herself comes from the middle class and who has succeeded in establishing herself in the public sphere, would appear to support cultivated women through her writing in this way. This does not mean that Mernissi undervalues proletarian women. Mernissi is concerned about the empowerment of women in rural Morocco. Her work in civil society and in the NGO projects shows

---

306   Mernissi 2002: 154.
307   Mernissi 2002: 158.
308   Mernissi 2002: 158.
309   Mernissi 2002: 158.

this (see: 2). Mernissi is also committed to protecting the rights of proletarian women, as exemplified by her interview with Mina, a proletarian working woman without the right to be insured (see: 2.2). What Mernissi seeks to emphasize in her presentation of proletarian women and the middle-class women is the importance of education. The role of education for Mernissi is crucial in emancipating women from illiteracy, and for preventing men's domination. Education and a university degree would enable women to succeed in all spheres of society, including the socio-economic sphere, the academic sphere, the political sphere, and—why not—in the religious sphere as well (see: 2.2). As Mernissi declares:

> For women of my generation higher education was regarded not as a luxury, but as a chance for survival and escape from the widespread contempt for women that characterized the traditional ordering of society a few decades ago.[310]

Hence, dictator leaderships will be frightened of educated women because their voices will be heard, and they will be a threat to them. Mernissi argues that "it was university women like those who surged into the streets in front of the presidential palace in Algiers to demand democracy"[311] who are the target of oppression by fundamentalist and dictator leadership.

In this line of thought, Mernissi refers to feminists who are persecuted by fundamentalists for voicing their demands in the Arab and non-Arab worlds. She names the Egyptian feminist Huda Sha'rawi, the Egyptian feminist Nawal el-Saadawi, and the Iranian sociologist Nayereh Tohidi.[312] In my opinion, el-Saadawi[313] is one of the most important feminist thinkers in the Arab world. In 1981, she was imprisoned for alleged crimes against the state under Anwar Saadat's rule. After the assassination of Saadat (see: 2.3), el-Saadawi was released. Her memoir, Memory of the Women's Prison (1994), chronicles her prison days. El-Saadawi wrote about women's emancipation. In her writings, she advocates women's rights and denounces male's dominance. Having been trained as a physician and psychiatrist, she is furious about the traditional ritual of female circumcision. In her view, this practice deprives women of their dignity and causes psychological damage to them. El-Saadawi sees that most Muslim male jurists determine the rights of women via a patriarchal interpretation of laws. As a result of her observation, she concludes that Islam specifically, and religion in general, are not *per se* oppressive against women, but they become

---

310 Mernissi 2002: 159.
311 Mernissi 2002: 158.
312 Mernissi 2002: 160.
313 For further insights into el-Saadawi's biography and intellectual work, see: Nawel el-Saadawi (2016): "Nawal El Saadawi and a History of Oppression: Brief Biographical Facts." In *Diary of a Child Called Souad* (pp. 153–158). London, United Kingdom: Palgrave Macmillan.

oppressive when adapted to existing patriarchal social structures. During her lifetime, el-Saadawi was charged with blasphemy. Her progressive ideas about women's rights were criticized even by Arab feminists. Even after her death in March 2021, el-Saadawi's thoughts on women's emancipation remained the target of fundamentalists activist.

What was described here by Mernissi is the social-political protest led by many Maghrebian women against the first war of Iraq (1991). Mernissi interpreted this protest as an indication of women's emancipation from their private sphere and their emergence in the public sphere. This emancipation, however, did not last. Women were subjected to religious procedures that aimed to stifle their right to protest and to express their opinion. I turn now to Mernissi's exploration of one of the socio-economic effects of the Gulf War: the increase in unemployment rates.

Mernissi explores the issue of unemployment as socio-economic phenomena in two of her books; in her dissertation published in the USA in 1975 under the title *Beyond the Veil: Male-Female Dynamics in a Modern Muslim Society* (2003) and in her book *Islam and Democracy: Fear of the Modern World* (2002). I start by analyzing her stance on the unemployment rate in the latter book, in which she provides statistics on the rate of the unemployment in most of the Arab states during 1990. In this regard, she declares:

> Unemployment is the gravest threat to stability in the Arab states. One of its causes is the annual rate of population increase—one of the highest in the world, 3.9 percent. From 1985 to 1990, the Arab population increased from 188 million to 217 million ... in just five years![314]

Mernissi relates the unemployment rate to the increase of the rate of population in the Arab world. She further argues:

> Women, as half this population, (108 million in 1990, almost equal to the population of France and western Germany combined)—most of whom are under twenty-five years of age—represent a large army of job seekers. [315]

To put it simply, unemployment primarily affects young women, who make up the majority of the population throughout the Arab world. Mernissi further explains

> When we talk about Arab women, therefore, we are not talking about mature, settled women; we are talking about *83 million job seekers* who will marry late because, like young men, they are concerned about their futures and want to get

---

314   Mernissi 2002: 164.
315   Mernissi 2002: 164.

an education first. Whereas early marriage used to be the rule, today the Arab world is seeing a spectacular delay in the age of marriage.[316]

Hence, the tradition of women marrying at younger ages has changed in modern times. This is an important social and cultural element which is emphasized by Mernissi. It is not the goal of most women in Arab countries to get married at a young age. Many women want to continue their university education as well as gain access to the job market. Indeed, having a job means being economically independent and establishing their own lives. However, women's access to university and demanding of jobs is a threat to most Arab regimes that are unable to satisfy the social and economic needs of their populations. Therefore, Mernissi asserts, Arab leaders will call for religious procedures to keep women from accessing the job market and to reduce unemployment rates. Most leaders will then impose veiling on women as a religious practice. Mernissi illustrates her investigation using Algeria as an example. She declares:

> The Algerian leader Shaykh Madani, who is a sociologist, knows the statistics well. By calling for the return to the *hijab*, the fundamentalists delegitimize the presence of women on the labor market. It is an extraordinary powerful political weapon.
> The *hijab* is manna from heaven for politicians facing crisis. It is not just a scrap of cloth; it is a division of labor. It sends women back to the kitchen. *Any Muslim state can reduce its level of unemployment by half just by appealing to the shari'a, in its meaning as despotic caliphal tradition.* [317]

Mernissi claims that calling for the hijab—the veil—is a religious procedure introduced by those in power to prevent women from entering public spaces and, consequently, to limit their prospects for employment. This argument may be relevant to 1990, when Mernissi conducted her socioeconomic empirical study. In the present time, both veiled and unveiled women are affected by high unemployment. Most veiled women have abandoned their domestic life and are looking for work. Nowadays, veiled women in most Islamic societies attend universities, and once they graduate, they go to employment offices to find work. In some cases, they have been successful in finding jobs and can be seen in higher positions such as those of teachers, professors, doctors, and politicians. Hence, the stereotype of veiled women as subordinate and traditional is superannuated today.

Within the scope of her book *Beyond the Veil: Male-Female Dynamics in a Modern Muslim Society* (2003), Mernissi not only analyses the socio-economic dimension of

---

316   Mernissi 2002: 165.
317   Mernissi 2002: 165.

unemployment as it relates to women, but she also speculates about men, who are also at risk of unemployment. As explained earlier, the problem of unemployment in most Arab states becomes more apparent when women enter the labor market. Mernissi discusses the example of Algeria, which relies heavily on religious customs, such as requiring women to wear a veil and to stay home to keep jobs free for men and reduce unemployment in the country. Thus, this traditional pattern of governance was designed to deny women the right to work, and to give men greater employment opportunities. In this regard, Mernissi further cites the example of Morocco to illustrate how the Moroccan code of family law, Mudawana, based on a patriarchal interpretation of Islamic law, makes women dependent upon men and forces them to stay at home:

> This just what happened in Morocco. In 1956–57, at the dawn of independence, a commission of ten men selected from the leading religious authorities and the most prominent functionaries of the Ministry of Justice met and drafted a *Personal Status Code*, which after some discussion, was adopted and become law. Article 115 of that Code affirms "Every human being is responsible for providing for his needs (*nafaqqa*) through his own means, with the exception of wives, whose husbands provide for their needs." [318]

Thus, Mernissi bases her argument on a critical analysis of the Moroccan Personal Status Code, Mudawana, created after independence. The family law code continued to exist during her 1990 socio-economic investigation. The family code was subjected to reform in 2004. (This will be explained below.) In this matter, what we need to understand is that Article 115 of the Moroccan code of family law is intended to ensure the economic subordination of women to men. Mernissi contends that this law contradicts the social realities in Morocco. The image portrayed of men who can provide for their own needs as well as the needs of their families does not correspond to the living conditions of most families. Mernissi notes: "In Morocco, racked by class divisions and constant inflation, the man in the street spends considerable time discussing virtually insoluble economic problems".[319] In fact, most men fail to find full-time jobs, and most women are forced to look for wage-labor outside the domestic sphere.[320] Based on these socio-economic facts, one can understand that women's work becomes a necessity not only because they want to secure their economic independence, but also because they want to help their husbands. Consequently, as Mernissi claims, these development challenge the traditional cultural system upheld

---

318 Mernissi 2003: 148.
319 Mernissi 2003: 148.
320 Mernissi 2003: 148.

by men who are economically dominant and women who consume their husbands' fortunes.[321]

As a follow-up to Mernissi's investigation, one could add that wives are not the only ones who support their husbands, but female daughters do the same for their parents. In modern Tunisia, illiterate females from the very lowest classes work as maids or in textile factories to support their families. Many of them come from rural regions of Tunisia and are working as child labor without any legal or social protection. In this line of thought, as was examined in 2.2 above, Mernissi highlights the condition of women workers in Morocco. In this context, she argues:

> What is new, and laden with consequences, is not the mere fact of women working (Moroccan women of the poor classes have always worked), but the fact that they are working in positions in which they are paid wages. In traditional Moroccan society only women of the plutocracy were inactive and led lives of leisure. The others worked hard, often without any remuneration whatever, in domestic services and also in economic sectors like crafts and agriculture. [322]

Access to the job market is an important step for women in their search for economic and social independence. Nevertheless, the employment of women is often plagued by negative elements. This is due to the way the employers exploit them. Mernissi describes the situation of proletarian women workers who are exploited economically in Moroccan society. Women who work in the labor sector are particularly affected by this situation. Chapter 2.2 of this study discussed women's illiteracy as a major obstacle in their struggle for economic and social rights. They have no idea about human rights treaties protecting their rights as workers. Mernissi argues once more that the privilege of education is a fundamental human right. Through education, individuals learn about their rights. In this respect, Mernissi's project engages in empirical research in order to draw attention to the lack of social and economic rights in Morocco. In what follows, I use recent statistics on female unemployment to place Mernissi's study of women's work in Morocco, completed in 1990, in the context of the current socio-economic situation in the Maghreb.

Current statistics show that in the third quarter of 2021, Tunisia's female unemployment rate was 24.1%, exceeding that of men by about 8%. Women's unemployment remained higher than that of men between 2017 and 2021, reaching 25 percent in the second quarter of 2020. As a result of the COVID-19 outbreak, the Tunisian labor market saw an increase in unemployment in that period. Similarly, Morocco has a higher rate of unemployment among women than among men. Women in Morocco are unemployed at 16.2%, while men are unemployed at 10.7% in 2020. Women

---

321 Mernissi 2003: 148.
322 Mernissi 2003: 152.

in the southern regions were experiencing the highest rates of unemployment, at 48%. Likewise, in 2019, the female and male unemployment rates in Algeria corresponded to approximately 20% and 9% percent, respectively. The unemployment rate for women has been significantly higher than that of men since 2010 and peaked at 20.7% in 2017.[323]

Thus, Mernissi's study of unemployment among women, dating back to 1990, remains topical in present-day Maghreb. Women in Maghrebian countries face a higher unemployment rate than men, based on current statistics. The high unemployment rate of women in the Maghreb region is caused by several factors: few workplaces, gender-blind economic policy, educational outcomes that do not match market demands, social and cultural constraints as well as, regulatory and policy issues.[324]

The empowerment of women is one of my suggestion for combating unemployment among women. There is no doubt that the approach of women's empowerment is an important one, as it advocates for the socio-economic and political rights of women and prevents them from being socially and economically exploited. In this regard, I would like to emphasize the approach to women's empowerment known as "Gender and Development" (GAD) by the United Nations (UN). The GAD project is influenced by the writings of postcolonial and cultural studies, which aim to defend the rights of women in the Global South. The aim of GAD is to ensure the social, economic, and political rights of subordinated and marginalized women by highlighting the necessity for changing their role in society, and to liberate women by deconstructing and understanding the patriarchal dominance that continues to affect them.[325] In fact, five strategies will be used to accomplish the empowerment of women: The first strategy, "well-being", is to satisfy the vital and essential needs of women. Second, women must have access to the fundamental institutions and structures of society. Third, "consciousness-raising" means that women should be aware that they can participate in various projects concerning their society, in the manner that "their sex is not a fatality and does not condemn them to servitude nor does it confine them to certain tasks rather than others" [translation mine].[326] Fourth is "mobilization" meaning that women should be able to make decisions in development projects. Five, "control" refers to the access of women to political decision making.[327]

Accordingly, the improvement of women's socio-economic conditions could not be achieved without a radical change in the political power system. The demonstra-

---

323 https://de.statista.com.
324 United Nations: Social Policy Brief 8: 2016.
325 Mestiri 2016: 109.
326 Mestiri 2016: 109.
327 Mestiri 2016: 110.

tions of Maghrebian women of 1991, seen by Mernissi as women's uprisings for their rights, continue up to the present. The lack of political, social, and economic rights described by Mernissi (also see 2.2) could be considered as one of the major manifestations of the corrupt regimes that controlled much of the Arab World and the Maghreb. As a result, in 2011, a revolt began to change the system of power. In most of the Arab world, oppressed individuals reacted against poverty, discrimination, and despotism. In fact, some corrupt regimes ended. Other political systems chose to undertake political, economic, and social reforms. In other cases, the revolts and demands for rights have turned into anarchism and absurd fundamentalism. I demonstrate in the following how Mernissi's 1990 study is still relevant today to show that social, political, and economic rights remained the most cherished rights of citizens during the 2011 revolutions in Maghreb countries.

In Morocco, a group of young Moroccans calling themselves the "February 20 Movement" (F20) recognized that the regime's democratization process remains stalled. Their demand for the democratization of their regime triggered the first wave of protests in early 2011. Several calls for demonstration were launched on social networks, the first on January 30. These calls were renewed on February 20, 2011, under the name "Dignity Day". [328]The demands of the F20 were freedom, equality, real democracy, social justice and dignity, issues that are linked to an international human rights discourse.[329] The claims expressed by the protest were an unprecedented blend of social, economic and political demands : The establishment of an elected Constituent Assembly, entrusted with the drafting of a new constitution to be submitted to a popular vote in a referendum; the recognition of Tamazight as an official language; the abandonment any repression against peaceful demonstration; the immediate integration of unemployed graduates into public service; the protection of citizens' purchasing power by limiting the cost of living, raising the minimum wage and improving working conditions; free access to social services for all citizens; the punishment of all those responsible for crimes against the people; and the punishment of all those responsible for plundering the country's wealth.[330] The socio-political protest in Morocco was not only sustained by young people, but also by political parties from different backgrounds, such as Parti social iste unifié, parti de gauche, Annahj Addimocrati, parti de la gauche radicale, Al Adl Wal Ihsane, mouvement islamiste, Ila Al Amame, mouvement marxiste, and Mou vement amazighe. It was also supported by several political associations. The most important of these are : La Ligue marocaine pour la défense des droits de l'homme, l'Association marocaine des droits humains, le Forum marocain pour la vérité et la justice, l'Association démocratique des femmes du Maroc, l'Association marocaine

---

328   Desures 2013: 410–411; Bennani-Chraïbi and Jeghllaly 2014: 3; Hamblin 2015: 186–190.
329   Brouwer and Bartels 2014: 16.
330   Radi 2017: 39.

des femmes progressistes, l'Association marocaine pour la citoyenneté et les droits de l'homme, and Organisation pour la liberté d'information et d'expression.[331]

In Algeria, the protest took the form of social demonstrations. They began on January 3, 2011, and were directed against the rising prices of certain basic foodstuffs. The manifestations were transformed into a political movement through the coordination of opposition parties and civil society representatives, as well as unofficial associations such as the "Rassemblement pour la Culture et la Démocratie (RCD)" and the "Coordination nationale pour le changement et la démocratie (CNCD)."[332] These political civil society organizations attempted to organize a demonstration in Algiers despite a ban by the political authorities. Several thousand demonstrators gathered in Algiers on February 12, 2011, to demonstrate against Algerian power.[333] This political movement in Algeria did not bring about a change in the political system. Currently, as well as in 2019 and 2021, demonstrations are taking place in Algeria one after another in different regions of the country, as well as in the diaspora. The protests started in 2019 and are called the Hirak movement. They were a popular movement which began following the announcement of the candidacy of President Bouteflika (he was the president of Algeria 1999–2019) for a fifth term, and led to his resignation. The protests were about reforming the political system. Protesters demanded democracy, civil liberties, and the rule of law.[334] The active role of women in the protests was remarkable. Women founded the feminist collective "Femmes algériennes pour un changement vers l'égalité" on March 16, 2019, in order to strengthen the political role of women in the protests.[335]

In Tunisia, the rule of one-party state dictatorship has continued for fifty-five years. Democracy and the modern political instruments of freedom of thought, press and expression have been completely absent for decades. On December 17, 2010, the first wave of protests was set off against the political regime of Ben Ali. The protests started in Sidi Bouzid after the self-immolation of Mohammed Bouazizi. This was an intense civil resistance that lasted 28 days. The protests were sparked by high unemployment rates, corruption, lack of political freedoms, and poor living conditions. ", "*Shughl, hurriyya, karama wataniyya* (Work, freedom, national dignity) [شغل,حرية,كرامة وطنية] was one of the most repeated slogans during the early stage of the protests. The notion of dignity ([كرامة] karama) was central in the narratives of the protests, which denounced the economic and political humiliation that Tunisians experienced on a daily level under the authoritarian regime."[336] The

---

331 Brouwer and Bartels 2014: 16.
332 Chena 2011: 106.
333 Volpi 2013: 107–109.
334 Volpi 2020: 153–154.
335 Djelloul 2020: 86.
336 Zeghal 2013: 7.

protests reached the capital, Tunis, on Dec. 27, where a thousand citizens expressed solidarity with the residents of Sidi Bouzid and demanded jobs. As a reaction to these massive protests, Ben Ali announced that he would not change the constitution, a move which would have allowed him to stay in power until 2014. Zemni (2013) notes that Bouazizi's self-immolation "was not so much the starting point of the Tunisian revolution but rather the rallying point for different types and forms of protest to converge into a national uprising".[337] He explains that activists from the labor movement, as well as "well-educated but unemployed youth, and some of the urban poor" contributed to the January 2011 revolution, alongside "a large proportion of civil servants, members of professional associations (lawyers, engineers, etc.), and sectors of the economic elite".[338] On January 14, 2011, Ben Ali resigned and dissolved his government and declared a state of emergency. On the same day, he fled the country to Saudi Arabia. Thus, "the revolution in Tunisia is presented as the result of an emptiness of the human, misery, despoliation, distress, resistance taken to its limit, to nihilism, to the immolation of Bouazizi" [translation mine].[339] The Tunisian protest turned into revolution. The regime of Ben Ali fell, and he left the country. "The period of mass protests that started on December 17, 2010—the day of the self-immolation of Mohamed Bouazizi—and ended on January 14, 2011—the departure of President Ben Ali from the country—was called a *thawra* [ثورة] by Tunisians, which can be translated by 'uprising,' 'revolt,' or 'revolution.'"[340]

Thus, Mernissi's thought is relevant for contemporary men's and women's struggles for their rights in the Maghreb region and the Arab world in general. The example of the Maghrebian protests/revolutions (2011) outlined here is an ultimate justification to affirm this. Mernissi refers to the UDHR in her writing of 1990 in which she considers it as the core principle of human rights still applicable today in Morocco, where protesters assert their rights based on the international human rights declaration. In addition, women's rights issues occupied a prominent place during and after the protests in Morocco, and they were the main contention.[341] Similarly, Mernissi's 1990 study that highlighted the importance of women's participation in the demonstration continues to be relevant for the 2011 Maghrebian demonstration in which Algerian women of different ideologies mobilized themselves and demanded their rights. Therefore "the Hirak of February 22, 2019 was an opportunity for Algerian women to reclaim the public space from which they had been excluded for decades".[342] Last but certainly not least, one can argue that the intellectual en-

---

337 Zemni 2013: 128.
338 Zemni 2013: 128.
339 Ben Said-Cherni 2016: 19.
340 Zeghal 2013: fn. 1.
341 Sadiqi 2016: 16.
342 Rouibah 2021: 585.

gagement of Mernissi is relevant to understand the current revolutions that took place in most parts of the Arab world—the Maghreb—to liberate people from oppression and despotism.

Nonetheless, as discussed above, Mernissi uses Morocco as an example to illustrate how Islamic law is still used to exclude women from public life after independence. This is not the case for all Muslim countries.[343] As a counterexample, I would like to emphasize Tunisia, as a Maghrebian country. Indeed, Tunisia was among the rare Muslim countries after colonization that promoted the social and political rights of women within the reform of the Islamic family law in 1956, as well as the implementation of the code of nationality in 1993.

Postcolonial Tunisia promulgated the Personal Status Code (CPS), giving Tunisian women their social and political rights. By enacting the CPS, polygamy was abolished, and traditional divorce rules were drastically altered, since husbands could no longer repudiate their wives verbally and without granting them their legal rights. Thus, the CPS allowed women to file for a divorce by judicial procedure, by which the divorce become a judicial affair and rights of alimony and child custody accrued to women. In addition, the promulgation of the CPS prohibited parents from forcing their daughters to marry against their will. A major social right accorded by the CPS was the right to education, which was granted equally to men and women.[344] As political rights, the CPS "gave Tunisian women the right to vote, and it is considered as one of the most liberal codes in the Arab World, particularly in terms of women's rights".[345] In 1993, Tunisian women were granted the right to pass on their nationality to their children. Indeed, "the Code of Nationality was amended in 1993 to allow mothers more rights to transfer their citizenship to their children".[346]

Tunisia was known in the Arab region as the most promising country for woman rights after the promulgation of the CPS in 1956. The CPS has provided important rights to Tunisian women, especially compared to other Arab Muslim countries. In Tunisia, however, some legal rules are still maintained by patriarchal domination, for example, regarding the transfer of citizenship from the mother to her children, which, despite its confirmation in 1993, is still not required by law, as just outlined. Also at issue are: conditions of marriage, guardianship, conjugal duties, relationship with children, pension, their last name, and the law of inheritance.[347] Moreover, the Tunisian woman remains vulnerable to several insecurities. For example, Tunisian women are subjected to physical and psychological violence in domestic and public

---

343 Hatem 1987: 816.
344 Charrad 2007: 1519.
345 Jules 2017: 373.
346 Moghadam 2005: 297.
347 Tunisia: Pact for Equality, Individual Freedom: 2018.

spheres. Furthermore, in many cases, the rights guaranteed by the CPS to Tunisian women are not enforced by law.

In this line of thought, since the code of family law remains based on religious law, it might be an important idea to rewrite it from the perspective of Islamic feminism. Thus, the participation of women scholars in reinterpreting religious texts is crucial to ensuring Tunisian women more legal rights. The approach to Islamic feminism is not very well developed in Tunisia, since the reformulation of the family law code was programmed by a nationalist feminist state project, which came after independence to suppress all forms of religious traditionalism.

One shall explain that the first approach to feminism in Tunisia was led by a man who contributed to the liberation process and won Tunisian independence in 1956. In Tunisia, Habib Bourguiba (the first president of Tunisia 1957–1987) was the first nationalist leader to assert women's rights. There is no doubt that Taher Haddad's emancipatory project for women inspired Bourguiba. Haddad was first and foremost a Tunisian pioneer of the women's movement. In his book *Muslim Women in Law and Society* (1930–2007), Haddad argued for more rights for women, arguing that the patriarchal interpretation of Islam hindered them.

According to the nationalist feminist project, women were encouraged to participate in the public sphere, i.e., national and social life. Therefore the institutions of the newly state met the needs of most citizens. Women and men could participate in the construction and conduct of a modern state and society. However, at that time, no theory of equality within the family existed. Thus, equal rights between men and women were not envisioned in two areas: the religious segment of the public space—that is, religious professions and religious ceremonies, in which women could not participate—and the private sphere of the family, which was governed by religion, so that the interpretation of family law was still subject to misogynist interpretations.[348]

Islamic feminism is often viewed as a traditionalist approach that devalues the secular rights granted to Tunisian women after independence. Indeed, the lack of intellectual engagement in interpreting Tunisian family law from an Islamic feminist perspective negatively impacts the achievement of Tunisian women's rights. In this sense, the drafting of the controversial Article 28 of the new 2014 constitution was the first political sign that there was an intensified need of a renewed interpretation of Islamic legacy to acquire more legal rights for women. The article challenges the privileges guaranteed to Tunisian women in the 1956 CPS. It "states that women are 'complementary' to men."[349] Based on religious tradition, the article asserts that in Islam, women cannot be equal to men; rather, women must complete men. Therefore women do not play an essential role in Tunisian society. A woman is viewed as an

---

348 Badran 2010a: 27–28.
349 Grami 2016 : 309.

object by a man; she is not treated as an autonomous subject. Grami argued that the concept of complementarity was interpreted in a conservative manner in order to achieve an "authentic" patriarchal culture.[350] Large demonstrations were promptly organized, with up to 6,000 women participating, in the capital Tunis on August 13, 2012, Tunisian Women's Day, protesting this article.[351] In this sense, women can demonstrate against the politics of their countries. Some of the women who participated in the 2012 demonstration belong to civil organizations. To mention a few of the organizations involved the demonstrations : The Democratic Women's Association, La Ligue Tunisienne des Droits de l'Homme and L'Association des Femmes Tunisiennes pour la Recherche sur le Développement.

In contrast to Tunisia, which fails to promote women's rights based on a feminist interpretation of the Islamic legacy and in which we are witness to the consequences of that failure, I want to explore the example of Morocco. In 2004, Moroccan feminist activists operating under the influence of Islamic feminism actively participated in the reformation of the Moroccan family code of 1957, which was described by Mernissi as the main source of the subordination of Moroccan women. Hence, the Moroccan code of family law (Mudawana) was successfully reformulated in 2004. The first code of personal status (Mudawana), instituted in 1957 in Morocco, was based on religious law to make it "sacred", and not subject to public debate. This law establishes women as minors and distances them from the public.[352] In fact, the Moroccan feminist movement was confronted by a serious challenge: the powerful Islamist movement. As a result, they pushed female politicians to advocate for women's rights from a religious standpoint. The main strategy used was a call for a more flexible rereading of the religious corpuses.[353] In other words, Moroccan feminist activists realized that reforming the family law, which is based on Islamic law, required reinterpreting the religious texts to claim their rights. That is considered a challenge to the ideologies of Islamists who used the religion as a justification to exclude women from public life and to deny their rights. One might affirm that the egalitarian philosophy of gender justice espoused by Mernissi enabled feminist activists to make gender issues a national issue for the first time in Morocco's history.

Mernissi discusses the modern socio-economic and legal rights of most women in the Maghreb. According to her, the Iraq War of 1991 sparked a female uprising, with women demanding the right to voice their opinions and to be seen in the public sphere. The majority of women have access to education and the labor market in the modern era. Unemployment remains a significant challenge for women and

---

350   Grami 2016 : 309.
351   Charrad and Zarrugh 2015 : 106 ; Grami 2016 : 309.
352   Sadiqi and Ennaji 2006: 20.
353   Sadiqi and Ennaji 2006: 21.

men. Most government policies have failed to solve the problem. They used traditional religious prescriptions to exclude women from social and economic life. The uprising of 2011 served as a testament to the relevance of Mernissi's investigation. The 2011 uprising highlights that most women in the Maghreb still face socio-economic difficulties, especially when it comes to legal rights and economic issues.

The reception of Mernissi's thought: secular and Islamic feminist approaches

Mernissi's thought was characterized by two approaches: "reconstructionist" (or "revolutionary") for her secularist approach, and "reformist" for her Islamic feminist approach.[354] In the following, I begin by examining the criticism against Mernissi's secularist approach to show how scholars such as Katherine Bullock (2010) and Lamia Zayzafoon (2005) understand Mernissi's views on gender relation in Islam.

Mernissi's secular feminist approach

Mernissi argues in her dissertation (1975) published under the title *Beyond the Veil: Male-Female Dynamics in Modern Muslim Society* (2003):

> Sexual equality violates Islam's premise, actualized in its laws, that heterosexual love is dangerous to Allah's order. Muslim marriage is based on male dominance. The desegregation of sexes violates Islam's ideology on women's position in the social order: that women should be under the authority of fathers, brothers, or husbands. Since women are considered by Allah to be a destructive element, they are to be spatially confined and excluded from matters other than those of the family. Female access to non-domestic space is put under the control of males.[355]

Bullock interpreted this stance as follows:

> [Mernissi concludes] that Islam views women's sexuality as dangerous, therefore needing to be controlled. She further argues that Islam views 'femaleness' as anti-divine, or sullying, and that Islam is against heterosexual love between husband and wife. Women threaten men's relationship to God, so must be covered, secluded and excluded from the Muslim community.[356]

One could argue that Mernissi desires to criticize the "official Islam"[357] to contest its religious authority. This is ignored by Bullock. As a counterexample, Bullock em-

---

354 Rhouni 2010: 5.
355 Mernissi 2003: 19.
356 Bullock 2010: 16.
357 Mernissi 2003: 82.

phasizes Islamic sources, the Qur'an and the Tradition, to show that Islam does not assert inequality between the sexes. Bullock affirms that Islam has a sexually positive outlook; all appetites harden the heart, only sexual desires soften it. She further argues that there is nothing in the Qur'an about women as dangerous sexual beings.[358] There is the notion that men and women are fundamentally alike, being created of a single soul, and being both recipients of the divine breath, and therefore the Qur'an is replete with verses stressing mutual material love and harmony, for instance in chapter 30, verse 21 of the Qur'an.[359] That verse asserts:

> Another of His signs is that He created spouses from among yourselves for you to live with in tranquility: He ordained love and kindness between you. There truly are signs in this for those who reflect. [360]

Along the same lines of thinking, Zayzafoon addresses a major criticism of Mernissi's secularist writings. Zayzafoon accuses Mernissi of promoting an orientalist notion of an Islamic culture that is homogeneous and unifying, dismissing the heterogeneity and diversity of Islamic cultures.[361] According to Zayzafoon, Mernissi neglects the cultural heterogeneity of the Maghreb region in relation to the Moroccan Berber-speaking population.[362] In the last chapter of this study, I discuss Mernissi's rejection of the notion of a homogeneous and unifying Islamic culture to show that she is aware of the different ethnicities that exist in the Arab and Islamic societies, referring to her novel *Scheherazade Goes West* (2001).

Furthermore, Zayzafoon argues, along with Bullock, that "Mernissi's claim that the entire Muslim order condemns love between a man and a woman, and a husband and his wife, presupposes a homogenous misogynistic Islamic tradition with no internal antagonistic or contradictory elements."[363]

In order to respond to Bullock and Zayzafoon's claim, I argue that Mernissi presents this thesis in her book *Beyond the Veil* (1975–2003), while in *The Veil and the Male Elite* (1987–1991), Mernissi offers an antithetical thesis, presenting the prophet as a lover who sought his wives' advice in all matters (see 2). As well, Mernissi published a book in 1986 entitled *L'Amour dans les pays musulmans* (Love in Muslim countries), "in which she precisely argues that love is central to Islam, but is one of its repressed or forgotten aspects."[364]

---

358   Bullock 2010: 16.
359   Bullock 2010: 16.
360   The Qur'ān, Chapter 30, The Byzantines; Verse 21.
361   Zayzafoon 2005: 2.
362   Zayzafoon 2005: 22.
363   Zayzafoon 2005: 24.
364   Rhouni 2010: 3.

Bullock and Zayzafoon, thus, focus on Mernissi's writings from 1975, which are written from a secular perspective. They see Mernissi as conforming to orientalist views of women in Islam. Their reception of Mernissi's work is incomplete because they fail to consider her Islamic feminist framework. Thus, I would like to cite the reception of Mernissi's Islamic feminist approach as an example of her anti-orientalist and, thus, reformist treatment of women in Islam.

Mernissi's Islamic feminist approach

By focusing on Mernissi's book, *The Veil and the Male Elite* (1987–1991), Barlow and Shahram present Mernissi as a moderate feminist thinker. They argue: "The impact of Islamic revivalism on Mernissi's feminism is manifest in *The Veil and the Male Elite*. In the preface to this book Mernissi is confident that "Muslim women can walk into the modern world with pride, knowing that the quest for … human rights … stems from no imported Western values, but is a true part of the Muslim tradition."[365]

In this respect, *Le Harem politique: le Prophète et les femmes*, first published in 1987, and mostly known as *The Veil and the Male Elite: a Feminist Interpretation of Women's Rights in Islam* (1991) has been considered as one of the first works which displays a new way of doing feminism, in which Mernissi breaks with her earlier secularist position. In this book, she focuses on the interpretation of the Islamic foundational texts, the Qur'an and Tradition. She does not denounce their legacy, but she introduces interesting conversations with these established texts of Islam.[366] Raja Rhouni explores the methods used by Mernissi to reinterpret those texts from the perspective of an Islamic feminist approach.

She argues that "By considering the political, social and psychological context of production of those verses, Mernissi's hermeneutics moves beyond the methodology of classical exegesis, or *Tafsir*, called *asbab al-nuzul*, "occasions of the revelation," which is a tool limited to the consideration of the immediate events which aroused the revelation of a particular verse".[367] Despite this claim, one could affirm that Mernissi does not totally reject the historical analysis of the '*asbab al-nuzul*'. In this sense, Rhouni clarifies that Mernissi's work can also be seen as building on this tradition since *asbab al-nuzul* is a historical tool of analysis, but this method does not include an analysis of the broader historical and social environment and their psychological dimension.[368] In this regard, Mernissi's reading of the established text of Islam is crucial in the way that she alternates between the traditional method of historical as well as sociopolitical analysis and a psychological assessment, as pointed

---

365 Barlow and Shahram 2006: 1486
366 Rhouni 2008: 105–106
367 Rhouni 2008: 106
368 Rhouni 2008: 106–107.

out in section 4 above, where I introduced her interpretation of the verse of the veil, including a linguistic analysis of the word 'veil' as well.

Another interesting method used by Mernissi to rethink the established text of Islam, as pointed out by Rhouni, is the method of verification. This method aims to prove the untruthfulness regarding the interpretations of the Tradition, which has been distorted by misogynist ideology.[369] As outlined earlier, Mernissi engages in a critique of the Tradition, which has been attributed to the prophet, concerning women' incapacity s to become political leaders (see 2). The method of the verification asks new questions, such as when the transmitter remembered this statement, and most importantly, in which political circumstances this act of remembrance occurred. In this context, Rhouni argues that Mernissi challenges the traditional methodology of reference, *isnad*, concerned with authenticating statements attributed to the prophet, by verifying the reliability of their transmitters.[370]

In a continuation of Rhouni's analysis of Mernissi's approach to reinterpreting religious texts, I discuss other Islamic feminist scholars who help developing Islamic feminism. The intent is to assert that Mernissi puts forth these methods in her intellectual Islamic feminist project. She thereby engages in Islamic feminism by combining different approaches of thinking.

a) The first method is the interpretation or explanation (*tafsir*) of the Qur'an.

Among other Islamic feminist thinkers interested in the interpretation of the Qur'ān, I introduce Amina Wadud, one of the most important figures of Islamic feminism today. Wadud is an Afro-American Islamic feminist. She converted to Islam in 1970. Wadud believes in the equality of men and women. She argues that the Qur'an contains many verses on women's rights. Nevertheless, the problem lies in the fact that the interpretation of the Qur'an is distorted by the ultraorthodox. As a result, Wadud calls for an "anti-sexist" interpretation of the Qur'an, meaning that Muslim women should contribute to the interpretation of the Qur'an. For Wadud, the veil should be regarded as a choice of clothing rather than as a sign of oppression. Furthermore, she argues that Islamic feminism is concerned with gender justice through the involvement of men in the gender discourse, and not their elimination from it.[371] Pakistani theologian Riffat Hassan is yet another feminist who contributes to the reinterpretation of the Qur'anic text. Hassan argues that the Qur'an text is the Magna Carta of human rights. She argues that the Qur'an upholds several general human rights, such as the rights to life, respect, justice, freedom, knowledge, sustenance, work, and privacy. She maintains that these rights are also

---

369 Rhouni 2008: 106–107.
370 Rhouni 2008: 106–107.
371 Wadud 1990.

applicable to Muslim women. Throughout her work, Hassan makes references to verses of the Qur'an that serve as principle references to defend her position.[372]

b) The second method focuses on reexamining the Tradition.

Azizah Al-Hibri, a Lebanese philosopher and legal scholar, is famous for reexamining Islamic law to promote women's rights.[373] The interpretation of the texts of Islam—the Qur'ān and the Tradition—is so controversial among Islamic feminist scholars as it concerns the background on which they ground their reasoning about Islamic sources. In this respect, I would like to clarify the connection between Islamic feminism and Islamist movements.

Islamic feminism is interconnected with the notion of Islam, which remains widely misunderstood and misused. Within the framework of political Islam, some Muslim feminist scholars advocate the establishment of an Islamic state. Other Muslim feminists advocate the idea of an Islamic society or community within a secular state. Still others, and this is more a phenomenon of late Islamism (1990s), act politically to gain the freedom to express their religious identity in public. Others promote "progressive Islamism," which calls for the rereading and interpretation of Islamic texts for the daily life of all Muslims.[374] Thus, the term "Islamic," which is connected to the approach of Islamic feminism, covers a wide range of meanings, from radical Islamism to the progressive Islam. With her intellectual project, Mernissi promotes an Islamic moral vision within a secular state by arguing for a renewed reinterpretation of the Islamic heritage (see 2.1).

In this regard, in her book, *The forgotten Queens of Islam* (1993), she differentiates between political Islam and spiritual Islam. According to her, political Islam means the use of Islam for political ends. By contrast, spiritual Islam expresses the relationship between human beings and God, instead of being used for political purposes. Islamic spirituality conveys the essential message (*Risala*) of Islam. In this context, she states:

> In order to avoid any misunderstanding or confusion, let me say that in this book every time I speak of Islam without any other qualification, I am referring to political Islam, to Islam as the practice of power, to the acts of people animated by passions and motivated by interest, which is different from *Islam Risala*, the divine message, the ideal recorded in the Koran, the holy book. When I speak of the latter, I will identify it as *Islam Risala* or spiritual Islam.[375]

---

372 Riffat 1996: 361–386.
373 Badran 2009: 247.
374 Badran 2001: 48.
375 Mernissi 1993: 5.

Contrary to Mernissi's approach to Islam, Cooke (1999) introduces the Egyptian Islamic feminist scholar Zayneb Al-Ghazali who presents herself as an Islamic feminist. Al-Ghazali is "adamant that the duty of the Muslim woman is to be a wife and mother first, and ... when she has satisfactorily fulfilled these duties, can she contemplate other activities."[376] Accordingly, Al-Ghazali views the first duty of a woman as fulfilling her family responsibilities. For Al-Ghazali, a woman's access to the public sphere and to work is not a necessary requirement to fulfil this duty. Al-Ghazali's claim can conform with patriarchal and traditional views of women. Alternatively, as explained earlier, Mernissi believes that the right to work in the public sphere is a prerequisite for a woman's emancipation (see 2.2, and 2.4 section 4).

c) The third method explores the history of Muslim women who were actively involved in the political and social lives of Islam.[377]

Algerian novelist, poet, and filmmaker Assia Djebar[378] commences her novel entitled *Loin de Medine: Filles d'Ismael* (1991), with a historical account of the death of the Prophet in Medina. As illustrated in the novel, there were many fascinating women in Medina, including Fatima, the daughter of the prophet, who is described as a new Antigone of the Islamic tradition, because she expressed her political opinion against Abu Bakr's succession to her father the prophet Muhammed. At the other extreme, Aisha, the widow of Muhammad, the most revered and the youngest, settles gradually into her role of telling the Tradition of the prophet. For Sunni Muslims, she is a trusted source of the Hadith. In addition, Djebar uncovers the history of migrant women from Mecca, the freedwomen, the wanderers, a whole chorus of anonymous people recounting the chain of "sayings" of the disappeared prophet. In particular, Djebar rehabilitates Aisha and Fatima, demonstrating how their voices are indispensable to better understanding the Tradition of the prophet. With the strength and breadth of a prose epic of Arabic inspiration, this novel by Djebar gives back to women the freedom of the body and their voice.[379] Alike Djebar, Mernissi used the paradigm of revealing the history of Muslim women who played a crucial role in the history of Islam. She cites the youngest wife of the prophet, Aisha, as an intellectual figure reporting the Hadith (see 2.4). In this way, Djebar and Mernissi uncover an emancipatory image of women in Islamic history that contrasts with the subjugated image of women in most of the modern Muslim world used to control women. In her pursuit of gender justice within Islam, Mernissi is combining the three methods of the Islamic feminist approach mentioned above.

---

376 Cooke 1999: 102.
377 Cooke 1999: 97.
378 Tlemçani 2016: 236.
379 Djebar 1991.

In summary, Mernissi employs transdisciplinary methods to examine women's rights within an Islamic feminist framework. These transdisciplinary methods include historical inquiry, socio-political analysis, and linguistic analysis, as well as empirical research. In addition, Mernissi expresses interest in applying pioneering methods to interpret Islamic corpora as an opportunity to renew the Islamic heritage. By addressing the issue of women's rights in Islam, Mernissi also combines insights generated by secular and Islamic feminism. In what follows, I present my interpretation of Mernissi's thought and show that in addition to her secular and Islamic feminist approaches, Mernissi also takes a transcultural stance in defending women's rights.

2.5 The relevance of Mernissi's feminist thought for a transcultural approach to feminism

One of the approaches that is gradually appearing in philosophical books and articles is the transcultural approach. As the name suggests, transculturality refers to the exchange and dialogue between different cultures. In other words, transculturality goes beyond a singular, isolated, and autonomous notion of what a culture is and refers to pluralistic cultural entities. One could argue that postcolonial thinking paves the way for the development of a transcultural approach to thinking. Postcolonial thought challenges homogeneous notions of identity, the simplified representation of foreign cultures, and Eurocentric universalism. Thus, postcolonial thinking advocates the use of pluriverse knowledge that can better reflect the diversity of the world and the heterogeneity of knowledge. Postcolonial thought engages with subaltern studies (see 2).

In this line of thinking, Islamic feminism is related to the transcultural approach. This is because Islamic feminism draws less on the experiences of women from Western cultures or former colonies and more on those of Muslim women who face specific social and cultural challenges in their societies or even in their communities. In other words, Islamic feminism critically engages with colonial studies of Islam, thus, detaching the question of feminism from its Western location where it was born.[380] Islamic feminism opposes the monolithic constitution of Islam and its misogynistic representation that conveys the notion of a sexist Muslim culture and religion.[381] In doing so, Islamic feminism emphasizes the distortion of cultural and historical knowledge about Islamic culture. Islamic feminism promotes dialogue and the participation of women from different cultures and religions to support transculturality (see: 2).

---

380 Lazreg 1994: 8.
381 Benbrahim 2014.

In this context, this chapter illustrates Mernissi's transcultural approach to feminism. The section begins by exploring Mernissi's effort to deconstruct the clichés of Orientalist misrepresentations of Muslim women that portray them as submissive to patriarchal orders. The chapter also emphasizes Mernissi's reactivation of the Islamic heritage of Sufism in order to highlight her goal of breaking down cultural boundaries. Mernissi's reactivation of Sufi thought is intended to promote transcultural dialogue and cultural exchange.

The deconstruction of myths as one of Mernissi's approaches to transcultural feminism

In her novel, *Scheherazade Goes West: Different Cultures, Different Harems* (2001), Mernissi debunks several myths about Islam and Islamic culture in general. Myths refer to a traditional representation developed over time in order to represent cultures. Mernissi aims to dispel the myth of a single Arabo-Islamic identity. Furthermore, Mernissi seeks to deconstruct the myth of the passive Muslim woman who lacks intellectual capacities. She further deconstructs orientalist representation of the harem as a place of sexual desire.

Mernissi attempts to deconstruct the myth of an essential Arabo-Muslim identity by asserting that there are different identities in the Muslim world. In doing so, she presents several identities in the context of Islam by pointing out the dynamics in the Muslim world today.[382] Thus, the Muslim world is culturally dynamic, and there is not just one identity, but a great diversity of identities.

Moreover, Mernissi emphasizes that despite the fact that there are different identities and ethnicities in the Muslim world, most women share the experience of a constant struggle against colonialism, patriarchy and political dictatorship. She writes: "Throughout the 1920s, Turkey had been the site of a radical struggle waged by a movement known as the 'Young Turks,' who fought against three things perceived to be intimately linked: despotism, sexism, and colonization."[383]

The struggle of Muslim women against dictatorship is reflected in their ambition to participate in political decision making and to become leaders in their Muslim countries. Their goal is to challenge male dominance in politics. Indeed, women with different ethnicities and identities in the Muslim world, such as Turkish women and Pakistani women, aimed to accomplish this goal. In this sense, Mernissi declares, "[their opposition of dictatorship] could explain why women have emerged, in spite of extremism, as political leaders in many Muslim countries, from Benazir Bhutto in Pakistan and Tansu Çiller in Turkey, to Megawati in Indonesia."[384]

---

382 Mernissi 2001: 22.
383 Mernissi 2001: 109.
384 Mernissi 2001: 23.

In addition, Muslims share the same cultural background regardless of their different ethnicities and identities. For example, the Arabs adopted the Persian name Scheherazade and wrote down her stories in Arabic literature. The different ethnic origins in the Muslim world are united in describing Scheherazade as a wise woman who convinces a man not to kill women by telling him stories every night. In her argument, Mernissi reactivates the Islamic heritage about Scheherazade to argue that Muslim women should be inspired to be like Scheherazade, with her strong determination and resistance. Despite her Persian identity, Scheherazade's narratives are disseminated and received throughout the Muslim world. Mernissi argues:

> Scheherazade is the Persian name of the young bride who tells the stories in *The Thousand and One Nights*. These stories are of 'various ethnic origins, Indian, Persian, and Arabic.' The tales, which are a symbol of Islam's genius as a pluralist religion and culture, unfold in a territory that stretches from Mali and Morocco on the Atlantic Coast of North Africa to India, Mongolia, and China. When you enter the tales, you are navigating in a Muslim universe that ignores the usual borders separating distant and divergent cultures.[385]

Connected to this myth of an essential Muslim identity is the myth of the subordinate Muslim woman, which Mernissi attempts to deconstruct. She does this by reactivating strong-minded women such as Scheherazade who is, according to her, an intellectual woman within the rich heritage of Islamic culture. Thus, I present Mernissi's deconstruction of the myth of Scheherazade as presented in orientalist works, in the German tale entitled *Die Herrin Subeide im Bade oder Von der Geschlechter Lust und List in den arabischen Nachten*, published in Germany in 1984, and in Sergey Diaghilev's Ballets Russes, performed in Paris in 1910. In these cultural and artistic Western products, Scheherazade is limited to a sexual and erotic dimension. In this regard, Mernissi relates:

> I spotted two of the few German words I knew, *"Arabischen Nachten,"* in the subtitle. What does *"Geschlechter Lust und List in den Arabischen Nachten"* mean? I asked Hans in a low voice, so that no one else would hear. "Sexual desire and voluptuousness in the Arabian Nights" was his instantaneous translation. The book was a recent edition (1985) of Scheherazade's tales, illustrated by an East German artist. Yet his rendition of the Muslim storyteller was totally unfamiliar to me. I would never think of Scheherazade as nude and plump. Even though the climate is temperate in the Arab world, only delusional women in mental asylums discard their clothes.[386]

---

385 Mernissi 2001: 43.
386 Mernissi 2001: 34.

Rather than the sexist Scheherazade represented in orientalist books, Mernissi emphasizes the intellectual Scheherazade. Indeed, due to her intellectual abilities, Scheherazade saves other women from slaughter. Mernissi sheds light on the prioritization skills of Scheherazade which she enumerates as three. Mernissi argues, "the first skill is of an intellectual nature, requiring a wealth of knowledge."[387] "Scheherazade had read the books of literature, philosophy, and medicine. She knew poetry by heart, had studied historical reports … She was intelligent, knowledgeable, wise, and refined. She had read and learned".[388] The second skill, as Mernissi declares, "is of a psychological nature: the ability to change a criminal's mind by using words alone."[389] The third strategic skill is, as Mernissi tells us, the "cold-blooded capacity to control her fear enough to think and lead the dynamic interaction with the aggressor instead of being led."[390] Ultimately, Mernissi claims that Scheherazade convinced Shahryar not to kill other women through her persuasive skills and intellectual capacities: "she is a super-strategist of the intellect."[391] As we can see, unlike Scheherazade as portrayed in one of the orientalist tales, Mernissi gives voice to the intellectual Scheherazade, who uses her intelligence to save other women from being murdered. In this way, Mernissi attempts to deconstruct the image of the Western Scheherazade who has no intellect. In addition, Mernissi refers to Scheherazade as performed in Sergey Diaghilev's Ballets Russes. Mernissi quotes from Joan Acocella's description stating that the ballet performer Vaslav Nijinsky, who plays Scheherazade, appears "in brown body paint, and grinning, and wound with pearls—not so much as a sex object but as sex itself, with all the accouterments of perversity that the fin-de-siècle imagination could supply: exotism, androgyny, enslavement, violence."[392] Mernissi uses this Ballet Russe to argue that both men and women are mispresented as mere sexual being. In fact, both men and women are reduced to their sexual desire, which is the only way they can relate to one another. Consequently, this orientalist ballet denies the possibility of an intellectual dialogue between men and women, and that Scheherazade and her stories represent.

Scheherazade has recently been appearing in decolonial writings on feminism; the phrase "Decolonizing Scheherazade" [translation mine] [393] is a perfect illustration of this. It is evident that the decolonization of Scheherazade from orientalist representation is also part of Mernissi's intellectual goals. As such, one can point

---

387 Mernissi 2001: 47.
388 Mernissi 2001: 47.
389 Mernissi 2001: 47.
390 Mernissi 2001: 48.
391 Mernissi 2001: 48.
392 Mernissi 2001: 69.
393 Mestiri 2016.

out that a decolonial aspect of Mernissi's thought is sometimes omitted, abandoned or misinterpreted by her feminist interpreters. Mernissi deconstructs prejudices by questioning what is conveyed through the classical imagery of Scheherazade: "a submissive, entrusted, even hostage woman of the private sphere, an object-woman sacrificed on the altar of male pleasure, a subaltern with no right to speech" [translation mine].[394] Consequently, Mernissi seeks to liberate Muslim women from sexist platitudes by decolonizing Scheherazade. According to Mernissi, women in Islamic culture have the freedom to pursue intellectual interests. In other words, Muslim women are neither mere sexual objects nor simply sexual subjects.

The myth of the harem is another aspect of Islamic culture that is restricted to sexuality in most orientalist representations. A woman resides in the harem, the place of sexual pleasure where naked and lascivious women frolic. In contrast, Mernissi wants to challenge this sexist representation of harem in her autobiographical novel, *Dreams of Trespass: Tales of a Harem Girlhood* (1994) and in her novel *Scheherazade Goes West: Different Culture, Different Harems* (2001).

Throughout *Dreams of Trespass*, Mernissi deconstructs orientalist myths about the harem. Mernissi presents powerful feminist perspectives among older, traditional, illiterate women who dislike patriarchy. Accordingly, Mernissi's presentation of the harem challenges the idea that Muslim women in patriarchy accept their subordinated situation to be under man and, thus, are unaware of their oppression. In this regard, Mernissi writes: "Right on our threshold, you could see women of the harem contesting and fighting with Ahmed the doorkeeper as the foreign armies from the North kept arriving all over the city".[395] In their confinement, women in harems invent fairy tales to escape their reality, giving them hope that their dream of trespassing the harem boundaries may come true. Mernissi recounts "Aunt Habiba's most popular tale, which she narrated on special occasions only, was about 'The Woman with Wings,' who could fly away from the courtyard whenever she wanted to."[396] In harems, women are aware that they are deprived of their rights. Mernissi declares: "Sometimes, she said that to be stuck in a harem simply meant that a woman had lost her freedom of movement. Other times, she said that a harem meant misfortune because a woman had to share her husband with many others."[397] Therefore, women in harems aspire to emancipation and know their rights, which include, as Mernissi tells us, "every woman was to have the same right to education as a man, as well as the right to monogamy—a privileged, exclusive relationship with her husband." [398]

---

394   Mestiri 2016: 39.
395   Mernissi 1994: 1.
396   Mernissi 1994: 22.
397   Mernissi 1994: 34.
398   Mernissi 1994: 35.

2. Background and methods in the thought of Fatima Mernissi 143

In this way, Mernissi portrays the harem as a place of women's revolt against patriarchal rules and their aspiration to rights that protect their dignity. Hence, Mernissi deconstructs the orientalist representation of harem, in which women are expected to be obedient and willing to be sexual objects. For her, in situations where women are held back by patriarchal rules and confined within a harem, nevertheless they seek freedom. The harem presented by Mernissi is the place of reclusion of women who only dream of emancipating themselves, playing with their talent and intelligence. These women are in fact those who populate the domestic harems of the 1940s in Fez, Morocco, where Mernissi grew up. Mernissi presents her individual childhood experience as a child born in a harem. Therefore, one cannot assume that all women who lived in harems were intellectually active or striving for emancipation.

In *Scheherazade Goes West*, Mernissi seeks to deconstruct the misogynist and patriarchal harem exclusively associated with Islamic culture. She states that the West also has its own harem. In this way, the myth of the harem is shared across cultures, but it has different meanings. In this regard, Mernissi affirms:

> Unlike the Muslim man, who uses space to establish male domination by excluding women from the public arena, the Western man manipulates time and light. He declares in order to be beautiful; a woman must look fourteen years old. If she dares to look fifty, or worse, sixty, she is beyond the pale."[399]

According to Mernissi, Western women's appearance is prescribed by Western men according to established beauty rules and norms, such as looking tiny and young. Hence, Western men discriminate against Western women on the basis of a 'body size' norm. When a woman is overweight, 'big,' she is seen as outside the mainstream of beauty and, thus, as aging. Western women need to look thin, in order to appear young. According to Mernissi, the 'Western harem rules,' which exploit the image of women and deny their age due to the passage of time, are more dangerous than the Eastern harem rules. In this sense, she declares:

> These Western attitudes, I thought, are even more dangerous and cunning than the Muslim ones because the weapon used against women is time. Time is less visible, more fluid than space. The Western man uses images and spotlights to freeze female beauty within an idealized childhood, and forces women to perceive aging—that normal unfolding of the years—as a shameful devaluation.[400]

---

399   Mernissi 2001: 213.
400   Mernissi 2001: 214.

As evoked in Mernissi's thought, the harem culture exists in both East and West, to the point that Western and Eastern women are equally dominated by men. Both Eastern and Western men seek to manipulate women's bodies. Eastern men manipulate women's bodies by hiding them in harems for fear of sullying the public sphere of Muslim believers, because women's bodies are seen as imperfection (*awra*). Likewise, Western men control women's bodies through the time harem, which prescribes beauty standards of body size. As a result, Western women are subjected to being treated as objects, as bodies, as forms of nothingness. Therefore, in both 'harems systems,' women are limited to sexuality and considered merely bodies without any other capabilities.

Thus, Mernissi applied a transcultural approach by deconstructing several notions of myths associated with Islamic culture. She challenged the clichés of one Muslim identity by arguing that there are Muslims who are not Arabs (Iranians, Turks, Chinese, et cetera). Hence there is a transcultural aspect of Muslim identity that encompasses different ethnicities and cultural identities. In the same vein as Mernissi, I would like to add other facts that show the interreligious and plurilingual nature of the Arab world. There are Arabs who are not Muslims (Arab Christians and Arab Jews) in the Arab world, so the Arab world cannot only be defined as a Muslim one; it is an interreligious one. A number of languages are spoken in the Arab world, such as Kurdish, Kabyle, and Hebrew. The Arab world is therefore multilingual, so it cannot be reduced to just the Arab language. As outlined above, Mernissi also intended to deconstruct the myth of the subordinated Muslim woman and the myth of the sexual harem that are prevalent in most orientalist representations. With her notion of 'Western harem,' Mernissi provocatively questioned the myth of the harem by connecting it to western culture, thus, transforming the concept of a harem into a transcultural phenomenon that transcends the boundaries of the 'Orient.' Accordingly, Florina Bernardi writes:

> Mernissi introduced a cross-cultural analysis of the production and reception of representations of Middle Eastern women. Through her profound examinations of the long-lasting intercultural antagonisms between the East and the West, Mernissi approaches the issue of Otherness, often dismissing familiar orientalist readings and emphasizing instead cultural complexity, in a way that makes often hitherto unthinkable or unexpected suggestions for western readers. [401]

The myth of cultural boundaries is another myth Mernissi strives to deconstruct, through her interpretation of the Sufi heritage and understanding of the Islamic concept of *Adab*—the art of dialogue and communication—which she employs as a means of fostering her transcultural feminist approach.

---

401 Bernardi 2010: 412.

A transcultural dialogue: The transgression of the myth of boundaries (*hudud*)

It is essential to engage in dialogue with other cultures when applying a transcultural approach. The idea of transculturality is explored at the end of Mernissi's book, *Islam and Democracy: Fear of the Modern World* (2002), in which she presents a poem by the Persian Sufi Farid al-din Attar, entitled *The Conference of the Birds*. The poem of Attar expresses a dream of a world without boundaries (*hudud*), where one could freely explore cultures without being arrested. Mernissi declares:

> It happened in Nishapur in Iran in the spring of A.D. 1175. A man dreamed of a world without fear, without boundaries, where you could travel very far and find yourself in the company of strangers whom you knew as you knew yourself, strangers who were neither hostile nor aggressive. It was the land of the Simorgh.[402]

The illustration of Attar's poem in Mernissi's book clearly conveys a feminist idea, which can be interpreted as dreams of most Muslim women to live in a world without boundaries, to escape their private sphere and to discover other cultures.

Although the dream of trespassing boundaries no longer exists, the poet Sufi Attar, who preached tolerance, peace, beauty, and divine love through his poem, was assassinated by a despotic ruler. In this regard, Mernissi affirms:

> In his long meditations in Nishapur, all by himself Attar imagined that land where strangeness only enriched what we are to the ultimate degree. He committed his dream to paper, a long poem that he called *Mantiq al-tayr* (The Conference of the Birds). It instantly became famous, but intolerance and violence knocked one night at Attar's door. Genghis Khan's Mongol soldiers murdered Attar in 1230. The poet died, but the dream lived on through the centuries and continues to haunt our imaginations.[403]

The murder of Attar reminds us of the murder of the Sufi Al-Hallaj (see 2.3), who was also murdered for his belief in self-determination. Like Al-Hallaj, Attar was assassinated because he demanded to cross borders and to achieve freedom. Despotic regimes are always directed against freedom and against people demanding their rights because it challenges their authoritarian regimes. In this sense, one could argue that Mernissi is trying to convey a political message against political despotism that goes beyond recalling the assassination of Attar. In addition, Mernissi tells the

---

402   Mernissi 2002: 172.
403   Mernissi 2002: 172.

story of the poet Sufi Attar to express another feminist stance. At this point, she suggests that the prohibition of the circulation of Attar's poem in the 'Orient' reminds us of the prohibition for most Muslim women to leave the confines of their private sphere and to express their thoughts freely, without being subjected to male control. She argues: "Since that time, the Simorgh, banned in the Orient of the palaces, has haunted women's tales and children's dreams".[404] Thus, most Muslim women are forced to hide and keep their dreams to themselves out of fear of being murdered by oppressive and misogynistic male relatives and leaders, who see women's steps into the public sphere and crossing borders as a threat to their patriarchal tradition and oppressive regimes.

Regarding Mernissi's transcultural approach, Bernardi contends that Mernissi, who "as a postcolonial, polyglot, female subject has lived, studied, and worked in both the East and the West," reinterprets the East and the West as visual landscapes rather than geographical or historical landscapes. She looks through Orient and Occident to promote dialogue between their civilizations.[405] For this reason it remains a viable intellectual achievement for Mernissi to overcome boundaries in order to achieve dialogue between the East and the West. According to her, the following two intellectual strategies should be employed to foster a transcultural dialogue between the East and the West:

The first strategy is presented in her article entitled "Palace Fundamentalism and Liberal Democracy: Oil, Arms, and Irrationality" (1996). In this article, Mernissi focuses on the responsibility of Western, Eastern, and Maghrebian intellectuals to "[make their] differences intelligible."[406] To do this, Western intellectuals should explore the Eastern and Maghrebian cultures, not only to prove that they are open to other cultures, but also to interact with their Eastern counterparts in the Arab world. A dialogue between East and West is conducted on the basis of promoting an equitable distribution of "the world's resources"[407] and strengthening "commitment to democracy."[408] In this regard, Mernissi urges:

> Let us rethink the entire approach to economic development and democratization in the Middle East, giving 'stability' and 'security' a different and more positive meaning. Western intellectuals and policy makers can make a great contribution in this regard by adopting a sense of responsibility and commitment to democracy commensurate with their great capacity to control the world's resources. Reversing earlier policies of support for autocratic regimes and nurturing

---

404 Mernissi 2002: 174.
405 Bernardi 2010: 412
406 Mernissi 1996: 263.
407 Mernissi 1996: 264.
408 Mernissi 1996: 264.

the revitalization of civil society in the Arab world would be a daring and constructive way to step into the twenty-first century.[409]

During an interview under the title "The New Arab Mass Media Vehicles of Democracy?" (2006), Mernissi expressed more of her ideas about global notion of justice, which one could add to Mernissi's notions of justice presented in (2.2). In this sense, she argues:

> I think that where there is not responsibility there should necessarily be one. We need a world where if you commit a crime, afterwards you can't hide yourself or excuse yourself saying that it was committed elsewhere. This means responsibility ... this is logical, you can't commit a crime with impunity. But why does that happen today? Because we don't have a global justice that deals with everybody in the same way, and I believe that if there isn't a global justice yet, we should establish it, otherwise it's chaos, because there are no more boundaries and so it's necessary that responsibility should be global.[410]

To establish transculturality between the East and the West, Mernissi holds on to the necessity of a responsible and engaged dialogue that improves justice in resource distribution, a democracy cultivated by the West and the East, and a responsibility to punish those responsible for crimes against humanity. Developing these principles promotes global justice. According to Mernissi's thinking, democracy and global justice are fundamental concepts which form the basis of her transcultural approach.

Mernissi highlights the second strategy for transcultural dialogue between the West and the East at the end of her book *Islam and Democracy* (2002) as well in the above-mentioned interview of 2006. In *Islam and Democracy*, Mernissi affirms that scientific advances have enabled a dialogue between the West and the East. Although it is virtual, cyberspace and satellites enable the crossing of boundaries. In this context, Mernissi affirms:

> We can bring a new world into being through all the scientific advances that allow us to communicate, to engage in unlimited dialogue, to create that global mirror in which all cultures can shine in their uniqueness. Nothing makes me more exuberant than the vison of this new world, and the fact that we must go forward toward it without any barriers no longer frightens me.[411]

The notion of democracy is always regarded by Mernissi as a framework for establishing dialogue and communication among cultures. In connection with this,

---

409   Mernissi 1996: 264.
410   Mernissi and Leccese 2006: 350.
411   Mernissi 2002: 174.

Mernissi believes the new Arab mass media has fostered democracy by allowing individuals with different worldviews to voice their opinion. A democratic system, in this sense, contradicts any form of extremism, as Mernissi points out in her interview: "Extremism, actually, consists in using violence against someone that is different, that has different opinions, to impose one's own."[412] In her view, the abolition of extremism is necessary to establish respect for differences and pluralism. In this sense, she argues:

> Nowadays in the Arab countries the élite don't have any more the control on decisions, and they have lost the control of information. Of course there is a difference between us and you ... now I am going to show you the difference that will make democracy in the Arab world set off at incredible speed ... within three years the Arab world that we know will be different because of the media [ellipses in the original].[413]

According to Mernissi, dialogue and communication are integral to the concept of *adab*; for her, "*adab* means to add other brains to yours."[414] In simple terms, *adab* is a dialogue between individuals who represent different perspectives. In most cases, it ends with convincing the opponent of one's argument. Mernissi further affirms:

> This *Adab* experience is very important to learn: when the power in office proved to be interested to dialogue with the *stranger* and didn't try just to control, *to make some mafia*, and so on, it won; when it used a military strategy it failed. [415]

The concept of *adab* does not consist of controlling the opinion of the opponent by force, but on mutual intellectual exchange between individuals who hold different opinions. Communication and conversation are basic components of *adab*, not violent extremism or military tactics. *Adab* is equated with *jadal* in secondary literature dedicated to Mernissi's thought on transculturality. In this sense, Bernardi claims:

> Teaching and practicing *jadal* – the art of dialog and debate – the digital revolution and the satellite are, in Mernissi's view, the means to foster dialog, undermine fundamentalism and spread a "Humanist Islam." The importance of such technologies is relevant to combating the way that, throughout the centuries, the ideologies of colonialism and neocolonialism have limited the reciprocal body of knowledge (or body of truth) about the East and the West, directing mutually

---

412 Mernissi and Leccese 2006: 347.
413 Mernissi and Leccese 2006: 351–352.
414 Mernissi and Leccese 2006: 348.
415 Mernissi and Leccese 2006: 349.

distorted gazes onto the Other, fixing rude and hostile biases and stereotypes – something that arguably became intensified even more after the 11 September terrorist attacks, when subsequent media coverage contributed to re-imposing or reinforcing a dominant image of the East as the source of a fundamentalist, unsettling and fatal ghost.[416]

For Bernardi, the digital age provides an advantage to the Arab Muslim world because it demonstrates a culture more open to communication and dialogue, which respects diversity and plurality. In the present time, digital technologies and social media have allowed the Global South and the Global North to become more open to one another. As an example, social media played an essential role in the Arab world during the 2011 revolutions. The social media platforms enabled protesters and bloggers from the Arab World to share, transmit, and report information about what was taking place in Tunisia, Egypt, and Syria to France, Germany, and the United States by simply logging onto one of the platforms. Due to social media, the world is becoming more open, one can travel without borders or passports.

Following Bernardi, it is correct to say that Mernissi has reactivated the notion of *adab*, i.e. *jadal*, in order to point out the humanism entailed in Islamic culture. Throughout her intellectual career, Mernissi dispensed with colonial, neocolonial, as well as orientalist stereotypes and clichés that portray the Arab Muslim world as misogynistic and extremist, where only male voices matter, and military weapons are the acceptable language.

One could further assert that Mernissi aims to challenge those representation through the revival of two Sufi practices: movement—in the sense of crossing boundaries (*hudud*)—and the art of dialogue and communication (*adab*). Mernissi reactivates Sufism as part of the Islamic heritage in order to claim that there was a rich philosophical tradition of dialogue, accepting different opinions, and being open to discovering other cultures. Indeed, Mernissi asserts that crossing boundaries is a fundamental element of Sufism. She writes:

> Therefore movement is important…and like Ibn 'Arabi, I like Sufism, because it means movement, there are no frontiers … your space is there, you are in your *dimension*, but you meet the *stranger*. This is globalization![417]

In addition, she recognizes that the notion of *adab*—the art of communication—is also integral to Sufi tradition. She declares:

---

416 Bernardi 2010: 412–413.
417 Mernissi and Leccese 2006: 347.

Sufis, who believed in the communication strategy (*Adab*), avoided links with the power and withdrew from public life. They chose to practice their teachings inside *zawaya* and transmitted their vision of life to the masses.[418]

Mernissi's advocacy of the Islamic heritage of Sufism was of interest even to Western scholars to initiate an intellectual debate to free Islam from extremist and misogynistic ideologies. For instance, the orientalist scholar Annemarie Schimmel (d. 2003) asserts that Sufism was practiced not only by Sufi men, but also by Sufi women who were mothers of male Sufis and who also taught Sufism. For her, Ibn 'Arabi has developed his spirit in the search for divine love under Sufi women. In this sense, Schimmel affirms:

> Indeed, no one less than Ibn 'Arabi, the *magister magnus* of Islamic theosophical mysticism (d. 1240) studied under two women saints in Spain, among whom Fátima of Cordova must have been a person of extraordinary power. (...) It seems highly probable that Ibn 'Arabi developed some salient features of his mystical thought under the influence of Fátima as well as of that of a young Persian lady whom he met in Mecca during the pilgrimage and who inspired him to write delicate mystical love poetry. The female element plays an important role in Ibn 'Arabi's system so that he even sees in woman the highest manifestation of the Divine.[419]

Thus, Schimmel's study of Sufism in Islam highlights the dialogue that brought Eastern and Western cultures together and broke down boundaries between cultures. Alike Mernissi, Schimmel contributes to the deconstruction of the notion that Arabo-Islamic culture is misogynistic and patriarchal, valuing only men intellectually.

one could argue that Mernissi takes a transcultural approach to feminism in her latest work. According to Mernissi, the transcultural approach to be promoted requires, above all, the deconstruction of myths and stereotypes that misrepresent Islamic culture. Mernissi corrects false representations depicting Muslim women as submissive and sexist through her transcultural approach. In her work, she analyzes the harem as a transcultural institution that is practiced both in the West and in the East. By doing this, she "brings terms back together ... that have been and still are deliberately separated, thus allowing for a better understanding and, ideally, less violence between 'Eastern' and 'Western' traditions."[420] Mernissi returns to the Islamic traditions of Sufism, which includes notions of dialogue across cultures. She thereby

---

418 Mernissi and Leccese 2006: 349.
419 Schimmel 1982: 148.
420 Mahboub 2016: 5.

"has built bi-, cross-, and transcultural bridges."[421] Mernissi's transformative work inspires us to continue promoting a much-needed dialogue between different cultures, religions, and societies.

2.6 Conclusion on the thought of Fatima Mernissi

The purpose of this first part has been to situate Mernissi's thought within the framework of *feminist philosophy*. Feminist philosophy defends gender justice as equal rights for women. Mernissi's feminist stance is based on *a transcultural approach* that introduces how feminism is practiced in other cultures. Mernissi's approach to feminism is characterized by her commitment to communicating across cultures and by combining different approaches to feminism.

A notable contribution of Mernissi's feminism is the combination of *secular and Islamic frameworks*. The secular feminism in most of the Muslim world emphasizes equality in the public sphere while retaining complementarity in the private sphere. This means that secular feminism does not advance equality in the religious domain, which is controlled by men, and the family law sphere, which is regulated by religion. This prevents women from participating in religious discourse. *Islamic feminism* aim at giving women more rights in both spheres through a full participation of women in the re-reading of Islamic religious texts for themselves in order to stand up for their rights. "Islamic feminism, which brings together interpretation and implementation, is a major force in the drive to move beyond patriarchy in Muslim contexts."[422] Thus, the purpose of Islamic feminism is to free Islam from misogyny, sexism, and fundamentalism by reinterpreting Islamic scriptures within a framework of gender equality.

The contribution of Mernissi to Islamic feminism is characterized by her *transdisciplinary approach*. As part of her defense of women's rights in Islam, Mernissi uses a variety of disciplines. She conducts linguistic research, for instance. She interprets the word 'veil' in Islamic legacy, and examines words such as freedom, innovation, and creation. Her linguistic study aims to correct false traditions and systemic beliefs that link words in Islamic corpuses and thought to their exact definitions without considering alternate meanings.

Another aspect of Mernissi's transdisciplinary approach is her *empirical research*, which is based on interviews, field work, and statistical analysis. Mernissi reveals the situation of women workers in subaltern positions. Her empirical studies contributes to improving the economic and social wellbeing of women by providing data that justify their demand for decent work. In addition to her empirical study,

---

421   Mahboub 2016: 6.
422   Badran 2010b: II.

Mernissi also conducts socio-political surveys to critique most despotic regimes in most Arab-Muslim countries. Her focus is primarily on religious extremism and religious interference in public life that stymie women's rights and other rights such as the freedom of thought and the right to pluralism and diversity.

Another element of her transdisciplinary approach is her historiographic study, which explores the pre-Islamic era, the period after the advent of Islam, and the history of Islamic civilizations. Mernissi examines various female figures who have made significant contributions to the history of Islam, presenting women as rebels, political leaders, deities, and intellectuals, to show that the Islamic heritage entails women with considerable abilities. The purpose of this approach is to reject patriarchal and orientalist clichés that aim to deny the significance of women in Islam. Thus, Mernissi offers a double critique of Western clichés and Islamic misogynist tradition.

In addition, her historiographical study is characterized by an analysis of the philosophical Arabo-Islamic heritage of the 8th to the 10th centuries, through which one can explore the meaning of the theories of justice, including: the concept of legal justice, which affirms the right to interpret the Islamic heritage and the pursuit of the common good for the individual; the concept of divine justice, which is based on the principle of self-determination and freedom of expression; and the concept of political justice, which requires that individuals be fully involved in decision-making, thereby limiting the power of the leader. Her historical research further underlines the humanist heritage of Islamic civilization characterized by an interreligious, transcultural, and multi-linguistic intellectual environment. Mernissi explored the crucial role played by intellectuals from different religions, cultures, identity positions, and ethnicities contributing to the improvement and flourishing of sciences. As for transcultural overtures, the method of translation is substantial for the opening up to other traditions of thought.

Justice plays a central role in Mernissi's thinking. Mernissi's claim that women and men should participate equally in political decisions is the foundation for her notion of political justice. For Mernissi, democracy enables equality between men and women, as well as respect for freedom of religion and freedom of thought.

Throughout Mernissi's conceptualization of gender equality across the public and private spheres, she advances a notion of legal justice, which applies both to the family (the private sphere) and to society (the public sphere of human interaction). Mernissi attempts to reform the patriarchal family law that limits the legal rights of women. Monogamy and unilateral divorce, for instance, are religiously sanctioned rights and fundamental entitlements for men, as is the concept of male authority over women. Throughout her writings, Mernissi challenges these patriarchal rules both by advocating international modern norms against religious tradition and, most importantly, by advocating women's rights using a renewed interpretation of the religious discourse.

The concept of social justice is understood from Mernissi's thinking through her advocacy for women's right to participate independently in the public sphere. To obtain economic independence, women must be able to work in favorable conditions. Mernissi advocated social and economic rights, such as the right to health insurance, a fair wage, and equal employment opportunities regardless of class or gender. The notion of social justice she advocated was based on a strong sense of egalitarianism, and thus was non-discriminatory.

According to Mernissi, the emancipation of women is primarily achieved through education. The education of women shall eliminate illiteracy and make them capable of exercising their rights and of fully participating in society. It is through education that women are able to achieve independence and develop their personalities. As a consequence, Mernissi's writing on equal access to education entails a plea for epistemic justice. A fundamental principle of epistemic justice is that everyone has access to the same knowledge and educational resources.

I conclude this part of the study as I began it, by noting the necessity of engaging with Mernissi's feminist thought in the present time. How is Mernissi's feminist stance to be located in this post-revolutionary context? What is the relevance of her feminism today for women's struggles in most Arabo-Islamic societies?

In 2011, the revolution overthrew oppressive and corrupt political regimes to establish a new democratic order based on equality and justice. Recent parliamentary elections, for example in Tunisia (2011, 2014, 2016), resulted in Islamist majorities. What are the implications of Islamist political ascendancy for equality and justice for women? As Islamists gain political power, some feminists worry that Islamists will roll back progress achieved by women's movements, especially in the sphere of personal status law. It is a particular danger in Tunisia that women will again be subjected to social restrictions in the name of Islam.

As this research revealed, religious and traditional rules continue to hinder women's aspirations for equality. In this sense, Mernissi's perspective on gender justice within an Islamic feminism framework does not undermine secular rights for women, but defends their rights within religious discourse. Thus, Mernissi's approach to Islamic feminism is essential for integrating women into the religious discourse in order to counter the hegemony of men.

The importance of Mernissi's advocacy of social rights cannot be overstated. In the post-revolutionary era, unemployment and social injustice have risen sharply for both women and men in most of the Arab world. Aside from that, religious traditions and patriarchal rules that protect men's 'honor' continue to oppress women, who are subjected to violence and social harassment as a result.

The renewed interpretation of the Islamic legacy is also a defining feature of Mernissi's thought. The goal is to rid Islam of extremist demands that impede the implementation of humanistic ideas within Islam and to purge Islam of patriarchal interpretations that deprive women of their rights. Through her writings, Mernissi defends the rights to democracy and freedom of thought and expression, which are essential in today's world. Freethinkers of Islam are still at risk of being murdered for freely expressing their opinions and allowing a reinterpretation of Islamic discourse.

Mernissi advocates a transcultural approach to feminism through cross-cultural dialogue. As women around the world are affected by racism and injustice, a transcultural approach to feminism could be an effective way to unite women's voices and ensure that they fight together for their rights, regardless of their religious, national, and cultural backgrounds.

3. Background and methods in the thought of Mohammed Arkoun

In the context of globalization, a transcultural perspective on justice is essential to understand how the idea of justice is conceived in other cultures and in other systems of thought. This second part of my study aims to theorize justice from an Arabo-Islamic perspective, focusing on the Maghrebian context and a postcolonial perspective. The study focuses on the contemporary intellectual project of Mohammad Arkoun, one of the key figures and pioneers of contemporary Islamic thought. Arkoun's intellectual project is relevant to several disciplines, including Islamic studies, history of Islamic thought, Islamic and/or Arabic philosophy, Qur'anic studies, and religious studies.

Arkoun's thought is important because it challenges both Muslim and non-Muslim perceptions of Islam. He opposes the fundamentalists and the orthodox frameworks by calling for a new understanding and reinterpretation of Islamic thought. His thinking also opposes the hegemonic constructions that give rise to Arab nationalism and Euro-modernism. Arkoun argues for the recognition of the diverse identities and cultural traditions that have shaped the Arab world. He also argues for a notion of justice expressed in equal participation in global intellectual and scientific production. His central project is based on an ethical humanist and cosmopolitan concept that promotes transcultural dialogue between cultures and religions. As a way of introducing Arkoun's thought, I first describe his life, work, and influence as an intellectual and researcher.

Insights into the person, life and work of Mohammed Arkoun

Mohammed Arkoun was born on February 1, 1928, into a poor family in Taurirt-Mimoun, a Berber/Amazigh village in the Great Kabylia, Algeria, which was already occupied by France at the time. His family led a traditional and religious life. During his first years of primary school, Arkoun left Kabylia and moved to a prosperous village of French settlers east of Oran, where he continued his primary education. Thanks to a scholarship, he graduated from high school and went on to study Arabic literature in Algiers. He also attended courses in law, philosophy, and geography, and studied

Arabo-Islamic philosophy. After leaving Algeria on the eve of the War of Independence, he continued his studies in Arabic language and literature at the Sorbonne, graduating with honors in 1956. He established himself academically in 1986 with his dissertation on Miskawayh, entitled *Contribution à l'étude de l'humanisme arabe au IVe/IXe siècle: Miskawayh (320/325-421) = (932/936-1030), Philosophe et Historien*. In his dissertation, Arkoun examines the multifaceted understanding of justice developed by Miskawayh as well as the intellectual impact of Greek philosophical thought on early Arabo-Islamic philosophy. It is this connection between Islamic tradition and Greek tradition that inspires the transcultural approach to thinking that is particular to Islamic thought.

In 1970 Arkoun started as a professor of Islamic history of ideas at the University of Vincennes (Paris VIII). In 1980 he became director of the Department of Arabic and Islamic History of Ideas at the Sorbonne Nouvelle (Paris III) and editor of Arabica. From 1993 until his death in 2010, he was professor emeritus and visiting professor at the Institute of Ismaili Studies in London.[1] He was also a fellow at the Wissenschaftskolleg in Berlin (1986–1987 and 1990).

Arkoun's childhood and adolescent experiences in Algeria, as well as his studies in Paris, played a crucial, even decisive, role in shaping his thought.[2] Through this biographical account, I have explored three themes that emerge from his intellectual project and that I seek to explore in more detail below: the implicit demand for a concept of justice, the defense of religious and ethnic minorities, and the incorporation of transdisciplinary and transcultural approaches.

First, as I mentioned earlier, Arkoun grew up in Kabylia, an Algerian tribal region. His family belonged to a lower social class. In Algeria, he lived in a village on the edge of successive dominant cultures and political configurations. He lived in a remote village far removed from the center of Arabism and Islam.[3] As a result, his writing may reflect a notion of social justice that he seeks to defend in the face of what he recognizes as social discrimination in order to assert the rights of minority social groups. Arkoun's call for a rethinking of Islamic thought, the main feature of his thought, is based on an ethical notion of justice. In this context, Arkoun's intellectual project can be seen as fundamental to the assertion of women's rights in Islam. This explains the feminist reception of Arkoun's thought as found in the work of Margot Badran, Raja Rhouni, and Malika Zeghal. Drawing on the work of these Muslim feminists, I show how Arkoun's thinking leads to the development of a concept of gender justice as a shared intellectual inquiry between him and Fatima Mernissi.

---

1   Günther 2004 a: 127–128; Günther 2013: 63.
2   Günther 2019.
3   Lee 1994: viii.

Second, Arkoun is affected by sense of diaspora. Arkoun is a Berber/Amazigh Muslim philosopher. Diaspora[4] is defined as the feeling of not belonging in the country where you were born and where you have your roots and identity; the feeling of being different and out of place because one has a different identity. Similar to Jacques Derrida, who is an Arab-Algerian, Jewish, and Francophone scholar, Arkoun is a Berber-Algerian, Muslim, and Francophone intellectual. I compare Arkoun to Derrida because the latter is a major influence on Arkoun's contemporary thought project. Arkoun's diaspora is crucial for his formation of a concept of justice in transcultural and postcolonial philosophical research. Arkoun lived under Algeria's Arab nationalist discrimination and French colonization. Subsequently, he learned what it was like to be an immigrant in France. He was exposed to the contempt of the Berber population in Algeria because he was neither an Arabophone nor a Francophone.[5] As a native Berber speaker, Arkoun learned French as a second language and then Arabic as a third.[6] In fact, he had to learn two languages at the same time in order to gain social status and communicate outside the Berber regions. At the same time, he had to overcome two systems of oppression: French colonial rule, which affected the entire population of Algeria – Berber and Arab – and the exclusion of Berber's population social rights, which was expressed in the ideologies of the Algerian national and political system. Thus, Arkoun experiences the phenomenon of Arabo-centrism, colonialism and Western hegemony. Moreover, he had to deal with the conflict of different social statues between Arab and Berber Algerians.[7]

One might argue that Arkoun's intellectual thought is characterized by the development of concepts concerned with the critique of the hegemonic discourse of religion and politics. He confronts orthodoxy, which is supported by Muslim and non-Muslim perceptions of and approaches to Islam, as well as the Arab nationalist discourse that has taken root in several postcolonial Arab countries. Berber Muslim intellectuals, for example, have sharply attacked Arab nationalism and religious fundamentalism in Algeria. In their view, Arab nationalism and religious fundamentalism are responsible for the imposition of orthodoxy and the exclusion of Berber

---

4   In his book *Global Diasporas: An Introduction* (2008), Robin Cohen points out four phases from which a definition of diaspora emerges. In the context of my claim that Arkoun was affected by the sense of diaspora, I refer to the third phase, which has been influenced by poststructuralist readings and social constructionists who argue that the concept of diaspora in a postmodern world encompasses more than the loss of home belonging and is not limited to the loss of ethnic or religious affiliation, but also includes a sense of identity. In the postmodern world, the very concept of identity has been deconstructed to affirm a form of diaspora (See: Cohen, Robin (2008): *Global Diasporas: An Introduction*, second edition. Taylor and Francis e-Library: Routledge: London).
5   Günther 2004a: 127.
6   Lee 1994: viii.
7   Günther 2004 a: 127.

rights in Arab countries. They demand that their language and culture be recognized that they be allowed to participate in political life, that discriminatory laws be renounced, and that resources be distributed equally.[8]

Furthermore, Arkoun's intellectual project introduces a subdivision of the traditions, ethnicities, and identities of the Arab world. For example, Arkoun uses the terms "Islamic context" or "Muslim context" to refer to Muslims living in Arab countries. Using these terms, Arkoun also considers different cultural traditions and civilizations related to the Islamic religion. Moreover, both terms refer to Muslims living in non-Arab countries such as Turkey, Iran, and Europe. In fact, Arkoun wants to challenge the normative and fixed classification of the Arab-Muslim world and argues that not all Muslim philosophers are necessarily Arabs and not all Arab philosophers are Muslims, but that there are Arabs who are Jews and Arabs who are Christians.[9]

Third, Arkoun gave seminars in Arabic and Islamic philosophy and history of ideas at the university of Vincennes-Saint-Denis. This intellectual experience had a decisive influence on the critical development of his thought. The university of Vincennes is known as one of the "avant-garde" universities in France. It had the ambition to create a new form of pedagogy, to teach new contents, to become transdisciplinary and open to the world.[10] Arkoun was welcomed as a lecturer at this university, because as a Muslim thinker, he presented early Arabo-Islamic thought to a Western university. This fosters a transcultural philosophical debate alongside the Western school of thought. Arkoun, thus, fuses philosophical concepts and ideas from the East and the West, making his thought extremely attractive for transcultural dialogue.

In addition, poststructuralist scholars such as Derrida also taught at the university of Vincennes.[11] Derrida's thought never fit into an institutional scheme. Throughout his life and in many different forms, Derrida aimed to expose and dismantle or deconstruct the oppressive domination that he believed was inherent in all institutions.[12] Derrida's poststructuralist thought influenced Arkoun in developing his critique of orthodoxy in Islam. This is crucial, considering that Arkoun invokes a normative theoretical foundation of Islamic ethics by deconstructing the orthodox and hegemonic reinterpretation of Islamic thought. The philosophical school of Vincennes continues to be inspirational and widely used by critical theorists in gender studies and political thought. In addition, it is taken as a basis

---

8   Layachi 2005:196.
9   Dübgen 2020: 893.
10 Soulié 1998: 48–49.
11 Soulié 1998: 49.
12 Borradori 2008: xi.

by postcolonial theorists to critique hegemonic discourse on language, culture, identity, gender, history, and politics.

In this context, one might suggest that Arkoun's thought is situated within the framework of postcolonial studies and critical theory because he challenges certainties and transcends the boundaries of the established understanding of Islam. Arkoun understands Islam not as a monolithic and homogeneous discourse, but as open to further reinterpretation. In his writings, Arkoun transcends the boundaries of Islamic studies by employing methods that are not traditionally considered part of Islamic studies. As a result, his concepts of and approaches to thinking are associated with the methods of poststructuralist criticism in Islamic studies.[13]

Postcolonial thought in the context of contemporary Arabo-Islamic thought is, thus, defined by three features expressed in Arkoun's intellectual project: Critique of orthodox religious discourse, critique of Arab nationalism, and critique of Euromodern capitalism. These notions of critique are explored in my analysis of Arkoun's contemporary intellectual project, as I highlight in the following account of the structure of my study.

Structure and outline of the study

The first chapter deals with the Islamic concept of justice according to the Muslim philosopher Miskawayh (d. 1030). First, I examine the multi-faceted ethical concept of justice according to Miskawayh by focusing on his book entitled *The Refinement of Character* (2002). Arkoun does not conceptualize justice himself, but engages extensively with Miskawayh's ethical theory and his respective concept of justice early in his career. I present Arkoun's reinterpretation of Miskawayh's concept of justice based on his dissertation entitled *Contribution à l'étude de l'humanisme Arabe Au IVe/ Xe siècle: Miskawayh philosophe et historien* (1970). Arkoun states that Miskawayh's idea of justice is developed through the connection between the ethical Islamic tradition and the Greek tradition.

The connection between the Islamic and Greek traditions that shaped Miskawayh's thought is used by Arkoun through an interpretive method to highlight his notion of philosophical humanism. Arkoun focuses on Miskawayh's humanistic approach, which has been previously neglected in scholarship, to uncover the transcultural approach that drove Miskawayh's thought. In early Arabo-Islamic thought, the concept of humanism indicated an openness to foreign philosophical traditions and a concept of transcultural dialogue beyond Arabic-centric and Islamic thought. The humanist approach also represents the approval of rational thought. In this sense, one could argue that Arkoun's rereading of Miskawayh's thought is important for today in order to translate and situate ethical-philosophical discourse in a

---

13   Günther 2004a: 125.

transcultural approach and to unite an epistemic dialogue between East and West in the process of globalization.

The second chapter is divided into three sections. This chapter explains Arkoun's method of providing heterogeneous and multifarious interpretations of Islamic thought, as well as the criticisms he makes of homogeneous and monolithic interpretations. The methods he uses to rethink "Islam as a cultural and religious system"[14] are influenced by early Islamic philosophy and poststructuralist Western philosophy. Thus, the first section is devoted to Arkoun's reinterpretation of the early Islamic philosophy of Al-Amiri (d. 992), focusing on Al-Amiri's method for interpreting Islamic thought. The focus is on Arkoun's article entitled "Logocentrism and Religious Truth in Islamic Thought: The Example of al-I'lam bi manaqib al-Islam [*An exposition on the merits of Islam*]" (2002).[15] Before I present the outline of this chapter, I would like to highlight the following ideas.

I note that Arkoun focuses on Persian philosophers in his respective method of rereading of Islamic thought. To me, this has an attractive intellectual significance. I understand that Arkoun wants to open the field of Islamic studies to connect and exchange with other philosophical traditions. If one looks into Arkoun's intellectual project, one can discover the thought of philosophers who come from Persia – modern-day Iran. Yet these philosophers belong to a different cultural tradition, which is not Arabic, and to a different religious tradition, which is not the Sunni religious

---

14   Günther 2013: 65.
15   In 2002, Arkoun compiled eight of his seminal articles into an interesting English book entitled *The Unthought in Contemporary Islamic Thought* (2002a), which I refer to in this second part of my study to introduce Arkoun's contemporary intellectual project. In this book, Arkoun seems to address his thoughts to international readers. Arkoun's eight essays, reflecting a lifetime in the field of Islamic studies, cover a variety of topics that encompass Islamic thought: Qur'ānic studies, revelation, faith, authority, power, law, and civil society (see: Ameer U. Shaikh (2002): *The Unthought in Contemporary Islamic Thought, Mohammad Arkoun*, London: Saqi Books, 2002, 352 pages; a review in The American Journal of Islamic Social Sciences 21:1 (pp. 100–102)).
I focus on this book because the most groundbreaking concepts and themes that Arkoun elaborated throughout his intellectual career are presented in this collection of articles, from his reactivation of early Islamic philosophy, his critique of Orientalist methods, and his rethinking of Islamic discourse and reason to his development of a concept for interreligious dialogue. In this study, which deals with Arkoun's intellectual project, I also refer to articles he wrote in French at the beginning of his intellectual career and others translated into English between 1973 and 2007. There is a German translation of some of his articles collected in a book entitled *Der Islam: Annäherung an eine Religion* (1999) introduced by Gernot Rotter und translated by Michael Schiffmann. These articles were also published in an English collection of articles under the title *Rethinking Islam: Common Questions, Uncommon Answers* (1994), translated by Robert. D. Lee.

tradition. Miskawayh, for example, had been a Zoroastrian and converted to Shi'ite Islam.

With this in mind, I interpret Arkoun's intellectual strategy of uncovering Persian philosophy as meaning that Arkoun wants to shed light on the unconventional school of Islamic thought, although Miskawayh's ethical project is considered groundbreaking in the field of Islamic ethics. Arkoun aims to counteract the intellectual dominance of Arabian thinkers by giving Persian philosophical tradition an intellectual voice.

Following this line of thought, one could affirm that Arkoun aims to bridge different Islamic traditions and shed light on the richness of Islamic heritage beyond the religious and political conflicts that characterize the relationship between Muslims of various religious sects today. Arkoun also addresses Western readers by presenting a notion of cultural and religious diversity rooted in Islamic culture that might be attractive to someone interested in the field of Islamic studies. In this context, the second chapter takes a closer look at the Islamic thought of Al-Amiri (d. 992) as interpreted by Arkoun.

Arkoun's rereading of al-Amiri project exposes al-Amiri's transdisciplinary, comparative, and rational methods. These methods of thought, established in early Islamic thought, are important in the field of Islamic studies in our day to reconcile the disciplines of philosophy and religion. In this regard, for Islamic thought to be rational, it must be viewed anew through the lens of philosophy. The thought of al-Amiri was attractive to Arkoun for showing that Islamic philosophy embodied a reconciliation between rational and religious thought. Arkoun wished to highlight Al-Amiri's intellectual genius in offering a rational method and a transcultural approach to the study of Islam. Al-Amiri and his contemporary Miskawayh were willing to engage in an intellectual dialogue with Greek philosophy in order to harmonize Greek thought with Islamic ethics.

Al-Amiri's rational philosophical and transcultural approaches are certainly crucial to Arkoun's contemporary thought. Like al-Amiri, Arkoun draws on Western philosophical thought to rethink Islamic thought, and he reconciles the fields of humanities and philosophy to improve the field of Islamic studies. During his intellectual career, Arkoun drew inspiration from various philosophical schools of thought, such as the secular modern thought of the Enlightenment, the skeptical methods of thought, the hermeneutic school of thought, and the poststructuralist school.

As mentioned earlier, Arkoun was an Algerian-North African intellectual who grew up in Islamic culture and religion and later became acquainted with French culture and intellectual thought. Throughout his life and intellectual career, Arkoun engaged in an intellectual discourse on Islam with French readers under the influence of the French language and both humanist Islamic and poststructuralist French thought. One of his focuses was to examine the ways in which Muslims in North America and Europe present Islam to non-Muslim publics, as well as the ways in which Muslims living in Muslim societies must deal with dictatorships, and with traditional and patriarchal sociopolitical and religious challenges. To counter these confrontations, which are directed against Islam as a culture and religion, Arkoun outlines a discourse of humanistic Islam that contradicts the image of a violent, terrorist, and fundamentalist Islam.

For this reason, his thought remains attractive in this post-revolutionary era to critique orthodox Islam and fundamentalist discourse in the Arab world and European countries. Arkoun familiarized himself with modern rationalist and critical poststructuralist methods of thought. In this contemporary intellectual project, Arkoun sought a radical reform of Islamic thought to free it from fundamentalism and orthodox manipulations, but less in the spirit of early Muslim thinkers such as Miskawayh and Al-Amiri. He analyzes Islam in purely rational and poststructuralist philosophical terms.

Sections two and three of chapter two introduce Arkoun's innovative method of deconstructing Islamic thought. Section two presents Arkoun's method of applied Islamology, which was introduced in 1973. Arkoun proposes his method of applied Islamology as a critical modern analysis for Islamic studies. Applied Islamology is critically directed against classical Islamic studies and Orientalist methods, which Arkoun believes are incapable of developing a study that can respond to the challenges facing most Muslim societies today.

To make this clear, the section begins by presenting the main features of applied Islamology. It exposes the discourses of classical Islamic studies that applied Islamology critically examines. The various articles I focus on to explore Arkoun's method of applied Islamology include his introduction in his book *The Unthought in Contemporary Islamic Thought* (2002a) and his article entitled "The Answers of Applied Islamology" (2007). In these materials, Arkoun develops his concept of applied Islamology in line with the current methods of poststructuralist thought. He urges the establishment of a discourse called the "discourse of the science of man and society,"[16] which aims to understand and interpret Islamic thought in relation to the development of most Muslim societies and the social challenges faced by most Muslim individuals. To this end, Arkoun proposes the dialectic of the thought and the unthought. The unthought is the sphere of prohibition, which to human thought is forbidden to understand. The unthought is that which traditional human societies block out and refuse to think about. In contrast to the unthought, the thought with its critical methods makes the unthought clear and reveals its forbidden perspectives. Arkoun uses this controversial dialectic to make the unthought, which is obscured by traditional culture, critically accessible to human thought.

Among the unthought perspectives that the discourse of the science of man and society seeks to critically improve is the situation of women in most Muslim soci-

---

16   Arkoun 1985 a.

eties. In this regard, the second section of chapter two highlights the relevance of the method of applied Islamology for Muslim feminist thinkers who use Arkoun's method of thought to evaluate and deconstruct concepts associated with the tradition of women's subordination in Islam. Arkoun considers the Qur'an as a spoken discourse first that was then transformed into a written text. For Arkoun, the manifestation of the Qur'anic text during that process of transformation was prepared and strongly influenced by socio-cultural conditions and political ideologies. Thus, he sees the Islamic law of Shari'a as a legal text, derived primarily from the Qur'an, which can be questioned and needs to be deconstructed with a critical framework in order to find plausible interpretations that advocate greater justice for women. As Katharina Völker argues, Arkoun's "application of concepts such as demythologization, deconstruction, rationalization and historization to the Qur'anic text earned him frequent accusations of heresy."[17] In other words, his thinking about the Qur'an is at odds with reformist and conventional theological understandings of Islam that avoid critically questioning how the Qur'an went from revelatory speech to written text.

In this line of thought, the third section of the second chapter presents how applied Islamology engages in shaping various traditions related to Islam based on a critical and deconstructive analysis of the Islamic legacy. The focus is on Arkoun's article "Rethinking Islam Today" (2003) and other articles in his book *Rethinking Islam: Common Questions, Uncommon Answers* (1994). In *Rethinking Islam*, Arkoun defines various concepts related to Islamic studies such as Qur'an, revelation, and Tradition. He examines these concepts using the poststructuralist methods of Michel Foucault's "épistème," Gilles Deleuze's "difference," and Jacques Derrida's "deconstruction" to reveal a multifarious understanding of Islamic legacy beyond a monolithic interpretation. Arkoun refers to the notion of exhaustive tradition, which is an ethical approach because it confirms the pluralistic and discursive cultural traditions in Islam. The exhaustive tradition affirms the right of excluded traditions of Islam to have their say and contributes to the reconstruction of multicultural Islam.

The third chapter deals with Arkoun's critique of the hegemonic discourse shaped in the spheres of religious, nationalist, and Western thought. First, Arkoun states that hegemonic discourse formulates orthodoxy through the manipulation of Islam in two stages: the stage of the Qur'anic fact and that of Islamic fact. Qur'anic fact is the oral revelation of the Qur'an to the Prophet Muhammad. At this stage, the Qur'an is sacralized without considering the possibility of distinguishing between the rational, which individuals can accept with their minds, and the mythical, which represents the Almighty.

The second stage is that of Islamic fact. This stage presents the collection and canonization of the Qur'an in a book called the *Muṣḥaf*. In this stage, the Qur'an

---

17   Völker 2014.

served as a pretext for the emergence of a socio-political context. Various aspects of Islamic fact are selectively used by orthodoxy for power-political purposes. Arkoun's distinction between these two stages aims to argue that Islam turns into a powerful and hegemonic discourse because it is reconstructed by official religious scholars to serve political purposes and orders. Arkoun's thinking aims to liberate Islam from hegemonic constructions by making it open to a range of interpretations and realizations.

Second, Arkoun claims that the hegemonic discourse is established by the Arab nationalism discourse in both Islamic fundamentalist and secular positivist ideologies. On the one hand, Islamic nationalism identifies Islam as the only religion of Arabs, followed by the Arab nation, which is the only ethnicity, and the Arab language, which is the only language. Arkoun believes that Islamic nationalism restores the concept of ummah – the community of Muslims – but in the process erases other religions such as Judaism and Christianity, which are also widespread in the Arab world. Islamic nationalism also denies the different cultural customs and languages spoken in Arab countries. The renewal of the concept of ummah in most postcolonial Muslim societies cannot take place without the promotion of democratic rules that defend pluralism and a justice that preserves human dignity. On the other hand, the positivist nationalist discourse promotes the idea of modern and secular societies, but in doing so, positivist nationalism denies the religious fact and neglects democratic rules to be functionalized with a notion of secularity. For Arkoun, religion is an essential part of human society and cannot simply be denied. Arkoun's goal is to make religion a discipline and a field of study that allows for the deconstruction of religion from orthodoxy and fundamentalism.

Following Arkoun's critique of radical Islamism and secularism within the hegemonic discourse of nationalism, I present Arkoun's concepts of secular humanism and intellectual modernity, which he offers as a critique of the concept of radical or militant secularism and Euro-modernism. Arkoun's concept of secular humanism preserves the individual's right to criticism, freedom of thought, and respect for different religious beliefs, thus, defending pluralism. Arkoun's concept of intellectual modernity is presented as a critique of the centrism of Euro-modernism, manifested in a capitalist agenda in which the globe is characterized by a hegemonic rupture between center and periphery. One of Arkoun's critiques of the capitalist structure aims to challenge the economic consumption and passivity of most Muslim societies, as well as the domination of developed countries in the distribution of economic and cultural sources. Arkoun calls for global participation in scientific research and economic development, as well as equitable distribution of goods. This would be plausible as part of a global or transcultural debate that emphasizes solidarity, global justice, hospitality, and religious tolerance.

Chapter four discusses Arkoun's concept of emerging reason. Emerging reason calls for an abolition of the binary division of the globe into the periphery and the center within the dominant ideologies and systems of thought, and presents instead a project of solidarity that aims to create a dialogue between cultures. This chapter concludes with a discussion of Arkoun's new ethos expressed in terms of individual autonomy, community, and cosmopolitan thought. These concepts are essential to civil societies in which individuals' rights to freedom of thought and belief, tolerance, and respect for differences should be promoted. Arkoun advocates and defends the project of interreligious dialogue to combat religious fundamentalism and extremism, both of which continue to pose a threat to our societies today. This chapter is a synthesis of Arkoun's thought with the aim of establishing a link between all the previous chapters in order to shed light on Arkoun's ethical and humanistic thought. The conclusion ends with an evaluation of Arkoun's contemporary intellectual project to show the relevance of his thought to our times.

3.1 Mohammed Arkoun's rereading of the Islamic thought of Miskawayh (d. 1030): A multifaceted concept of justice[18]

This chapter deals with the Islamic concept of justice according to the Muslim philosopher Miskawayh and the contemporary thinker Mohammed Arkoun. Justice in Arabo-Islamic philosophy describes how Muslim individuals should behave and treat each other. By definition, "justice is in accordance with the highest virtues which establish a standard of human conduct".[19] Humans are encouraged to adhere to a minimum standard of duties and to act in accordance with the divine virtues as much as possible.[20] The divine virtues are laid down in revelation-the Qur'an and Tradition, but Muslim philosophers have derived their concept of justice not only from Islamic sources but also from Greek and Persian philosophers.[21]

In this reflection, I would like to introduce the concept of justice according to the Muslim philosopher Ahmad ibn Muhammad Miskawayh (d. 1030). I chose Miskawayh because he is one of the most important Muslim philosophers to whom Arkoun devotes a study. In addition, as mentioned earlier, Arkoun did not develop an explicit concept of justice in his contemporary project. Early in his academic career, he dedicated his dissertation to Arabo-Islamic philosophy, entitled *Contribution à l'étude de l'humanisme arabe au IVe/Xe siècle: Miskawayh, philosophe et historien* (1970), and to

---

18 This chapter is based on the following article: Karoui, Kaouther (2021): "The Theory of Justice between the Humanism of the Classical Muslim Thinker Miskawayh and the Contemporary Thought Project of Mohammed Arkoun". In Sebastian Günther Yassir El Jamouhi (eds.), *Islamic Ethics as Educational Discourse: Thought & Impact of the Classical Muslim Thinker Miskawayh (d. 1030)*. Tübingen: Mohr Siebeck, pp. 321–336.
19 Khadduri 1984: 107.
20 Khadduri 1984: 107.
21 Khadduri 1984: 107.

Miskawayh's humanist thought. As a Muslim researcher studying at the Sorbonne, Arkoun aims to communicate and translate the ethical and humanistic tradition of Islamic philosophy to Western readers and to sensitize 'Arab' Muslims to their humanistic heritage. For this reason, in addition to my presentation of Miskawayh's theory of justice, I would also like to present how Arkoun, as a contemporary thinker, interprets and reflects on Miskawayh's concept of justice.

I give a brief overview of Miskawayh's thought to highlight the importance of his intellectual project. Indeed, Miskawayh is considered the most important philosopher to occupy a central place in the Muslim tradition of philosophical ethics.[22] Miskawayh was also an ethical philosopher himself, for he refined some of the Greek ethical theories and reformulated them in the context of Islamic morality.[23] In addition, Miskawayh was an active scholar in many fields of knowledge. His main contribution was in two fields of study: history and ethics.[24] I focus on the field of ethics, which concerns the concept of justice and is the main topic of this chapter. His most important and influential work on ethics is *The Refinement of Character: Tadhib al-Akhlaq* (2002). *The Refinement of Character* is an important book because it occupies a prominent place in Muslim ethical literature. It deals with a wide and diverse field, including Islamic religious tradition, literary studies, and especially ethical philosophy.[25] The book refers to the Greek science of ethics as part of practical philosophy.[26] In doing so, Miskawayh draws on the Greek ethical theories of Plato and Aristotle and on some of the later Greek writers who lived in the late period of the Roman Empire.[27]

This chapter is divided into three main sections, extended by two excursions to explain in more detail, in agreement with Arkoun, that the concept of justice is introduced in early Islamic thought within two approaches to thought: Islamic legacy and Greek rational thought, which decipher the humanistic and rational approaches to Arabo-Islamic philosophy.

The first section introduces Miskawayh's concept of justice on two levels: Divine justice and human justice. Divine justice is presented in terms of the spiritual relationship between man and the divine. Human justice is reconstructed in terms of transactional and social theories of justice. I argue that in his study of the concept of justice, Miskawayh combines the metaphysical concept of justice – divine justice – and the practical concept of justice, a combination that is a hallmark of studies of humanity.

---

22   Zurayk 2002: xvii.
23   Khadduri 1984: 111.
24   Zurayk 2002: xiii.
25   Zurayk 2002: xv.
26   Zurayk 2002: xv.
27   Zurayk 2002: xv.

The second section presents Arkoun's interpretation of Miskawayh's concept of justice. Arkoun claims that Miskawayh's concept of justice is based on Plato's idea of 'universal justice,' which establishes a link between the concepts of divine justice and human justice. Arkoun also interprets Miskawayh's concept of human justice in line with Aristotle's political thought. Arkoun explores how Miskawayh's concept of justice is influenced by Greek thought. He further assumes that Miskawayh's political thought was developed in conjunction with the Islamic political legacy.

The first excursion presents the 'Three Laws' that govern social and political justice in the realm of human interaction. I would like to emphasize that Miskawayh's concept of justice is based on the Islamic perspective. Therefore, the convergences and divergences between Miskawayh's, Plato's and Aristotle's concept of justice will be presented in order to claim that Miskawayh unites Islamic religious tradition and Greek philosophical ethics. This translates his humanist approach and shows that Miskawayh is not simply an interpreter of the Greek philosophical tradition.

The third section deals briefly with Arkoun's concept of philosophical humanism, which he introduces at the end of his dissertation on Miskawayh. The concept of philosophical humanism plays a crucial role in Arkoun's contemporary intellectual project, in which he affirms that religious thought should be interpreted through reason to avoid orthodoxy. This assessment would confirm Arkoun's central claim about Miskawayh's independent philosophical achievement in terms of Islamic humanism.

The second excursion introduces the Islamic doctrine of 'voluntarism' to claim that the Islamic ethical doctrine enables philosophical humanism and, thus, rational thought. In this regard, 'voluntarism' supports that justice is determined by reason. Since individuals are responsible and self-determined, they can make choices and control their moral behavior. Thus, with the help of reason, individuals can decide what is appropriate for them in the realm of ethical behavior and take responsibility for their choices.

Miskawayh's theory of justice and the influence of Plato's and Aristotle's ethos

Miskawayh wrote a groundbreaking ethical treatise in Arabic, *Tahdhīb al-akhlāq* (1961), which appeared in English under the title *The Refinement of Character* (2002). Considering this manuscript, the concept of divine justice as an expression of the purification of the soul will be explained below based on Miskawayh's Islamic philosophical ethics. In addition, Miskawayh's detailed analysis of justice as it relates to human action is presented, which states justice in terms of human social interaction. As part of my commentary on Miskawayh's concept of divine justice and justice in human interaction, I point out his references to Plato's *Republic* and Aristotle's *Nicomachean Ethics*, which have been remarked upon by scholars such as Majid Khadduri (1909–2007) and Majid Fakhry (1923–2021), making an interesting contribution to Islamic theory of justice. Thus, the key to denoting Miskawayh's Islamic philosophical ethic is to highlight his mediation on Plato's and Aristotle's theories of justice and, most importantly, to show that Miskawayh was not a pure imitator of the Greek philosophical thought, but he associates aspects of Islamic religious ethics with Greek philosophical ethics.

Divine justice as an expression of the purification of the soul: Based on the metaphysical virtues of Plato

The concept of justice in Arabo-Islamic philosophy is discussed on two levels: divine and human justice.[28] For this reason, I present Miskawayh's concept of justice both on the level of divine justice and on the level of human justice to make it clear that he provides a multifaceted examination of the concept of justice by examining it on different levels.

Let us first briefly discuss divine justice as it is portrayed in the Islamic legacy with emphasis on the Qur'an and early Islamic philosophy. Divine justice is expressed in the Qur'an as follows: God is never unjust to His servant;"[29] "My Lord commands righteousness;"[30] "God does not love evildoers;"[31] "Let harm be requited by an equal harm ... He does not like those who do wrong."[32] These Qur'anic verses clearly show that the Divine calls upon humans to do justice. Therefore humans must embody justice in their behavior, because the Divine strictly commands it.

Majid Fakhry argues that the most explicit prediction of divine justice occurs in another verse of the Qur'an; the verse states: "God commands justice, doing good, and generosity towards relatives and He forbids what is shameful, blameworthy, and oppressive. He teaches you, so that you may take heed."[33] Fakhry also mentions that divine justice is described in terms of adjectival nouns. These nouns are in the list of the 99 'beautiful names' of God.[34] Names of God are names attributed to God in the Islamic legacy. Some names are known from either the Qur'an or the Tradition, while others are found in both sources. One of these nouns is al-'adl. The Just meaning that God is just and ensures that justice prevails in the behavior of people. Divine justice in the Islamic legacy, then, is about how Muslims can embody justice, a value prescribed in the Islamic scriptures that God requires of Muslims.

Earlier Islamic philosophy does not contradict Islamic legacy on the issue of divine justice. Islamic philosophy sees that divine justice is about the relationship be-

---

28   Khadduri 1984: 107.
29   The Qur'ān, Chapter 3, The Family Of 'Imran; Verse 182.
30   The Qur'ān, Chapter 7, The Heights; Verse 29.
31   The Qur'ān, Chapter 3, The Family Of 'Imran; Verse 57 and Verse 140.
32   The Qur'ān, Chapter 42, Consultation; Verse 40.
33   The Qur'ān, Chapter 16, The Bee; Verse 90.
34   Fakhry 1991: 14–15.

tween humankind and the divine and that humankind must embody justice, and also sets out how it is possible for humankind to do so. Therefore, Islamic philosophy has raised the issue of the soul, as it is stated in the Qur'an in Chapter 91 entitled *The Sun*, which states that the soul should be purified in order to achieve justice. The verses of this Qur'anic chapter declare "(...) by the soul and how He formed it and inspired it [to know] its own rebellion and piety! The one who purifies his soul succeeds and the one who corrupts it fails."[35] Indeed, both Islamic legacy and early Islamic philosophy reflect how it is possible for humankind to embody divine justice. In this sense, divine justice is achieved by human beings when they find a balance between the faculties of their souls to achieve happiness, perfection and excellence, which are characteristics of a just person.

As a Muslim philosopher, Miskawayh develops his concept of divine justice based on Islamic legacy and philosophy by showing the characteristics of the soul's faculties and explaining how the soul can be purified to achieve justice. In this context, I will address the questions: How does the soul attain the virtue of justice? And how does the purification of the soul enable humankind to approach the divine?

In the first discourse of *The Refinement of Character*, subtitled "The Principle of Ethics: The Soul and its Faculties; the Good and Happiness; Virtues and Vices," Miskawayh discusses the nature of the soul. He affirms "Having found within man something which, by its definition and properties, is opposite to bodies and parts of bodies and, by its actions, is opposite to the actions and properties of the body."[36] Hence, the soul is both the opposite and a part of the body. The soul is part of the body because it lives in the body, which is its abode, but the action of the soul is opposite to the actions of the body because the soul is a substance, and the body is accidental. The soul claims eternity and intelligence, while the body claims contingency.

To explain the characteristics of the soul, Miskawayh claims that the soul strives for the sciences and forms of knowledge to constitute its virtue.[37] Indeed, the human shall "pay greater attention to his soul and puts in [strives with] all his power and capacity to renounce the things which hinder him from achieving the virtue".[38] Like Plato in his theory of the soul, Miskawayh distinguishes between the soul and the body, and joins a virtuous characteristic to the soul. This is to claim that the soul is the essence of humankind because it is incorporeal and immortal. Miskawayh also, like Plato, perceives that the soul is striving for knowledge to achieve virtue. This is achieved by training the soul to perform rationally. The question must be asked: How can the soul abandon desire and realize virtue?

---

35 The Qur'ān, Chapter 91, The Sun; Verses 7- 8- 9-10-11.
36 Miskawayh 2002: 5
37 Miskawayh 2002: 10.
38 Miskawayh 2002: 10.

Based on his interpretation of Plato's metaphysical values, Miskawayh argues that there exist three faculties of the soul, which human beings shall temper to achieve virtue: "The rational faculty is called the kingly, and the organ of the body it uses is the brain. The concupiscent faculty is called the beastly, and the organ of the body which it uses is the liver. The irascible faculty is the leonine, and the organ of the body which it uses is the heart."[39] This is similar to how Plato classifies the soul. Indeed, for Plato, reason, spirit, and appetite are the three faculties of the soul: Appetite enhances the worldly desires and selfishness; the spirit soul is courageous and has a strong will; reason is to calm desire and selfishness caused by the appetite-soul, and balance the bold and strong will that characterizes the spirit-soul.[40]

As we see, Plato accords a principle role to the rational soul. In this way, we understand that the rational soul is the responsible agent for moderating yearnings. In the same line of thought, Miskawayh conceives that the rational faculty is an intermediary between the beastly and the leonine faculties. The rational faculty produces virtuous acts because the rational soul is supervised by reason. When the soul is guided toward knowledge it will not act wrongly. As Miskawayh explains, when the activity of the rational soul is moderate, and when the soul seeks true knowledge, it achieves the virtue of knowledge followed by that of wisdom. When the activity of the beastly soul is moderate, when it yields to the rational soul, and does not reject what the latter allots to it, and when it does not indulge in the pursuit of its own desires, it achieves the virtue of temperance followed by that of liberality. Similarly, when the activity of the irascible soul is moderate, when it obeys the rational soul and what it allots to it, it achieves the virtue of magnanimity followed by that of courage.[41] "Then, when all these three virtues are moderate and have the proper relation one to another, a virtue is produced, which represents their perfection and completeness, namely the virtue of justice."[42]

Besides the discussion of the nature of soul underlying its faculties to achieve purification, in the fourth discourse of *The Refinement of Character*, which clearly deals with the matter of justice, Miskawayh goes on to cite a statement by Plato, from which he highlights the question of how the soul of humankind, by the achievement of the virtue of justice, as the completeness of the other virtues, becomes nearer to God. Miskawayh argues when man acquires justice, every part of his soul illumi-

---

39   Miskawayh 2002: 15.
40   See: Plato, The Republic: book 4 which explain in detail three parts of soul. Or, among other places, books 8 and 9 of the Republic.
41   Miskawayh 2002: 15
42   Miskawayh 2002: 15–16.

nates every other part. Thereby all the other virtues are achieved in the soul in the best possible way. This is the happy man's nearest approach to God.[43]

In this regard, we note that Miskawayh's concept of divine justice is "defined not as governing the moral relationship among gods but as the relationship between God and man."[44] One can understand that Miskawayh bases the concept of divine justice on the Islamic principle of the oneness of God. Therefore, he rejects the multiplicity of gods as emphasized in ancient Greek thought and trusts in the oneness of God. I argue that belief in the oneness of God is the pillar of a monotheistic religious tradition called *Tawhid*. This observation also underscores Miskawayh's intellectual humanism and transcultural approach, by which he links two traditions together as "… an effort to achieve harmony of Greek philosophy and religion."[45]

The main characteristic of divine justice, according to Miskawayh, consists of the harmony between the soul and the body. Divine justice is realized only if man is able to harmonize the excesses of his natural passions by equilibrium or proportion (*i'tidāl*). It exceeds materiality and seeks the apprehension of the intelligible. In a word, divine justice is a spiritual relationship between God and man. It transcends the relationship between man and nature or between man and man.[46] On the one hand, I assume that it is pivotal to rethink the abstract conception of divine justice that encourages the self-divinization of humankind, where the soul as divine agent could moderate the corporal. However, I want to highlight that the conception of divine justice introduced by Miskawayh, under Plato's influence, is still insufficient in the realm of practical ethics. The conception of divine justice is restricted to the individual sphere of the human being and his relationship with God. Indeed, it does not include justice in the social sphere of human interaction. This prompts me to discuss how Miskawayh thinks about the concept of justice as it relates to human interaction.

Justice in relation to human social interactions: Based on the practical ethics of Aristotle

Human justice in Islamic ethics deals with the ability of human beings to imitate or to reproduce the value of divine justice in the sphere of human interactions, for instance in terms of economic, political, and social spheres. Miskawayh believes that the measure of establishing justice on a practical level is related to the concept of equality. He argues that equality gives meaning to justice. Therefore, equality is established between individuals and in all spheres of human interactions when justice

---

43   Miskawayh 2002: 110–111.
44   Khadduri 1984: 111
45   Khadduri 1984: 111
46   Fakhry 1975 a: 246; Fakhry 1975 b: 42; Khadduri 1984: 111–112.

is applied as a principle. Miskawayh defines the term equality as follows: "the etymology of the word equality indicates to you its meaning. For counterbalance (*'idl*) in loads, equilibrium (*i'tidāl*) in weights, and justice (*'adl*) in actions are all derived from the meaning of equality (*musawah*)".[47] He observes that the notion of equality "in its basic meaning, it is unity or a shadow of unity".[48] Thus, as I understand it, equality could not be a principle of measuring to define economic and social justice. For this reason, Miskawayh draws on Aristotle's concept of proportion to realize human justice. He explains: when we cannot attain that equality which is sameness within multiplicity, we resort to proportion (*i'tidāl*) to achieve equality.[49]

In Aristotelian terms, to proportion is to equally grant distributive justice between individuals on their own merits.[50] In this respect, Miskawayh distinguishes between three types of proportions to establish justice: discrete proportion, continuous proportion, and geometrical proportion.[51] In line with these proportions, Miskawayh enumerates three types of justice regarding human activity: The first is justice relating to the division of money and honors; second is justice relating to the division of voluntary transactions such as selling, buying and exchange; and third is justice in involuntary transactions, in which injustice and violation of rights could be committed.[52]

In order to promote a clear understanding of Miskawayh's theories of justice in the realm of human activities and in accordance with their proportions, I propose to refer to the first and second kinds of justice as transactional justice, by which I mean economic exchange between individuals. The third kind of justice – that of involuntary transaction – I will call social justice, which deals with mutual assistance between humans.

I shall now explain the three types of justice and how they function with their appropriate proportion (*i'tidāl*) to determine equality. Miskawayh explains that the first type, which is justice according to the division of money and honors, a type of transactional justice, takes the form of a discrete proportion. An instance of this is the equitable distribution of privileges between people of the same rank. The second type of transactional justice, justice according to the division of voluntary transactions such as selling, buying and exchange, sometimes takes the form of discrete and continuous proportions. The discrete proportion entails that, in economic exchange,

---

47 Miskawayh 2002: 101.
48 Miskawayh 2002: 101.
49 Miskawayh 2002: 101.
50 In *Nicomachean Ethics*, Book 5, Aristotle discusses "distributive justice in accordance with geometrical proportion." Aristotle claims "awards should be 'according to merit;' for all men agree that what is just in distribution must be according to merit in some sense."
51 Miskawayh 2002: 101.
52 Miskawayh 2002: 102.

each man shall share the same transaction as others in the same rank.[53] I understand this to mean that the notion of transactional justice has the same meaning as Aristotle's concept of distributive justice, in that distributive justice involves dividing benefits and burdens fairly among members of a community.[54] The third, justice of involuntary transaction, which I call social justice, is nearer to the geometrical proportion. It deals with human relationships between one man and another. When the latter annuls this relation by doing injustice to the former, justice requires that the former does the same injustice to the latter by involuntary action.[55] As a result, the concept of social justice is equivalent to Aristotle's notion of distributive justice. In this sense, distributive and social justice reestablish a fair relationship between individuals.[56]

In sum, human justice is dealing with justice in actions. It is produced in the realm of human interaction as in the economic – distributive – and social spheres. It is to provide a fair and just distribution of goods among individuals in the transactional realm; further, it calls for just conduct among individuals.

One could argue that Miskawayh's theory of justice is shaped through a multifaceted concept. In this regard, Khadduri comments on Miskawayh's concept of divine and human justice by claiming that Miskawayh brings together two levels of justice.[57] Divine justice is "(…) a spiritual relationship between man and God (…), it is the fulfillment of man's legal and religious duties toward God".[58] Human justice is expressed with a praxis notion of justice, dealing with the relationship among natural and physical bodies, or between humans.[59]

In other words, there exists divine justice; it only exists in terms of the transcendental relationship between the individual and God to determine divine virtues. Human justice deals with human relationships. It is to determine a just and good conduct of individuals in the sphere of social interactions and economic exchanges. I suggest that Miskawayh develops a notion of humanism (*al-ansana*) as the main achievement of the connection between the notion of divine justice and human justice. In this manner, "Humanism – in particular, *humanista studia* – was the key to the success of this symbiotic relationship (i.e., between theory and praxis)."[60] As theory, justice refers to the relationship between God and man, while as practice justice refers to human relationships.

---

53   Miskawayh 2002: 102.
54   See Aristotle, *Nicomachean Ethics*: 67–74, 76; 1129a–1132b, 1134a.
55   Miskawayh 2002: 102.
56   See Aristotle, *Nicomachean Ethics*: 67–74, 76; 1129a–1132b, 1134a.
57   Khadduri 1984: 111–112.
58   Khadduri 1984:112.
59   Khadduri 1984: 111.
60   Radez 2015: 32.

In addition, humanism (*al-ansana*) is developed by Miskawayh through the concept of reason. Reason realizes divine justice when the rational soul triumphs over the concupiscent and irascible faculties to achieve it. Furthermore, the faculty of reason exists to monitor human behavior in the realm of human interaction, because when they use the faculty of reason, humans will act in a correct manner. In this case, I agree with Radez who claims that Miskawayh not only made a connection between Platonic and Aristotelian ethics, but also placed moral knowledge in a rationalist context.[61] In doing so, he uses reason to regulate human behavior in the realm of human interaction and as a principle to achieve divine justice.

Arkoun's interpretation of Miskawayh's theory of justice

Focusing on Arkoun's interpretation of Miskawayh's theory of justice, my working material consists of Arkoun's dissertation on Miskawayh entitled: *Contribution à l'étude de l'humanisme arabe au IVe/Xe siècle: Miskawayh, philosophe et historien* (1970), and the part on *"Conditions d'accès au bonheur"* [conditions for access to happiness]. I structure this section as follows: First, I emphasize that Arkoun interprets Miskawayh's concepts of divine justice and human justice as interconnected. Arkoun sees that Miskawayh was influenced by Plato's idea of universal justice, which a wise man must hold. Second, I present Arkoun's interpretation of Miskawayh's detailed analysis of the concept of justice. The point is to illuminate how Arkoun shows that Miskawayh's political ideas were inspired by Aristotle's political philosophy.

At the first level of Arkoun's interpretation of Miskawayh's concepts of divine justice and human justice, which are interconnected in reference to Plato's idea of universal justice, Arkoun emphasizes that Miskawayh points out the general orientation of the virtue of justice, dependent upon the works of Plato.[62] The general orientation of the virtue of justice signifies Plato's concept of divine justice, which Arkoun understands as being possible once humankind achieves a harmonization between divine and human justice.[63] Arkoun indicates that Miskawayh developed the concept of justice on three levels: Divine justice, is the expression of unity and perfect existence.[64] Natural justice, then, is determined by the unity of celestial bodies and by the equality of the bodies around us.[65] Human justice exists in two realms: There is justice resulting from free choice or voluntary justice and institutional justice. Vol-

---

61   Radez 2015: 33–34.
62   Arkoun 1970:292.
63   Arkoun 1970:293.
64   Arkoun 1970:293.
65   Arkoun 1970:293.

untary justice results of the equilibrium between the three faculties of the soul,[66] and institutional justice concerns the equitable economic exchanges.[67]

Arkoun interprets Miskawayh's concept of justice in line with Plato's concept of the idea of universal justice as combination between divine and human justice. In this regard, Arkoun explains that the divine justice, and voluntary as well as institutional justice, are mutually and reciprocally correlated. Although voluntary justice and institutional justice deal with justice in human interaction activities, the key to ethical and good behavior is seen in the ability of human beings to achieve unity between divine virtues and human virtues of justice, therefore, of the *Unity* through proportion (*nisba*), equality and equilibrium.[68] Since there is homology of structures between the order of the world, the arrangement of the soul, and the organization of the city.[69]

Additionally, Arkoun explains that once humans achieve harmonization and union between divine and human virtues of justice, they attain an idea of universal justice.[70] Therefore, humans imbued with this idea of universal justice will be a living link between the upper world and the lower world.[71] In a word, the idea of universal justice represents a correlation between the divine and human virtues of justice. Humans should realize the idea of universal justice in order to act in the lower world in accordance with the divine virtues. In addition, Arkoun states that the human who embodies the idea of universal justice will be the embodiment of Beauty and Truth which are the content of Plato's idealism.[72] Arkoun maintains that Miskawayh emphasized the idea of universal justice more than other Muslim philosophers and in line with Plato's idealism.[73]

Like Arkoun, Khadduri explains the idea of the union of the divine and human virtues of justice in Miskawayh's thought. Khadduri quotes him (Miskawayh): "'The truly just man,' Miskawayh said, 'is he who harmonizes all his faculties, activities, and states in such a way that none exceeds the others ... desiring in all of the virtue of justice itself and not any other object ... He can achieve this only if he possesses a certain moral disposition of the soul out of which, and in accordance with which, all his activities come forth'".[74] In the following, I explain who this "just man" is, who will promote a universal idea of justice as a link between divine and human justice.

---

66   Arkoun 1970:293.
67   Arkoun 1970:293.
68   Arkoun 1970:293.
69   Arkoun 1970:293.
70   Arkoun 1970:293.
71   Arkoun 1970:293.
72   Arkoun 1970:293-294.
73   Arkoun 1970: 293–294.
74   Khadduri 1984:113; Miskawayh 2002: 100.

In his article entitled "Greek thought in Arab ethics: Miskawayh's theory of justice" (2000), Yasien Mohamed, in contrast to Arkoun, assumes that Miskawayh adopted Plato's theory of justice of the soul and developed his concept of social justice following Aristotle.[75] For Mohamed, the general orientation of the virtue of justice or the universal concept of justice, thus, develops following Plato and Aristotle, and not only through Plato, as Arkoun depicts it.

Arkoun explores the question of who is the person capable of promoting divine justice in the realm of human interaction based on his interpretation of Miskawayh's concept of justice. In other words, the question must be asked: Who is this man who has appropriated the idea of universal justice and succeeded in reproducing the divine virtues of justice in the subordinate world of human interaction? In this regard, Arkoun declares that Miskawayh "was haunted by the Iranian ideal of a righteous ruler, the figure of the Imam, master of Justice, and the daily spectacle of a city gone astray" [translation mine].[76] As Arkoun affirms, Miskawayh, like Plato, was sensitive to the need to overcome the contingency of history by opening moral and political leadership to the transcendence.[77] In addition, Arkoun argues that the figure of the righteous Imam could be interpreted as Socrates, and what's more, as Plato and Aristotle's idea of the wise man. When, according to Plato and Aristotle, the virtue is formed and reached by the wise man, every man is capable of discerning and choosing the Good in all circumstances.[78]

From a comparative perspective, I would like to briefly point out the divergence between Plato's and Miskawayh's concepts of the 'sage' that Arkoun does not address. The main characteristics of 'wise men' according to Plato are that they must be the embodiment of the idea of good; they must be heroes, supermen, and demigods. From among these men, the one who possesses the qualities of leadership, which are wisdom and strength, is chosen to be a political leader.[79]

Thus, I claim that Plato, from a purely philosophical point of view, asserts that every man is capable of knowing virtue, but that man should be a philosopher who provides the quality of wisdom. Wisdom and political power must be united in one man, who provides the leadership of a philosopher-king.

Contrary to this Greek philosophical tradition, and following the Arkoun based interpretation of Miskawayh's concept of the 'wise man,' I understand that Miskawayh justifies his notion of universal justice as being led exclusively by the Imam with the Islamic political heritage when it is stated that only the Imam is qualified to

---

75 Mohamed 2000: 242.
76 Arkoun 1970: 294.
77 Arkoun 1970: 294.
78 Arkoun 1970: 298.
79 Plato, The Republic Book 5: 476a-b; 476d; 476e-477e.

3. Background and methods in the thought of Mohammed Arkoun 177

lead the citizens politically. That is regarding to the Shi'ite Islamic political tradition, where the Imam leader is transcendent as God.

Indeed, 'transcendence' in Arabic is called *tanzih*. Transcendence is only asserted to God, where Muslims must submit and surrender to God, first because of His unity, uniqueness, and perfection, second because of His omnipotence and majesty, and finally because of His specifically transcendent attributes of infinitude and everlastingness.[80]

Just as these divine virtues are meant to describe God, they are emphasized above by Arkoun in his account of the divine attributes of the Imam as the 'master of Justice.' In the same perspective as Arkoun, Fakhry sees that the Imam, the ruler, acts on behalf of God.[81] As we can see, the Imam is immanent to God, and therefore Shi'ite Muslims should submit to the Imam because he represents divine virtues in the lower world. As a religious icon, the Imam has the authority to politically control individuals.

As a result, Arkoun understood that Miskawayh's theory of justice is presented in the same perspective as Plato's idealism through the idea of universal justice resulting from the harmonization between divine and human justice. I have highlighted a point of divergence between Miskawayh's and Plato's theory of the wise man that was not explored by Arkoun in his presentation of the idea of who will embody the concept of universal justice. For Plato, the wise man is a philosopher with political power; for Miskawayh, he is a ruler who holds religious leadership. Therefore I conclude that Miskawayh's concept of the wise man is exclusively linked to an Islamic political legacy.

On the second level of Arkoun's interpretation of Miskawayh's detailed concept of justice, Arkoun's dissertation focuses on the fifth discourse of *The Refinement* of Miskawayh, which deals with the concepts of "love and friendship." I mention this to illustrate that Arkoun begins with an interesting introduction to the section of his dissertation on Miskawayh that deals with "*la justice dans la cité*" [justice in the city]. In it, Arkoun affirms the necessity of human sociability as a principle of Greek moral and practical philosophy, which for him inspired Miskawayh's thought on justice.[82]

In fact, Arkoun explains that happiness, which is the result of good moral behavior between individuals, cannot be reduced to a spiritual relationship between God and the individual. Therefore, the individual is intent on attaining his own happiness, living in isolation and at a distance from other individuals.[83] However, Arkoun explains to us that happiness in Greek practical philosophy has its meaning in relation to individuals among themselves. Happiness must be shared between individ-

---

80   Graham 1982: 8.
81   Fakhry 1991: 115.
82   Arkoun 1970: 302.
83   Arkoun 1970: 302.

uals and is perceived in the sphere of social human interaction.[84] In my own words, individuals live in a social group. For this reason, they need the support of other individuals, just as other individuals need their support. Thus, when individuals treat and support each other justly, human justice arises in the sphere of socio-political interaction, followed by happiness.

Following on from this, I understand the reason Arkoun comments on Miskawayh's detailed concept of justice by focusing on the fifth discourse of *Refinement*, which is about love and friendship. Arkoun does this because "love" and "friendship" are the cornerstone for strengthening human relationships and spreading happiness. I will not reproduce in detail in this study Arkoun's analysis of Miskawayh's concept of love and friendship as a cement for strengthening human social relations. This is because I note that Arkoun merely repeats Miskawayh's definition of love and friendship. In what follows, I am more concerned with presenting Arkoun's engagement with Miskawayh's detailed concept of justice. The purpose is to examine how the concept of political justice is articulated in Miskawayh's thought and examined in accordance with Aristotle's political philosophy and within the Islamic political tradition. I begin by presenting Arkoun's interpretation of Miskawayh's detailed concept of justice, which Arkoun conceived on the basis of Aristotle's thought.

Arkoun declares that Miskawayh develops a certain definition and a particular description of the detailed concept of justice – or a 'particular' notion of justice – under the influence of Aristotle.[85]

To confirm what Arkoun says, I turn to Miskawayh's book *The Refinement of Character* to demonstrate that Miskawayh clearly draws on the Greek philosophy of Aristotle to develop his detailed concepts of justice. Thus, Miskawayh affirms, "[r]esuming our discussion of justice, we say: Aristotle divided justice into three categories."[86] In fact, for Aristotle, there are two types of justice: distributive justice and remedial or corrective justice. Distributive justice implies that the state should divide or distribute goods and wealth among citizens according to their merit. Again, remedial justice is divided into two, dealing with voluntary transactions and with involuntary transaction. Further, Aristotle added commercial and cumulative justice to the above-mentioned types of justice.[87] Since remedial justice is divided into two cate-

---

84 Arkoun 1970: 302.
85 Arkoun 1970: 292.
86 Miskawayh 2002: 106.
87 Aristotle, *Nicomachean Ethics*, Book V, chapters. 1–2. In his book *Refinement of Character*, Miskawayh, following Aristotle, also presents three categories of justice. The first category of justice is what people do toward God. The second category is what people perform, one towards another. The third category of justice is what people must do as an obligation, such as paying their debts (see Miskawayh (2002): *Refinement of Character* (p: 106)). I examined these categories of justice in the first section of this chapter, which dealt with Miskawayh's concept of divine justice and his concept of justice in relation to human social interaction.

gories of justice, voluntary and involuntary transactions, one could argue that Aristotle presents three categories of justice. Therefore, Arkoun's claim that Miskawayh derives his detailed concept of justice from Aristotle is accurate in that Miskawayh clearly cites Aristotle as the reference on which he relies to ground his concept of justice, which he conceptualized in three categories as did Aristotle.

I continue by presenting Arkoun's interpretation of Miskawayh's political thought. Arkoun explains that all of Miskawayh's political ideas were developed in terms of Greek thought.[88] He further explains that Miskawayh's political ideas were summarized in the book IV, which deals with justice, and the book V, which is devoted to love (*mahabba*).[89] Nevertheless, Arkoun explains that Miskawayh does not provide a deeper analysis of the concepts of the machinery of government, the possible constitutions, and the concrete relations between citizens.[90] For Arkoun, this means that Miskawayh does not know Aristotle's book of *Politics*, since he adheres to Aristotle's political ideas set forth in the *Nicomachean Ethics*.[91]

In addition, Arkoun emphasizes that Miskawayh was an intellectual celebrity at the time of the Buyid dynasty. Arkoun affirms that Miskawayh defined the social function of religion and the responsibility of the ruler in terms that were clearly dictated the Buyid Dynasty[92]. Arkoun states that most of Miskawayh's primary intellectual works were written during the period of Buyid rule. He further asserts that Miskawayh served as librarian and instructor to Abu-l-Fath Ibn al-'Amid (360–366).[93] In agreement with Arkoun, one could argue that it is important to point out this biographical fact about Miskawayh in order to shed light on the fact that Miskawayh places his political ideas within the legacy of Persian political tradition, for he is a Shi'a intellectual who was among the intellectuals who occupied a prominent position in the intellectual assemblies of the Buyid viceroys.[94] This leads Miskawayh to a positive assessment of Buyid rule and the Islamic political tradition.

Thus, one can argue that Arkoun interprets Miskawayh's detailed concept of justice in two realms: the realm of social interaction, where Arkoun focuses on the two

---

88   Arkoun 1970: 302–303.
89   Arkoun 1970: 302–303.
90   Arkoun 1970: 302–303.
91   Arkoun 1970: 302–303. See the section "Justice in relation to human social interactions," in which I examine Miskawayh's notion of human justice based on Aristotle's books of *Nicomachean Ethics*.
92   Arkoun 1970: 302. The Buyid Dynasty is a Shi'a Persian dynasty that originated from Daylaman in Gilan. They founded a confederation that controlled most of modern-day Iran and Iraq in the 10th and 11th centuries. See: Husain Syed, Muzaffar, Sayed Saud Akhtar, and Babuddin Usmani (eds) (2011): *A concise History of Islam* (pp.183). New Delhi: Vij Books.
93   Arkoun 1970: 65.
94   Kraemer 1993: 54.

principles of love and friendship to strengthen human interactions; and the realm of the political, in which he attempts to understand Miskawayh's political ideas in the light of Aristotle's political theory. According to Arkoun's interpretation of Miskawayh's political ideas, Miskawayh does not provide an implicit definition of what political justice is. Therefore political justice is still related to the other categories of divine justice and human justice. Following the same line as Arkoun, Mohamed explains the fact that Miskawayh developed his theory of justice following Aristotle, because "both Aristotle and Miskawayh share the view that justice is the kind of virtue that embraces all virtues as it does not apply to justice to oneself alone, but also to others."[95]

Arkoun claims that Miskawayh's concept of justice is embedded in an Islamic legacy.[96] As mentioned earlier, Arkoun refers to the ruler, the infallible Imam, who should promote a notion of universal justice as a link between divine and human justice. However, I argue that Arkoun does not deal in depth with Miskawayh's notion of laws. For Majid Fakhry, the concept of law is the principle for regulating the social or political behavior of individuals in the realm of human interaction.[97] Arkoun does not refer to Miskawayh's fourth discourse on *The Refinement of Character* in his analysis of Miskawayh's thought, which I think demonstrates a lack of attention to Miskawayh's concept of law. Instead, Arkoun focuses more on the fifth discourse. With this in mind, the next section of this study will discuss the three laws that are said to govern justice in the transactional and social realms. My primary concern is to emphasize more strongly that Miskawayh's theory of justice is influenced not only by the Greek philosophical ethos but also by the Islamic legacy, in order to show Miskawayh's transcultural approach to justice as a link between two traditions of thought: Greek and Arabo-Islamic.

Excursion 1: The Three Laws: *The Islamic law of Shari'a, a principle law between a just ruler and money*

The focus here is on the fourth discourse of *Refinement of Character*, to introduce "The Three Laws" that govern the social and political ideas of justice. My main goal is to point out that Miskawayh's theories of ethical justice are rooted in Islamic legacy in addition to the philosophical thought of the Greeks.

Law is used to regulate the conduct of individuals. Law is also related to particular traditions of society or community. To define justice, Miskawayh uses laws that are in connection to the Islamic tradition. Miskawayh argues that there exist three laws by which justice should be established in the sphere of human interaction. He

---

95 Mohamed 2000: 243.
96 Arkoun 1970: 356.
97 Fakhry 1991: 115.

declares "the highest law is from God (blessed and exalted is He!), the ruler is a second law in His behalf, and money is a third law."[98]

Paraphrasing Miskawayh's words, the "highest law" is the Islamic law, Shari'a, which is revealed by God. The second is the just ruler, identified by Miskawayh with the Caliph or Imam, who acts in the image of God and, thus, is the only being who can justly imitate the Islamic law of Shari'a to establish the sense of justice between individuals because he is infallible. The third is money, which is only an imitator.[99] In contrast to Aristotle, who "derives the Greek nomisma (money) from nomos (law)"[100] by considering money as the principal law for establishing justice, Miskawayh introduces the Islamic law of Shari'a as *the principal law* for determining justice, whereby *the ruler, the imam, is an imitator* and *money is a means*.

Miskawayh argues that while Shari'a is the supreme law, the ruler (Imam) and money play an important role in promoting justice. Money is a means of promoting justice in the social sphere – in the context of distributive justice and economic exchange. The ruler should promote justice in the political sphere. Thus, in the absence of either the righteous ruler or money, social and political justice cannot be established.[101]

To explain this idea of the dependency relationship between the Shari'a law, the ruler and money, Miskawayh gives the example of the distribution of jobs between workers of different ranks. He affirms that although the workers have different positions, they are related one to the other. Thus, when they accomplish their respective duties, justice will be done.[102] He declares "there is nothing to prevent a small labor from being equal to a considerable labor [of another kind]. For instance, the engineer does little supervision or labor, but his supervision is worth a considerable amount of labor on the part of people who toil under him and conduct his plans".[103] Similarly, Shari'a law, the just ruler, and money are all associated to ensure equality, but if one of them is not pursued, social and political justice will not be established. Therefore "the most unjust man is he who does not accept the religious divine Law (al-shari'ah), and refuses to abide by it; he also does not accept the decision of the just ruler; therefore he will not earn money but usurps it, giving to himself more than what is his due and others less than what is due to them."[104] In his commentary on Miskawayh's theory of dependence on laws, Majid Fakhry states, "he who clings to the divine law will act in accordance with the precepts of justice and thereby acquire

---

98   Miskawayh 2002: 103.
99   Fakhry 1975 a: 248.
100 Zurayk 2002: 204.
101 Miskawayh 2002: 103–104.
102 Miskawayh 2002: 103–104.
103 Miskawayh 2002: 103–104.
104 Miskawayh 2002: 103–104.

perfection of character and happiness. He who deals with his fellowmen equitably in money matters will contribute to the prosperity of the state, which is the essence of 'political justice'".[105] I argue that Shari'a law is an important law for promoting justice, but it is tied to the ruler and money. In fact, without ruler and money, there is no social or political justice.

In addition, Miskawayh distinguishes between three categories of men to show who among them is best suited to be the custodian of Shari'a law. These men are also divided into three different ranks. Miskawayh argues that the first man is the Imam, the one who purifies man and belongs to those who have a noble heritage and lineage; the second man is the one who has a noble heritage; and the third man is the reasonable man, who is said to be the wise man.[106] In addition, Miskawayh declares that the "rational men, however, deem it to be the prerogative of the wise and wisdom, for only wisdom and virtue bestow real authority and sovereignty, and it is they that have placed the first and the second in their proper rank and [conferred upon them] their virtue." [107]

Thus, this assumption confirms that Miskawayh does not give the rational man a privileged position. This is because Miskawayh clearly affirms that the righteous Imam is the guardian of the supreme Islamic law. In this context, he declares "the just imam, who rules according to equality [...] acts as the deputy [yakhluf] of the Custodian of the Law."[108] As mentioned earlier, Miskawayh states that the second law is the righteous ruler, the Imam, who imitates the supreme Shari'a law because he acts on behalf of God, and is, thus, the guardian of the Islamic divine law.

Putting Miskawayh's theory of law for determining justice into other words, one could argue that for Miskawayh, Shari'a law is the fundamental law for establishing justice. This is to emphasize that Miskawayh's theory of justice is rooted in elements of Islamic legacy – and Greek thought. Hence, "justice as the whole of virtue is ethical justice, which Miskawayh maintained is quite consistent with Islamic teaching, as moral principles, enshrined in the Law and Traditions, are the ultimate goals of the Islamic religion."[109]

Arkoun's concept of philosophical humanism as ethos for rational justice

In the following, I examine the idea that justice in Arabo-Islamic thought can be determined by the faculty of reason. Arkoun's concept of philosophical human-

---

105 Fakhry 1975 a: 248.
106 Miskawayh 2002: 105.
107 Miskawayh 2002: 105.
108 Miskawayh 2002: 105.
109 Khadduri 1984:113.

ism, which he defends in his contemporary intellectual project to rethink Islamic thought, favors this perspective.

At the end of his doctoral dissertation (1970), mentioned earlier, Arkoun highlights three forms of humanism: religious humanism, literary humanism – in the sense of humanitas (*adab*) – and philosophical humanism (*adab discipliné*).[110] In this regard, I introduce here the characteristics of philosophical humanism. Arkoun affirms that philosophical humanism integrates elements of religious humanism and literary humanism, but philosophical humanism is the most promising and relevant of the three. I point out characteristics of philosophical humanism, which "is distinguished by a more rigorous intellectual discipline, a more restless, more methodical, more solitary quest for truth on the world, on humankind and on God" [translation mine].[111] That is, philosophical humanism is based on reason, which guarantees a rational understanding of religion to get beyond the dogmatic closure of thought.[112] Therefore it is fruitful to indicate that Miskawayh's humanist project is elaborated within the method of logical reasoning. In this manner, Arkoun demonstrates that Miskawayh adopted the methods of logical reasoning illustrated in the Organon of Aristotle.[113] Arkoun holds that Miskawayh displays a rationalist bent in his scientific posture. This rationalist tendency is reinforced by rigor, exactitude, and consciousness – qualities which dominate Miskawayh's style.[114] Thus, I contend that the method of thinking shaped through the theoretical approach of philosophical humanism is not applied to the approach of *humanitas adab*, as it is to the concept of literary humanism. The term *humanitas*, like *adab*, designates a complete culture or a faultless knowledge highlighted by moral elegance, an agreeable outfit, refined manner, and a high sense of social relation.[115] Thus, *humanitas adab* is related to the aristocracy of the spirit, wealth and power.[116] I clarify the meaning of *humanitas adab* to remind the reader that Miskawayh's philosophical humanism, *adab discipliné*, differs from *humanitas adab* in its methodological and epistemological way of thinking. It is beyond the scope of this study to detail the method of logical reasoning introduced in the project of Miskawayh. Still, it helps our understanding to mention that Arkoun develops his contemporary project of rethinking of Islamic thought based on Miskawayh's philosophical humanism. In this context, Arkoun develops a more critical approach to the relationship between human reason and religious thought.

---

110   Arkoun 1970: 356.
111   Arkoun 1970: 357.
112   Arkoun 1970: 195.
113   Arkoun 1970: 196.
114   Arkoun 1970: 213.
115   Arkoun 1970: 357.
116   Arkoun 1970: 357.

Excursion 2: The Islamic ethical doctrine of 'voluntarism': The demand of human responsibility and self-determination to establish rational justice in Islam

Following Arkoun's concept of philosophical humanism, there is the theory of voluntarism, which initiates the debate on human responsibility and self-determination in order to establish a concept of rational justice. Voluntarism states that human beings are responsible for their moral behavior and therefore are free to determine their own lives. Thus, human beings are distinguished by their capacity to reason because they can make choices and freely participate in determining their moral behavior. Therefore, I examine the earlier controversial debate of Islamic teachings on how a concept of rational justice can be possible.

So before I elaborate on the doctrine of voluntarism, I would like to emphasize that philosophical justice, according to modern Western thought, states that justice is not determined within the religious framework, but according to the capacity of reason. Nevertheless, most Muslim philosophers in early Islamic thought intend justice to be defined and determined in accordance with both reason and revelation.[117] To put it simply, most Muslim philosophers intend to make justice intelligible to the individuals without necessarily compromising the creed and without challenging the authority of revelation.[118] I mention this to make it clear that justice in Islam is linked to religious duties and therefore must be determined within the framework of revelation.[119] However, this statement does not allow me to claim that there is no recommendation in the revelation on the concept of human responsibility and self-determination, which are the pillars of the Islamic doctrine of voluntarism. To corroborate this, I refer to Majid Fakhry's work entitled *Ethical Theories in Islam* (1991).

Indeed, Fakhry focuses on revelation, i.e., the Qur'an, and the Tradition, to show that human responsibility and self-determination are permitted in the Islamic legacy. Therefore I begin with an introduction to Fakhry's commentaries on the Qur'an. Fakhry reminds us that there are several verses in the Qur'an that address people by asking them about their righteous and wrong deeds on the Day of Judgment.[120] He refers to chapter 16 verse 56, which asserts, "They set aside part of the sustenance We give them, for [idols] about which they have no true knowledge. By God! You will be questioned about your false inventions;"[121] chapter 29 verse 13, which claims, "They will bear their own burdens and others besides: they will

---

117   Khadduri 1984: 79.
118   Khadduri 1984: 79.
119   Khadduri 1984: 107.
120   Fakhry 1991: 18.
121   The Qur'ān, Chapter 16, The Bee ; Verse 56.

be questioned about their false assertions on the Day of Resurrection;"¹²² and last but not least, chapter 37 verse 24, which says "[Angels], gather together those who did wrong, and others like them, as well as whatever they worshipped beside God, lead them all to the path of Hell, and halt them for questioning: 'Why do you not support each other now?'--no indeed! They will be in complete submission on that Day--and they will turn on one another accusingly."¹²³

Fakhry says, "in some of these verses the unbelievers (*kafirun*) or polytheists (*mushirkun*) are stated *to be answerable* to God Almighty for their misdeeds or their unbelief on the Day of Judgement."¹²⁴ In addition, Fakhry maintains that "apart from knowledge or consciousness, the most fundamental precondition or ground of human responsibility is that freedom." ¹²⁵ Hence, "in the absence of such a precondition, the human agent is reduced to the status of an automaton, as all forms of mechanism and determinism logically presuppose, or that of a slave of the almighty, as all forms of theistic determinism (or predestinationism) entail." ¹²⁶

This statement reveals that humans must explain their actions or decisions before God, which in turn means that in Islamic legacy, human beings are recognized as responsible and capable of giving an answer. Therefore, Islamic legacy assumes that human beings are responsible and self-determined. I argue that human beings are not determined agents. If they are determined, there will be no Day of Judgment when individuals will be questioned about their moral behavior. This is because, according to Islamic ethics, individuals are responsible and self-determined. In fact, they will be judged according to their moral behavior.

In addition to the Qur'an, from which Fakhry sets out the verses that affirm human's responsibility and self-determination, Fakhry refers to the Tradition to introduce testimonies in which the concepts of human self-determination and responsibility are presented. It is not my intention to present the texts of the Tradition to which Fakhry refers, as they are so diverse. Rather, I would like to present Fakhry's achievement in interpreting the Tradition cited by Al-Bukhari. In this context, Fakhry focuses on the Book of Logic – *Kitab-al Manaqib* – by al-Bukhari. He tells us that al-Bukhari "[...] reports a Tradition [which] illustrates very well the preoccupation of the early Muslim community with the question of right and wrong and its bearing on religious belief." ¹²⁷

However, according to Fakhry's commentary on al-Bukhari's cited Tradition, Fakhry concludes that "this tradition does not give us a definition of what the good

---

122   The Qur'ān, Chapter 29, The Spider ; Verse 13.
123   The Qur'ān, Chapter 37, Ranged in Rows ;Verse 24.
124   Fakhry 1991: 18; emphasis added.
125   Fakhry 1991: 19.
126   Fakhry 1991: 19.
127   Fakhry 1991: 23.

and evil referred to really are."[128] In this sense, the concept of human actions or works (*a'mal*) is coupled with the concept of intention (*niyyat*); a certain degree of self-determination is presupposed as a prerogative of humans. Therefore, the two concepts of human action and intention are not at all opposed to libertarianism.[129] In other words, the cited Tradition does not clearly express the concepts of responsibility and self-determination. I define the Islamic doctrine of voluntarism to show that, according to early Islamic thought, humans are responsible for their moral behavior. In this regard, justice is to be determined by reason. In this context, I refer to Majid Khadduri's book entitled, *The Islamic Conception of Justice* (1984).

Khadduri maintains that "the Kharijites were the earliest thinkers in Islam to initiate the debate on justice, and they discussed not only its political aspect but also its ethical implications. Although they advocated the doctrine of *qadar* (voluntarism) and held that man is responsible for his actions on the political plane",[130] "the doctrine of voluntarism was by no means acceptable to all believers."[131] This is because the Qur'an and the Tradition are not clear whether they are in favor of voluntarism or involuntarism.[132] This led to different opinions about the relationship between religious and moral duties.[133]

This reveals a controversial debate about the doctrine of voluntarism in the earlier Islamic tradition, in which two schools of thought are represented: the Qadarites and the Jabarites.[134] Hence, "the Qadarites asserted the principle of voluntarism by virtue of which man possesses the capacity to choose between good and evil and is held responsible for all his moral acts."[135] While the Jabarites held that man's acts, predicated by God, must be considered valid as an expression of His will, and therefore the question of good and evil is irrelevant.[136] As a result, the key to justice according to the Jabarites is predicated by God, and must be subordinated to His will, and moral issues should be settled in accordance with the religious Law.[137] Conversely, the Qadarites argue that "justice is connected with morality and determined by Reason (in accordance with the doctrine of qadar, voluntarism)."[138] Putting the Qadarites' concept of justice in other words, I claim that their concept of justice is

---

128   Fakhry 1991: 24.
129   Fakhry 1991: 26.
130   Khadduri 1984: 107.
131   Khadduri 1984: 107.
132   Khadduri 1984: 107.
133   Khadduri 1984: 107.
134   Khadduri 1984: 108.
135   Khadduri 1984: 108.
136   Khadduri 1984: 108.
137   Khadduri 1984: 108.
138   Khadduri 1984: 108.

founded on egalitarian justice. In this sense, Qadarites claim that individuals are responsible according to their reason to determine their moral behavior, because reason is the common faculty shared between human beings. Reason is the standard for determining morality.

This leads me to ponder the following ethical and religious question, "Can God do injustice?."[139] Considering the doctrine of voluntarism, I argue that justice is grounded in human reason. Thus, man is the only one responsible for his right and wrong acts. This means that God does not prescribe wrong actions. Thus, humans commit wrongs because they are responsible for their actions. Consequently, God cannot commit injustice, but injustice is the responsibility of humans. This is in line with Khadduri's statement when he asserts, "God commends as the individual's moral acts, each man is responsible for his own wrongdoing: 'Guidance comes from God,' [...] 'but wrongdoing comes from man.'" [140] I further note that the argument about God's fairness and perfection is based on the idea of divine justice, explained earlier. Thus, considering that God cannot cause injustice and that God can only do justice, divine justice must consequently be realized. When individuals embody God by aligning the faculties of their souls, they are virtuous. Consequently, justice is regulated in the realm of human interaction.

If one takes a closer look at the Islamic doctrine of the Qadarites, one can see that the Qadarites defend voluntarism. According to this, human free will is the fundamental principle to determine moral behavior. Therefore humans are responsible for their actions and can control their lives. Although the Qadarites affirm man's responsibility to determine justice, I contend that the question of who is capable of establishing political justice remains controversial. Hasan al-Basri (d.728), who is considered a Qadarite scholar, makes a distinction between ethical and political justice. He explains that man is responsible for ethical justice, but not for political justice. [141] He argues that revelation is clear on issues of political justice. Verse 59 of chapter 4 states: "You who believe, obey God and the Messenger, and those in authority among you."[142] Hence, "since political justice is an expression of the will of the Sovereign, the final decision on all questions of political justice must be made by the Caliph himself, presumably as God's representative on earth."[143]

In this context, Khadduri explains that the strength of the idea that political decisions should be made only by political authority could be justified by the particular historical and social circumstances of the time, in order "to repudiate all the political agitation which the leaders of the heterodox sects had aroused against Sunni's rule."

---

139 Khadduri 1984: 108.
140 Khadduri 1984: 109.
141 Khadduri 1984: 108.
142 The Qur'ān, Chapter 4, Women, Verse 59.
143 Khadduri 1984: 108.

[144] Thus, I argue that Hsan al-Basri and Miskawayh conflated religion and politics to establish their notion of political justice. In this sense, they argue that a religio-political authority should make political decisions. One deviation is that Hsan al-Basri argues that the caliph should be the final decision-maker in the political realm because he is the representative of God on earth. This is consistent with the Sunni tradition of the caliphate. Miskawayh, on the other hand, as mentioned much earlier, states from an Iranian Shi'ite religious tradition that political decisions should be made by the Imam, who acts on behalf of God.

This chapter introduced the multi-faceted concept of justice in the context of Arabo-Islamic philosophy. As a basis for understanding Arkoun's contemporary intellectual project of an ethical theory of justice, this chapter returned to the early thought of the Muslim philosopher Miskawayh by pointing to Miskawayh's reference to the Greek thought of Plato and Aristotle. Miskawayh elaborates his concept of justice within the concept of *"humanista studia"* by establishing a link between the two levels of justice: divine and human justice; a theoretical and a practical concept of justice.

This chapter presented Arkoun's interpretation of Miskawayh's thoughts on justice. Arkoun points out that Miskawayh's theory of justice is a link between Greek philosophy and Islamic legacy. Thus, Plato's idea of 'universal justice' and Aristotle's political thought are both representative of Miskawayh's concept of justice. In addition, Arkoun notes that Miskawayh's concept of justice is mediated by the Islamic legacy of the righteous ruler who embodies justice and acts on behalf of God. I also argued that Miskawayh's concept of divine justice is based on the concept of the oneness of God. Miskawayh's connection between the Greek and Islamic traditions, thus, establishes his humanistic thought and proves an earlier transcultural approach to justice in the tradition of Islamic thought.

To further assert that Miskawayh applies Islamic legacy to establish his notion of justice, I have also shown in my first excursion that the most important law governing social and political justice in the sphere of human interaction is the Shari'a law, a fundamental law to be applied by the righteous ruler in the political sphere, and a fundamental law for promoting distributive justice in the sphere of economic exchange when money is a means.

The chapter further introduces Arkoun's notion of philosophical humanism, a concept which Arkoun defends in his contemporary intellectual project – this will be further emphasized in the following chapters – and which he develops from Miskawayh's notion of humanism, which shows that the Islamic legacy can be interpreted through reason to develop a rational notion of justice.

Following Arkoun's notion of philosophical humanism and in order to show that early Islamic thought has a scope of rational thought, in my second excursion I have

---

144 Khadduri 1984: 108.

referred to the doctrine of voluntarism as an early Islamic doctrine indicating that justice can be determined by reason. In doing so, I emphasized that humans are responsible for determining their behavior and choices, to make the point that Islamic ethics recognizes the value of human responsibility and self-determination. Consequently, voluntarism, which assumes that justice must be determined by human reason, is indeed feasible in terms of a humanistic and rational conception of justice as expressed in Islamic thought.

3.2 The method of applied Islamology: A transcultural and transdisciplinary key for the renewal of Islamic studies

This chapter examines Arkoun's method of applied Islamology as key to the renewal of Islamic studies. One can argue that Arkoun's contemporary thought project is characterized by transcultural and transdisciplinary methods, and, thus, represents a global intellectual project for the renewal of Islamic studies. Arkoun's project is transcultural because he combines different philosophical traditions of Islamic thought from the early Islamic philosophy of Al Amiri (d. 992)[145] and from Western poststructuralist thought.

I have chosen to address Arkoun's reinterpretation of al- Amiri's early Islamic thought in this chapter rather than in the first chapter, even though al-Amiri is an early Muslim philosopher, because in this chapter I focus on the methods Arkoun employs in his contemporary intellectual project to renew the field of Islamic studies. In this context, I argue that Arkoun develops his methods based on his interpretation of al-Amiri's work from early Islamic philosophy. Moreover, this chapter explores how Arkoun' applies the poststructuralist methods of Foucault's épistème, Deleuze's difference, and Derrida's deconstruction as a deconstructionist analysis of Islamic archive – the Qur'an and Tradition. Arkoun's project is also transdisciplinary, combining multiple disciplines such as history, sociology, linguistics, and philosophy to examine Islamic thought.

This chapter is divided into three sections: The first section begins with an analysis of Arkoun's rereading and reinterpretation of al-Amiri's early Islamic thought. Arkoun examines three approaches to understanding al-Amiri's methods aiming to rethink Islamic thought, which I chose to name the transdisciplinary approach, the

---

145 Abu'l-Hasan Muhammad ibn Yusuf al-Amiri (d.381/992) is a Kurasanian philosopher. He is one of the immediate disciples of Al-Kindi (d.873). Al-Amiri was from eastern Iran and spent most of his life there. The titles of some twenty-five of al-'Amiri's works are known, and of these six (or seven, depending on a contested attribution) are extant and have been published. *The most eloquent testimony to al-'Amiri's views on reason and revelation is his best-known work, An Exposition on the Merits of Islam* (Rowson 2008: 405–406). Indeed Arkoun dedicated his subsequent study to that work.

comparative approach, and the rational approach. The transdisciplinary approach means combining several disciplines such as philosophy and religion. The comparative approach is the study of the similarities and differences between religions with the aim of finding criteria that unite them. The rational approach is the use of logic as a rational thinking tool to reinterpret Islamic thought. Hence, by analyzing Arkoun's relationship to al-Amiri's early work, Islamic studies can be subjected to the perspectives present in al-Amiri's early work.

The second section deals with Arkoun's method of applied Islamology. Applied Islamology combines different fields of research; it also establishes a link between Islamic thought and poststructuralist Western thought. The goal is to show that applied Islamology critically challenges the framework of the Orientalist-historical method for studying Islam. Unlike Orientalists who study Islam primarily from a historical perspective without examining its relationship to the present time or the process of Islamic thought, Arkoun views Islam as a discourse in development rather than a rigid discourse. It is a discourse in change and development according to the progress of man in society. This section ends by presenting an interpretation of Arkoun's intention in his use of the method of applied Islamology. An important implication of applied Islamology is to liberate Islamic thought from traditional and orthodox perspectives. Specifically, I examine how feminist Muslim scholars use Arkoun's critical method of applied Islamology as a new method for interpreting Islamic legacy to analyze patriarchal, Islamist, and nationalist discourses that paint a discriminatory picture of women in Islam.

The third section shows how Arkoun applies poststructuralist methods to deconstruct the Islamic archive – the Qur'an and the Tradition. Poststructuralist methods serve as the basis for introducing the concept of exhaustive tradition. This means that the deconstruction of the Islamic archive aims to create a subdivision of traditions in Islam rather than discussing a single tradition. The exhaustive tradition consists of discussing the marginalized traditions in most Arab-Islamic societies. It manifests itself as the concept of a cosmopolitan and global ethic for marginalized Muslim minorities to have their rights recognized and appreciated by policy makers.

The transdisciplinary, comparative, and rational approaches: Arkoun's rereading of the intellectual project of Al -Amiri (d. 992)

The purpose of this section is to show that early Islamic philosophy required a reinterpretation of Islam based on what I call transdisciplinary, comparative, and rational approaches. Arkoun's contemporary intellectual project is influenced by early Islamic philosophy, which shaped the progress in rethinking Islamic thought. The analysis of Arkoun's intellectual project involves a chronological study to go through all the concepts that characterize his thought. In doing so, I begin with his earlier work entitled "Logocentrism and Religious Truth in Islamic Thought: The Example of *al-I'lam bi- manaqib al-Islam*" [*An exposition on the merits of Islam*] (1972–2002 a), in which Arkoun examines the thought of the Muslim thinker al-Amiri.

Transdisciplinary Approach: The possibility to reconcile philosophy and religion

Arkoun reminds us first and foremost of the purpose of his rereading of Al-Amiri's intellectual project. He argues:

> I wanted to react against the prevailing scholastic division of Islamic thought into a specialized disciplines (theology, philosophy, historiography, law, literature) without pointing out a more significant unifying differentiation, using the criteria of *epistémè* and discourse analysis.[146]

One can understand that Arkoun draws on the thought of Al-Amiri to explore the transdisciplinary approach through the reconciliation between the fields of religion and philosophy. In this regard, Arkoun examines Al-Amiri's argument about the plausible harmonization between the fields of philosophy and religion on two levels: First, the level of opposition means the reconciliation between two opposing disciplines to examine Islamic thought. There is the philosophical realm, which is called science (*al- 'lam*), and the religious realm (*Islam*).[147] Or in other words, the intensity of opposition reveals the opposing characteristics of philosophy and religion. The goal of philosophy is to investigate and/or resolve questions about religion based on rational thought. In contrast, religion does not require reason, but faith and trust in religious scriptures.

Second, the level of harmonization involves the simultaneous use of philosophical and theological lexicons. According to Al-Amiri, Arkoun points out, the Qur'an contains both philosophical, in the sense of scientific or rational, vocabularies and religious vocabularies.[148] Hence there are parallel uses of rational and religious vocabularies in the Qur'an, as the following figures show: "Among the terms most frequently employed are *'aql* [reason] (40 occurrences), *'aqil* (14), *'ilm* [science] (46), and *sina'a* (in the sense of scientific technique) (49). In comparison, the terms used by al-Amiri are *din, adyan* [religion or religious] (43+55), *mila, milal* [sect or sects] (17), *'ibada* [acceptance] (32), *i'tiqad* [belief], *i'tiqadat* [convictions] (24), etc."[149]

By emphasizing that the Qur'sn contains both scientific and religious vocabularies at the same time, one can argue that Arkoun is rereading Al-Amiri's project

---

146 Arkoun 2002a: 32.
147 Arkoun 2002a: 180.
148 Arkoun 2002a: 180.
149 Arkoun 2002 a: 180.

to confirm the possibility of reinterpreting and explaining the Qur'an using rational methods. In this sense, "Al-Amiri attempted to reconcile religion with philosophy by arguing that a theological conclusion that is reached through philosophically correct procedure is the same as that directed by the religion of Islam."[150]

Thus, Arkoun was interested in Al-Amiri's thought to show that it is not problematic to explain the Islamic sources using philosophical thought. Moreover, one can affirm that the reconciliation between the fields of philosophy and religion confirms the notion of a transdisciplinary approach that characterized Al-Amiri's thought in the 10th century. Thus, Al-Amiri's genius was to show that rational thought cannot contradict the revealed truths of Islam. Al-Amiri was concerned with showing how philosophy could be used to answer theological questions and how philosophy and Islam could be reconciled as complementary paths to truth.[151] The possibility of interpreting Islamic sources with rational methods and the transdisciplinary approach that characterized Al-Amiri's Islamic thought influenced Arkoun's contemporary project, in which he argued for the possibility of establishing a link between different disciplines for the study of Islam. I will show this below.

Comparative approach: A harmony between different religions

The comparative approach evaluates the similarities and differences between religions. Rather than separating religions, the comparative approach identifies what religions have in common. The comparative approach is a means of the concept of interreligious dialogue. This requires bringing different religions together in a climate of dialogue to discuss concerns that might unite them. A fundamental aspect of Arkoun's intellectual project is his appeal for interreligious dialogue. In this regard, Arkoun examines Al-Amiri's reference to verse 17 of the 22 chapter of the Qur'an to show how this Qur'anic verse cites different religions and religious sects to argue that they share the same fate of God's judgment as a fundamental commonality between religions.[152] The verse reads, "As for the believers, those who follow the Jewish faith, the Sabians, the Christians, the Magians, and the idolaters, God will judge between them on the Day of Resurrection; God witnesses all things."[153]

For Arkoun, Al-Amiri uses two criteria to compare Islam with the religions mentioned in the verse. There is on the one hand the objective criterion, dealing with the characteristics that the monotheistic religions have in common. In this regard, Arkoun affirms "the term 'objective criteria' is used to mean all of the truths received

---

150   Gaskill 1998: 207.
151   Rowson 2008: 407.
152   Arkoun 2002a: 186.
153   The Qur'ān: Chapter 22 The Pilgrimage; Verse 17.

through 'common sense'".[154] Examples of these truths include: monotheistic doctrine, which postulates the existence of one God, a Revelation, angels, prophets, souls, etc.; and the necessity for Resurrection, for a distinction between true and false, good and evil, and, thus, a fundamental schism between believers and non-believers.[155] In religious discourse, the distinction between believers and non-believers raises the question of whether tolerance between the religious and the non-religious is possible, or whether it reproduces or exacerbates existing conflicts of religious intolerance. The subjective criterion refers to religious practices that differ between religions and distinguish one religion from another. Arkoun affirms that subjective criteria "expressed the moral values established by 'the experiences of the nations' and reinforced with the authority of the prophets, sages, mystics and great princes who had given them incisive formulations."[156]

Interpreting Arkoun's intent behind his rereading of Al-Amiri, one could argue that Arkoun wants to show that Al-Amiri uses a comparative approach between religions by examining their convergence and divergence to resolve a conflict between different religious beliefs; Al-Amiri thereby calls for religious tolerance based on the objective criterion of monotheism. In our present time, it is imperative that we revive this tolerant tradition of Islamic thought in order to create societies that respects everyone's freedom, opinions and attitudes. As part of his intellectual project, Arkoun is committed to religious dialogue and the promotion of tolerance between religions.

Rational approach – The science of language (*kalam*): The opening of the gate of *Ijtihad*

Arkoun claims that Al-Amiri's thought is characterized by an epistemological criterion and a methodological criterion aimed at understanding and interpreting the religious language of Islam. First, the epistemological criterion, as Arkoun says, "emerges from the classification of the sciences. It confirms the well-known opposition between the philosophical sciences and the religious sciences, one using logic, the other language, as its instrumental science."[157]

However, Arkoun affirms that Al-Amiri does not intend to make a disconnection between the two sciences of religion and philosophy.[158] This has already been explained above, where I argued that Al-Amiri's project is characterized by the com-

---

154 Arkoun 2002a: 187.
155 Arkoun 2002a: 187.
156 Arkoun 2002a: 188.
157 Arkoun 2002a: 189.
158 Arkoun 2002a:192.

bination of philosophy and religion and that one can interpret religious language with logic as a scientific and rational tool of thought appropriate to philosophy.

In this sense, Arkoun affirms that "Al-Amiri juxtaposes two theoretical discourses on logic and language, rather than comparing them and looking for common criteria."[159] According to Arkoun, Al-Amiri applies logic as a philosophical science in the study of Islamic religious discourse to show how logic can be used to study language as a linguistic system that reflects religious discourse. Arkoun argues by defining logic and language:

> On the one hand, logic is presented as a universal language of reason focused on eternal intelligibilities; on the other, language is conceived and practiced as the instrument for achieving and communicating the most nuanced, the most profound and the most unexpected meanings.[160]

Given the symbolic, allusive, and enigmatic aspects of language, then, one could argue that logic is used as a rational tool to understand the enigmatic properties of language. Following Arkoun, logic is, thus, used for the rational interpretation of religious language. 'Logic' (Greek: λογική, logikē) is the formal, systematic approach to reasoning grounded in formative rules of definition, argumentation, validity, and fallacies developed by the Greek philosopher Aristotle in his work Organon.[161]

Second, Arkoun affirms "the methodological criterion is concerned with what technical procedures to employ to arrive at the desired truth."[162] By technical procedures, Arkoun means the religious sciences of *kalam* and *fiqh* that are aiming to examine the religious texts of the Qur'ān and Tradition.[163] In what follows, I discuss the science of language (*'Ilm-kalam*) and Islamic legal theory (*fiqh*). This is important because Islamic legal theory is a hermeneutic system from which ethics and politics are to be prescribed. For Muslims, Islamic legal theory is a source of legislation.

As Arkoun tells us, the science of language (*'Ilm-kalam*) "defends holy religion and enables the individual to join an élite that can reject or approve a thing with total clarity of vision."[164]

By the same token, one could argue that the science of language (*'Ilm- Kalam*) is an approach by which Islamic reasoning is sought through Aristotelian dialectics. In Arabic, the concept of the science of language means knowledge about speaking. The science of language (*'Ilm-Kalam*) in Islamic thought is based on the search for theological premises through debate and argumentation within the framework of ratio-

---

159 Arkoun 2002a:192.
160 Arkoun 2002a:192.
161 Aoude 2011:1.
162 Arkoun 2002a: 193.
163 Arkoun 2002a: 193.
164 Arkoun 2002 a: 193.

nal discussion. In short, the science of language is the science in which the Islamic legacy is understood not only within the framework of the Qur'ān or Tradition or the opinions of the first three generations of Muslims (7th century), but also through the reasoning of scholars. Thus, the science of language was the forerunner of the later stylized argumentation methodology called logic (*mantiq*), which was introduced by Aristotle, to denote the Islamic instrument of argumentation.[165] Put simply, Muslim scholars use Aristotelian logic to understand and interpret Islamic legacy. Based on Aristotelian logic, the science of the language of Islamic theology opens a door to the interpretation of Islamic heritage through intellectual reasoning and the formation of a theory of law termed Islamic legal theory (*fiqh*). In this regard, Arkoun argues:

> (*fiqh*) is at it were 'an intermediary between the *hadith* and *kalam*,' consisting in an effort of reflection (*ijtihad*) to distill from the texts those standards without which no royalty (*mulk*) is possible; and language, finally, is (as we have seen) the instrument used in these practices.[166]

In other words, Islamic legal theory is to discover the law of God. Islamic legal theory is crucial because it is the law by which individuals behave in a manner that is acceptable to God. It serves the very purpose of finding the rules enacted by God. Islamic legal theory is meant to open the gate of Islam to *ijtihad*, the maximum effort of the jurist to master and apply the principles and rules to discover the divine law.[167] One can state that Islamic legal theory (*fiqh*) follows strict procedures to understand and interpret the case in question by the intellectual (*mujtahid*).[168]

In this context, Arkoun claims that the principle of analogy (*qiyas*), as an instrument of Islamic legal theory, is the most controversial method among scholars to reach a consensus on a judgment. According to traditionalist Muslim scholars, the use of analogy (*qiyas*) is not permissible in either the Qur'an or the Tradition. Therefore, one should trust the Tradition as they were proclaimed by the companions of the Prophet, because they lived at the time of the Prophet and witnessed the circumstances of the revelation and the elaboration of the Tradition when they took place.[169]

In the same line as Arkoun, Wael El-Hallaq explains how difficult it is sometimes to find consensus – accord – among scholars about a legal deliberation. El-Hallaq clarifies that the *mujtahid* can try to find the legal verdict in an unprecedented religious argument by using the procedure of *qiyas* (analogy). But before embarking on this task, he must first search for the legal judgment in the works of well-known

---

165 Aoude 2011: 2.
166 Arkoun 2002 a: 193.
167 El-Hallaq 1984: 4.
168 El-Hallaq 1984: 4.
169 Arkoun 2002 a: 193.

jurists. If he does not find it in these works, he can look for a similar religious argument, where the consequences of a legal deliberation are different, but the causes of the legal deliberation are the same. If he is unsuccessful, he must turn to the Qur'an, Tradition, or *ijma'* (consensus) to find a literal legal judgment as formed by the preceding jurists. In this case, the mujtahid must apply *qiyas* (analogy) to see if this legal judgment is applicable to the religious case in question.[170]

In the 8th century of Islam, the science of language as an equivalent of Greek logic was initially considered part of the foreign sciences; so much so that many traditionalists Muslim scholars refused to accept logic as something valuable for the development of Islamic philosophy and for the reinterpretation of Islamic law.[171] I briefly introduce the work of Ruth Mas, who specializes in the study of Islamic philosophy with its early and modern traditions. She divides Islamic philosophy into two approaches of rational scholars who defend the use of the science of language to interpret Islamic thought by emphasizing the need to open the gate of *ijtihad* to interpret Islamic sources. Among these scholars, Mas introduces al-Farabi (d. 950). Al-Farabi is considered the first and greatest commentator on Aristotelian logic, a logician in his own right. Al-Farabi is considered one of the influential Muslim thinkers who helped introduce Aristotelian thought into Islamic literature.[172] In contrast to al-Farabi, there is the approach of traditionalist Muslim scholars who reject logic and argue that it is an alien tool designed to eradicate the Islamic faith. Among these scholars, Mas mentions Ibn Taymiyya (d. 1263). Ibn Taymiyya is considered a dogmatic theologian and jurist who frequently made polemical accusations against Greek logic.[173] It is important to mention this intellectual conflict between earlier Muslim philosophers to show that al-Amiri, like his predecessor al-Farabi, is one of the defenders of reason in Islam. This intellectual conflict between the rational and the traditionalist scholars of Islam has not ended even in our time. This study addresses this issue and aims to revive the thinking of the rational thinkers of Arabo-Islamic philosophy within the early and modern/postmodern schools.

I shall now outline the rational approach I take following Arkoun's interpretation of al-Amiri's position on logic as a rational method for interpreting Islamic thought. One can argue that al-Amiri defends a rational approach based on epistemological and methodological criteria to interpret the Islamic legacy. The epistemological criterion requires the study of the Islamic legacy through the approaches of philosophy and religion. According to the methodological criterion, the Islamic legacy is under-

170 El-Hallaq 1984: 4.
171 Aoude 2011: 2.
172 Mas 1998: 114.
173 Mas 1998: 122.

stood through the categories of the science of language (*'Ilm-kalam*) and Islamic legal theory (*fiqh*), using analogies from this theory.

One can further observe that Arkoun draws on al-Amiri's intellectual project because Arkoun subjects Islamic thought to rational interpretation. Arkoun combines several disciplines to examine Islamic thought. He also supports a project of solidarity between religions. Like al-Amiri, Arkoun is open to other traditions and schools of thought to provide a rationalist interpretation of Islam. As a Muslim scholar who has studied, taught, and lived in Paris, Arkoun draws on the intellectual perspective and achievements of contemporary Western philosophy, which include an emphasis on human reason as opposed to dogmatic religious belief and the application of poststructuralist methods. In this sense, Arkoun's approaches to reinterpreting Islam converge with the rationalism of Descartes, the critique of Kant, the structuralism of Saussure, Barthes, and Hjemslev, and the semiotics of Greimas.[174] Arkoun also drew inspiration "from the methods of Paris School poststructuralism."[175] It was Claude Cahen, a member of the French Annales school,[176] who introduced Arkoun to the ideas and concepts of the Annales schools of historians.[177] Thus, Arkoun critically engages with various belief systems, traditions of exegesis, theology, and jurisprudence in order to liberate Islamic thought from dogmatic paradigms.[178] Arkoun seeks to subject Islamic thought to historical critique in order to strip it of the sanctity and grandeur associated with it.[179]

Nevertheless, there is also a pragmatic shift between Al-Amiri's and Arkoun's thought project. Arkoun's thought is in flux. It evolves in line with intellectual, political, social, and cultural changes in contemporary Muslim and European societies. Arkoun also argues for poststructural and deconstructivist methods to rethink Islamic thought. Arkoun's critical thinking about Islam goes beyond the rationalist approaches that characterized early Islamic and Greek thought, for he seeks a radical reform of Islamic thought.

In the following, I present Arkoun's method of applied Islamology. The aim is to show that applied Islamology emphasizes transdisciplinary, transcultural, rational

---

174 Soekarba 2006: 80; Khalil and Khan 2013: 35.
175 Soekarba 2006: 80.
176 The Annales school emerged in the second half of the twentieth century. It was one of the most important currents in the study of history, not only in France but also in many other parts of the world. In the Annales school, history was studied with an emphasis on interdisciplinary research with other social sciences. Instead of focusing on events and telling the story of great personalities at the center of history, the Annales school emphasized the study of historical problems through investigation (see: André Bruguière: The Annales School: A New Approach to the Study of History, Odile Jacob: Paris/New York).
177 Günter 2004 a: 128.
178 Khalil and Khan 2013: 34.
179 Shiyab 2014: 406.

approaches as well as deconstructivist and emancipatory norms in order to liberate Islamic thought from orthodox perspectives.

Applied Islamology: A modern analytical criterion for the renewal of Islamic studies

This section examines Arkoun's method of applied Islamology as a modern analytical criterion for Islamic studies. First, the main features of applied Islamology are outlined. Second, the section introduces three types of discourse that reconstruct the field of Islamic studies. Third, the section examines the alternative discourse that Arkoun introduces to rethink the unthought sphere of Islamic thought. The section ends with an examination of the intellectual purpose beyond Arkoun's use of applied Islamology and rethinking Islamic thought: I situate Arkoun's thought within the perspective of feminism in Islam.

Carool Kersten, in his article "The Applied Islamology of Mohammed Arkoun" (2010), claims that Arkoun first introduced the concept of applied Islamology in 1973.[180] This is correct. However, one could argue that the final explanation of applied Islamology can be found in the introduction to Arkoun's book *The Unthought in Contemporary Islamic Thought* (2002 a). In this book, Arkoun presents a collection of eight articles he wrote in French in the 1970s and 1980s. These articles were translated into English in 2002, making the book accessible to a wider audience. In addition, Arkoun discusses his concept of applied Islamology in his final article, "The Answers of Applied Islamology" (2007). In this article, Arkoun provides a comprehensive explanation of his applied Islamology and its relationship to poststructuralist thought. Arkoun also points out some emancipatory implications that the applied Islamology approach brings to women's rights in Islam. I begin with an introduction to Arkoun's definition of applied Islamology as he presents it in the introduction to his book *The Unthought in Contemporary Islamic Thought* (2002 a). Arkoun defines applied Islamology in many systematic terms. I refer to his definition of applied Islamology as he explained it to avoid misinterpretation of his thought. In this context, Arkoun explains that applied Islamology

> is a way of thinking, rather than essays in traditional scholarship based on primary sources. Not that I do not use such sources extensively, but my interpretation of them is informed by a strategy which differs from that usually employed for the purpose of providing a descriptive, narrative, factual and cumulative presentation of what they contain. My intention is to combine a critical review of modern studies devoted to early and contemporary periods of what is generally called 'Islam,' with the systematic deconstruction of the original texts used

---

180 Kersten 2010: 3.

3. Background and methods in the thought of Mohammed Arkoun

in these studies as sources of genuine information. Primary and secondary texts are not read in order to discuss the facts themselves, but to **problematize** the epistemic and epistemological framework underlying the articulation of each discourse. [emphasis in the original] [181]

To put it simply, applied Islamology contrasts with the descriptive and narrative methods of traditional scholarships, which neglect a critical approach to the study of Islam. In applied Islamology, the original text of Islam, the Qur'an, and Tradition are critically examined. An important goal of applied Islamology is to learn more about the socio-historical and cultural background that has shaped Islam. Moreover, Arkoun claims that his approach to applied Islamology is innovative in the field of Islamic studies. As a result, applied Islamology subjects Islam to historical epistemology and philosophical criticism when examining the history of Islam. Arkoun argues:

This cognitive strategy has never been used before in interpreting the types of discourse produced by Muslims to express their Islam, or in approaching them as a subject of study, alongside the Western literature on Islam and Muslim societies. From this perspective, **historical epistemology** has a priority over the purely descriptive, narrative presentation of what 'Islam' teaches, or what Muslims say, do or achieve as social and historical protagonists. ... Such an itinerary can be proposed and achieved only by those who accept the need to combine respect for the rules of scientific research with the capacity to submit to philosophical criticism every stance of reason, every intellectual and every question arising therefrom. For a time, during the late 1970s, I called this approach 'applied Islamology' following the example set by a group of anthropologists who started the practice of 'applied anthropology'. [emphasis in the original] [182]

This quote forms the basis of my strategy to introduce the method of applied Islamology in order to explore the fact that applied Islamology criticizes the Orientalist method; to show the alternative discourse that applied Islamology proposes; and to interpret the ethical purpose of applied Islamology by disapproving the patriarchal system that prevents women, minorities, and other socially oppressed groups from realizing their rights.

Scholars have commented on Arkoun's method of applied Islamology as follows: Kersten claims that applied Islamology is a critical modern analysis for Islamic studies.[183] "Applied Islamology was envisaged as an *epistemological* reflection that [aims]

---

181 Arkoun 2002a: 10.
182 Arkoun 2002a: 10.
183 Kersten 2010: 4.

to: (1) critically re-read the so-called 'exhaustive Muslim tradition, free from the dogmatic definitions of the existing literature'; and (2) historicize contemporary Muslim discourse in order to unveil its ideological prejudices. Ideology critique is one of the major tasks of Applied Islamology, says Arkoun."[184] Kersten further explains that in elaborating the method of Applied Islamology, Arkoun was influenced by the achievements made in the Western human sciences during the twentieth century and by the Applied Anthropology (1971) of the French ethnologist and sociologist Roger Bastide (1998–1974).[185]

Abu Zayd affirms that Arkoun establishes the approach of applied Islamology to call for abandoning the methods practiced by conformist and orthodox Muslim scholars to study Islam. Applied Islamology moves to an applied critical analysis of Islamic thought.[186] He further explains that applied Islamology aims to provide a critical analysis of religious texts in order to renew Islamic thought. It transforms Islamic discourse from a unified and systematic reading into different interpretations and from a conservative and traditionalist interpretation into a liberal and progressive interpretation.[187] Moreover, el-Ayadi affirms that applied Islamology deals with Islamic discourse according to the necessities of critical reason. It questions the construction of discourse; that is, any discourse that has become a dogmatic certainty.[188] Thus, applied Islamology subjects Islamic thought to critical scrutiny. It analyzes the representations and the discourses that construct Islam. In what follows, I explain what Arkoun means by Islamic discourses. What discourses is applied Islamology critical of? And what discourse does Arkoun propose as an alternative that is consistent with the critical method of applied Islamology?

Three categories of discourse: A tenuous and fixed study of Islamic Tradition

Islam consists of the Qur'an and Tradition. The majority of orthodox Muslim scholars interpret these texts in a way that cannot be critically analyzed or evaluated over time. In this regard, Arkoun, in his article entitled "Current Islam Faces its Tradition" (1985a), defines three discourses that stand for a monolithic study of the Tradition:

> 1) Current Islamic discourse, which tends to dominate all the others by its political power and great social and psychological scope. It is deeply rooted in the mythical dimension of the Tradition while unwittingly secularising the religious contents of that Tradition. 2) Classical Islamic discourse, which explains the Tradition in the period of its being formed and fixed in authentic texts. 3) Orientalist

---

184 Kersten 2010: 4.
185 Kersten 2010: 4.
186 Abū Zayd 2006: 84.
187 Abū Zayd 2006: 83.
188 El-Ayadi 1993: 48–49.

discourse,[189] which applies to the forming and fixing stage a philological and historical critique, predominantly historicist and positivist and which belongs to the nineteenth century.[190]

What these discourses have in common is that they have developed a rigid study of the Islamic Tradition that does not consider the socio-historical context in which it was developed. These discourses have also disconnected from the actual socio-historical changes in most Muslim societies. In what follows, I examine Arkoun's critique of the Orientalist methods of working on Islam. However, considering that Orientalism is a critical concept according to Edward Said and one of the frameworks for postcolonial theory, Arkoun was not a rabid critic of the Orientalist camp as inspired by Said and postcolonial theory. Arkoun directs his criticism primarily against the working methods of some Orientalists-historians who, he notes, fail to develop an evaluative and transdisciplinary approach that incorporates the sciences of man to study Islam, as practiced in his applied Islamology.

Applied Islamology: As critique of Orientalist method

Before discussing Arkoun's criticism of the Orientalist method, one can note that Arkoun's criticism of Orientalist historians cannot mask his praise for the intellectual achievements of classical Islamic studies developed in the West. Rather, Arkoun's main criticism is of the extravagance of pragmatic Islamology, which was pushed by a younger generation of Islamists with a background in social science rather than philology and which succeeded in marginalizing classical Islamology in the 1980s and 1990s.[191] In other words, Arkoun criticizes the method of Orientalist historians who attempt to study Islamic Tradition through narratives without recognizing how the earlier account of Islam is relevant to actual Islamic practices. In an article published in the Oxford Encyclopedia of the Islamic World under the title "Islamic Studies" (2009), Arkoun criticizes the Orientalist method by asserting:

> Orientalism has accepted the traditional account of Muhammad's life, the articulation of the Qur'ān in Mecca and Medina, and the early formation of the Muslim community (…). Radical source criticism of the Qur'ān and other early Islamic texts has been attempted by very few orientalist scholars.[192]

---

189 Based on the secondary literature dealing with Arkoun's critique of Orientalism, I will refer to Arkoun's critique of Orientalism not as Orientalist discourse, but as Orientalist method. As far as I understand, Arkoun specifically criticizes the Orientalist historians' method of studying the Islamic Tradition.
190 Arkoun 1985 a: 92.
191 Kersten 2010: 3.
192 Arkoun, "Islamic Studies": in The Oxford Encyclopedia of the Islamic World: 2009.

Unlike some Orientalists, Arkoun advocates the study of Islamic Tradition through a transdisciplinary approach that incorporates social sciences, philology, history, anthropology, linguistics, and philosophy. For the study of Islam, Arkoun calls for the creation of a network of critical thinking. He notes, for example, that some Orientalists overlook the positive contributions of the humanities and social sciences to Islamic studies. As a result, they refuse to engage in epistemological discourse in the field of Islamic studies.[193] Arkoun affirms that Orientalist method only questions texts that are assumed a priori to belong to a religious tradition, thought, or culture.[194] In addition, Arkoun notes that in most Muslim societies, Islam is studied only to a limited extent and is carefully controlled by the authorities to protect political objectives and maintain the legitimacy and continuity of their power. Islam is , thus, an ideological lever, a subject of an ideological lever, a subject of offensive or defensive apology.[195] In this sense, one can say that Arkoun directs his criticism both at the method of studying Islam as developed by some Orientalists and at Muslim scholars who subjected and controlled their study of Islam for political ends.

In contrast to the working method of Orientalist and Muslim scholars, Arkoun argues that Islam must be liberated from the essentialist and substantialist postulates of classical metaphysics.[196] In other words, Islam is presented in most Orientalist history accounts as a specific, unchanging system of traditions, beliefs, and non-beliefs. I also interpret the essentialist and substantialist postulates that characterize the study of Islam by some Orientalists in terms of non-evaluative and fixed approaches to thought, following Arkoun's description of the approaches that some Orientalists use to study Islam, which he describes as "decidedly fixed, articulated, and evaluated with selections, eliminations, fragmentations, marginalization, and minimizations by those who write, read, and teach orthodox norms on the official state level of social construction."[197]

One can argue that Arkoun's engagement with the Western discipline of Islamic studies was a critique of the positivist historians of the 1960s. Arkoun's critique of Orientalism preceded Edward Said's critique in *Orientalism* (published in 1978).[198] While Said criticizes Orientalism, he refers to the simplistic, stereotypical, and pejorative notions that Western scholars have of Arab and Asian cultures. Said's critique of Orientalism places us in the context of the discriminatory division that exists in the global cultural system between those who describe and decide and those who obey and observe. According to Said, Orientalist research is based on power

---

193 Arkoun 1985 b: 95–96.
194 Arkoun 1989: 2.
195 Arkoun 1989: 2.
196 Arkoun 1989: 2.
197 Arkoun, "Islamic Studies": in The Oxford Encyclopedia of the Islamic World: 2009.
198 Abu- Uksa 2011: 187 fn. 63.

differentials in the process of knowledge production. Arkoun paved the way for the critique of Orientalism in 1973. "His critique of Orientalism was methodological in nature."[199] He denounced that some Orientalist historian does not consider the new methodological principles recently elaborated by social scientists and historians to allow an evaluative and more critical understanding of Islam.

Arkoun mostly adopts a critical attitude toward the Orientalist method and seeks to liberate the field of Islamic studies from that which he argues does not promote a more critical examination of the sources of Islam and does not relate them to human societies. For Arkoun, Orientalism is presented only to examine what Tradition has said, without seeing if that Tradition is still applicable in today's Muslim context.

In addition, an important part of Arkoun's critique of "Orientalist European Islamology"[200] – that is, what I have previously called a critique of the Orientalist method – may be his desire to create a dialogue between European and Arabo-Muslim intellectuals on the subject of Islamic studies in order to reduce the pejorative study of Islam by some Orientalist thinkers. Thus, Arkoun aims to promote dialogue between Muslim intellectuals and their Western counterparts on the challenges facing Islam today. Throughout his intellectual career, Arkoun has studied both Islamic and Western schools of thought. In Arkoun's view, intellectuals have a key role to play in expressing the concerns of their societies. Their role should be to provide understandable and accessible information about political and social issues affecting their societies and to link these to a global intellectual critique.[201]

To simply put, Orientalist method does not address the social, political, and cultural concerns and problems associated with contemporary Muslim societies. Therefore, the question arises: what is the alternative discourse that Arkoun offers to Islamic studies that embodies the characteristics of an applied Islamology?

The discourse of the science of man and society: Disclosing the "Unthought" of Islam as a subversive strategy

Arkoun introduces the discourse of the science of man and society as an alternative to the Orientalist method of studying Islam and as a more evaluative and critical discourse to the Islamic Tradition. It is in fact the fourth discourse, following the other three enumerated above:

> The discourse of the sciences of man and society, which aims to rework the preceding three to emphasise in each instance those questions that are repressed as

---

199 Abu-Uksa 2011: 187 fn. 63.
200 Rhouni 2010: 20.
201 Völker 2015: 214.

unthinkable or "unthought", and, thus, to make possible a *current* critical revival of the problem of the Tradition and traditions in Islam.[202]

In other words, the discourse of the science of man and society aims at critically questioning the previous discourses on Islam. It seeks to place Islam within the framework of the critical disciplines in order to interrogate the unthinkable, the unthought; that is, the hidden and concealed features associated with Islamic thought. Next I examine the main features of the thinkable and the unthinkable, i.e., the thought and the unthought, in order to clarify Arkoun's intention in his proposing the discourse of the science of man and society that examines Islamic thought within critical approaches. Arkoun first defines the sphere of the unthinkable, which has anchored Islamic thought in a tradition of thought that renders reason incapable of critically engaging in rethinking Islam. In this context, he claims:

> When the field of the unthinkable is expanded and maintained for centuries in a particular tradition of thought, the intellectual horizons of reason are diminished, and its critical functions narrowed and weakened because the sphere of the unthought becomes more determinate and there is little space left for the thinkable.[203]

As Arkoun affirms, the unthinkable exists in religious, political, and legal realms that cannot be critically thought. He writes:

> Islam everywhere has been put under the control of the state (*étatisé*); but the religious discourse developed by the opposing social forces shifted to a **populist** ideology which increased the extent of the **unthought**, especially in the religious, political, and legal fields. [emphasis in the original] [204]

Arkoun believes that the state, through its institutions, engages in the manipulation of the unthinkable sphere and the distortion of the critical thinking framework. He declares:

> There certainly is a clash, but it is between collective **imaginaries** constructed and maintained on both sides through **unthinkables** and **unthoughts** cultivated by the education systems, the discourse of political and academic establishments, and the media that feed on this rhetoric and seek to increase their following

---

202   Arkoun 1985 a: 92.
203   Arkoun 2002 a: 12.
204   Arkoun 2002 a: 15.

by outdoing each other with anticipations of interpretations from the leading minds. [emphasis in the original][205]

Thus, Arkoun asserts that the unthinkable is subject to the control of the state, which contributes to the formation of collective ideas about religion that influence law and politics. In other words, the unthought refers to religious restrictions and prohibitions that the thought cannot critically question. In this regard, Margot Badran, a Muslim feminist thinker, argues that Arkoun's concept of the unthought corresponds to the religious segment of the public sphere; that is, the realm of religious professions and performance of rites, and the private family sphere, which is legally regulated by religion.[206] In both spheres, public and private, women are not allowed to participate and be active according to the patriarchal interpretation of Islamic legacy. Likewise, the thought is forbidden to question the unthought aspect of religious rituals and traditions promoted by religious orthodoxy. According to Ursula Günther, the concepts of thought and the unthought aim to open Islamic studies and thought to critique by questioning certainties and pushing thought beyond the boundaries of orthodoxy.[207]

One can assume that Arkoun, through the discourse of the science of man and society, seeks to examine Islam in relation to the real change that most Muslim societies face and to question the silent and forbidden aspect of the Islamic Tradition. In doing so, Islamic studies should consider that Islam as a religion must be critically assessed and evaluated. I agree with Ursula Günther who says that "Arkoun ... goes beyond the boundaries of Islamic Studies by appropriating methods that traditionally are not part of what is considered to be Islamic Studies or the study of Islam."[208] This leads me to present how applied Islamology, through its transference to the discourse of man and society, can challenge some unreflective systems regarding the issue of women in Islam.

The relevance of applied Islamology for feminist thought: An exemplary case for its emancipatory functions

An intrinsic emancipation norm that applied Islamology seeks to improve is Islam's equality policy. Applied Islamology examines the forbidden and hidden aspects of human societies that are not considered in the critical framework. Injustice and discrimination against women in the legal and political spheres are among the unthinkable issues that applied Islamology seeks to address. As Arkoun points out:

---

205   Arkoun 2002 a: 18.
206   Badran 2010: 28.
207   Günther 2004 a: 125.
208   Günther 2004 a: 125.

Women represent a particularity disadvantaged social body; it is they who have to suffer the oppression of regimes that instrumentalize religion to compensate for their own lack of political legitimacy; the resistance of the popular mentality to any questioning of the status of women as fixed by God Himself in the Qur'ān; and the weight of beliefs and customs they have themselves internalized through the rearing process handed down by their mothers and grandmothers in the lineage of an ancient feminine memory.[209]

The laws governing the legal conduct of women are both prescribed in the scriptures of Islam and the subject of traditional customs that influence the prescription of women's rights in Islam. Here, the method of applied Islamology critically examines the traditional constructs that continue to restrict women's right. Arkoun exemplifies the potential of applied Islamology to critically investigate gender issues in the following way:

> Applied Islamology first proceeds with the sociological analysis of the evolution of the structures and functions of parenthood in Islamic contexts. There too, one discovers the simultaneous disintegration of the traditional structures and codes, and the imposition by the state of traditionalist policies that protect the official religion and divine Law from 'blasphemy.' This means that family law remains unalterable; women can vote, but still they do not enjoy the same rights as men. [210]

In other words, women in Islam live in a dichotomy between the religious tradition of Islam and global modern rules. The example Arkoun gives of women having the right to vote but not enjoying other important rights and freedoms is an apt example that illustrates this dichotomy. The right to vote has to do with the modern rules of citizenship that many Muslim countries are forced to accept as part of the world, but family law, which determines a woman's social and political status in relation to her society, continues to be manipulated by patriarchy. The feminist project of Fatima Mernissi (d. 2015), presented in the first part of this research, consisted of her study of the feminist task within modern secular rules and Islamic traditions, showing that one cannot apply secular and modern rules to the Muslim world without modernizing Islamic discourse itself. For this reason, Mernissi's idea was to reconcile the secular and 'Islamic' feminist movements. In Arkoun's words, reconciliation between secular and Islamic feminism means reform. It means reforming Islamic thought to reconcile with modernity, but with some preservation and critique of Western modernity itself. This will be presented in chapter three. The critique of

---

209 Arkoun 2002 a: 22.
210 Arkoun 2007: 23–24.

Western modernity marks an important difference between the methodological and normative strategies of both thinkers.

In this regard, Muslim feminists recognize that there is a political reform (*islah*) beyond Arkoun's approach of applied Islamology. This is the defense of gender justice in Islam. Indeed, Malika Zeghal begins her article "Veiling and Unveiling Muslim Women: State Coercion, Islam, and the Disciplines of the Heart" (2012) by addressing the question of feminism in Tunisia between secular and Islamic thought. Zeghal shows that Arkoun's intellectual endeavor to reform religious discourse and transform political discourse on gender provides a promising gender discourse on the eve of postcolonial Tunisia. She contends that there is a contradictory discourse about women in postcolonial Tunisia; that is, a deep, hidden, and unstable convergence in the terminologies used in the debate about women between the secular nationalist elites and "those who 'expressed in Islamic terms' a 'hankering for cultural authenticity'".[211] Put simply, secular nationalist elites use the same vocabulary of cultural authenticity that includes Islamic terms. Likewise, Islamist activists refer to the national expression by calling Tunisian women virtuous citizens. Arkoun's intellectual project offers a way to make intelligible this contradictory discourse between the nationalist secular discourse and the nationalist Islamist discourse in the postcolonial period of most Muslim societies by showing that both the secular and Islamist discourses share an orthodox and hegemonic conception. They both serve to create fundamentalist, authoritarian, and discriminatory discourses about religion, culture, gender, and identity. This will be discussed in more detail in the third chapter of this study.

In her critical stance on the theory of Islamic feminism, Raja Rhouni also describes Arkoun as a "post-foundationalist islamic gender critic."[212] It would be equally accurate for her to describe Muslim feminist scholars who critique patriarchally controlled interpretations of Islam as post-foundationalist scholars who subscribe to Arkoun's "global epistemological project of applied Islamology."[213] Rhouni sees that the method of "Islamic feminism" calls for women's rights in Islam within the "androcentric assumptions of Islamic jurisprudence."[214]

There are several approaches associated with the field of feminism in Islam, such as state feminism, secular feminism, and Islamic feminism. In Zeghal's work, we saw how state feminism uses the same term that secular or Islamic feminist movements use to demand women's rights. Influenced by Arkoun's foundational critique of traditional Islamic thought, Rhouni uses a lower-case "i" to distinguish between rationalist scholars and traditionalist scholars in Islamic feminism (see part one of

---

211 Zeghal 2012: 129.
212 Rhouni 2008: 103; Rhouni 2010: 17.
213 Rhouni 2010: 20.
214 Rhouni 2010: 20.

this study, on Fatima Mernissi). Indeed, she claims that one should be careful with the approach of Islamic feminism because sometimes Islamic feminist scholars use their method of "'picking-and-choosing'"[215] to pick up or drop an idea that correctly represents women in Islam, but they do not offer a deconstructionist approach to the study of Qur'anic verses or Tradition that would also explain the predominant position of women in Islam.

In this sense, Rhouni sees that Arkoun's post-foundationalist critique of religious discourse and Mernissi's critical study of patriarchal religious interpretation of Islamic texts share commonalities.[216] Arkoun and Mernissi aim to open Islamic discourse to a new rational interpretation.

Thus, one can see how Arkoun's method of applied Islamology is important for contemporary gender scholars to classify and distinguish Muslim thinkers according to their thought processes when it comes to demanding gender justice in Islam. To reiterate, applied Islamology is an important method of analysis for Islamic studies. It is distinguished by its transdisciplinary and deconstructionist approaches to the study of Islam. It is directed against the simplistic, aestheticizing Orientalist method. Its main concern is to provide a rational and scientific discourse on man and society that penetrates into the realm of the unthinkable/unthought of Islamic thought. The emancipatory norms inherent in applied Islamology can be exemplified by Arkoun's efforts to emancipate women from patriarchal and fundamentalist constructs.

Exhaustive Tradition: The emergence of a subdivided Tradition in the Islamic archive using the methods of poststructuralist thought

In this section, Arkoun's method of exhaustive tradition is presented as an additional methodological tool within his transdisciplinary method of applied Islamology. The exhaustive tradition involves Arkoun introducing the methods of post-structuralist Western philosophy to examine Islamic religious discourse. When one engages with Arkoun's intellectual project, one can understand that the method of applied Islamology aims to establish an exhaustive tradition in Islam. Arkoun uses the term exhaustive tradition to refer to the marginalized cultural traditions of various religious sects that are excluded from the study of Islam. In this sense, the exhaustive tradition subjects the Islamic corpus to multiple and polythetic interpretations. The exhaustive tradition releases Islamic thought from logosphere. By logosphere, Arkoun refers to a restrained and structured interpretation of the Islamic corpora – Qur'an and Tradition – based on a unified interpretation of their language and the context of their emergence. Thus, this section presents the three poststructuralist

---

215 Rhouni 2010: 20.
216 Rhouni 2010: 35.

analytical methods, épistème, différence, and deconstruction, that Arkoun uses to interpret the Islamic corpora, which he refers to as the Islamic archive. By the Islamic archive, Arkoun means the two teachings of the Islamic religion, the Qur'an and Tradition, which have degenerated into a simplistic interpretation and do not submit to the framework of critical and evaluative thinking.

Three analysis methods to deconstruct and rethink the Islamic archive: Épistème, Différence, and Deconstruction

In "The Answers of Applied Islamology" (2007), Arkoun refers to Western poststructuralist thinkers who have subjected classical and metaphysical Western thought to a critical framework. Through their critical work, they provide new methods and concepts that allow us to reevaluate our notions about values, religion, and law to cite only a few. Arkoun introduces these thinkers to demonstrate the plausibility of using their methods of critical analysis to open the Islamic archive to diverse interpretations. He declares:

> Jacques Derrida warns us that, as a singular item, the archive (*arkheion* – that which is ancient) is a query about the future itself, made by a rational mind in the tradition of Freud and Nietzsche – and later pursued with varying degrees of pertinence by Arendt, Deleuze, Foucault, Levinas, Ricoeur, Lacan, Legendre, etc. Those names may let one think that this archive is a matter solely for those philosophers and psychoanalysts who have replaced classical metaphysical wishful thinking with a genealogical critique of their subject matter, of 'values,' of the Law (as the art of legal interpretation) and of the references to foundational texts as a revealed given.[217]

Among these scholars, Arkoun refers in particular to the critical analysis approaches of Foucault, Derrida, and Deleuze to demonstrate his strategy of subjecting the Islamic archive to rational and critical analysis.

Foucault's notion of the épistème and the disclosure of the logosphere

I begin by examining the concept of épistème, which Arkoun introduces to free the Islamic archive from its outdated, rigid interpretation and place it within the actual social implications of most Muslim societies. Arkoun writes:

> As Foucault points out, the social and political sciences and the human sciences are so subservient to the pressing managerial requirements of our bureaucratic, industrial and urbanized societies that they pay little attention to 'the possibility

---

217   Arkoun 2007: 21.

of a discourse which could go back and forth (between clinic and critique) without becoming discontinuous, a dual articulation of the history of individuals on the subconscious of cultures, and the historicity of the latter on individual subconsciousness."[218]

Epistème means the social analysis; it examines the Islamic corpora of the Qur'an and Tradition to situate them in their social content and to see if what they claim is still applicable in today's Muslim societies or not. Epistème aims to discover and reveal the implicit structure of the discourse. Foucault's epistème method asks for the meaning of a discourse by uncovering the process of its development and evaluation. In this regard, Arkoun argues: "Epistème is a better criterion for the study of thought because it concerns the structure of the discourse – the implicit postulates which command the syntactic construction of the discourse."[219]

For Foucault, epistème is not about a question of knowledge described in its progress toward an objectivity in which our contemporary science might recognize itself, but epistémè means to investigate the realms of knowledge considered outside any criterion related to their rational value or to their objective forms.[220] In other words, epistème describes a system of meanings and cognitive schemes of values/categories that form the basis for knowledge, science, and philosophy at a given time. This refers to all ideas, religious doctrines, and postulates that have an impact on a system of thought and channel discourse – the way people talked about reality in a particular era.[221]

One can affirm that Arkoun applies the method of epistème to release the Islamic archive from the logosphere system of language. As briefly mentioned earlier, the logosphere is based on a limited, narrow, and mystifying understanding of language that constructs the Islamic archive and renders it incapable of being subjected to a renewing interpretation. This means that the language of the Qur'an, if considered only as written sacred sources, does not allow for any other interpretation. Logosphere is the confinement of thought to the norms of social, political, and cultural constructions as described in the archive. In this regard, Arkoun sees that logosphere refers to the inability of reason to express itself either internally, externally or in writing without the assistance of language. The limits of language do not necessarily coincide with the limits of thought. As a free activity, thought is continuously capable of expanding the scope of language and increasing its effectiveness.[222] To put it simply, for Arkoun, the logosphere manipulates thought ac-

---

218   Arkoun 2007: 21.
219   Arkoun 2003: 20.
220   Foucault 1966: 13.
221   Günther 2004 b: 267; Schönberger 2010: 6.
222   Arkoun 2002 a: 173.

cording to language. Language formulates and constructs and limits interpretation in a strict sense. One can understand that by text, Arkoun means the religious texts that should be studied according to the transdisciplinary approach of the history of ideas, which examines a religious text by combining the fields of sociology, science, philosophy, literature, and so on.

Thus, Arkoun realizes that the text must be understood by placing it in its contemporary context. According to Arkoun, the relationship between writing/text/reading must be revived in all its complexity in order to make use of documents dealing with the history of ideas. A text, once written, eludes its author and takes on a life of its own, whose richness or poverty, expansion or desiccation, oblivion or revival, is now decided by readers.[223] In other words, by placing the archive – the text – within the framework of the history of ideas, the archive submits to the reader's understanding and relinquishes authority and control over the language used by the author. The text is interpreted differently from reader to reader, and thought becomes active in giving the text different meanings, interpretations, and explanations. In this vein, Arkoun argues:

> Only rarely does the reader comprehend a text in all the meanings intended by the author. Very often it is something he recites to free himself from his own internal discourse. In this case the text is being exploited as an excuse, rather than used properly as a channel of information. It becomes the setting for an intense dialectic between reader and author. … All these movements, exchanges and interactions help determine the life of the *logos*, in other words the mind embodying itself in a language and giving birth to many languages. Each language, in turn, can remain at the stage of the spoken word or extend itself into writing.[224]

Carool Kersten notes that Arkoun coined the term logosphere in reference to Derrida's notion of logocentrism.[225] As a result, Arkoun seeks to explain how the Islamic archive – the text – is involved in the manipulation and control of logocentric language. Arkoun assumes that the transdisciplinary approach to the history of ideas overcomes a restrained interpretive content of the Islamic archive and interrogates it in terms of contemporary social problems of Muslim societies. In this way, Arkoun attempts to overcome a restricted interpretation of Islam. In addition to the analytical method of epistémè, Arkoun also uses the analytical methods of difference and deconstruction to liberate the Islamic archive from its logosphere enclosure of language.

---

223 Arkoun 2002 a: 172.
224 Arkoun 2002 a: 172.
225 Kersten 2010: 3.

Arkoun's adaptation of Difference and Deconstruction to liberate the Islamic archive and open up possibilities for new interpretations

Arkoun refers to Deleuze's book *Difference and Repetition* (1968–1994) to explain the features of the method of difference that he applies to liberate the Islamic archive of the Qur'an and Tradition from the logosphere control of language. Arkoun conceptualizes the role of difference as a method of analyzing a written text as follows: difference "would be to put an end to the repetition of a given form of writing after making a detailed study of its limitations, describing its internal mechanism, evaluating its role and tracing its correlations." [226] In this line of thought, Deleuze introduces repetition as a paradigmatic opposition to difference, he explains, "far from grounding repetition, law shows, rather, how repetition would remain impossible for pure subjects of law – particulars." [227] By pure subjects of law, I understand texts that have the role of determining a law, such as the texts of the Qur'an and Tradition. For Deleuze "there are as many constants as variables among the terms designated by laws."[228] Indeed, the Qur'an and the Tradition are an object of law and the basic text of legislation, and they are determined by repetition. For this reason, it is impossible to give a pure sense of legislation when the text itself is determined by repetition. Thus, as Deleuze affirms, repetition condemns pure subjects of law to change. [229]

Therefore one might question to what extent repetition affects the text of the law? Can repetition lead to a pluralistic interpretation or does it rather preserve the rigid meaning of the text?

In this context, Deleuze explains, repetition accords "*an empty form of difference*, an *invariable form of variation*, a law compels its subjects to illustrate it only at the cost of their own change."[230] Simply put, repetition represents a meaningless understanding of the law, i.e., the text. It is important to note that repetition conveys a simple and singular official meaning of the text and prevents the text from being open to multiple interpretations. Arkoun, in fact, aims to create a difference in the Islamic legal corpora in order to liberate the Islamic written texts from their fixed meanings enforced by conformist repetition and official interpretation. The difference leads to the creation of a pluralistic understanding of the Islamic archive, i.e. text. Thus, the understanding of the text is not bound to a limited explanation, but is open to different explanations.

---

226 Arkoun 2002 a: 173–174.
227 Deleuze 1994: 2.
228 Deleuze 1994: 2.
229 Deleuze 1994: 2.
230 Deleuze 1994: 2.

3. Background and methods in the thought of Mohammed Arkoun 213

In addition to his use of the method of difference to create differences in the interpretation of the Islamic archive, Arkoun refers to Derrida's book *De la grammatologie* (1970) to introduce his concept of deconstruction as a criterion of analysis of the Islamic archive. For Derrida, deconstruction is "an unclosed, unenclosable, not wholly formalizable ensemble of rules for reading, interpretation, and writing."[231] Thus, one can state that deconstruction is behind a closed interpretation of the text. Deconstruction is crucial to liberate the text from its narrowed explanation and, thus, achieve a plausible understanding of the text. Indeed, "the task of deconstruction is to liberate the text, to deliberately develop its ambiguity, to uncover its suppressed ambiguity, to reveal its self-contradiction, and to identify the flaw, which is the condition of the possibility of every text."[232] The notion of law is fundamental in Derrida's work, which he expresses with the concept of "aporia" that blocks the understanding of the meaning of the text. Deconstruction aims to free the text from that flaw, that aporia, in order to make it intelligible.[233] Arkoun points out

> Since the publication of J. Derrida, *De la grammatologie*, an interesting discussion has ensued concerning the deconstruction of classical metaphysics. It was more than a new field of research in the history of ideas as still practiced, especially in the history of Islamic thought. Derrida was aiming to introduce new cognitive strategies in the interpretation of the long philosophical tradition of thought in the ontological framework of classical metaphysics which has influenced theological thinking in the three 'revealed' religions.[234]

For Arkoun, deconstruction is a revolutionary method within the framework of classical metaphysics. In particular, Arkoun locates Derrida's deconstruction in the field of Islamic studies. Arkoun understands deconstruction as a new strategy of interpretation that can change the theological framework. In this regard, deconstruction is a crucial method for decoding the cognitive strategy of Islamic thought and liberating it from the logosphere construction of language and, thus, from a limited understanding of the text.

As just explained, Arkoun applies the method of difference and deconstruction to liberate the Islamic archive from an essentialist and simplistic, singular and controlled official interpretation. In what follows, I explain how Arkoun applies these deconstructionist methods to the two theories of revelation, i.e., the Qur'an – as revealed discourse – and Tradition.

---

231 Derrida 1983: 40.
232 Binder 1988: 92.
233 Binder 1988: 92.
234 Arkoun 2002 a: 31.

Arkoun's deconstructivist rethinking of the theories of Revelation and Tradition

As part of his critical study of Islamic thought, Arkoun questions the theories of revelation and Tradition, which are the fundamental texts that elaborated the Islamic legacy. In Islamic legacy, revelation means the word of God transmitted to his chosen messenger, Prophet Muhammad. Tradition is the Prophet's customs as prescribed by his companions so that Muslims would know how to behave according to the Prophet's words and deeds. Arkoun assumes that every discourse was subject to social conditions that changed and reshaped it during the writing process. To examine Arkoun's critical thinking about revelation and Tradition, I refer to his book *Rethinking Islam: Common Questions, Uncommon Answers* (1994) and to his article "Rethinking Islam Today" (2003). I begin by examining how Arkoun explores the question of the theory of revelation. In this context, he notes that "the Islamic conception of revelation is called *tanzīl* (descent), a fundamental metaphor for the vertical gaze humans being are invited to cast toward God, transcendence."[235]

Hence, the Qur'an was at first a revealed discourse. It was articulated as discourse to the prophet Muhammed. Arkoun wants to question the process of the writing of this revealed discourse. He argues that "the putting into writing of the whole of the revealed discourse comes under the reign of third caliph, 'Uthman, between 645 and 656."[236] Arkoun attaches great importance to the process of transforming the revealed discourse of the Qur'an into a written text, because for him the revealed discourse of the Qur'an takes a great deal of time to be fully written in a book: from the time of the Prophet's life until the reign of the third caliph. Arkoun presents the process of the development of the theory of revelation from a revelatory discourse proclaimed to the Prophet Muhammad to a written text in the Qur'an as follows:

> A very small group of believers followed Muhammad, a charismatic leader related to the known paradigm of prophets and messengers of God in the history of salvation common to the "People of the Book." Muhammad, supported and inspired by God, had the ability to create a new relationship to the divine through two simultaneous and interacting initiatives as all charismatic leaders do with different levels of success and innovation. He announced the absolute truth in an unusual Arabic form of expression, and he engaged the group in successive, concrete experiences of social, political, and institutional change. The Revelation translated into a sublime, symbolic, and transcendental language the daily public life of the group whose identity and *imaginaire* were separated from the hostile,

---

235   Arkoun 1994: 31.
236   Arkoun 1994: 30.

non-converted groups (called infidels, hypocrites, enemies of God, errants, and bedouins.[237]

According to Arkoun, one must historicize the revelatory event and place it in the socio-cultural context of its origin, considering what people could add to this revelatory discourse from their daily lives and experiences. Arkoun believes that what has been proclaimed as the revealed truths of Islam should not be taken as guaranteed. He criticizes in particular the method by which the revelation is developed from speech to written text and then studied in narrative approaches without examining it. In this regard, he states "When we write the history of these twenty years (612–632) during which Muhammad created a new community, we mention the principal events in a narrative style. We neglect to point out the use made of these events by later generations of believers."[238] Arkoun introduces two approaches to analyze the event of revelation: "The first is to index, describe, and articulate all the significant events and facts that occurred in each period; the second is to analyze the mental representations of these events, facts, and actions shaping the collective *imaginaire* which becomes the moving force of history."[239] In other words, the study of the event of revelation requires that each articulated speech should be studied according to the circumstances of its revelation. Moreover, one should consider the cultural and traditional facts that play a crucial role in the development of the theory of revelation.

To put it simply, for Arkoun, revelation, i.e., the Qur'an written down in a book called *muṣḥaf*, is subject to the circumstances and facts of the time in which it came into being. The Qur'an is not the absolute truth that it is assumed to be. Arkoun does not consider the revelation as a sacred truth transmitted by God to the Prophet Muhammad. Arkoun questions the transformation of the Qur'an from a discourse of revelation into a written text. In this line of thought, Völker comments on Arkoun's understanding of the theory of revelation as follows. Völker conceives that Arkoun's emphasizing the history of the Qur'an as that of human manipulations allows doubt about how much revelation, or original divine word, the Qur'anic text really contains. For her, Arkoun seems to deny any participation of the Divine in these manipulations, as it is sometimes put forward by Islamic teachings. In her view, Arkoun excludes what he considers mythological elements like the idea of Jibril and Muhammad editing the text together, or that God gave Muhammad's followers superhuman memories.[240]

---

237 Arkoun 2003: 34–35.
238 Arkoun 2003: 34–35.
239 Arkoun 2003: 34–35.
240 Völker 2014.

In other words, Arkoun holds that the Qur'an is a human creation subject to human manipulation and has nothing to do with supernatural or divine forces writing it. This was Arkoun's understanding of Mu'tazila's theological quest to gain recognition for "Khalq al-Qur'an" (God's created speech). Simply put, his position that the Qur'an is a human creation is inspired by the Mu'tazila theory, which makes this exact claim. Mu'tazila aimed to establish a similar thought that would legitimize the rationalist interpretation of the Qur'an, in contrast to their opponent, who contended that the Qur'an was not created but was the literal word of God. In the same spirit of the Mu'tazila, Arkoun distinguished between "the Qur'anic event" and "the Islamic event or phenomenon" (I examine the Qur'anic event/fact distinction in chapter 3) in order to separate the period of revelation from the historical consequences that were manifested in the establishment of state, dogma, institutions, and legal and ethical systems during and after the seventh century.[241]

Regarding Tradition, Arkoun asserts that in addition to the Qur'an, which is the main foundation of the Shari'a – Islamic law – there is a second source or foundation (aṣl): the prophetic Tradition known through the Hadith, the utterances of the Prophet in his role as leader of the community of believers.[242] Arkoun affirms that the prophetic Tradition is a second basis for the elaboration of the Islamic legacy, which he believes is limited to a collection of "authentic" texts recognized in each community: Shi'i, Sunni, and Khariji.[243] In this sense, Arkoun "sought to replace the monolithic fundamentalist perception of Islam (in Sunni, Shi'i and Khariji Islam) with a discursive and pluralistic notion, free from the manipulation of power."[244] This becomes even clearer when he introduces his concept of exhaustive tradition, which means to create a pluralistic, discursive, and subdivided concept of Islam by opening it up to what is considered to be the marginalized and non-fundamental tradition of Islam.

Arkoun draws our attention to the fact that the writing of the Tradition took much more time than the compilation of the Qur'anic text. Importantly, the selection and editing of the Tradition gave rise to ongoing controversies among the three Muslim communities: Shi'a, Sunni, and Khariji.[245] Arkoun emphasizes the complexity of transforming a discourse, like revelation, into a written text. The Tradition took a long time after the Prophet's death to become a text. It is important to question the authenticity of the Tradition, how it was transmitted, under what circumstances it was transmitted, by whom, and whether the source is infallible. One should keep in mind that the Tradition of the Prophet is understood and interpreted differently by

---

241 Abu-Uksa 2011: 174.
242 Arkoun 1994: 45.
243 Arkoun 2003: 21.
244 Abu-Uksa 2011: 176.
245 Arkoun 1994: 45.

3. Background and methods in the thought of Mohammed Arkoun 217

different Islamic schools. There are some sources of transmission that are neglected by some, and considered infallible by other Islamic schools.

Arkoun notes that revelation and Tradition continue to reconstruct our understanding of Islam without subjecting them to critical analysis to examine the origins of their development. Thus, as part of his deconstruction of Islamic thought, Arkoun seeks to subject the theory of revelation and Tradition to the framework of critical analysis. Thus, one can say that Arkoun uses the analytical criterion of deconstruction to examine the sources of Islam that construct a form of dogmatic belief. In fact, Arkoun seeks to re-emphasize the marginalized meaning, the hidden or forgotten meaning that has contaminated the discourse of the revelation and Tradition.[246] In this context, Soekarba claims that Derrida offers critical processes to analyze written discourse.

As outlined earlier, this critical process, referred to as 'deconstruction,' is a tool to uncover different meanings in Islamic archive. "Derrida writes of liberation, but specifically of liberation of the text in the sense of its openness to possible meaning."[247] Indeed, Arkoun has paid particular attention to the method of deconstruction in an attempt to reinvent meanings that have been marginalized or forgotten through the closure and freezing of Islamic thought.[248] In my own words, deconstruction serves to shake up, expose, and transform the mutual repetition that constitutes thought, written text, or spoken discourse. I further argue that Arkoun employs a schematic and organized set of analytical criteria to examine Islamic thought, beginning with a deconstructionist examination of its implicit foundations, moving through the discovery of its various traditions, and ending with the deconstruction of the conventional belief system.

As a result, the analytical criteria of epistème, différence, and deconstruction open the Islamic archive to further interpretation. Thus, a subdivision of traditions into Islamic traditions is developed. I agree with Khalil and Khan who explain that Arkoun believes that deconstruction of discourse should be followed by reconstruction after it has been freed from constraints, freezes, and distortions.[249] Thus, Arkoun has a goal that goes beyond his deconstruction of the Islamic archive. He believes that deconstruction must be followed by ethical reconstruction. I argue that Arkoun's use of deconstruction is based on an implicit emancipation norm, as it aims to liberate the Islamic archive from logosphere manipulation. Therefore, "the term 'deconstruction,' according to one of its champions, Jacques Derrida, is more than merely a method for interpreting texts; it is a mode of political action as well, though it is not 'political action' as that term is ordinarily understood. ... The deconstruction

---

246   Khalil and Khan 2013: 35.
247   Binder 1988: 91.
248   Soekarba 2014: 80–81.
249   Khalil and Khan 2013: 35.

of texts is essentially and emphatically a political act. ... Deconstruction has political consequences – ... it is a new way of constituting 'the world.'"[250]

In this respect, deconstruction opposes the dominant religious and political interpretation of Islam. It emancipates the Islamic archive from its logosphere enclosure and gives marginalized minorities of Islam the right to emerge, speak, and contribute to a modern *ijtihād* (intellectual struggle) on Islamic legacy. "Arkoun's deconstruction [of the Islamic archive of the Qur'an and Tradition and his proposals for reformulating the Shari'a] placed him in a frontal clash with conservatives and with political-Islamic movements." [251]

Exhaustive tradition: On the ethical necessity of speaking about the marginalized cultural traditions of Islam

According to Arkoun, the Islamic archive neglects the various cultural traditions that are part of Islam. Based on his concept of exhaustive tradition, Arkoun attempts to critique the dominant tradition of Islam by including other cultural traditions to bring the marginalized cultures more into focus. In this context, Arkoun affirms:

> Islam holds historical significance for all of us, but at the same time, our understanding of this phenomenon is sadly inadequate. There is a need to encourage and initiate audacious, free, productive thinking on Islam today.[252]

To accomplish this, Arkoun proposes to critically examine "silent Islam" to explore all the cultures and systems of thought associated with pre-Islamic, pagan, polytheistic societies as well as modern secular societies that remain unthinkable and are therefore unthinkable in orthodox Islam.[253] Simply put, Arkoun tries to open the sphere of the unthinkable, outlined earlier, to criticism. This will make it possible to identify the silent cultures and traditions that have influenced Islam's development, rather than reducing Islam to one tradition.

Arkoun argues "if we add to the Qur'an and Hadith, the methodology used to derive the Shari'a and the *Corpus juris* in the various schools, we have other subdivisions of the three axes of Islamic Tradition." [254] One could understand that Arkoun wants to apply the exhaustive tradition approach to the four predominant Islamic schools of law of the Maaliki, Shaafa'i, Hanafi, and Hanbali in order to derive a pluralistic and heterogeneous interpretation of the Islamic law of the Shari'a as the main law of Islamic legislation.

---

250   Zuckert 1991: 336.
251   Abu- Uksa 2011: 176.
252   Arkoun 2003: 18–19.
253   Arkoun 2003: 20 .
254   Arkoun 2003: 21 .

Thus, the application of the exhaustive tradition will produce a variety of interpretations of the Islamic textual sources that are consistent with each Islamic school. Hence Arkoun declares "I tried to introduce the concept of an exhaustive tradition worked by a critical, modern confrontation of all the collections used by the communities, regardless of the orthodox limits traced by the classical authorities."[255] In fact, the exhaustive tradition is at odds with the orthodox and classical methods of studying Islam. The exhaustive tradition is characterized by its critical approach.

One might note that the concept of 'exhaustive' is associated with the concept of tradition. Here one should explain the difference between the Tradition of the Prophet and tradition as cultural traditions related to Islam. Arkoun explains the latter as follows: "the concept of tradition as it used in anthropology today – the sum of customs, laws, institutions, beliefs, rituals, and cultural values which constitute the identity of each ethno-linguistic group."[256] In this context, Arkoun emphasizes that one should not confuse Tradition in the sense of prophetic Tradition – the sayings and actions of the Prophet Muhammad, as explained earlier – with tradition in the sense of the entire Islamic heritage (*turāth*).[257]

Hence, Arkoun understands Islam as a set of cultural traditions. The understanding of Islam should not only correspond to the different schools of Islam such as Shi'a, Sunna and Khariji, but also depend on the original and instinctive tradition of the people before the advent of Islam. That is, in terms of each folk tradition that emerges, grows and lives in contemporary Islamic societies. In Arkoun's view, the study of Islam from its various traditions requires a critical framework that asks the questions:

> How do we speak of or interpret the so-called popular culture? Who uses the words magic, superstitions, paganism, polytheism, heterodoxies, or sects to refer to wrong beliefs, underdeveloped cultures, anarchy, rebellion as opposed to political order, the writing of book culture, reason, high culture, civilization, and so forth?[258]

Using a transcultural research method, Arkoun's theory of exhaustive tradition addresses the excluded cultural traditions of people in the Islamic realm, in contrast to the conventional theological understanding of Islam developed by historian Orientalists and even contemporary Arabo-Islamic scholarship. Günther affirms that exhaustive tradition is an approach that views Islam as a holistic and comprehensive religion, marginalizing and suppressing parts that are labeled heterodox. The

---

255 Arkoun 2003: 21.
256 Arkoun 1998b: 209.
257 Arkoun 1994: 47–48.
258 Arkoun, "Islamic Studies": in The Oxford Encyclopedia of the Islamic World: 2009.

exhaustive tradition is another example of Arkoun's ability to create space beyond orthodox definitions. The exhaustive tradition accounts for internal discontinuities within Islamic thought, such as cosmopolitanism and plurality of doctrines. The exhaustive tradition recognizes external discontinuities in the simultaneous connection with Europe and/or the Western world and intellectual modernity.[259] In other words, Arkoun's exhaustive tradition serves as a critique of orthodox thought that seeks to manipulate Islam. An exhaustive tradition advocates heterodoxy in Islam by supporting its pluralistic traditions. Thus, the exhaustive tradition is at odds with a monolithic reconstruction of Islam. It offers a transcultural study of Islam beyond the hierarchical manipulation of the most powerful Islamic tradition of the Arab Muslim Sunna and the Persian Muslim Shi'i. Exhaustive tradition means claiming the right of Muslim minorities to stand up for their rights. Exhaustive tradition as an intellectual, ethical and political project ensures the multiculturalism of Islam in terms of cultural diversity, without excluding different Islamic schools or Islamic religious sects and traditions.

Arkoun's approach to an exhaustive tradition is rooted in and resonates with his biography as a Kabyle-Berber Algerian Muslim intellectual belonging to a marginalized ethnic group in the Maghreb. Thus, exhaustive tradition makes marginalized popular traditions in Arab Muslim countries emerge in the face of dominant social, political, and cultural repressions. The Berber community in Algeria recognized marginalization after and before independence. In most Maghrebian countries, Berber are still struggling to secure their economic, social, and political rights.[260] Indeed, Berber militants fought the government in the early 2000s, demanding their economic, political, and cultural rights. This conflict is not new, but it has found firm and persistent expression since 2001. This has included occasional clashes with security forces, in which more than eighty Berber demonstrators have died and several people have been arrested.[261]

The militant repression and resistance of the Berber ethnic group in the Maghreb during these years challenged the realization of one of their cultural rights. In 2016, the Tamazight language – the Berber language, which is the second largest spoken language after Moroccan and Algerian dialects – was declared an official language in Algeria and Morocco.

Yet Arkoun was not a political activist, nor was he directly involved in politics. When Arkoun was asked in an interview, "Why is the political aspect absent from

---

259 Günther 2004 a: 155, fn. 14.
260 In this context See: Chaker Salem (1992): "La question Berbère dans l'Algérie indépendante: La fracture inévitable ?". In *L'Algérie incertaine* (No 65, pp. 97–105). Revue du monde musulman et de la Méditerranée.
261 Layachi 2005: 196.

your works?" he answered, "No, the political exists on every single page, and in every single concept I use, it is evident in the scientific content." [262] One can understand that Arkoun's critical analysis of Islamic thought has a political and ethical basis that leads to liberating most Muslim people from the injustice and alienation they experience because of their different ethnicities, as stated above. Arkoun's writings on the exhaustive tradition can reflect the struggles that marginalized Muslim ethnic groups face on the ground to defend their rights. The emancipation of the Berber population was, thus, accompanied by the intellectual engagement of several Berber intellectuals, such as Arkoun, whose critical concepts implicitly championed the Berber cause in the Maghreb.

To summarize what this chapter explored: Arkoun offers transdisciplinary, transcultural, and rational approaches of thinking about the study of Islam, taken from Al-Amiri's Islamic philosophy. Arkoun's methods of thinking further combine concepts from poststructuralist Western philosophies. This chapter presented Arkoun's method of applied Islamology, which is a critical, modern analysis of Orientalist/classical Islamic studies and aims to develop a new discourse for the study of Islam. His concept of exhaustive tradition, which is a post-structuralist approach, also serves to deconstruct/reconstruct Islamic legacy. Applied Islamology and exhaustive tradition contribute to creating an implicit ethical norm through the emancipation of most Muslim women from patriarchal rules, the liberation of Islamic thought from logosphere, and finally the emancipation of the popular tradition from the hegemonic religious and political systems. The following chapter examines Arkoun's critique of the various levels of hegemonic discourse manifested in the spheres of religion and politics and expressed in postcolonial discourse and Western Eurocentrism.

---

262 Arkoun's interview by Turki al-Dakhīl on the Alarabiya satellite channel: "Iḍa'āt: Mohammed Arkoun;" Abu- Uksa 2011: 172).

3.3 Toward an emancipation from hegemonic constructions: The critique of orthodoxy, Arab nationalism, and Euro-modernism

This chapter addresses Arkoun's critique of the hegemonic discourse[263] that constructs the thought through notions of religious orthodoxy, nationalist political ideologies, and Euromodernism. According to Arkoun, texts and discourses are politically constructed and, thus, instruments of power. For Arkoun, hegemonic discourse manifests itself in religion as an influential factor in the formation of orthodoxy. Arkoun draws attention to how religious texts – of the Qur'an and Tradition – have been hegemonically interpreted and manipulated by official religious scholars to protect political interests. According to Arkoun, hegemonic discourse manifests itself not only in religious discourse but also in the political discourse of Arab nationalism, both Islamist and modernizing. Thus, Islamist Arab nationalism in most Muslim countries calls for the eradication of the cultural traditions and religious beliefs of minorities, and in order to unite Arab Muslim countries, Islam must be propagated as the religion of the nation, Arabic as its language, and Arab as the ethnic group of the nation.

The hegemonic discourse is also evident in Arkoun's critique of modernist Arab nationalist and Euro-modernity discourses. Arkoun opposes a secularism that establishes itself as a coercive regime which eliminates the fundamental right to religious freedom. Arkoun emphasizes a humanistic secularism in which people are free to express their religious beliefs. He believes that in secular societies, everyone should respect the differences of others, in a climate of democracy and tolerance. In addition, Arkoun speaks about capitalist modernity, which he believes manipulates the world economic system by placing powerless countries under the control and exploitation of powerful countries. Arkoun considers that modernity in most Muslim countries is limited to consumption, subordinating itself to the scientific and economic development of developed countries instead of participating in transcultural

---

263 Arkoun uses the concept of hegemony, attributed to various discourses (religious, nationalist, Western), to explain that a thought becomes hegemonic when it is not subjected to critical evaluation. A thought acquires hegemony when it is characterized by a structured and rigorous discourse that manipulates thought and is led by official and authoritarian representatives. Massimo Campanini has examined the philosophy of Muslim scholars who seek to liberate Islamic thought from "hegemonic ideologies of politics." Campanini draws on Arkoun's critique of hegemonic discourse. He asserts that "a change in [thought] requires a change in socio-political and ideological relations in society, as Antonio Gramsci argued." Following Gramsci, Arkoun calls Islamic thought hegemonic because it is based on a set of hegemonic discourses created by religious orthodoxy and nationalist political ideologies that manipulate Islamic thought. See: Massimo Campanini (2009) "Qur'anic Hermeutics and Political Hegemony: Reformation of Islamic Thought" in The Muslim World Hartford Seminary (pp. 124–133); published by Blackwell.

scientific exchange and economic development through trade fairs. While criticizing the concept of capitalist modernity, Arkoun invokes the concept of intellectual modernity, which is the result of intellectual research and the participation of Arab intellectuals in humanism and critical thinking discourse.

This chapter is divided into two sections to illustrate how hegemonic discourse shapes orthodoxy, Arab-nationalism, and Euro-modernism. The first section explains what the hegemonic discourse and orthodoxy are. This is to illustrate how hegemonic discourse manipulates religion by creating orthodoxy. Arkoun deconstructs the hegemonic discourse to show how religious texts are under the control of official religious scholars to protect political ideologies and interests. Through his critical examination of hegemonic discourse, Arkoun seeks to liberate religious discourse from orthodoxy and, thus, from official control. The second section examines how hegemonic discourse determines nationalist discourse in most postcolonial Muslim countries. The aim is to highlight Arkoun's critique of both Islamist and modernist nationalist discourses involved in the creation of a closed identity, cultural closure, and religious dogmatism. The chapter ends with an exposition of Arkoun's concepts of humanistic secularity and intellectual modernity, which he advocates for Muslim societies and European countries as basic principles of Enlightenment philosophy to create notions of religious tolerance and pluralistic democracy.

The hegemonic discourse as an influential factor in the formation of orthodoxy within the Qur'an

The first focus here is to show how hegemonic discourse creates orthodoxy with religious discourse. The second focus is on the two levels of orthodoxy that make Islam a hegemonic discourse manipulated by official religious scholars for political purposes.

In this sense, orthodoxy is shaped in two stages: The first stage is that of the Qur'anic fact; the revelation – as mentioned in chapter 3.2 – is oral. This is the transmission of the Qur'an to the prophet Muhammed in the form of speech. Orthodoxy manipulates the revelation by not making it open to different horizons of interpretation and knowledge. Thus, the revelation, or the Qur'anic fact, is systematized and does not logically distinguish between the mythical and the rational. The second stage is that of Islamic fact. It means the collection and canonization of revelation in a Qur'anic book, the *Muṣḥaf*. Orthodoxy here used the revelation as a pretext for the socio-political context that developed as a power. Some aspects of Islamic fact are selectively used for power purposes. Orthodoxy is established by official religious scholars who are employed by political power to protect their political authority. Here the revelation is no longer open, but narrowed to the Arabic-language understandings that orthodoxy constructs.[264]

In this context, I introduce what Arkoun means by hegemonic discourse to understand its impact on the creation of orthodoxy in Islam. In his article entitled "From Inter-Religious Dialogue to the Recognition of the Religious Phenomenon" (1998 a), Arkoun presents the concept of hegemonic discourse as follows:

> What I mean by [hegemonic reason[265]] is that all exercise of reason aims at attaining a procedural and cognitive sovereignty able to resist all denials and make itself indispensable for all time to every human intelligence. This quest for a durable and inescapable cognitive validity which applies to everyone is psychologically legitimate: it conveys at once the desire for eternity, the nostalgia of being, and the desire to know, which haunt every human being; but it becomes hegemonic when reason imposes through political, economic and social constraints cognitive systems beyond the reach of free criticism.[266]

In other words, hegemonic discourse constructs a valuable discourse about Islam that is inviolable and valid for all times and places. Arkoun sees that hegemonic discourse becomes a threat when it is used as an instrument of power to manipulate human reason. One could argue that hegemonic discourse manipulates Islam through the creation of orthodoxy. In this sense, orthodoxy prohibits other understandings and interpretations about religion and forces individuals to think the same without subjecting religious discourse to critical examination. In this context, Arkoun introduces the concept of orthodoxy as follows:

> Orthodoxy refers to two values. For the believers, it is the authentic expression of the religion as it has been taught by the pious ancestors; the "orthodox" literature describes opposing groups as "sects." For the historian, orthodoxy refers to the ideological use of religion by the competing groups in the same political space, like the Sunnis who supported the caliphate – legitimized afterwards by the jurists – and who called themselves "the followers of the tradition and the united community." [267]

Arkoun uses the term orthodoxy to refer to the official religion established by the majority of official religious scholars – 'ulamā' – to protect political power. He

---

264 Hashas 2015.
265 In this study, I prefer to use the term "hegemonic discourse" because hegemony is installed in various forms of discourse – religious discourse, nationalist discourse, and Western discourse – and not just Islamic reason as hegemonic reason.
266 Arkoun 1998 a: 126.
267 Arkoun 2003: 22.

claims, according to Pierre Bourdieu, that orthodoxy systems are based on mutual exclusions, manifested, for example, in the contradictions between orthodoxy and heresy.[268] I refer to Bourdieu to show that orthodoxy means straightforward thinking to which one should adhere, in contrast to heterodoxy, which means the creation of various critical approaches to thinking. In Bourdieu's terms:

> Orthodoxy, straight, or rather *straightened* opinion, which aims, without ever entirely succeeding, at restoring the primal state of innocence of doxa, exists only in the objective relationship which opposes it to heterodoxy, that is, by reference to the choice – hairesis, heresy – made possible by the existence of competing possibles and to the explicit critique of the sum total of the alternatives not chosen that the established order implies. It is defined as a system of euphemisms, of acceptable ways of thinking and speaking the natural and social world, which rejects heretical remarks as blasphemies. [269]

Focusing on Islam, one can understand that opinions and interpretations that lead to a different understanding of religious texts are considered heresy, i.e., a deviation from orthodoxy, from the usual approach to understanding Islamic religious texts. As mentioned earlier, Arkoun recognizes two stages in the emergence of orthodoxy in Islam – particularly in the Qur'an: The stage of Qur'anic fact and the stage of Islamic fact.

Arkoun declares: "At the stage of the 'Qur'anic fact,' God presents Himself to man in a discourse articulated in the Arabic language."[270] Hence the Qur'anic fact refers the revelation of the Qur'an to the Prophet Muhammad in the form of speech. Regarding the second stage of the Islamic fact, Arkoun clarifies, "the 'Islamic fact' retains and exploits this dimension of the 'Qur'anic fact' as an area of sanctification, of spiritualization, transcendentalization, ontologization, mythologization, ideologization through all the doctrinal schemes, all the legalistic, ethical, and cultural codes, all the systems of legitimation put in place by the *ulamā*".[271] To put it simply, the Islamic fact is the use of the Qur'an by official religious scholars as a sacred phenomenon to manipulate the legal and ethical systems. In this way, the Qur'an becomes a powerful and hegemonic discourse that manipulates humanity and establishes a monolithic understanding of Islamic law without allowing for open interpretation. Indeed, as Arkoun affirms, "it is to the 'Islamic fact' that the development and historical action of what is called Muslim law should be linked, especially the aspect that is applied as positive law *(fiqh)*."[272] Arkoun believes that the Qur'an

---

268 Schönberger 2010: 7; cf. Günther 2004b: 60.
269 Bourdieu 1977- 2005: 169.
270 Arkoun 2002 a: 262.
271 Arkoun 2002 a: 262.
272 Arkoun 2002 a: 262.

can be interpreted to produce a just Islamic law that promotes human dignity and rights. Consequently, the Qur'an survives the canon of orthodoxy and official control because of its openness to interpretation.

In the same line of thought, Günther clarifies the concepts of Qur'anic fact and Islamic fact to show how they determine the framework of the Qur'an and how they promote orthodoxy in Islam. She asserts:

> Qur'ānic and Islamic fact/event allow a differentiation between a linguistic event and the consolidation of the new religion, that is, between the period of revelation shaped by the Qur'ānic or prophetic discourse which ended with death of Muhammad in 632, and the fixation of revelation as a written document resulting in a determination of the reading which is supposed to have been effected from 661 on. Thus these concepts describe the historical process of the coming into being of a new religion, effected and supported by social, political, and cultural actors. Furthermore, the concept of the Islamic fact/event takes into account that Islam, as a system of belief, has been used for ideological and political purposes in order to legitimize and maintain power. [273]

In her understanding of Arkoun's concepts of Qur'anic fact and Islamic fact, Günther notes that the Qur'an is manipulated by orthodoxy in order to protect ideologies and preserve political interests. The Qur'an becomes a hegemonic text so that it cannot be interpreted differently outside the canon of orthodoxy. Günther understands Arkoun's view that the Qur'an is subject to fixed and monolithic interpretations, making it an established, powerful text used to manipulate individuals in support of political actors, similar to John Armajani, who states that "Arkoun understands the initial revelation of the Qur'an and its subsequent interpretations as existing along a continuum; the interpretations of the Qur'an throughout Islamic history are related to peoples' perceptions of the importance of the book, and individuals who have held power throughout much of Islamic history have utilized their interpretations of the Qur'an to their own advantages."[274]

Arkoun, thus, understands that the Qur'an is manipulated within the framework of orthodoxy. Historically, the Qur'an has been used by orthodox scholars as an instrument of political power and ideology to protect political interests. Indeed, a major criticism of Arkoun's is directed at the political powers that use the Qur'an to protect their political goals and manipulate and control their populations. "Though his focus was Islamic history of ideas, he also gave space to comparative theology, violence and religion, power and hegemony, which are issues that intertwine in making the current Arab world bloody and chaotic. His overall work does not point a (bad)

---

273 Günther 2004 a: 143.
274 Armajani 2004: 116.

finger to the divine *per se*, but to corrupt power that hides behind orthodoxy."[275] Arkoun's project critically engages the Islamist and political ideologies that use religious discourse to secure their extremist and fundamentalist view of Islam. His critique of hegemonic discourse remains compelling in that it establishes a renewed interpretation of Islam that grants Muslim individuals greater rights and freedom. Arkoun makes it clear that the hegemonic discourse is developed not only in the field of religion through the creation of orthodoxy, but also in most nationalist political ideologies that have emerged in the post-colonial era in several Muslim countries.

The hegemonic discourse as an influential factor in the formation of the nationalist discourse in most Muslim countries – The Maghreb

This section examines how nationalist discourse creates internal hegemony in most Muslim countries. Arkoun's work facilitates the redirection of postcolonial debates of the 1950s on Arabo-Islamic reason driven by nationalist and Pan-Arabist political preoccupations.[276] As part of his critique of the nationalist discourses that emerged in most Muslim countries after independence, one can argue that Arkoun intends the nationalist movement of the Maghreb[277] countries in his critique of nationalist discourse.

Historically, the Mediterranean as a unified geo-cultural and mental space has played a marginal role in the Arab-Muslim countries of the eastern and southern regions of the Mediterranean. The intellectual history of these countries was dominated during the second half of the twentieth century by Pan-Arabism and by Islamic perceptions of a cultural and political identity that left little room for the Maghrebian/Mediterranean countries. In general, the idea of a Mediterranean region was common among Arab and Muslim intellectuals with Francophone backgrounds, including Arkoun himself. Arkoun's perception of the Mediterranean was more sophisticated and comprehensive. The most important difference lay in the fact that his views about the Mediterranean were not embedded in national theory, but in the post-national context; Algerian nationalism did not play a significant role, but Islam as part of the Mediterranean identity did.[278] Put simply, by criticizing the hegemonic nationalist discourse that developed in most Muslim countries after independence, Arkoun aims to show that Maghrebian countries have also suffered from nationalism, which may not be accounted for in Arabo-Muslim intellectual history. Thus, he challenges the idea of Arab nationalism, which is restricted to the

---

275   Hashas 2015.
276   Yacoubi 2020: 114.
277   The term "Maghreb" is used here to refer to the western Mediterranean region of coastal North Africa in general, and to Algeria, Morocco, and Tunisia in particular.
278   Abu-Uksa 2011: 178.

well-known nationalist movements in the Arab-Muslim countries of the eastern and southern region of the Mediterranean.

In addition, Arkoun argued in his dissertation (1970) and in *Humanisme et Islam Combat et Proposition* (2008) that the Mediterranean culture of Islam had already experienced humanism in the ninth and tenth centuries. This contradicted the thesis of Jacob Burckhardt, who attributed humanism exclusively to the Renaissance in Western Europe. For Arkoun, religions around the Mediterranean in the tenth century shared a religious humanism that was heavily influenced by Greek philosophy. In the contemporary context, Arkoun uses this historical assertion to argue that Islam does not fundamentally reject philosophy and free thought, but rather shares European modernism – while he retains a critique of the concept of Euromodernism.[279] In this sense, Arkoun sees in the Mediterranean "the epitome of human pluralism and interaction throughout the centuries."[280]

According to Arkoun, the Western Mediterranean region of the Maghreb cannot be subjected to the nationalist and conformist discourse on religion and identity, because nationalism excludes the culture of diversity that characterizes the Maghrebian peoples and civilizations that have populated the Maghreb and shaped its cultural, ethnic and religious pluralism. Arkoun directs his criticism at the conservative and positivist nationalist discourses that are interchangeably involved in the construction of hegemony in most Muslim countries – the Maghreb – through the establishment of religious fundamentalism, closed identities, and intellectual closure. Beyond Arkoun's critique of the discourse of political hegemony, he calls for the creation of a democratic and humanistic ethic that includes respect for different religious beliefs, respect for human dignity and rights.

In his book entitled *Rethinking Islam: Common Questions, Uncommon Answers* (1994), Arkoun defines the notion of nationalism as "the historical and semantic deterioration of a symbolic universe into a collection of signals operating in contemporary societies".[281] Simply put, nationalism is identification with one's nation and support of its interests. Arkoun explores the concept of nationalism as an important political event in the postcolonial history of most Muslim countries. For Arkoun, nationalism promised the suppression of religious and cultural pluralism. Arkoun argues for religious and cultural pluralism rather than identification with only one religion or culture. In doing so, he explores the following question: "Which culture has been supported, chosen and imposed by all the post-colonial states since the 1950s? Is it the emancipating, liberating, liberal, pluralist modern culture, or its antithesis, the ideological, restrictive, alienating, oppressive culture?."[282]

---

279 Abu-Uksa 2011: 178.
280 Hashas 2015.
281 Arkoun 1994: 28.
282 Arkoun 2002 a: 303.

According to Arkoun there are two systems of nationalism: the "so-called national or religious identities" and "those of the already well-established modern democratic regimes."[283] I commence by examining the first model of the conservative nationalist discourse, as Arkoun defines "the so-called Islamic regimes or rather regimes which claim Islam to be the official religion of the state."[284]

The nationalist conservative discourse: The foundation of closed Islamists identities

Arkoun is critical of the nationalist conservative discourse that supports the idea of "'national identities' and 'collective identities' as a springboard for seizing political power."[285] This nationalist conservative discourse fosters "the monolithic closed image of fundamentalist Islam [which] has led to the marginalization, and eventually the elimination, of other cultures, which have been rejected and ignored both by the state policy of education and the powerful political movements of Islamisation of the surviving remnants of idolatry and 'savage' cultures."[286] Consequently, the intellectual implications of fundamentalists and Islamists politic imply that "liberal philosophy and political institutions are rejected and maintained in the domain of the unthinkable, in order to avoid the dissolution of Islamic belief".[287]

One could understand that Arkoun means by the concept of liberal philosophy the ideas of freedom of thought, including freedom of religion beliefs, which allow the creation of cultural and religious diversity in societies. These liberal ideas have not been supported by most nationalist conservative discourse. This is because most Islamic nationalists view liberal ideas as a challenge to their orthodox understanding of Islam in order to protect their political interests. Consequently, most nationalist Muslim elites invoke the experience of the Prophet Muhammad, who had the religious mission of spreading Islam and the political mission of uniting the ummah – the community of Muslims. In this sense, Arkoun argues that Islam celebrated the non-separation between the state and the religion, recognized with the experience of the prophet Muhammad in Medina, where the prophet of Islam intended to establish the ummah. He was a prophet who had a religious mission to spread Islam, and at the same time a political leader the community of Muslims. At that time, Islam was *din-dawla* – religion state.[288]

---

283   Arkoun 2002 a: 299.
284   Arkoun 2002 a: 303.
285   Arkoun 2002 a: 304.
286   Arkoun 2002 a: 303.
287   Arkoun 2002 a: 304.
288   Arkoun 2002 b: 84.

Abdou Filali-Ansary, one of the greatest commentators on the rejection of Islamic religious nationalism and author of an important book on Arkoun's thought, rejects religious nationalism as much as Arkoun did. Filali-Ansary critically examines the concept of the ummah that was used by several Arab nationalists to establish the religious nationalism after independence. In this sense, Filali-Ansary argues that nationalist Islamists give legitimacy to their discourse by invoking the historical, social, and political experiences of the Prophet Muhammad and his principle of building the ummah. Muslim scholars would enforce religious laws in civil affairs to legitimize an Islamist political system.[289]

Filali-Ansary explains that the basis of the theory of ummah is not possible because it refers to the establishment of a political power that was established after the death of the Prophet Muhammad under the political system of the caliphate. Specifically, Filali-Ansary directs his criticism at the monarchy of the caliphate, which turned religious law into a political institution. For Filali-Ansary, the change from co-opted and religiously inspired rulers to a monarchical caliphate is a kind of coup d'état, which is a violation of the principles associated with the advent of Islam and the integrity and freedom of the ummah. For Filali-Ansary, the monarchical system based on the caliphate that ruled over Muslim communities was accepted as more or less inevitable. However, it was not considered entirely legitimate. Over the centuries, the title of caliph lost prestige.[290] In this sense, one can understand that the caliphate system established after the Prophet's death violated the ethics that the Prophet wanted to promote during his lifetime by demanding freedom and equality among Muslims. However, these norms were changed to reduce the Prophet's ethical message after his death to a political message aimed at subjugating Muslims to the caliph's monarchy.

As Arkoun and Filali-Ansary agree, most Muslim nationalists revive the concept of ummah, which is based on the concept of Islamic religious identity as used by the caliphate monarchy to establish an Islamic state and create a modern-political monarchy that is religiously governed. This goes hand in hand with supporting religious orthodoxy by rejecting a rational interpretation of religious discourse.

Völker evaluates Arkoun's critique of Islamist nationalist discourse from two perspectives. On the one hand, she sees that Arkoun believes that nationalism always relies on a mythologized Islam that supports the interpretation of Islam by official religious scholars ('ulama). In this regard, nationalism is a political system favored by numerous Islamic countries, and one such attempt to unite Islamic nations is the establishment of the Arab Islamic League.[291] On the other hand, Völker considers that this creation of Arabo-Islamic unity must be understood

---

289   Filali-Ansary 2012 b: 2–3.
290   Filali-Ansary 2012 b: 1.
291   Völker 2015: 212–213.

as a reaction by Islamic countries to the perceived Western dominance to "cure" Islamic cultures.[292] Simply put, Arabo-Islamic nationalism is a response to Western colonialism, to liberate Islamic cultures from Western imperialism. This could be seen as a right to affirm one independence. But this independence from Western colonization should be based on a greater notion of democracy, guaranteeing human dignity and freedom. As Völker explains, the unification of the Arabo-Muslim community should not be an artificial union imposed on a still illiberal people in whom democratic structures have no future.[293] Following on from this, Arkoun looks for democratic rule to be introduced in most Muslim countries and especially in the Maghreb.

In addition to his criticism of the Islamist nationalist discourse, Arkoun also criticizes the positivist nationalist discourse that aims to create secular and modern Islamic states without improving the right to democracy and freedom of thought and religious beliefs. However, the notion of secularity and modernity that they want to create is still informed by a notion of political despotism when the idea of secularity and modernity coincides with undemocratic rules.

The nationalist positivist discourse: The establishment of a modern political dictatorship

In his article entitled "Positivism and Tradition in an Islamic Perspective" (1984), Arkoun refers to the theory of Kemalism, which can be understood as a reference to the political regime of Mustafa Kemal Atatürk (1881- 1938)[294] in Turkey, during which Atatürk built the modern, secular society. Arkoun critically evaluates the policies of Atatürk, who, in his opinion, promoted a violent model of forced secularization according to the Western values of secularism by eliminating all access to the Islamic heritage.[295] For Arkoun, Kemalism "introduced a certain mobility into political, institutional and cultural life, but at the cost of a serious break with Islamic her-

---

292   Völker 2015: 212–213.
293   Völker 2015: 212–213.
294   Mustafa Kemal Atatürk was a Turkish field marshal, revolutionary statesman, writer, and the founding father of the Republic of Turkey, of which he was the first president from 1923 until his death in 1938. He conducted far-reaching progressive reforms that modernized Turkey into a secular industrial nation. An ideological secularist and nationalist, his policies and sociopolitical theories became known as Kemalism. Because of his military and political achievements, Atatürk is considered one of the most important political leaders of the 20th century. See: Cuthell Jr., David Cameron (2009). "Atatürk, Kemal (Mustafa Kemal)": In Ágoston, Gábor and Masters, Bruce (eds.). Encyclopedia of the Ottoman Empire. New York: Facts On File, Inc. pp. 56–60.
295   Arkoun 1984: 97.

itage."²⁹⁶ Arkoun defines the Islamic heritage as a religious fact. In this sense, the religious fact means that religion is an essential part of the cultural and social heritage of the population and therefore cannot be displaced from the life of the people. One can understand that Arkoun criticizes Atatürk's regime for promoting secularism, a product of the French system, by completely rejecting and excluding religion. An essential part of Arkoun's position is his rejection of secular thought *which denies the existence of religion as an essential phenomenon*. Völker convincingly explains Arkoun's concept of secularism as follows:

> Reflecting on a potential frame for a civilian society, Arkoun is indeed sceptical about French laicism, or 'militant secularism.' However, he was a member of the 'Committee for Laicism' in France. Arkoun's view on secularism is mainly a critique of the idea that separating state and religion on legal and administrative levels is at all possible because religion still influences society. He is not denying the need for such artificial divisions, but he calls for a secularism which is not blind to the religious fact as social fact.²⁹⁷

One can realize that Arkoun has an ambivalent view of secularity. On the one hand, he believes that secularism is essential for the separation between politics and religions and, thus, for the improvement of civil rules and liberal thought. On the other hand, Arkoun rejects secularism in the sense of a complete rejection of religious fact, which he considers part of social reality, and which cannot be successfully denied. In this context, Arkoun argues that "France is not truly enlightened since it actively and forcefully opposes public expressions of faith."²⁹⁸ For Arkoun, therefore, a state that promotes the ideas of the Enlightenment should respect the freedom of religious belief as seen by Enlightenment philosophers as its foundation.

In the same line of explication, Völker understands that for Arkoun "a truly enlightened state should be aware of the religious fact (*fait religieux*) and its mechanisms within society and does not on the contrary chose to ignore or even fight it."²⁹⁹ Following on from this, I would like to elaborate on Arkoun's concept of secularism. Specifically, I pose the following question: How can Arkoun argue for secularism while holding on to the idea of religion if secularism is understood to mean the separation of state and religion, or in its radical sense, a complete rejection of religious belief?

---

296   Arkoun 1984: 97.
297   Völker 2015: 212.
298   Arkoun 1994: 77.
299   Völker 2015: 211.

Toward an understanding of Arkoun's ambivalent concept of secularity based on the recognition of the religious fact

In an important article entitled "Mohammed Arkoun ou l'ambition d'une modernité intellectuelle" (1993), Mohammed el-Ayadi examines Arkoun's secular concept in a remarkable approach, presenting Arkoun's concept of humanist laicity as protecting the right to religious belief. In this context, el-Ayadi notes that Arkoun urges distinguishing between the concept of laicity and that of laicism. In fact, Arkoun uses the term laicism, just outlined, to refer to a 'militant laicism' that consists of rejecting religion. According to el-Ayadi, Arkoun does not adopt a notion of laicism in the sense of a radical rejection of religion. Rather, he openly advocates a concept of laicity that respects the freedom of religious belief.

Arkoun, thus, strives for a humanist laicity in the public space of civil society. Humanist laicity means that citizens of different religious beliefs can live together and that equal and common rules should apply to protect the social and political interests and rights of citizens regardless of their religious, ethnic and cultural affiliations.[300] Consequently, humanist laicity differs from laicism in that it respects people's religious diversity and does not require rejection of religious belief. Importantly, according to Arkoun, the concept of a humanistic laicity, as seen by el-Ayadi, requires a critical sense of religious orthodoxy in order to take root. Indeed, a humanist laicity opposes religious discourses that do not promote critical thinking toward religious orthodoxy.[301]

In other words, promoting critical thinking over religious orthodoxy would help get rid of the manipulated understanding of religious discourse established by official religious scholars who promote patriarchal and fundamentalist ideas about Islam to secure political power and use Islam for political purposes. The importance of humanism here is seen in the ability of individuals to use their reason to rationally rethink religious discourse. Further promotion of renewal interpretations in religious discourse could eventually lead to a situation where different faiths and religious beliefs are no longer seen as a threat to each other but rather serve to preserve democratic rules. One interpretation of the Islamic legacy is based on respect for other religious beliefs and a view of democracy, for example, in the Islamic legal notion of the common good (*maslaha*); the protection of individual freedom and rights. Of course, other reformist thinkers have long invoked Islamic precedents (especially in the Qur'an) to legitimize or reject democracy.

Furthermore, one can argue that Arkoun's concept of humanist laicity is consistent with the philosophy of Enlightenment. To this end, I explain Arkoun's idea of Enlightenment, which he understands as emancipation from religious orthodoxy

---

300   El-Ayadi 1993: 69.
301   El-Ayadi 1993: 69.

and obscurantism in order to create democratic societies where religious pluralism and cultural diversity are respected. In this context, Arkoun introduces the concept of autonomy of reason as one of the three major directions of the development and expansion of Enlightenment philosophy. He argues:

> The conquest of the autonomy of reason relative to the dogmatic excesses of religion; socially, in Europe, this meant the rise of a liberal bourgeoisie which tended to secularize institutions and to struggle with the clergy and the nobility for power over them. [302]

Arkoun emphasizes that Enlightenment thought limits religious dogmatism and celebrates the autonomy of reason. The autonomy of reason could be useful in liberating Muslims from the political monarchy that uses religion to maintain power. Unlike the European Enlightenment, which was led by the bourgeoisie, Arkoun believes that the revolution against dogmatism and political monarchy should be shared, generated and spread by all people and without discrimination. The right to enlightenment should be a global and collective right. People need the right to think and free their minds from religious dogmatism to be autonomous. This leads to a great egalitarian achievement in the intellectual field of education and society and enriches the critical thinking of individuals. In this context, el-Ayadi notes that for Arkoun, the emergence of an intellectual revolution should be grounded in the participation of all social classes.[303]

In addition, one can insert that Arkoun prompts the principle of autonomy of reason to argue that it is the basis for the emancipation of the Muslim individual from the constraints of orthodoxy, defined earlier. Autonomy of reason is to challenge the dogmatic and tyrannical notion of religion, manipulated by the official religious scholars. The autonomy of reason is not foreign to rational Islamic thought. Thus, it is presented under the quest of (*ijtihad*), the intellectual struggle, which encourages rational deliberation and the use of individual reason to interpret the religious discourse (see 3.1 and 3.2). For Arkoun, the Enlightenment project is a crucial intellectual and political event that could be used to promote the ideas of democracy, including freedom of thought, belief, and equality in the postcolonial era.

Arkoun repeatedly refers to the adventure of secularism in Turkey during Atatürk's regime, noting that this secular model was not aimed at promoting Enlightenment values based on the promotion of democracy in societies. Hence, the most poorly studied aspect of this great historic adventure is no doubt the effective place of Islam in Turkish society compared to the perception which Atatürk and

---

302   Arkoun 1984: 84–85.
303   El-Ayadi 1993: 67.

his partisans had of it. Most authors – Turkish or Western– have allowed themselves to be enclosed in tenacious ideological oppositions such as religion and secularism, tradition and modernity, the Ottoman decadence and the power of the Western model, Islamic conservatism and the progress of civilization, etc.[304] Consequently, the so-called modern secular political regimes after independence are determined by the absence of rethinking the Islamic religion in order to free Islamic thought from dogmatism; the absence of psychological, cultural, historical or anthropological studies that would allow a strong link between the philosophy of the Enlightenment and the message of Islam; and the absence of speaking of an inner necessity in Islamic civilization that could explain the constant confusion between secular and religious authorities. [305]

Arkoun examines the modern nationalist system through the example of the theory of Kemalism to confirm that laicity requires the autonomy of reason as a central principle of Enlightenment thought in order to be successful. This allows individuals to think critically and independently. Secularism cannot be improved by forcibly rejecting religion in societies where dictatorship still manipulates the right of individuals to express their thoughts differently.

There remains a comment directed against Arkoun's ambivalent concept of secularism: Völker calls Arkoun's relationship to secularism a love-hate relationship,[306] meaning that Arkoun does not take a clear position on the concept of secularism, i.e., whether he believes that religion must be banished from human societies for good, or whether he finds another, nuanced form of secularism in which religion need not be completely disavowed.

To respond to this comment, one could argue that Arkoun develops his ideas on secularity further, conceding that religion is an inherent feature of society, in 1994 when he discovers the ethical and political thought of Jürgen Habermas. Arkoun argues:

> To follow this complex and ambitious course, one should at the outset elaborate the circumstances in which modern thinking is debated, putting theoretical knowledge in critical perspective. A reference to the critical analysis of Jürgen Habermas on the "philosophical discourse of modernity" should suffice to indicate the size of the task I am targeting.[307]

Indeed, Habermas, one of Europe's leading secular liberal thinkers, argues in his article entitled "Secularism's Crisis of Faith" (2008):

---

304 Arkoun 1984: 83.
305 Arkoun 1984: 87.
306 Völker 2015: 211.
307 Arkoun 1994: 114.

> Secular citizens in civil society and the political public sphere must be able to meet their religious fellow citizens as equals. ... So, if all is to go well, both sides, each from their own viewpoint, must accept an interpretation of the relation between faith and knowledge that enables them to live together in a self-reflective manner.[308]

Taking a comparative approach, one could argue that Arkoun joins Habermas in advocating a non-rejection of religion, thus, affirming the democratic right to protect religious pluralism. Habermas affirms that citizens in civil society should freely express their religious beliefs and that citizens should be treated equally despite their different religious affiliations. This contributes to peaceful participation in the public sphere. In our contemporary times, Arkoun's approach of humanist laicity and Habermas's notion of post-secularity are attractive for those who wish to unite and embrace pluralism and live in a dynamic democracy. Nevertheless, the notion of post-secularity cannot work when professing a religious position in a thoroughly secularized world – as in the case of Islam in European countries – can be a dangerous undertaking. It is an even greater problem when the faith one professes is viewed as suspect or threatened by the dominant group within one's own society. When a community's deeply held beliefs, the basis of its identity, spiritual life, and cultural norms, are seen as backward, oppressive, undemocratic, and unenlightened, it is easy for that community to internalize these accusations and to close itself off in its religious lifeworld, refusing to engage with the broader society in a non-antagonistic and/or open way. [309]

The divergence between Arkoun's and Habermas's conceptions of secularity is that Habermas relates his thoughts about post-secular rules to the European Christian community, which comes from an Enlightenment heritage and is accustomed to religion's reform. As Arkoun says, "Christian theology had to cope with the challenges and political revolutions initiated by a dynamic capitalist bourgeoisie and the efficient alternatives offered by reason of enlightenment."[310] In contrast, Arkoun directs his notion of humanist secularity to most Muslim countries, where the understanding of Islam is not linked to religious reformation and is in tension with the rational heritage of Islam. In this context, Arkoun states:

> In the case of Islamic thought, the triumph of two major official orthodoxies with the Sunnis (since the fifth century Hijra) and the Shi'a (first with the Fatimids and second with the Safavids in Iran) imposed a mode of thinking narrower than those illustrated in the classical period (first to fifth century Hijra). Contemporary Islamic thought is under the influence of categories, themes, beliefs, and

---

308   Habermas 2008: 29.
309   Byrd 2017: 3–4.
310   Arkoun 2002 a: 206.

procedures of reasoning developed during the scholastic age (seventh to eighth century Hijra) more than it is open to the pluralism which characterized classical thought.[311]

The dogmatic closure of Islamic thought remains relevant. As I have explained, Islamic thought is dominated by a hegemony that codifies orthodoxy, which has implications for the future construction of cultural, political, and social actors in the postcolonial era. In this context, Arkoun argues that most postcolonial nationalist leaders prioritize pragmatic action over political control to protect their authoritarian regimes.[312] Arkoun goes on to claim that authoritarian regimes manipulate human reason by creating an epistemological break not only with Enlightenment thought but also with early Islamic humanism. This means that they are creating a rupture with the most important studies that deal with rational Islamic thought.[313]

Arkoun borrows the notion of epistemological break from Gaston Bachelard, who assumes that scientific progress always reveals a break, or constant ruptures, between ordinary knowledge and scientific knowledge.[314] Arkoun presents this distinction of knowledge as a break between the rational and orthodox interpretations of Islam. What Arkoun means by the epistemological break, then, is the interruption of Islamic thought with the philosophical and scientific achievements of its humanistic heritage. Islamic thought at the time of its humanistic framework explored a variety of topics with different emphases. It dealt with strictly religious matters, ethics, jurisprudence, politics, social and economic questions, theology, and philosophy. Linguistics, esthetics (literature, music, painting, and architecture), science and technology, and history, geography, and cosmogony were other fields of inquiry.[315]

Arkoun, thus, invokes the great intellectual and scientific achievements of early Islamic thought to argue that they are indispensable to the progress of contemporary Arab-Islamic thought in order to promote its participation in the current age of modernization. In fact, the epistemological break with the rational Islamic thought led most Islamic countries to be dependent on the hegemony of Euro-modernism. This will be explored below.

---

311   Arkoun 2003: 27.
312   Arkoun 1984: 86.
313   Arkoun 1984: 86.
314   Bachelard 1938–2002: 5.
315   Arkoun 1977: 19.

Arkoun's concept of intellectual modernity: As a critique of the subordination of most Muslim societies to Euro-modernity-centrism

Here I introduce Arkoun's concept of intellectual modernity as a counterpart to the concept of material modernity[316] or civilization, i.e., a concept of materialism. As explained above, Arkoun criticizes orthodoxy in religious discourse as well as religious fundamentalism and political dictatorship in nationalist discourse. Arkoun proposes a notion of secularism as a humanistic concept that guarantees religious freedom and respect for pluralism. In the following I explore Arkoun's critique of the subordination of most Muslim societies to Euro-modernism hegemony. According to Arkoun, 'Euro-modernism' in the materialist sense has emerged within the capitalist system and prevents poor, underdeveloped countries from participating in and contributing to global economic and scientific development. As a result, most underdeveloped countries remain economically dependent on rich and developed nations. In this way, the underdeveloped countries are controlled by the dominant countries and are subject to their economic and political systems. This leads to an unjust global power system in which the center of the globe dominates the periphery.

Arkoun criticizes the manipulation of industrialized countries at the global level of political and economic spheres, and does not attempt to accept the fate of most Muslim societies as a destination of control and subjugation to Eurocentric modernity. Rather, he seeks to liberate most Muslim countries from this manipulation, invoking his concept of intellectual modernity, which he uses to encourage most Muslim individuals to embrace the positive aspects of modernity based on scientific and intellectual inquiry. Importantly, Arkoun directs his critique at the culture of materialism in which most Muslim societies are enmeshed; he sees that they are large consumers of Western products and unable to contribute to global cultural, scientific, and economic production.

In this context, and in order to establish a notion of justice on a global scale, Arkoun understands that a notion of intellectual modernity should be introduced in most Muslim societies, and especially in the Maghreb, in order to participate in and contribute to global economic and scientific development. He believes that most Muslim societies are still dependent on developed European countries because the concept of modernity, as they have realized it, is based on consumption without participating in economic and scientific development themselves. Arkoun believes that the economic achievements of Europeans were built gradually, starting with

---

316 Arkoun uses the term "material modernity" in his book (1994). In his article (2003), he uses the term "material civilization." Both terms are used to criticize different forms of neo-capitalism.

3. Background and methods in the thought of Mohammed Arkoun 239

religious reforms, scientific advances in various fields and disciplines, and finally through industrial progress. In this sense, he argues:

> Intellectual modernity started with Renaissance and Reform movements in sixteenth-century Europe. The study of pagan antiquity and the demand for freedom to read the Bible without the mediation of priests (or "managers of the sacred," as they are sometimes called) changed the conditions of intellectual activities. Later, scientific discoveries, political revolutions, secularized knowledge, and historically criticized knowledge (historicism practiced as philosophies of history) changed more radically the whole intellectual structure of thought for the generations involved in the Industrial Revolution with its continuous consequences.[317]

As can be understood, Arkoun relies on the concept of modernity in the sense of intellectual achievements in various fields. For Arkoun, religious reform, the freedom to interpret and reform religious discourse, and, thus, the emancipation of religious discourse from the power of religious authority are the first steps on the road to intellectual modernity. In his view, most Muslim countries do not promote such reform because they cling to the tradition of closing the gate of interpretation of religious discourse that has been followed through the 12 centuries of Islam (see 3.2), when religious discourse was manipulated by religious orthodoxy. As a result, most Muslim societies have been cut off from scientific progress. In this context, Arkoun explains:

> This evolution was achieved in Europe without any participation of Islamic thought or Muslim societies dominated, on the contrary, by a rigid, narrow conservatism. This is why Muslims do not feel concerned by the secularized culture and thought produced since the sixteenth century. It is legitimate, in this historical process leading to intellectual modernity, to differentiate between the ideological aspects limited to the conjunctural situations of Western societies and the anthropological structures of knowledge discovered through scientific research. Islamic thought has to reject or criticize the former and to apply the latter in its own contexts.[318]

For Arkoun, the key to intellectual modernity lies in the promotion of scientific research. Scientific research is essential to understanding the anthropological structure of knowledge; for example, understanding how religious discourse has been rigorously structured by orthodox assertions. It is important to note that Arkoun highlights the need to reform and rethink religious discourse as a key feature of his contemporary intellectual project. For Arkoun, the emancipation of Islamic thought

---

317 Arkoun 2003: 27–28.
318 Arkoun 2003: 27–28.

from orthodoxy is the cornerstone for the creation of a modern intellectual Muslim society that can contribute to global scientific progress.

As explained above, however, for Arkoun, intellectual modernity does not take place in most Muslim societies; rather, a sense of material modernity has taken hold. Most Muslim societies are described as being on the periphery, outside the global center of economic development and scientific research. According to Arkoun, material modernity or material civilization becomes threatening when it has capitalist and materialist effects on societies that are outside the modernization process.[319]

In this context, Arkoun points to the concept of material modernity or material civilization, referring to its elaboration by Fernand Braudel. With this concept, Braudel draws attention to those societies that stand outside the formal process of economic production, referring to them as expressions of material life or material civilization.[320]

Moreover, Arkoun believes that material modernity or civilization not only has a significant impact on the subordination and submission of most Muslim countries to Euro-modernity, but also replaces Islamic values of human solidarity and hospitality with a materialism that is a culture of consumption. As a result, most people are more interested in how to get rich than in cultivating their minds toward an ethical and intellectual perspective. Arkoun underscores this point in his statement:

> Material modernity has disrupted traditional solidarities and replaced values of fidelity, loyalty, mutual assistance, unconditional solidarity, constancy, generosity, hospitality, and respect for promises, human dignity, and the property of others with strategies of getting rich quickly, for social and economic ascent, and for gaining power.[321]

Consequently, El-Ayadi points to Arkoun's critique of the material modernity that characterizes most Muslim societies, as most Muslims are subjected to material consumption and modernity is reduced to its material aspects.[322]

Arkoun believes that Muslim countries can emancipate themselves from material modernity by participating in global scientific progress. To this end, Arkoun argues for a modernity based on scientific and intellectual achievement, rather than a modernity based on materialism and exclusion of others, and for a humanistic and ethical project based on the concepts of solidarity and hospitality. With his ethical and humanistic project, he wants to unite the South and the North of the world by overturning the power relations that define our world today.

---

319   Arkoun 2003: 39 fn. 6.
320   Braudel 1992: 23.
321   Arkoun 1994: 118.
322   El-Ayadi 1993: 69.

In this chapter, I have examined Arkoun's critique of the hegemonic discourse that shapes the fields of religion and politics in most postcolonial countries in the Arab world and also gives rise to Western Eurocentrism. According to Arkoun, hegemonic discourse has several manifestations: It shapes religious discourse by organizing orthodoxy, it determines nationalist discourse by ordering religious identities, and it establishes authoritarian regimes by promoting enforced secularism. The hegemonic discourse also determines Euro-modernism, in which there is no equal contribution and participation in global economic development and scientific research. Thus, Arkoun proposes the concepts of humanistic secularity and intellectual modernity to emancipate Islamic thought from the hegemony of the aforementioned constructions of religion and politics. His innovative thought on secularity and modernity is crucial in today's global world for creating democratic societies where pluralism and global economic and epistemic justice are promoted. Arkoun's concept of humanistic secularity aims to promote the right to freedom of belief, which is one of the cornerstones of democracy and leads to people with different religious beliefs being able to live together in an atmosphere of tolerance and acceptance of each other's differences. His concept of intellectual modernity is an emancipatory key to initiate the participation and contribution of the Global South to global economic and scientific development. In this sense, one can argue with Mohammed Hashas, who claims that "Arkoun needs to be our companion in building a tolerant and ethicist future – "our" here stands for "we" especially the Mediterraneanists, Arabs, Europeans, etc.".[323] Consequently, Arkoun's intellectual project is crucial to rejecting racism and global injustice in the contemporary era as he seeks to create a culture of solidarity, hospitality, and tolerance. As just outlined, in the final chapter of this part of the study, Arkoun's concept of emerging reason is explored in more detail as an analysis of his democratic and cosmopolitan project.

3.4 The concept of emerging reason: A key for a democratic and cosmopolitan project

This final chapter addresses Arkoun's concept of emerging reason and explores his intellectual, democratic and cosmopolitan project. I have chosen to examine Arkoun's concept of emerging reason in order to systematically trace his thought because I understand that Arkoun's agenda to rethink Islamic thought prepares the ground to launch his project of emerging reason which he introduced in 1996.[324] As a result of his emancipatory endeavor to liberate Islamic thought from the hegemonic constructs of orthodoxy, nationalism, and materialism, Arkoun develops the

---

323   Hashas 2015.
324   Kersten 2011: 35.

concept of emerging reason in his final writing. According to this view, emerging reason is a new reason that emerges from the rethinking of Islamic thought. Emerging reason is the product of applied Islamology (see 3.2), in the sense that it is a liberated reason, free from monolithic constructions about Islam and rigid traditions. Emerging reason in itself represents Arkoun's democratic and cosmopolitan project, which calls for dialogue and solidarity between different cultures.

The chapter is divided into two sections: First, I introduce the concept of emerging reason. The focus is on examining the epistemological and cognitive strategies that emerging reason employs, based on philosophical inquiry, to open thinking to broader perspectives and to develop an understanding that different cultures and nations can interact. Emerging reason, thus, represents Arkoun's humanist attitude based on rational and philosophical frameworks that aim to critique the canons of religious discourse and secular reason. "This concept was characterized by humanist, pluralistic and decentralized leanings that broke with the Euro-centrism of modernity."[325] Thus, I show that the concept of emerging reason embodies a notion of an epistemic and relational solidarity project and of transculturality between different philosophical traditions in order to deconstruct knowledge from a Eurocentric perspective. In this sense, emerging reason is an ethical concept that gives marginalized and silenced traditions of thought the right to emerge and speak.

The second section deals with the new ethos Arkoun wants to build on the basis of his humanistic attitude. His new ethos is based on interrelated concepts that promote a way of life guided by moral principles that favors the harmonious coexistence of people from different cultures and religious traditions in civil societies. Three concepts are presented: *the concept of individual autonomy*, which promotes democratic rights to freedom of thought and belief, which involves ending the triad of violence, sacredness, and truth. Violence serves as a means of expressing fundamentalist and extremist principles rather than promoting dialogue. The sacred is therefore not oriented toward critical thinking and leads to dogmatism and orthodoxy within religion, a concept that Arkoun sharply criticizes (see 3.3). Truth means that everyone believes every discourse to be true and believes in it, which leads to individuals dogmatically believing in their own thinking as the truth without considering or accepting the opinions of others.

The concept of community is intermingled with the concept of individual autonomy, which also preserves the notions of democratic rules. Arkoun builds his notion of community based on civil society, where human rights to freedom of thought and belief are respected. These notions should be established by breaking with the notion of religious orthodoxy (see 3.3) and the social imaginary, which does not reflect

---

325 Abu-Uksa 2011: 177.

on the reality of the society, but rather represents the system that determines the social structure of the collective community. Importantly, Arkoun bases his concept of community as free of orthodoxy and social imaginary on a historical epistemological approach by reviving early Islamic thought of the 10th century in which rationality was pitted against traditionalism and dogmatism.

After liberating the individual from the prevailing religious orthodoxy and socio-cultural traditional systems and building democratic rules based on freedom of thought and freedom of religious belief, Arkoun's third concept, the *concept of cosmopolitanism*, seeks to cultivate a notion of dialogue and recognition between different cultures and religious traditions. Arkoun bases cosmopolitanism on interreligious dialogue – a concept he defends together with participants from different religions. Thus, interreligious dialogue is a promising antidote to religious fanaticism and extremism, which lead to conflicting ideological systems between people of different faiths in which one religion is considered superior to another and lays claim to absolute, sacred truth, while other religions are inferior or distort the function of their holy book.

A global dialogue between religions requires that people with different religious traditions from around the world come together to discuss the ethical commonalities that unite them rather than divide them. In this way, it is possible to achieve a humanistic attitude of tolerance and justice by not discriminating between ethnicities, cultures and religions, and by being open and understanding of differences. This would promote a peaceful environment between people, especially when it comes to religious beliefs, because religions are often the root of conflicts, especially when they are misused for purely political purposes.

Emerging reason: The need to adopt a different worldview, or *Weltanschauung*

The concept of emerging reason contrasts with the binary division of the global order into North and South. It embodies a new way of thinking that aims to accommodate diverse opinions and incorporate different philosophical traditions of thought. The concept of emerging reason is brought forth in the introduction of *The Unthought in Contemporary Islamic Thought* (2002 a). Arkoun identifies the concept of emerging reason as following:

> Emerging Reason goes beyond the punctual, particular methodological improvements actualized in some fields of research, or in some disciplines applied to the study of different aspects of Islam and other non-Western cultures. It is concerned with the philosophical subversion of the use of reason itself and all forms of rationality produced so far and those which will be produced in the future so

as not to repeat the ideological compromises and derivations of the precedent postures and performances of reason."[326]

Emerging reason is a critical reason that opposes hegemonic reason (see 3.3). As mentioned in chapter two, hegemonic reason mostly creates three modes of thinking to manipulate reason: religious discourse, nationalist discourse, and Euro-modernist discourse. Emerging reason seeks to liberate Islamic thought from the constructs of hegemonic reason and to connect it to other fields of philosophical inquiry, particularly poststructuralist/deconstructionist approaches (see 3.2). Emerging reason is an approach to thought that Arkoun advocates as the future reason of Islam because it is free from the ideological manipulations that orthodoxy has produced in the past. According to Arkoun, the establishment of an emancipatory reason depends on the contribution of social and political scholars who use philosophical approaches to critically challenge the prevailing construction that manipulates Islamic thought. In this regard, he states

> Social and political scientists are supposed to share this fundamental concern [of using philosophical thought to examine the dominant epistemological postures of reason] not only in their contributions to theoretical confrontations, but even more in the process of working out their concepts and articulating their discourse.[327]

For Arkoun, the interweaving of emerging reason is a philosophical task of solidarity. It relies on philosophers from different schools of thought and traditions to participate in the task of liberating the humanities from hegemonic constructions. Emerging reason is a reason that is in harmony with its time, which deals with its problems and advocates the emancipation of human beings. This reason pushes aside the prejudices and transcends the canons and established genres.[328]

Arkoun notes, however, that "many western philosophers, not to mention the vast majority of scholars, limit their epistemological control to the western historical logosphere."[329] Arkoun's point is that some Western philosophers are unwilling to leave the canon, applying conventional and centered interpretation and conceptualization over other cultures and traditions of thought. Consequently, Arkoun urges some western philosophers to open their worldview to other cultures and philosophies. He suggests that intellectuals of the world should make their "common *weltanschauung* ... criticized, revised, opened."[330] In order to create a project of solidar-

---

326 Arkoun 2002 a: 23–24.
327 Arkoun 2002 a: 24.
328 El-Hassan 2019: 118.
329 Arkoun 2002 a: 24.
330 Arkoun 2002 a: 24.

ity between different schools of thought and to engage in a transcultural dialogue, philosophers must abandon their constructed view of other traditions of thought that differ from their own.

From that perspective, the concept of Weltanschauung traces its origins to Immanuel Kant and his notion of a world concept, or Weltbgriff. "This term functioned as an idea of pure reason to bring the totality of human experience into the unity of a world-whole, or Weltganz."[331] One can argue that the concept of Weltanschauung is similar to Arkoun's concept of emerging reason, as the creation of integrating and uniting dialogue between different cultures. This is an important assessment illustrating that Arkoun relates this concept to that of overcoming the idea of reason or thought exclusively related to one dominant tradition or system of thought, by delaying and excluding other philosophical traditions. In addition, Arkoun refers to the concept of worldview to give voice to marginalized and silent people. By defending the rights of oppressed and marginalized groups to be heard and to express themselves, emerging reason itself embodies an emancipatory and just reason. According to Arkoun, "We have to be able to hear voices reduced to silence, heterodox voices, minority voices, the voices of the vanquished and the marginalized, if we are to develop a reason capable of encompassing the human condition."[332]

In other words, the concept of emerging reason is a global reason, as it includes all humans to engage in a promising transcultural dialogue about the future of humanity from a global perspective. Furthermore, emerging reason goes hand in hand with what Arkoun calls a humanistic attitude. This is a democratic practice and consists in subjecting everything to criticism, including fundamentalist and orthodox religious beliefs and enforced secular reason.[333] Emerging reason can be understood as a critique of enforced secular reason, which aims to ignore religion as an essential component of human mentality and society, so that it cannot simply be denied (see 3.3). The exercise of forced secularism means denying individuals the right to practice their religious beliefs democratically. As argued in chapter three, the right to practice a religious belief goes hand in hand with the subjugation of religious discourse itself to criticism in order to free it from fundamentalist and orthodox frameworks.

This prompted me to recall Arkoun's humanistic stance developed in his dissertation (1970) on Miskawayh (see 3.1). Arkoun's humanistic stance is based on subjecting religious discourse to criticism and rational thought as a philosophical framework. That is, the humanist stance is based on philosophical approaches to reason that guarantee a rational understanding of religious discourse in order to overcome the dogmatic closure of thought.

---

331   Naugle 2002: 9.
332   Arkoun 2002 a: 22.
333   El-Hassan 2019: 119.

Arkoun links his contemporary intellectual project to the idea that Islamic thought must free itself from orthodoxy and hegemony in order to be rethought. Consequently, the rationalist-humanist stance to liberate Islamic thought goes hand in hand with emerging reason. In addition, the liberation of Islamic thought paves the way for the development of democratic and cosmopolitan attitudes. Ali Mirsepassi also supports this claim. He comments on Arkoun's concept of emerging reason as a reconstruction of democracy and cosmopolitan attitudes, affirming that Arkoun's "project of cosmopolitan and democratic restructuring of collective belief is idealized through hopes for Emerging Reason."[334]

Arkoun's democratic and cosmopolitan project: The emergence of a new ethos

For Arkoun, emerging reason is only possible after freeing Islamic thought from hegemonic constructs. A key principle of emerging reason is the liberation of thought from established ideas systematized and ordered by hegemonic structures (see 3.3), with the aim of promoting transcultural dialogue between different philosophies and ways of thinking.

This could be done through the mediation of a global and transcultural approach, which should be realized through the formation of new ethos. Arkoun's new ethos is about promoting democratic and humanistic attitudes based on the autonomy of the individual; the right to individual thought and free choice; the coexistence of people from different cultures and religions; the right to criticize and interpret religious discourse in a way that ensures peace within the framework of religion; and interreligious dialogue.

First, one can understand that the formation of democratic societies, in which *individual autonomy* is an essential characteristic, leads individuals to think freely without depending on traditions and belief systems. Individual autonomy enables individuals to join with others and contribute to a creative dialogue that is free from the prejudices of cultural stereotypes and clichés. In this sense, according to Arkoun, humanism is crucial in creating a global interaction between different individuals from different cultural traditions so that they can interact globally.[335]

With the term humanism, Arkoun emphasizes that individuals should come together despite their religious, cultural and traditional differences. Arkoun is a humanist thinker influenced by the Louis Massignon tradition of political action committed to the peaceful coexistence of different peoples and religions.[336] However, the construction of societies in which individuals can interact and coexist despite their

---

334 Mirsepassi 2014 b: 146.
335 Arkoun 2002 a: 255.
336 Mirsepassi 2014 b: 136.

differences is implemented through the self-determination of individuals to make their own choices and shape their destinies. As Arkoun explains, the autonomous person is "free in his choices and commitments to lead his own existence in solidarity with his society and change in the modern world."[337] The coexistence of and solidarity between different individuals, despite their different religious and cultural traditions, could be strengthened by the principle of criticism of the triangle of "violence, sacred, truth."[338] In Arkoun's words: "It is certainly the relationship between violence, sacred, and truth that has mobilized men for millennia and continues to arouse them against false divinities in the name of the one true God."[339]

In other words: Taking all religious traditions as God's word and religious truth leads to orthodox beliefs and to people holding on to their beliefs without considering alternative perspectives in religious debate. In the following, I explain what Arkoun means by violence, sacred and truth, which do not allow the democratic principle of individual autonomy and, thus, the coexistence of people of different cultures and religious beliefs. Arkoun criticizes the concept of violence, which he believes is a fundamental threat to the peaceful coexistence of people of different cultures and religions.

The violence arises when people use the language of terror and fundamentalism against each other instead of choosing a culture of dialogue and intellectual debate. This points to the dangers of violence and abuse of power in collective mobilization strategies. Arkoun's political individualism, however, is not based on the solitary ego associated with intellectual virtue, but on a notion of Enlightenment humanism based on the self-forming civic community.[340]

The civic community is used here to describe individuals who have official status, enjoy rights, and live together in a community. The civic community is set in a humanistic atmosphere where people of different cultures and religions cohabit and coexist together. In addition to the concept of violence, there are other threats to peaceful coexistence caused by the phenomenon of the sacred. The sacred is the unthinkable, which cannot be evaluated or criticized. It is a dogmatic way of thinking, in which thinking ceases to develop its ability to open the sacred to rational examination. The sacred is seen as justified because it expresses the orthodox and conventional belief systems and traditional discourses that people believe in and accept without critical reason. When people hold to their dogmatic belief in the sacred, there is no openness to other perspectives that question the sacred, so interreligious dialogue is not possible.

---

337   Arkoun 2002 a: 255.
338   Arkoun 2002 a: 284.
339   Arkoun 2002 a: 255.
340   Mirsepassi 2014 b: 136.

Similarly, the concept of truth is linked to the concepts of violence and the sacred, which makes coexistence impossible. By truth, Arkoun means precisely the "ultimate truth"[341], i.e. absolute truth, which makes rethinking Islam as a religious and cultural framework impossible. Ultimate truth leads to dogmatism and orthodox thinking, when each individual believes in his or her own sacred aspect of thought, which prevents interaction with others and examination of what they believe to be true. In contrast to the dangerous and conventional notions of violence, the sacred, and truth, Arkoun proposes a humanistic ethos based on the autonomy of the individual and freedom of thought and belief, allowing interaction between people of different cultures and religious beliefs.

Second, Arkoun wants to establish a democratic concept of *community*, which is supported by civil society and is to be based on the individual's right to freedom of thought. This is a democratic pillar and essential for the emancipation of the individual from the orthodoxy established in religious discourse. In this regard, Arkoun explains that, without the freedom to think, to explore, publish, and debate previously forbidden fields of research, the horizons of interpretation and spiritual investment of what he called religious discourse could never be properly expanded.[342] Arkoun is aware that the freedom of thought, and the freedom of intellectual research are important to open the religious discourse – which is a hegemonic discourse (see 3.3) – with the means of criticism and examination.

Arkoun's concept of a community based on the individual's right to freedom of thought, however, is at odds with the concept of a community built on collective societal and cultural traditions. Arkoun believes that in the modern democratic context, it is imperative to deconstruct societal and cultural traditions in order to introduce a concept of critical thinking so that emancipated identities can emerge.[343]

As mentioned earlier, Islamic thought is maintained by the hegemonic construction of orthodoxy as the societal and cultural traditions that constitute the social imaginary. In this sense, Arkoun argues that it is wrong to consider the "thinkable" as the only aspect of the "historical development of a tradition of thought."[344] For the thinkable is dominated by the social imaginary, which ensures that "every period of thought is marked by the limitations of the unthinkable and the unthought."[345]

Arkoun implies that religious thought must be free and subject to renewed interpretation. This leads to detaching the religious thought from the driving force of

---

341 Günther 2013: 65.
342 Arkoun 2002 b: 89.
343 Mirsepassi 2014 b: 136–137.
344 Arkoun 2002 a: 75.
345 Arkoun 2002 a: 95.

the social imaginary, but only if the triangle of violence, sacred, truth [as previously explained] is broken.[346]

I have discussed Arkoun's claim that religious thought must be reconsidered in order to free it from orthodoxy and traditional thinking. Arkoun believes that religious thought is manipulated by a social imaginary. He follows Castoriadis, who criticized the self-proclaimed "natural status" (i.e., necessity) of the modern secular imaginary as a value-neutral category.[347] Castoriadis denounces the imaginary of modern secular thought, which establishes its superiority as derivative of the Western colonial legacy and the dominant narrative thought that has influenced and shaped the imagination of most modern states. Likewise, Arkoun condemns both the secular coercive thought that has taken root in most postcolonial states and the hegemonic discourse of Eurocentrism (see 3.3). In addition, he discusses the concept of the imaginary, which associates with the religious thought, making it orthodox and conventional as well.

In this regard, Arkoun uses the concept of the social imaginary to critique orthodoxy and show how Islamic thought is manipulated within a collective creation of myths and supernatural narratives that remove the religious framework from the scope of critical and rational analysis. "Arkoun contends that the societies that adopted the Islamic event [that means orthodoxy or official religion; see 3.3] still embrace certain metaphysical perceptions of existence that characterize pre-modern societies: circular perception of time; messianic expectation of the Mahdi; millennium hopes; taboo perception of any renewal; limitation of social frameworks; a central role for the myths and oral stories for the formation of the imaginary; and the importance of the collective over the individual".[348]

In addition, one can argue that Arkoun's concept of community to build his new humanist ethos in civil societies is "informed by Foucauldian historical epistemology."[349] One outcome of this historical epistemology approach is the formation of new perceptions, and thus, a new periodization of Arabo-Islamic intellectual history. According to this approach, the historical phases are based on analysis of the evolution of the Arab Muslim epistemology. The epistemological approach organizes Islamic history into five main periods: the Qur'anic period and the formation of Islamic thought (622–767); the classical period (767–1058); the scholastic period (1058–1880); the renaissance or al-Nahḍa period (1880–1950); and the postcolonial national period (1950-). Arkoun contends that the first three periods were formative for Islamic thought.[350] As explained earlier in the context of this study, for Arkoun

---

346 Mirsepassi 2014 b: 137.
347 Castoriadis 1975: 259–60-305.
348 Abu- Uksa 2011: 175.
349 Mirsepassi 2014 b: 140.
350 Abu- Uksa 2011: 174.

the most important period in the history of Arabo-Islamic thought is the classical or early Islamic period, which Arkoun studied following the thought of Miskawayh and Al-Amiri. This classical/early period of Islam saw the development of humanistic and rational thought adopted by generations of Muslim scholar-philosophers who were influenced by 'foreign sciences,' namely Greek philosophy, and who were opposed to dogmatic, and traditionalist thought (see 3.1 and 3.2).

Thus, Arkoun focuses on the problem of dogmatism – both religious and metaphysical – as a modern crisis of thought,[351] referring to the postcolonial period of Islamic thought. As Ali Mirsepassi explains, quoting Arkoun's words, Arkoun intends a consistent critique of religious discourse, arguing the use of human and social sciences to eliminate the problem of religious discourse in relation to the dogmatic mind. Religious discourse should then be critically examined in favor of the liberation which teaches that individual religion is able to achieve its own interpretive tradition.[352]

Thus, one can perceive that Arkoun wants to build a community within the framework of democratic rules, freeing the perception of the community from orthodoxy and imaginary thinking about religion. As a civil community, freedom of thought and research about religion is protected, so that each individual can discover his own personal understanding of religion.

Third, Arkoun builds his concept of the *cosmopolitan* on the basis of interreligious dialogue. This includes opening religious discourse to different interpretive approaches, which necessitates a comparative study of Islam within the broader tradition of monotheistic religions, thus, creating a cosmopolitan theory of the Islamic tradition.[353] Arkoun states that the comparative study between the monotheistic religions is to be justified by "the role of interreligious dialogue".[354] In this regard, Arkoun addresses the epistemic barriers dividing and conjoining the three monotheistic religions.[355] In other words, to achieve interreligious dialogue, Arkoun turns to the historical, epistemological, and sociopolitical facts that make interreligious dialogue, especially in relation to Islam, Christianity, and Judaism, a dialogue that is not yet entirely conventional.

From that perspective, Arkoun argues that "(...) despite or perhaps because of the Holocaust tragedy the Judeo-Christian dialogue has been able to make more tangible progress."[356] Holocaust means 'burnt offering.' Since 1945, the word has become almost synonymous with the murder of European Jews during the World War II,

---

351 Mirsepassi 2014 b:139.
352 Mirsepassi 2014 b: 139.
353 Mirsepassi 2014 b: 139–140.
354 Arkoun 1998 a: 128.
355 Mirsepassi 2014 b: 140.
356 Arkoun 1998 a: 130.

even though its use began before the World War II. Both European Jews and Christians suffer from the human catastrophe caused by the World War II. According to Arkoun, European Jews and Christians try to open up to each other to forgive their past, emphasizing that tolerance and forgiveness are fundamental concepts in both religions. For this reason, they understand that interreligious dialogue is essential to heal what national and discriminatory policies have done. In this regard, Arkoun argues that "Christians and Jews are familiar with the whole of the Bible."[357]

Turning now to the relationship of Islam with Christianity and Judaism, Arkoun finds that "the Islamo-Christian dialogue has been particularly active."[358] However, Arkoun argues that "for well-known political reasons, the Judeo-Islamic dialogue has practically not started; worse still, the presence of Judaism in the Islamo-Christian meetings is always desired but unfortunately systematically deferred."[359]

I submit that Arkoun means the Arab-Israeli conflict when he says, "well-known political reasons." He does not explain these political reasons nor mention this conflict, but he does base his explanation on religious conflict issues.

Arkoun speculates on the religious grounds that explain why interreligious dialogue between Islam, Christianity and Judaism has not yet begun. He argues that one of the reasons is that "Muslims do not always agree to make the educative effort to read the Bible and the Gospels outside the polemical framework in which the Qur'ān has fixed representations on the issue of the 'distortion' (*Taḥrīf*) of the scriptures of the peoples of the Book (*Ahl al kitab*)."[360]

By 'peoples of the Book' or societies of the book, Arkoun refers to Jews and Christians who have a book as the Bible and the Gospels. Societies of the book is a concept that emphasizes patterns of societies that embrace theological perceptions of prophecy and the holy book. The holy book plays a central role in the relation between knowledge and power, and in the relation between the social and the political. The historical dynamics of these fields gave the book, in ancient monotheist cultures, the status of a closed holy text that is preserved by a religious institution or political power (such as the church, or the caliph).[361]

As explored in various parts of this study, Arkoun critiques the phenomenon of the sacred book, which he views as an official, closed corpus that is not subjected to critical scrutiny and, thus, manifests itself as sacred in the sense of holy in order to protect institutional systems. Arkoun argues for the necessity of opening up the official closed corpus by situating it in a comparative approach "that will enable Muslim readers (...) to better assess the stakes in a scientific problematization of

---

357 Arkoun 1998 a: 130.
358 Arkoun 1998 a: 129.
359 Arkoun 1998 a: 129.
360 Arkoun 1998 a: 129.
361 Abu- Uksa 2011: 188 fn. 73.

orthodox vocabulary inherited from a theological theory of values resistent to every critical examination."[362]

However, most Muslims, the representatives of Islam, reject the comparative approach, which comes into play as a promising method to eradicate orthodoxy and end the ongoing conflicts between religions. The reason is that they believe that the Bible and the Gospels are forged scriptures. This means that the Bible and the Gospels are subject to alterations. Only the Qur'an has not been seen as distorted or corrupted. As Arkoun asserts, this allows Islam to not enter into fruitful, face-to-face discussions with other religions by clinging to the "heresiographic literature" that claims the Qur'an was never distorted.[363]

Thus, if Islam adheres to the orthodox belief that the Bible and the Gospels are forged books, then interreligious dialogue with the peoples of the Book is impossible, because Islam has a prejudice against other religions from the very beginning and makes itself the best and uncorrupted religion, which, as the only true religion, does not adhere to a forgery. Arkoun argues interreligious dialogue could not be available without "a comparative history of theologies [incorporating] the analysis of the cognitive strategies developed within each tradition."[364] In Arkoun's view, the study of religions and the development of interreligious dialogue are possible through a comparative history of theologies that examines the commonalities that unite the three monotheistic religions and that can make fruitful dialogue possible.

Arkoun's approach to interreligious dialogue in the context of comparative history of religions starts from the early Islamic thought of Al-Amiri (see 3.2). By interpreting Al-Amiri's project, Arkoun recognizes that one of the promising features of Al-Amiri's thought is to initiate an interreligious dialogue based on a comparative study that creates a notion of religious tolerance that we desperately need today.

Consequently, Arkoun's project of a new ethos requires the autonomy of the individual, that is, freedom of thought and liberation from dogmatic and traditional beliefs. This is consistent with the Enlightenment project, which emphasized rebellion against religious dogma and superstition. In addition, Arkoun implies the concept of community, the coexistence of people in civil societies that respect cultural and religious differences. However, this cannot be achieved without freeing common sense from the collective social imaginary, in order to promote the critical spirit of the individual towards any dogmatic and orthodox discourses. This, in order to promote respect for others. Cosmopolitan is therefore the term introduced at the end of my analysis of Arkoun's project for a new ethos. Cosmopolitan explains that interreligious dialogue would be necessary to nourish and enrich the shared public space

---

362   Arkoun 2002 a: 64.
363   Arkoun 2002 a: 75.
364   Arkoun 2002 a: 75.

through critical engagement with dogmatic beliefs. Interreligious and cultural dialogue, which Arkoun promotes as a new ethos in his contemporary project, thus, facilitates the exchange of ideas and mutual recognition among individuals of the world to reject hegemonic notions of superiority and false stereotypes about religion and culture.

Völker comments on Arkoun's idea of an interreligious dialogue leading to a peaceful coexistence of people from different religious traditions, arguing that Arkoun was part of the project of the Swiss scholar Hans Küng (1928–2021). Küng attempts to define stable social values with reference to religious consciousness. According to Völker, Arkoun is among the representatives of Islamic religious denominations. He was often asked by Hans Küng for advice and support for his interreligious project and respect for religious affiliation in civil societies. Arkoun, along with other scholars, signed the "Universal Declaration of a Global Ethic" (UDGE), which was presented at the first Parliament of the World's Religions in 1993. The principles of this declaration were as follows: Commitment to a culture of non-violence and respect for life, commitment to a culture of solidarity and a just economic order, commitment to a culture of tolerance and a life of truthfulness, commitment to a culture of equal rights and partnership between men and women.[365] Völker notes that the democratic values outlined in the UDGE are "in one form or another, at the heart of Arkoun's overall project".[366] The principles of the UDGE, thus, represent the new ethos outlined above, which Arkoun defends in his intellectual project.

With this in mind, I recapitulate this chapter by arguing that Arkoun's concept of emerging reason is an essential concept because it eclipses the canon of thought and the division of the world into systematized approaches of thought. Emerging reason is a promising concept that calls for a pluralistic and transcultural dialogue between different traditions and systems of thought, namely the openness of Western philosophy to other traditions of thought. In this way, philosophers around the world should engage in philosophical debates about the current problems and concerns that occupy humankind. Arkoun's concept of emerging reason introduces the new ethos he seeks to establish based on individual autonomy, community, and cosmopolitan attitudes. In his plea for interreligious dialogue, Arkoun argues that a civil society in which justice and freedom of thought and belief are respected is essential.

---

365   Völker 2015: 207.
366   Völker 2015: 207.

3.5 Conclusion on the thought of Mohammed Arkoun

In this second part of this study, the aim was to examine Arkoun's contemporary intellectual project based on his rethinking of Islamic thought. The purpose was to develop a transcultural approach to create a postcolonial concept of justice. My methodology for reading Arkoun's thought was based on a systematic examination of the various concepts he develops throughout his intellectual career.

The first chapter, then, dealt with Arkoun's interpretation of Miskawayh's multifaceted concept of justice, which was examined by turning to Miskawayh's ethical theory of justice, characterized by his combination of ideas from both Plato and Aristotle. Arkoun's interpretation of Miskawayh's concept shows that Miskawayh is not a mere translator of Greek philosophical thought. Arkoun emphasizes this point to show that Miskawayh's humanism is a combination of Islamic tradition and Greek philosophical tradition. Miskawayh's humanistic thought is based on opening the realm of Islamic ethics to rational and philosophical frameworks.

As part of a rereading of early Islamic thought, and in addition to Arkoun's reinterpretation of Miskawayh's ethical project on justice, the second chapter examined three approaches of thought that characterizes Al-Amiri's early intellectual project. The transdisciplinary approach means that Al-Amiri reconciles the fields of religion and philosophy by using different disciplines to study Islam. The comparative approach to the study of religions aims to convey the tolerant message that Al-Amiri wants to defend by attributing a common characteristic to the different religions in terms of belief. The rational approach is based on interpreting Islam through the rational method of thinking, logic, a thinking tool inherited from Greek thought, which could be promoted within the Islamic legacy. The chapter showed that Arkoun's reinterpretation of the early Islamic thought of Miskawayh and Al-Amiri provides the framework for his contemporary intellectual project, which is based on a rethinking of Islamic thought and a defense of a rational and humanistic stance. Arkoun is a contemporary of the post-structuralist thought of Western philosophy. He, thus, includes an influence of both systems of thought, the rational and humanist Islamic thought and the poststructuralist Western thought. Based on this transcultural approach, Arkoun introduces the concept of applied Islamology, which aims to adapt Islamic discourse to the context of current sociocultural Muslim societies. Applied Islamology also has an emancipatory meaning through a rational interpretation of religious discourse to promote women's rights within the discourse of feminism in Islam. The chapter examines Arkoun's concept of exhaustive tradition, understood as opening the Islamic tradition to more than one tradition to include the marginalized cultural tradition of Islam.

In the third chapter, I examined Arkoun's critique of hegemonic discourse to understand how it is shaped to create and construct orthodoxy in religious discourse, fundamentalist identity and radical secularism in nationalist discourses, and Eurocentrism in a capitalist framework of modernity. The chapter examines Arkoun's critique of orthodoxy through his notions of Qur'anic and Islamic facts to show how the Qur'an, as revealed discourse, was transformed into a written text influenced by past traditional and cultural events and adopted by religious officials to protect political interests. Through Arkoun's notions of humanistic secularism and intellectual modernity, the chapter aims to promote pluralistic and democratic ideas based on freedom of thought, freedom of religion, and equal scientific and economic production on a global scale.

Chapter four explores Arkoun's concept of emerging reason, developed in opposition to hegemonic approaches to thought. Emerging reason emphasizes transcultural dialogue between different systems of thought. The humanistic stance Arkoun advocates in his contemporary intellectual project is explored through his notions of individual autonomy, community, and cosmopolitan concepts. In his writings, Arkoun emphasizes the importance of promoting democratic rules in Muslim societies where critical thinking and intellectual inquiry are encouraged.

To evaluate Arkoun's thinking based on the transcultural approach, postcolonial thinking, and the concept of justice, I argue that Arkoun's project is related to the transcultural approach that forms the basis for this study. Arkoun develops a transcultural approach by combining different traditions of thought, such as the Western poststructuralist school of thought, by which he is influenced in developing his critical methods for rethinking Islamic thought. He is also a reader and a great interpreter of the thought of early Muslim scholars, from whom he transfers their transcultural, humanistic, and rational thinking to our thinking about Islam today. Arkoun's project is transdisciplinary in that he combines various research disciplines, such as sociology, history, linguistics, and philosophy, represented in his method of applied Islamology, to develop a new approach of thinking in the field of Islamic studies.

Arkoun's project is postcolonial in that he opposes the hegemonic construction about Islam and the socio-political, economic, and cultural division of the globe into center and periphery. Arkoun criticizes the postcolonial discourse of religious nationalism, Arab centrism, and an imposed notion of modernity that developed in several post-independence Muslim societies. In addition, Arkoun criticizes modern capitalism, which he argues promotes an unequal distribution of production that makes the global South increasingly dependent on the global North and prevents it from participating in global economic and scientific activities. Arkoun's Enlightenment thinking is perceived as ambivalent, as he see democratic rules and a civil society as cornerstones for the enforcement of freedom of thought and belief. However, he is critical of a radical secularism that enforces a total denial of religion. For Arkoun, Islam is a religious reality; it promotes the cultural tradition of the individual. Islam must be fundamentally reformed to be well received in our contemporary world. Arkoun argues for a humanistic attitude based on respect for the individual and the promotion of his ability to think and criticize.

Justice is a matter of course in Arkoun's thought. As a result of a thorough interpretation of Arkoun's contemporary project, I can identify a wide range of concepts of justice, which I call transcultural justice, gender justice, procedural justice, egalitarian justice, epistemic justice, and distributive justice. To illustrate this, the first chapter of the study introduces the concept of justice in early Arabo-Islamic thought, focusing on Miskawayh's early Islamic thought on justice and Arkoun's interpretation of Miskawayh's thought. In the first chapter, the concept of divine justice is explored in order to understand what in the divine appears to man as just and what man promotes in his soul. The concept of human justice is to be understood in the context of what humans promote in the realm of social interaction and in the realm of distribution when they treat each other equally. Following Arkoun's interpretation of Miskawayh's theory of justice, this chapter explores Miskawayh's development of *transcultural justice* by combining Islamic ethical thought and Greek philosophy.

By introducing the concepts of applied Islamology and the exhaustive tradition in chapter two, I have shown that there is a notion of gender justice and procedural justice behind the use of these concepts. Applied Islamology has been used by Muslim feminist scholars as a methodological framework for reinterpreting Islamic texts to seek women's rights in Islam and to call for the promotion of *gender justice* in the religious and political spheres of society.

The exhaustive tradition incorporates a notion of *procedural justice* by asserting the right of the marginalized tradition in most Muslim societies to speak out and be heard, thus, enforcing non-discriminatory policies toward groups of minorities based on their status as non-Arabs. Arkoun demands that non-Arab Muslims living in Arabo-Muslim societies should have equal access to political, social, and economic rights, and not be excluded.

Arkoun defends a concept of *egalitarian justice* that emphasizes equality and equal treatment of different religious beliefs based on his concept of secular humanism. Arkoun believes that in secular societies, citizens must be treated equally despite their different religious beliefs. For Arkoun, secularism should not be directed against religion, but rather against the use of religion for political purposes. Arkoun argues for democratic and civil societies that protect citizens with different religious beliefs to ensure their rights and equality.

In addition, Arkoun's thought articulates a concept of *epistemic justice* based on his plea for scientific and cultural dialogue among different traditions of thought and equal participation in scientific and cultural products and achievements. Taking into account global equality in economic production, Arkoun argues for *distributive justice* that ensures that goods should be distributed equally between the North and the South.

It is important to engage with Arkoun's thought today and in this study, because his thoughts are still relevant to the recent upsurge of popular democratic movements in many Muslim countries demanding cultural and political expressions of democratic or egalitarian aspirations. Arkoun's thoughts are alive to the building of civil societies in which democratic rules are promoted. Arkoun advocates a rational rethinking of Islamic thought, which is necessary, but he rejects a total exclusion of Islam in the public sphere. His thinking about Islam is a reformatory impetus for the individual's ability to think and criticize, and for a nonviolent process toward secular and democratic ways. Throughout his intellectual career, Arkoun defends a heterogeneous Islam; an Islam that is diverse and derives from a complex and rich history with multiple traditions. Arkoun's thinking continues to oppose the political nationalism that has emerged in terms of Arab-centrism or Eurocentrism. "This constitutes a potential trigger to popular action and nonviolent democratic paths so long as we reject old or new fixed mental habits of tyranny and exclusion."[367] Arkoun argues for a new ethos based on a humanist stance that offers the prospect of a democratic transformation of the rich resources of thought shaped by a multicentric dynamic of globalization based on transcultural and interreligious dialogue.

I would now like to shed light on some of the difficulties in dealing with Arkoun's intellectual project, which I point out. In this way, I reflect on why Arkoun's intellectual project has not been fully received in Arab academies. Arkoun critically challenges stereotypical ideas about Arab identity and the Islamic religion. Thus, his thinking contradicts the notion of an Arab identity that is firmly established in many Arab countries. Arkoun also contradicts interpretations of Islam that defy criticism and propagate fundamental ideas about Islam. For him, Islam is not a monolithic and homogeneous religious tradition. Islam should be interpreted by recognizing the subdivided Islamic traditions in the Muslim world. This assertion is not to deny the intellectual efforts of contemporary Muslim intellectuals who, like Arkoun, seek a transcultural understanding of Islamic religion and culture, and employ poststructuralist thought as a method of deconstructing Islamist religious thought and Western thought, as is the case in the thought of the Maghrebian thinkers Mohammad

---

367   Mirsepassi 2014 b: 155.

Abed al-Jabri (1935–2010)[368] and Abdelkebir Khatibi (1938 –2009)[369] – to name only two.

The lack of translation and publication of Arkoun's writings is also a problem. Arkoun himself states that his thought is met with a lack of understanding, especially by readers unfamiliar with the poststructuralist critique as it relates to Islamic studies.[370] Arkoun writes in French; it is difficult for intellectuals, especially from the Middle East, to recognize his thought; and despite the translation of several of his books into Arabic by his student Hisham Saleh, Arkoun's thought does not seem to be very present in the Arabo-Islamic intellectual debate. In addition, Western "postcolonial" and critical theorists have not yet located Arkoun as a postcolonial thinker, considering him to be a pure Islamologist.[371]

Most of the relevant secondary literature dealing with Arkoun's thought ignores the aspect of the reception of his thought within the Islamic feminist approach. The feminist reception of his thought by Margot Badran (2010), Raja Rhouni (2008; 2010), and Malika Zeghal (2012) helped me to look at Arkoun's thought from a different perspective by presenting his thinking on gender justice as a shared intellectual inquiry between him and Fatima Mernissi (see part one of the study).

Ali Mirsepassi claims that "Arkoun's discussion takes place on an abstract and theoretically rarefied level."[372] This is because Arkoun's project is characterized by a lack of systematization, which makes understanding his thoughts difficult and ambiguous for the readers. Arkoun himself understands this claim as a blockage that results in his thought not being discussed in most Arabic scholarship.[373] For this reason, my study of Arkoun aimed to systematically connect the various concepts and

---

368   Al-Jabri's thought was characterized by three requests, which could be described as deconstruction of Arab thought, overcoming of traditional thought patterns, and a plea for freedom of thought. See: Sonja Hegasy: Portrait of the Philosopher Mohammed Abed al-Jabri: Critique of Arab Reason (2009). In: https://en.qantara.de/content/portrait-of-the-philosopher-mohammed-abed-al-jabri-critique-of-arab-reason-0.

369   "Trained in sociology and a prolific writer of poetry, plays, fiction, and essays, Khatibi is best known for his writings on cultural decolonization and for his reflections on language, both in fiction and in his numerous essays. He was also one of the first theorists to establish historical and theoretical parallels between deconstructive and decolonial thought, supplementing the deconstruction of Western philosophy with what he calls "pensée-autre" ("other-thinking") and "double critique: a reciprocal dismantling of Western and Arab systems of thought." See: Olivia C. Harrison: "Abrahamic Tongues: Abdelkebir Khatibi, Jacques Hassoun, Jacques Derrida." In *Transcolonial Maghreb: Imagining Palestine in the Era of Decolonization*, 1st ed., 101–28. Stanford University Press, 2016. https://doi.org/10.2307/j.ctvqsds4d.10.

370   Arkoun 2008: 5.
371   Dübgen 2020: 896.
372   Mirsepassi 2014 b: 155.
373   Arkoun 2008:7.

themes that characterize his intellectual project in order to highlight his ethical and humanistic approaches that lie behind his rethinking of Islamic thought.

I would like to conclude my study of Arkoun's intellectual project by pointing out the contributions dedicated to him as an intellectual pioneer in the field of contemporary Arabo-Islamic thought, the first of which appeared during his lifetime in an interesting book on his relevant thought, and the last after his death.

In an interesting volume realized as a tribute to Arkoun, Filali-Ansary writes, "Professor Mohammed Arkoun was a prominent and influential figure in Islamic Studies. In a career of more than thirty years, he was an outstanding research scholar, a searching critic of the theoretical tensions embedded in the field of Islamic Studies, and a courageous public intellectual who carried the banner of an often embattled Islamic modernism and humanism".[374] In an obituary dedicated to Arkoun, Ursula Günther, one of the best-known commentators on Arkoun's thought, affirms "Mohammed Arkoun was not only a sharp-witted intellectual and humanist from the depth of his heart, with a subtle sense of humour. He was also a passionate, charismatic speaker and a dedicated teacher. He felt a part of all that is capable of opening up new links to intelligence, as he put it, and saw himself as 'an intellectual in revolt.' May his idea that thoughts develop a life of their own prove right, continuing to take effect beyond the walls of cognitive demarcations and dominant ideologies."[375]

Arkoun advocates a new ethos based on humanistic principles that promote openness, hospitality, tolerance, and democratic principles against all forms of discrimination and injustice. Currently, his work needs to be reactivated to challenge the remaining orthodoxy and hegemonic constructs that influence religion, culture, gender, and identity.

---

374   Filali-Ansary 2012 a: 7.
375   Günther 2010.

4. Epilogue: Theorizing justice in contemporary Arabo-Islamic philosophy

The intellectual heritage of Anglo-American and European scholars, as assembled by leading philosophers and theorists since the Enlightenment, continues to dominate debates about how to define and legitimate human relations in a world of diverse cultures. As explored in the previous chapters of this research, Mernissi and Arkoun offer a transdisciplinary and transcultural approach to the debate on justice that aim at constructing viable social and political ideas for human flourishing based on an in-depth analysis of the experiences of Islamic societies in a dynamic world full of diverse individuals, groups, and cultures.

Arabo-Islamic philosophy has not yet realized its importance for the justice debate because justice theory so far remains heavily influenced by Western normative debates. This study proposed a transcultural concept of justice to enrich the justice debate and move it beyond its Western orientation. What lessons, therefore, can philosophers from the Global South and North draw from the need for a transcultural dialogue on justice?

I emphasize the importance of being open to different perspectives on justice in different philosophical traditions in order to propose a cosmopolitan theory of justice that is based on a transcultural approach and promotes humanistic ideals. To this end, the first section of this epilogue recapitulates what I see as common intellectual approach in the thought of Mernissi and Arkoun in order to develop a concept of justice in Arabo-Islamic philosophy. Following that, I conclude by focusing on the promising cosmopolitan debate on justice from a transcultural perspective in order to discuss how this debate represents a new enrichment of the justice debate and how the inclusion and understanding of different debates on justice can help to make cultural and traditional differences more accepted.

4.1 The common approach to theorizing justice by Fatima Mernissi and Mohammed Arkoun[1]

Based on what has been explained in the previous parts of this study, I first argue that the thought of Mernissi and Arkoun is characterized by the critique of Orientalist discourse and method in order to free Islamic thought from a distorting, pejorative, and essentializing account.

In her plea against Orientalist discourse, Mernissi directs her critique at the symbolic representations of a monolithic Arab Islamic identity and religion. She claims that Islam is not only linked to Arab ethnicity, but that there are different ethnicities within Islam. She further notes that Arab ethnicity encompasses different religions, so that not all Arabs are necessarily Muslims, and not all Muslims are Arabs. Furthermore, Mernissi seeks to deconstruct the myth of the passive Muslim woman who lacks intellectual capacity. She refers to the figure of Scheherazade, who saved the lives of other women from a murderous and authoritarian man through the use of her knowledge and her intellectual abilities as a storyteller. Mernissi also deconstructs the Orientalist representation of the harem as a place of mere sexual desire. For example, she recounts her experiences as a child born in the harem, to show that women who lived in the harem were not always submissive, but aspired to emancipation. In this way, Mernissi promotes a critical examination of Western prejudices against Islamic culture, aiming to liberate women in Islam from stereotypes and Orientalist clichés and a patriarchal position that precludes women's access to basic rights.

While Mernissi's main criticism is directed against the Orientalist discourse, which represents a stereotypical image of the women of the Global South, Arkoun criticizes the Orientalist method used by some European historians. Arkoun conceives that the Orientalist method studies Islamic texts without critically analyzing them. According to him, Orientalist historians do not study Islamic texts in relation to the socio-cultural needs of Muslims in their contemporary societies. They do not problematize, for example, the socio-political conditions, in which certain verses of the Qur'an were revealed or by whom and under what circumstances certain Hadith (sayings of the prophet) were transmitted. Based on his methodological critique of Orientalist methods, Arkoun strives to critically examine and analyze Islamic discourse and not to view it merely as a form of monotheistic discourse.

Second, the contemporary intellectual project of Mernissi and Arkoun is characterized by the application of transdisciplinary approaches to liberate Islamic

---

1   This sub-chapter is based the following article: Karoui, Kaouther (2020): "Relektüren des Klassisch-islamischen Erbes für eine Gerechtigkeitsgrammatik der Gegenwart". In: Transkulturelle Perspektiven auf Gerechtigkeit, Special Issue for: Deutsche Zeitschrift für Philosophie, (Vol. 68, No. 6, pp. 915–927), Berlin: De Gruyter.

thought from hegemonic, fundamentalist, and patriarchal constructions. In this sense, both scholars plead for a reason-based critical-deconstructive analysis of the religious scriptures. Arkoun argues that 'Holy Scripture' such as the Qur'an should be open to historical, sociological, and anthropological analysis. Likewise, Mernissi aims to open Islamic discourse to new interpretations by using the methods of Islamic feminism such as the critique and deconstruction of classical Qur'anic exegesis, the historical contextualization of some Hadith and some Qur'anic verses through the use of linguistic analysis and grammatical explanations. Her approach to Islamic feminism is directed against prototypical traditionalist, misogynist scholars.

Using poststructuralist and hermeneutical approaches, both scholars emphasize the importance of cultivating the human intellect ('aql) and independent reasoning (ijtihad) in modern Islamic societies. Hence, both call for a rational new interpretation of Islamic corpuses and for opening up the Islamic intellectual discourse to dialogues with differing religious and cultural traditions. However, Arkoun's methods for reinterpreting the religious Islamic scriptures, however, are more critical than the methods used by Mernissi. Arkoun, for instance, uses Foucault's analysis discourse and Derrida's deconstructive approach to texts in order to address the question of how the Qur'an evolved from speech to text.

Third, Mernissi's and Arkoun's reactivation of early Arabo-Islamic philosophy can help contemporary Arabo-Islamic societies to overcome the orthodox traditional and patriarchal understanding of Islamic normativity by raising Muslims' and non-Muslims' intellectual awareness of the diversity and rationality of early Arabo-Islamic thought. Their reinterpretation of early Arabo-Islamic thought reveals Islamic thought as a combination of Greek philosophy and Islamic religious ethics to show that there is no contradiction between the two registers. In this regard, Mernissi's and Arkoun's reinterpretations of early Islamic thought reminds Muslim readers that early Muslim thinkers were open to the Greek-Western philosophical tradition. Both scholars refer to pre-existing written intellectual heritage –particularly from the early flowering of Arabo-Islamic philosophy – which is interpreted as a transcultural fusion between Greek philosophy and Islamic thought.

Mernissi and Arkoun also seek to transmit the rationalism and humanist ethics of early Muslim scholars to Western readers, challenging their often narrow understanding of Islamic culture by asserting that there was a fruitful, well-reasoned, and inspiring debate between different philosophical traditions in the early stage of Islam. Arkoun and Mernissi have drawn inspiration from this rationalist and humanist ethos that characterized early Arabo-Islamic thought to make Islam an ambivalent point of reference to be subjected to a critical re-reading – and to adapt it to the challenges and living conditions of Muslims today.

As a point of divergence, Mernissi and Arkoun use different methods to renew early Arabo-Islamic philosophy. While Mernissi rediscovers marginalized positions in the history of thought in Islam and affirms them positively to justify her call for gender justice and democracy in contemporary societies from an Islamic perspective, Arkoun takes a critical approach to established religious texts and seeks to deconstruct and reinterpret religious discourse on the question of revelation. He aims at encouraging self-criticism and calls for a critical reappropriation of theological rationalism. Arkoun sees the production and reading of texts as political acts, and texts as instruments of power.

Finally, Mernissi and Arkoun illustrate the theorist-strategic possibility of limiting the discourse of religion as a patriarchal and fundamentalist discourse and its influence on political control by using secular and modern expressions of equality. One can assume that "the post-Enlightenment secularism and modernity have habitually been seen in Islamic sectarian discourses as Western diseases, spread by colonialism, infecting and weakening the once great Islamic civilization".[2] In response to this assertion, Mernissi and Arkoun evaluate this discourse, which was shaped in most post-independence Arab-Islamic countries, by pointing to the richness of early Islamic thought and civilization, as mentioned earlier, and by examining both critically the concepts of secularity and modernity as used in Western discourses.

What is interesting about Arkoun's writing is that his assessment of modernity and Islam is not based on traditional religious arguments, but on postmodern theory. Arkoun is a Francophone North African who has studied and taught in Paris for most of his life. Postmodern theory has played an influential role for both Northern and Southern scholars in critiquing colonialism.[3] On the one hand, Arkoun sees the use of the rational attitude of Enlightenment thought as central to the emancipation of Islamic thought from dogmatism and obscurantism. He describes Enlightenment thought as emancipatory and insists on freedom of thought and freedom of religious belief in order to create pluralistic democratic societies within the Islamic world. On the other hand, Arkoun criticizes French secularism, as it evolved, which leads to the alienation of religion from society and contributes to an Islamophobic discourse. His criticism is also directed at Euromodernism, which promotes neocolonial structures based on political, military, and economic control of the Global South.

Alike Arkoun, Mernissi is a Muslim intellectual with a Western education, able to analyze and criticize Western thought on its own terms. Like Arkoun, she has written for a Western audience and for those Muslims who read Western languages and are familiar with Western critical theories. Therefore, her critique of traditionalist, male-oriented interpretations of Islam has more influence among Western non-Muslim intellectuals than among Muslim intellectuals. Moreover, like Arkoun,

---

2   Martin, Richard C., Mark. R. Woodward and Dwi S. Atmaja 1997: 204.
3   Martin, Richard C., Mark. R. Woodward and Dwi S. Atmaja 1997: 204.

Mernissi is a Francophone North African Arab who is also familiar with postmodern criticism as well as Islamic social movements.[4] Her critique of the colonial structure is based on the denial that French colonization served to create social and educational rights for native Moroccan women. During the colonial system in Morocco, women did not exercise their right to education, a fundamental right promoted by France. As a male-patriarchal interpretation of Islamic legacy overrode women's rights, native Moroccan women remained trapped in their private spheres. The Enlightenment-critical thinking that France advocated did not serve as an effective tool to challenge this patriarchal system. Thus the French protectorate in Morocco did not aim to liberate, civilize, and modernize the native population, as it claims. For Mernissi, however, secular thought could be emancipatory for Muslim women, so that religion does not intrude into the public sphere of human interaction. She repeatedly emphasizes that secular humanism is not against religion, but against the intrusion of religion into the public sphere, and that humanism promotes the right to use human reason for critical thinking.

Mernissi and Arkoun thus choose a secular and modern humanistic approach to defend human rights and to establish democracy. In this way, both scholars offer alternatives to Eurocentric and colonial conceptions of secularism and modernity. Indeed, they understand these concepts from a humanistic and cosmopolitan perspective. Their notion of secular humanism encourages critical thinking vis-à-vis any traditional and orthodox framework. Their notion of modernity is fostered by a transcultural fusion between the Global South and the Global North in various fields of knowledge. In their works, they analyze the demands for equal rights to political participation, gender equality, overcoming social discrimination (nationally and transnationally), and emancipating human reason from religious dogma as manifestations of secular humanist ideals.

For Mernissi, theorizing gender justice needs to be based on a cosmopolitan and transcultural debate between women from the Global South and the Global North. Mernissi argues persistently that openness to debate and new ideas is a necessary stance for Muslims in a late modern world increasingly characterized by cultural pluralism and political contestations.

Arkoun believes that Islamic thought needs to be renewed to promote a cosmopolitan ethos that emphasizes interreligious dialogue and detaches the canon of thought from a hegemonic discourse. In addition, his conception of a cosmopolitan ethos defines a dialogue between different philosophical perspectives and aims at a transcultural debate between different schools of thought.

Mernissi's and Arkoun's contemporary intellectual projects culminate in a call for a new humanism based on transcultural debate and a cosmopolitan horizon that puts forward a new grammar of justice, especially as a contribution to the discourse

---

4   Martin, Richard C., Mark. R. Woodward and Dwi S. Atmaja 1997: 206–207.

strands of transnational political justice, economic justice, and postcolonial gender justice.

4.2 On the relevance of a cosmopolitan theory of justice based on a transcultural approach

This research presented the contemporary intellectual projects of the Moroccan feminist thinker Fatima Mernissi and the Algerian philosopher Mohammed Arkoun to broaden the hermeneutical horizon for the normative discourse on justice by incorporating Arabo-Islamic philosophy. The research was divided into two main parts. The research began with a study of Mernissi's and Arkoun's thought, outlining and explaining their biographical and intellectual trajectories and presenting the meaning and characteristics of their ethico-political projects. It brings to light a detailed analysis and study of their engagement with the early and contemporary context of Arabo-Islamic thought, focusing on the cultural and socio-political context of the Maghreb countries to develop a philosophical thought that condemns orthodox hegemonic constructions.

Through a cosmopolitan ethos and the demand for religious freedom, the research challenges orthodoxy and fundamentalism. It promotes a better understanding of human rights and gender equality to combat patriarchal, discriminatory and racist structures. A key characteristic of Mernissi's and Arkoun's thinking is their blend of positive and negative views about the concepts of modernity and secularism. On the one hand, they criticize the modern Western thought for its hemogenic constructs formed in the discourse and methods of Orientalism, the discourse of Euromodernism, and the discourse manifesting neo-imperialism. On the other hand, based on their analysis, they find that modern secular thought contributes to the emancipation of humanity from orthodox religious beliefs. Importantly, secular thought serves the purpose of liberating women from the manipulation of religious discourse under patriarchal power. The secular thought defended in this study preserves the place of religion in societies as a spiritual and cultural sphere that can be criticized and evaluated, but does not use religion as a means to intervene into politics.

Mernissi's and Arkoun's re-reading of early Islamic thought is characterized by an exploration of the rational and humanistic approaches that shaped the ideas of early Muslim thinkers. A rational approach inherited from Greek thought as well as humanist ideals link Islamic ethics to Greek philosophy. The research confirms that the reevaluation of early Islamic thought is an ongoing task that not only challenges the established interpretations within Islamic orthodoxy, but also corrects the Western world's misinterpretations and generalizations about the rich Islamic intellectual heritage.

The contemporary intellectual project of Mernissi and Arkoun was studied from a transcultural perspective emphasizing their transdisciplinary approaches and their reference to different cultures. A comparison of modern Western and early Islamic thought revealed that both thinkers mediate between different traditions. Both scholars rethink Islamic thought using poststructuralist methods and early Islamic logics, hermeneutics, and Greek classical logic. They also draw on various disciplines such as linguistics, -and sociological empirical research. Through these multifarious approaches, Islamic thought is removed from a monolithic framework of theological interpretation and opened up to multifarious rational interpretations.

Highlighting Mernissi's and Arkoun's rethinking of Islamic philosophy aims at the inclusion of intellectual voices of scholars from the Global South in the justice debate. The goal is to develop a cosmopolitan theory of justice that opposes the exclusion of diverse perspectives of thought. In contrast, a cosmopolitan debate, as they advocate it, includes both sides of the globe in order to build a transcultural dialogue between different cultures and systems of thought.

A plea for an epistemic diversity and intersectional analysis

Following the contemporary intellectual project of Mernissi and Arkoun, which is analyzed in the context of this study, I would like to propose in this epilogue how a cosmopolitan debate on justice can be made plausible on the basis of a transcultural approach.

To establish justice via a transcultural approach, I argue first and foremost that intellectuals who are deeply engaged in their societies are well-equipped to critically examine the injustice in their specific contexts. Thus, intellectuals from around the world need to come together, reflect, and engage in a collaborative dialogue to transform the debate on injustice from a Western, Euro-Atlantic to a transnational, global level. To grasp the full extent of what is going on at the global level is something no single scholar can do alone, but only through collective efforts we may develop a global debate that includes the epistemology of the South.[5]

In addition, colonial structures still dominate the world. Colonialism has not ceased, only its language has evolved through the various structures that hierarchically separate the metropolitan societies of the former colonizers from the underdeveloped countries of yesterday's colonized, as well as through the division of humanity into human beings worthy to live and those destined to die.[6] For this reason, it is essential to abolish the hegemonic structures and languages that divide the world

---

5   Santos 2007: 55.
6   I refer to Achilles Mbembe's concept of Necropolitics, by which he means that specific humans are forced to remain in a suspended state of being located somewhere between life

into metropolitan societies and neo-colonial territories, so that the world can come together without hierarchical distinctions.[7]

To this end, and to apply a cosmopolitan justice debate based on a transcultural approach, a transnational "global cognitive justice"[8] that incorporates diverse knowledge systems and worldviews against the manipulation of knowledge within a single system of thought, and opposes the hierarchical division between subaltern and dominant knowledge, is indeed a promising and vital conception that is gradually being incorporated into the justice debate. I would therefore like to make the following suggestions for its implementation: First, I argue for transcultural dialogue between scholars from the Global South and the Global North. Secondly, I call for epistemological diversity of knowledge informing justice theory, and third, I argue for an intersectional conception of justice.

1. As just mentioned above, the concept of transnational cognitive justice is based on the development of a *transcultural dialogue*, especially starting from academia, which would promote and enable cross-cultural studies between different cultures and systems of thought.[9] This would set the stage for research in the humanities to become more sensitive to other social and political structures as well as multiple forms of injustice that play a role in different places around the world. As long as we believe that justice is a virtue that serves all people as a common good, we must free the academic debates about justice from discriminatory structures that monopolize and commodify our thoughts. Rather than focusing on a monolithic Western perspective and vision of thought, we should be open to heterogeneous worldviews. In this way, we can recognize the different systems of power and injustice in the world (see Introduction).

2. Transnational cognitive justice accounts for *epistemological diversity* by recognizing the existence of a plurality of knowledge .[10] For example, transnational cognitive justice demands that we combine rational with religious knowledge. In addition, it transgresses the divide between marginalized knowledge, which belongs to the unthinkable realm of inquiry, and hegemonic knowledge, which belongs to the thinkable realm of knowledge. Thus transnational cognitive justice refers to the recognition of a plurality of heterogeneous knowledge systems and the dynamic connection between them.[11]

---

and death. See Mbembe, Achille (2003): "Necropolitics", transl. by Libby Meintjes. In: Public Culture (Vol. 15, No. 1, pp. 11–40), Durham, North Carolina: Duke University Press.

7   Santos 2007: 46.
8   Santos 2007: 53.
9   Dübgen 2016.
10 Santos 2007: 67.
11 Santos 2007: 66.

In this respect, combining different forms of knowledge, especially by including religious thought in the field of philosophical thought, promises to enrich the philosophical debate on justice and promotes a transdisciplinary and transcultural approach to thinking. In this regard, in this epilogue, I would like to recapitulate what this study contributes to fulfilling the call for more transnational cognitive justice before I turn to my third argument.

Religious diversity and gender justice

Indeed, as shown in this study, the incorporation of religious thought into the field of feminist philosophy to gain an idea of gender justice has deprovincialized the field of feminist philosophy from its Western core to include different approaches in the feminist struggle by incorporating feminist voices from the Global South. Through the approach of Islamic feminism, women of different religious affiliations, veiled and unveiled women, women from the Global South and the Global North contribute to claiming their rights based on a renewed interpretation of religious discourse. Islamic doctrine has been controlled by men and subject to misogynistic interpretations that exclude women from participating in the religious sphere, which is considered a sphere forbidden to women. Islamic feminism further offers transdisciplinary approaches to the field of philosophical feminism by incorporating the method of religious hermeneutics and exegesis into the field of feminism and by promoting various disciplines related to linguistics, sociology, and history. Indeed, the link between religion and feminism underscores "the efforts of believing women of the monotheistic faiths to subject their religious texts to a feminist rereading, or to locate and emphasize the women-friendly and egalitarian precepts within their religious texts, are to be supported."[12]

Hence feminism, in this sense, refers not only to a discourse that demands gender equality based on modern and secular claims, but deals with multiple methods and approaches that should be used to assert the claim for women's rights. The starting point here is the realm of religious discourse as a powerful and patriarchal discourse and source of exclusion of women's rights. Thus the inclusion of religious and secular thought in the discourses defending women's rights serves to achieve a complementarity between religious and secular knowledge to ensure the emancipation of all women.

Rethinking secularism and modernity from a transcultural angle

This study aimed at deconstructing and rethinking secularism and modernity, disclosing their Eurocentric roots. First, I have demonstrated that secular thought does

---

12   Moghadam 2002: 1162.

not systematically imply an exclusion of religion by considering religion as irrational discourse. Rather, this study defends a secular thought that advocates for the right of religious citizens to exist and participate in civil society. The secular state must protect its citizens and grant them rights, without discrimination based on religious and political affiliations. In this sense, "all citizens should be equal before the law, with equal rights and obligations. Civil, political, and social rights of citizens should be protected by the state and by the institutions of civil society."[13]

From the hegemonic scientific point of view, religious discourse is considered the opposite of rational discourse and thus reduced to the realm of the unthinkable. In contrast, this study has pointed out that religious discourse must be considered a field of critical analysis and is open to multiple interpretations that correlate with the needs of people in their contemporary societies. In other words, religious discourse must be critically rethought and must be considered as an important field of knowledge that should not be simply dismissed. In fact, acknowledging the connection between secular and religious thought can help "to improve the status of women and to modernize religious thought."[14] In this way, poststructuralist and postmodernist methods, in conjunction with the field of religious hermeneutics, can be used to liberate religious discourse from extremist, fundamentalist, and dogmatic interpretations that lead to violence between religions as well as between the religious and the non-religious actors.

Moreover, this study includes a significant analysis of the concept of modernity. Based on my readings of Mernissi, I argued that the idea of modernity as a liberal and emancipatory thought is valuable for the emancipation of humanity from the constraints of religious orthodoxy and dogmatism. Considering that the discourse of modernity is linked with important treaties of human rights, furthermore, "a counter-hegemonic use"[15] of the concept of modernity can criticize any neo-capitalist and neo-colonial appropriation. This neo-capitalist and neo-colonial appropriation of modernity is manifest in global injustices and discourses of civilizational superiority.[16] It refers to a hierarchical distinction between states that advance civilization and those that obey and consume what developed states command. This study seeks to break down this hegemonic division of the globe by illuminating the possibility of the Global South, labeled "underdeveloped countries," to contribute to the intellectual and ethical advancement of the Global North. In this regard, rather than cultivating a neo-capitalist modernity, the study cultivates the idea of an intellectual modernity that focuses on the enlightenment of thought and the emancipa-

---

13   Moghadam 2002: 1163–1164.
14   Moghadam 2002: 1162.
15   Santos 2007: 70.
16   Santos 2007: 59.

tion of the human spirit. In this way, intellectual modernity calls for philosophical dialogue between different cultures and different systems of thought.

The quest for a cosmopolitan ethos: Transgressing the boundaries between philosophy and religion

In this sense, the call for a transcultural approach to justice was demonstrated in this study following the re-reading of early Arabo-Islamic thought, which is characterized by the connection between Islamic religious ethics and Greek philosophical ethics. This connection between Islamic legacy and philosophical thought reveals the heterogeneity and plurality of knowledge that constitute early Islamic thought in order to establish a concept of divine justice and a concept of human justice that grants justice in the social and distributive realms. Furthermore, rational thought proved to be an essential idea in early Islamic thought. It has been argued that early Muslim philosophers placed importance on formulating standards for Islamic discourse based on logical terms borrowed from Aristotle's *Organon*. This connection between rational and religious thought demonstrates how important early Islamic thought was in incorporating different perspectives of knowledge and opening itself up to other schools of thought.

In the context of this study, the relevance of the transcultural paradigm was anchored in the cosmopolitan ethos, which is central to cognitive justice between the Global South and the Global North. This book advanced the method of deconstruction as a conceptual tool to challenge monolithic conceptions – particularly the notion of "culture" – as mere intellectual constructs and strives to demonstrate the permeability, flexibility, and dynamism of cultural phenomena by insisting on the need to engage with different cultural perspectives and use different scales of analysis.[17]

Thus, the transcultural paradigm was demonstrated in this study by exploring the concept of *interreligious dialogue as cosmopolitan ethos*, which embodies the principle of tolerance as a necessary value to promote peaceful coexistence in civil societies. In this study, not only was interreligious dialogue embodied as a cosmopolitan ethos grounded by the transcultural paradigm, but also a cosmopolitan approach to feminism that deconstructs the stereotypes about Muslim women, who are oftentimes seen as religious and traditional women who have no perspective for self-emancipation in the tradition of Orientalist discourse. This study shows a different way of perceiving Muslim women by deconstructing these Western stereotypes. This approach is inspired by the Islamic doctrine of Sufism, which promotes the principle of openness to other cultures and thus cross-cultural dialogue within pluralistic identities rather than constructed homogeneous identities.

---

17 König 2016: 101.

"Global social injustice is, therefore, intimately linked to global cognitive injustice. The struggle for global social justice must, therefore, be a struggle for global cognitive justice as well".[18] Thus cognitive justice, as argued above, is crucial for creating global justice on a transnational scale by making connections between different fields of knowledge, such as religion and philosophy, and by removing the hierarchy of knowledge systems in order to deconstruct concepts, methods, and ideas from their hegemonic use to more heterogeneous, pluralistic, and intercultural networks and worldviews. A cosmopolitan ethos emerges when there is a transcultural dialogue based on cognitive justice that connects the Global South with the Global North. Following this line of thought, I conclude this epilogue to my study with the suggestion that intersectional justice is essential for promoting a transcultural approach to justice and also for the global justice debate.

3. *Intersectional justice* recognizes that discrimination can result from a variety of reasons and sources. Individuals can be discriminated against on the basis of gender as well as ethnicity, religion, or cultural background, as seen in the many different ways that women of color and minorities are discriminated against in their local societies. In this sense, global justice must serve the good and progress of all human beings in all sectors of society and in the various institutions. Therefore, the transcultural approach can be seen as a starting point for a critical debate that considers injustice in its global and local manifestations. As I indicated above, it is the task of engaged philosophers and theorists to talk about the various forms of injustice that exist on different levels of analysis. They could bring the forms of injustice into the global academic debate through more transcultural dialogue.

As an example, this study critiqued "nationalism" as one sphere of injustice related to other sides of oppression. It exposed how Arab nationalism has been used to exclude and discriminate against marginalized ethnicities and religions and deny them their rights. In addition, the study presented sociological empirical research that describes intersectional injustices such as socio-economic inequalities, ethnic discrimination, and gender inequality in their interrelatedness. In order to shed light on people's experiences and their struggles for social justice in the post-revolutionary era, the study focused primarily on the Maghreb region in North Africa.

In this context, I argued that intersectional injustice remains pervasive in the Maghreb region, particularly for women. Despite the increasing presence of women in public life who see their emancipation in education and access to high university degrees as a means to their liberation and emancipation, women continue to face inequalities in family law. They still depend on patriarchal dominance, as women still do not predominate in the field of religious knowledge despite the rise of the Islamic feminist studies. In Algeria, for example, polygamy and male repudiation remain legal; women cannot marry without a male-controlled guardianship, and an

---

18   Santos 2007: 53.

identity card is issued automatically to the male head of household while a woman needs to apply separately for one.[19] In Tunisia, Algeria, and Morocco, women are still largely responsible for childcare and care of the elderly. The free market economy has not benefited women as promised by neoliberal economic policy-makers. Economic liberalization has not generated more jobs for women, and certainly no well-paid jobs. To the extent that economic challenges – income inequality, poverty, unemployment, and inadequate social and physical infrastructure – prevent the material empowerment of women in the region, women's full participation in public life still needs to be achieved as well.[20] The division of access to the educational system and job opportunities is highly stratified based on the geographical divide between rural areas and metropolitan cities.

Highlighting the inequalities and forms of discrimination that still exist in the Global South leads me to conclude this study by emphasizing the need to deepen transcultural dialogue and matters of justice. The transcultural approach to justice requires philosophical principles to consolidate and develop the emergence of a cosmopolitan ethos based on the recognition of diverse experiences and traditions of thought. The study seeks to make a contribution to consider justice from the perspective of non-Western thought, focusing on the understanding of justice from the perspective of Arabo-Islamic philosophy. In addition, the study highlighted the mutual influence of Western and Islamic thought in enriching the debate and method of promoting justice during earlier stages of Arabo-Islamic philosophy.

The renewal of our philosophical terminology about justice becomes a necessity in a world where genocides, neo-colonialism as well as various forms of exclusion persist, and where communication between cultures, nations, and religions is repeatedly hampered by serious misunderstandings and prejudices.

---

19   Moghadam 2020: 480.
20   Moghadam 2020: 480.

Bibliography

Abu-Uksa, Wael (2011): "Rediscovering the Mediterranean: Political Critique and Mediterraneanism in Mohammed Arkoun's Thought". In: Journal of Levantine Studies (No. 1, pp. 171–188). Jerusalem: The Van Leer Jerusalem Institute.

Abu Zayd, Naṣr Ḥāmid (2006): *Reformation of Islamic Thought*. Amsterdam: Amsterdam University Press.

Ahmad, Aijaz (1994): "Orientalism and After". In: Williams, Patrick and Laura Chrisman (eds.), *Colonial Discourse and Postcolonial Theory* (pp. 162–171). New York: Columbia University Press.

Ahmed, Laila (1982): "Feminism and Feminist Movements in the Middle East, a Preliminary Exploration: Turkey, Egypt, Algeria, People's Democratic Republic of Yemen". In: Women's Studies Int. Forum (Vol. 5, No. 2, pp. 153–168). Oxford, England: Pergamon Press Ltd.

Al-Hibri, Azizah (1982): A Study of Islamic Herstory: Or how did we ever get into this mess? In: Women's Studies Int. Forum (Vol. 5, No. 2, pp. 207–219). Oxford: Pergamon Press Ltd.

Al-Jabiri, Mohammad Abed (2009): *Democracy, Human Rights and Law in Islamic Thought*. London: I.B. Tauris & Co. Ltd.

Amin, Samir (2009): *Eurocentrism Modernity, Religion, and Democracy: A Critique of Eurocentrism and Culturalism*, transl. by Russel Moore and James Membrez. New York: Monthly Review Press.

Angenot, M (2001): *D'où venons-nous? Où allons-nous? La décomposition de l'idée de progrès*. Montréal: Ed. Trait d'Union.

Aoude, Safia (2011): "Classical Logic in Islamic Philosophy: Creating Dichotomy or Catalyst?" http://aoude.dk/islamiclogic.pdf (last accessed: 1 June 2020).

Arab Charter of Human Rights (ACHR), adopted by the league of the Arab State in September 1994, https://www.equalrightstrust.org/ertdocumentbank/Arab%20Charter%20on%20Human%20Rights.pdf (last accessed: 2 November 2021).

Aristotle: *Politics*, transl. by Ernest Barker. Oxford: Oxford University Press (1946).

Aristotle: *Nicomachean Ethics*, transl. by Harris Rackham. Cambridge: Harvard University Press (1975).

Arkoun, Mohammed (1970): *Contribution à l'étude de l'humanisme Arabe au IV /X siècle Miskawayh (320/325–421) (932/936–1030) Philosophe et Historien*. Paris: J. Vrin.

Arkoun, Mohammed (1972): "Logocentrisme et vérité religieuse dans la pensée islamique: d'après al-I'lam bi-manaqib al-Islam d'al-'Âmirî". In: Studia Islamica (No. 35, pp. 5–51). Paris: Maisonneuve et Larose.

Arkoun, Mohammed (1977): "Scholars whose learning knew no bounds." In: UNESCO Courier: A Golden Age of Arab Culture (pp. 19–22). France: Paris.

Arkoun, Mohammed (1984): "Positivism and Tradition in an Islamic Perspective: Kemalism". In: Sage Journal (Vol. 32, No. 127, pp. 82–100). Paris: University of Paris III.

Arkoun, Mohammed (1985a): "Current Islam Faces its Tradition". In: Serageldin, Ismaill (ed.), *Space for Freedom* (pp. 92–103). London: Butterworth Architecture.

Arkoun, Mohammed (1985b): "Discours Islamique, discours orientalistes et pensée scientifique". In: Comparative Civilisations (Vol. 13, No. 13, Article 8, pp. 90–107). Paris: Université Sorbonne Nouvelle.

Arkoun, Mohammed (1994): *Rethinking Islam: Common Questions, Uncommon Answers*, transl. and ed. by Robert D. Lee. San Francisco, Oxford: Westview Press.

Arkoun, Mohammed (1995): "'Westliche'" Vernunft kontra 'islamische' Vernunft? Versuch einer kritischen Annäherung". In: Michael Lüders (ed.), *Der Islam im Aufbruch? Perspektiven der arabischen Welt* (pp. 261–277). München, Zürich: Piper.

Arkoun, Mohammed (1998 a): "From Inter-Religious Dialogue to the Recognition of the Religious Phenomenon", transl. by John Fletcher. In: Diogene (Vol. 46/2, No. 182, pp. 123–151). Granada: The commission of Catalonia and Andalusia for UNESCO.

Arkoun, Mohammed (1998 b): "Rethinking Islam Today". In: Kurzmann, Charles (ed.), *Liberal Islam. A Source Book* (pp. 205–222). Oxford: Oxford University Press.

Arkoun, Mohammed (1989): "Actualité du problème de la personne dans la pensée islamique". In: Die Welt des Islams, New Series (Vol. 29, No. 1/4, pp. 1–29). Leiden: Brill.

Arkoun, Mohammed (1999): *Der Islam Annäherung an eine Religion*, transl. by Micheal Schiffmann. Heidelberg: Palmyra Verlag.

Arkoun, Mohammed (2002 a): *The Unthought in Contemporary Islamic Thought*. New Delhi: Saqi Books.

Arkoun, Mohammed (2002 b): "Islam et démocratie. Quelle démocratie? Quel Islam?" In: Cités (No. 12, pp. 81–99). France: Cairn Info: Presses Universitaires de France, https://www.cairn.info/revue-cites-2002-4-page-81.htm (last accessed: 22 May 2023).

Arkoun, Mohammed (2003): "Rethinking Islam Today". In: Annals of the American Academy of Political and Social Science (Vol. 588, Islam: Enduring Myths and Changing Realities, pp. 18–39). Los Angeles, London, New Delhi: Sage Publications, Inc. in association with the American Academy of Political and Social Science.

Arkoun, Mohammed (2007): "The Answers of Applied Islamology". In: Theory, Culture and Society (Vol. 24, No. 2, pp. 21–35). London, Thousand Oaks, New Delhi: SAGE.

Arkoun, Mohammed (2008): Humanisme et Islam Combat et proposition. Rabat: Editions Marsam.

Armajani, Jon (2004): *Dynamic Islam: Liberal Muslim Perspectives in a Transnational Age*. Dallas: University Press of America.

Bachelard, Gaston (1938–2002): *The Formation of the Scientific Mind: A Contribution to a Psychoanalysis of Objective Knowledge*. Avon: The Bath Press.

Badran, Margot (2001): "Understanding Islam, Islamism, and Islamic Feminism". In: Journal of Women's History (Vol. 13, No. 1, pp. 47–52). Baltimore: John Hopkins University Press.

Badran, Margot (2002): "Islamic Feminism: What's in a Name?" In: Al-Ahram Weekly Online 17–23 January (No. 569), http://weekly.ahram.org.eg/2002/569/cu1.htm (last accessed: 5 June 2023)

Badran, Margot (2009): *Feminism in Islam: Secular and Religious Convergences*. London: Oneworld Publications.

Badran, Margot (2010 a): "Où en est le féminisme Islamique?" In: Critique Internationale (No. 46, pp. 25–44). France: Presses de Sciences Po.

Badran, Margot (2010 b): "Re/placing Islamic Feminism". In: Critique Internationales (No. 46, No. 10, pp. I–XXI). France: Presses de Science Po.

Barlow, Rebecca and Shahram Akbarzadeh (2006): "Women's Rights in the Muslim World: Reform or Reconstruction?" In Third World Quarterly (Vol. 27, No. 8, pp. 1489–1494). Published by Taylor and Francis Group.

Basheer, Nafi M. (2005): "Tahir ibn 'Ashur: The Career and Thought of a Modern Reformist *'alim*, with Special Reference to His work of *tafsir*". In: Journal of Qur'anic Studies (Vol. 7, No. 1, pp. 1–32). London: Edinburgh University Press.

Bayat, Asef (2007): *Islam and democracy: What is the real question?* Amsterdam: Amsterdam University Press.

Ben Said-Cherni, Zeineb (2016): "La révolution en Tunisie: transformation, immanence et post-Humanisme". In: El Khouni, Mohsen, Mouldi Guessoumi and Mohamed-Salah Omri (eds.), *University and Society within the Context of Arab Revolutions and New Humanism* (pp. 19–26). Tunis: Rosa Luxemburg Foundation.

Benalil, Mounia (2010): "Du mythe au concept: barbarie et historicité dans les essais de Fatima Mernissi". In: Porté (Vol. 38, No. 3, pp. 19–27), http://id.erudit.org/iderudit/045613ar (last accessed: 5 June 2023).

Benbrahim, Yasmina (2017): "Comprendre le féminisme musulman: bribes de réflexion adressées à tous, même ceux qui se croient à l'abri des préjugés". In: Sciences Po Monde Arabe, https://sciencespomondearabe.wordpress.com/2014/10/17/feminisme-et-islam-au-dela-des-cliches (last accessed: 13 August 2022).

Bennani-Chraïbi, Mounia and Mohamed Jeghllaly (2012): "The Protest Dynamics of Casablanca's February 20th Movement", transl. by Sarah Louise Raillard. In: Revue française de science politique (English Edition) (Vol. 62, No. 5–6, pp. 1–41), France: Cairn Info, https://doi.org/10.3917/rfsp.625.867 (last accessed: 5 June 2023).

Benthouhami, Hourya (2017): "Phénoménologie politique du voile Philosophiques". In: Philosophiques (Vol. 44, No. 2, pp. 271–284), https://doi.org/10.7202/1042334ar (last accessed: 29 May 2023).

Bernardi, Florina (2010): "Gazes, targets, (en)visions: reading Fatima Mernissi through Rey Chow". In: Social Semiotics (Vol. 20, No. 4, pp. 411–423), https://www.tandfonline.com/doi/full/10.1080/10350330.2010.494394 (last accessed: 29 May 2023).

Binder, Leonard (1988): *Islamic Liberalism: A Critique of Development Ideologies*. Chicago, London: University of Chicago Press.

Borradori, Giovanna (2008): "Pure Faith in Peace". In: *Islam and the West: A conversation with Jacques Derrida* (pp. xx–xxii). Chicago: University of Chicago Press.

Bouamrane, Chikh (1978): *Le Problème De La Liberté Humaine Dans La pensée Musulmane*. Paris: Libraire philosophique J. Vrin.

Bourdieu, Pierre (2005): *Outline of theory of practice*, transl. by Richard Nice. Cambridge: Cambridge University Press.

Boutni, Khadija (2017): شهادات نساجات تازناخت عن فاطمة المرنيسي. In: Talahite, Fatiha and Rachida Ennaifer (eds.), *Fatema Mernissi et la pensée féministe au Maghreb* (pp. 30–37). Tunis: Editions Journées féministes Maghrébines.

Braudel, Fernand (1992): *Civilization and Capitalism, 15th–18th century, Vol. I, The Structure of Everyday Life: The Limits of the Possible*. Berkeley, Los Angeles: University of California Press.

Brouwer, Lenie and Edien Bartels (2014): "Arab Spring in Morocco: Social Media and the 20 February Movement". In: Afrika Focus (Vol. 27, No. 2, pp. 9–22). Leiden: Brill.

Bruguière, André (2019): *The Annales School: A New Approach to the Study of History*. Paris, New York: Odile Jacob Publishing.

Bullock, Katherine (2010): *Rethinking Muslim Women and the Veil: Challenging Historical & Modern Stereotypes*. London: International Institute of Islamic Thought.

Byrd, Dustin J. (2017): *Islam in a Post-Secular Society: Religion, Secularity and the Antagonism of Recalcitrant Faith*. Leiden, Boston: Brill.

Cairo Declaration of Human Rights (CDHR), 1990, https://www.fmreview.org/sites/fmr/files/FMRdownloads/en/FMRpdfs/Human (last accessed: 2 November 2021)

Castoriadis, Cornelius (1975): *L'institution imaginaire de la société*. Paris: Seuil.

Campanini, Massimo (2009): "Qur'anic Hermeutics and Political Hegemony: Reformation of Islamic Thought". In: The Muslim World, Hartford Seminary (pp. 124–133). Naples: Blackwell Publishing.
Charrad, Mounira M. (1997): "Policy Shifts: State, Islam and Gender in Tunisia, 1930s–1990s". In: Social Politics: International Studies in Gender, State & Society (Vol. 4, No. 2, pp. 284–319). Oxford: Oxford University Press.
Charrad, Mounira M. (2001): *States and Women's Rights: The Making of Postcolonial Tunisia, Algeria, and Morocco*. Berkeley, Los Angeles, London: University of California Press.
Charrad, Mounira M. (2007): "Tunisia at the Forefront of the Arab World: Two Waves of Gender Legislation". In: Washington and Lee Law Review (Vol. 64, No. 4, pp. 1513–27). Lexington: Washington and Lee University.
Charrad, Mounira M. and Amina Zarrugh (2015): "Equal or Complementary? Women in the New Tunisian Constitution after the Arab Spring." In: Khalil Andrea (ed.), *Gender, Women and the Arab Spring* (pp. 100–113). London: Routledge.
Chena, Salim (2011): "L'Algérie dans le 'Printemps Arabe' entre espoirs, initiatives et blogages". In: Confluences Méditerranée (No. 77, pp. 105–118). France: Cairn Info, https://doi.org/10.3917/come.077.0105 (last accessed: 23 June 2023).
Christiano, Tom and Sameer Bajaj (2021): "Democracy". In: Edward N. Zalta (ed.), The Stanford Encyclopedia of Philosophy (Fall 2021 Edition), https://plato.stanford.edu/entries/democracy/ (last accessed: 2 October 21).
Cohen, Robin (2008): *Global Diasporas: An Introduction*, second edition. Taylor and Francis e-Library. London: Routledge.
Cooke, Miriam (1999): "Feminist Transgression in the Postcolonial Arab World". In: Critique: Journal for Critical Studies of Middle East (Vol. 8, No. 14, pp. 93–105). Oxford: Oxford University Press.
Cuthell Jr., David Cameron (2009): "Atatürk, Kemal (Mustafa Kemal)": In Ágoston, Gábor and Masters, Bruce (eds.). *Encyclopedia of the Ottoman Empire*. New York: Facts On File, Inc.
Daiber, Hans (2013): "Humanism: A Tradition Common to both Islam and Europe". In: Filozofija I Društvo Xxiv (1) Religijski I Filozofski Pluralizam: Susret Istoka I Zapada (pp. 293–310). Belgrade, Serbia: Institute for Philosophy and Social Theory.
Dawisha, Adeed (2016): *Arab Nationalism in the Twentieth Century, From Triumph to Despair*. London: Princeton University Press.
Djebar, Assia (1991): *Loin de Medine. Filles d'Ismael*. Paris: Albin Michel.
Deleuze, Gilles and Felix Guattari (1986): *Nomadology: The War Machine (Semiotext(e) / Foreign Agents)*, transl, by Brian Massumi. Los Angeles, USA: Semiotext(e).
Deleuze, Gilles (1994): *Difference and Repetition*, transl. by Paul Patton. New York: Colombia University Press.

Derrida, Jacques (1983): "The Time of a Thesis: Punctuations". In: Montefiore, A. (ed.), *Philosophy in France Today* (pp. 34–51). Cambridge: Cambridge University Press.

Derrida, Jacques (2016): *Of Grammatology*, transl. by Gayatri Spivak, introduction by Judith Butler. Baltimore: Johns Hopkins University Press.

Desrues, Thierry (2013): "Mobilizations in a Hybrid Regime: The 20th February Movement and the Moroccan Regime". In: Current Sociology (Vol. 61, No. 4, pp. 409–423), https://doi.org/10.1177/0011392113479742 (last accessed: 30 May 2023).

Dhouib, Sarhan and Franziska Dübgen (2016): "Der Begriff der Gerechtigkeit: Inter- und Transkulturelle Perspektiven". In: Goppel, Anna, Corinna Mieth and Christian Neuhäuser (eds.), Handbuch Gerechtigkeit (pp. 47–52). Stuttgart: J. B. Metzler.

Dhouib, Sarhan (ed.) (2016): *Gerechtigkeit in transkultureller Perspektive*. Germany: Velbrück Wissenschaft.

Djelloul, Ghaliya (2020): "Femmes et Hirak: pratiques de 'Desserrement' collectif et d'occupation citoyenne de l'espace public". In: Mouvements (Vol. 2, No. 102, pp. 82–90). France: Carin Info, https://doi.org/10.3917/mouv.102.0082 (last accessed: 5 June 2023).

Dobie, Madeleine (2021): "Politics and the Limits of Pluralism in Mohamed Arkoun and Abdenour Bidar"; special focus: Pluralism in Emergenc(i)es in the Middle East and North Africa. In: Review of Middle East Studies (Vol. 54, No. 2, pp. 252–268). Cambridge: Cambridge University Press.

Donnelly, Jack (1999): "Human Rights, Democracy, and Development". In: Human Rights Quarterly (Vol. 21, No. 3, pp. 608–632). Baltimore: Johns Hopkins University Press.

Dübgen, Franziska (2016): "Epistemic Injustice in Practice". In: Wagadu: A Journal of Transnational Women's and Gender Studies (Special Issue, Vol. 15, pp. 1–10).

Dübgen, Franziska (2020): "Transkulturelle Perspektiven auf Gerechtigkeit", Special Issue for: Deutsche Zeitschrift für Philosophie (Vol. 68, No. 6, pp. 891–898). Berlin: De Gruyter.

Dübgen, Franziska (2020): "Scientific Ghettos and Beyond: Injustice in Academia and Its Effects on Researching Poverty". In: Beck, Valentin, Henning Hahn and Robert Lepenies (eds.), *Dimensions of Poverty: Measurement, Epistemic Injustices, Activism* (pp. 77–95) Heidelberg: Springer.

Eddouada, Souad (2008): "Implementing Islamic Feminism: The Case of Moroccan Family Code Reform". In: Anitta Kynsilehto (ed.), *Islamic Feminism: Current Perspective* (pp. 37–46). Finland: Tampere Peace Research Institute.

El-Ayadi, Mohamed (1993): "Mohammed Arkoun ou l'ambition d'une modernité intellectuelle". In: Tozy, Mohamed and Abdou Filali-Ansary (eds.), *Penseurs maghrébins contemporains* (pp. 43–71). Casablanca: Editions Eddif.

El-Hassan, El-Mossadak (2019): *Raison Théologique et Raison Critique: Arkoun et la Reconstruction de la Pensée Islamique*. Casablanca: Centre Culturel du Livre, Edition et Distribution.
El-Saadawi, Nawel (1994): *Memories from the Women's Prison*, transl. By Marilyn Booth. Berkeley, Los Angeles: University of California Press.
El-Saadawi, Nawel (2016): "Nawal El Saadawi and a History of Oppression: Brief Biographical Facts." In *Diary of a Child Called Souad*. London, United Kingdom: Palgrave Macmillan.
Ennaji, Moha (2020): "Mernissi's Impact on Islamic Feminism: A Critique of the Religious Approach". In: British Journal of Middle Eastern Studies (Vol. 49, No. 4, pp. 2–23), https://doi.org/10.1080/13530194.2020.1840963 (last accessed: 30 May 2023).
Esposito John L. and John O. Voll (1996): *Islam and Democracy*. New York: Oxford University Press.
Esposito, John L., Tamara Sonn and John O. Voll (2016): *Islam and Democracy after the Arab Spring*. Oxford: Oxford University Press.
Fakhry, Majid (1975 a): "Justice in Islamic Philosophical Ethics: Miskawayh's Mediating Contribution". In: Journal of Religious Ethics (Vol. 3, No. 2, pp. 243–254). Blackwell Publishing Ltd., https://www.jstor.org/stable/40014897 (last accessed: 22 May 2023).
Fakhry, Majid (1975 b): "The Platonism of Miskawayh and its Implication for his Ethics". In: Studia Islamica (No. 42, pp. 39–57). Paris: Maisonneuve and Larose.
Fakhry, Majid (1991): *Ethical Theories in Islam*. Leiden: Brill.
Fanon, Frantz (1965): *A Dying Colonialism*. Grove Press: New York.
Filali-Ansary, Abdou and Aziz Esmail (2012 a): *The Constructions of Belief: Reflection on the Thought of Mohammed Arkoun*. London: Saqi Books.
Filali-Ansary, Abdou (2012 b): Introduction. In: Ali Abdel Razek, *Islam and the Foundations of Political Power* (pp. 1–17). Pakistan: Aga Khan University: Institute for the Study of Muslim Civilizations.
Flikschuh, Katrin, Rainer Forst and Darrel Moellendorf (2013): "On The Role of the Political Theorist Regarding Global Injustice". Interview by Valentin Beck and Julian Culp for Global Justice: Theory Practice Rhetoric (Vol. 6, pp. 41–53). Frankfurt am Main: Universitätsbibliothek Johann Christian Senckenberg.
Forst, Rainer (2002): *The Contexts of Justice: Political Philosophy beyond Liberalism and Communitarianism*, transl. by J. M. M. Farrell. California: University of California Press.
Foucault, Michel (1966): *Les mots et les choses. Une archéologie des sciences humaines*. Paris: Gallimard.
Gaskill, Tom (1998): "Al-Amiri, Abu'l Hasan Muhammad ibn Yusuf". In: Craig, Edward (ed.), Routledge Encyclopedia of Philosophy (pp. 207–208). London: Taylor and Francis.

Geoffroy, Eric (2010): *Introduction to Sufism: the Inner Path of Islam*, transl. by Roger Gaetani. United States: World Wisdom.

Grami, Amel (2016): "The Debate on Religion, Law and Gender in Post-Revolution Tunisia". In: Seyla Benhabib and Kaul Volker (eds.), *Toward New Democratic Imaginaries* (pp. 301–313). İstanbul Seminars on Islam, Culture and Politics. Heidelberg: Springer.

Grami, Amel (2018): "Women, Feminism and Politics in Post Revolution Tunisia". In Feminist Dissent (Vol. 3, pp. 23–56), https://journals.warwick.ac.uk/index.php/feministdissent/article/view/292 (last accessed: 30 May 2023).

Graham, William A (1982): "Transcendence in Islam". In: Edwin Dowdy (ed.), *Ways of Transcendence: Insights from Major Religions and Modern Thought* (Vol. 4, pp. 7–23). Australia: Bedford Park.

Guessous, Nouzha (2016): "Le(s) féminisme(s) de Fatéma Mernissi", Article développé par l'auteure, Nouzha Guessous, à partir de la présentation orale qu'elle a faite à la 6éme édition du Festival Méditerranéen des Ecrits de Femmes organisées par l'association le Féminin Pluriel au Rabat (Maroc), les 28 et le 29 avril 2016 (en cours de publication dans les actes du colloques), http://economia.ma/content/les-f%C3%A9minismes-de-fat%C3%A9ma-mernissi/ (last accessed: 6 June 2023).

Gutas, Dmitri (1998): *Greek Thought, Arabic Culture. The Graeco-Arabic Translation Movement in Baghdad and Early 'Abbasid Society (2nd–4th/8th–10th centuries)*. London, New York: Routledge.

Günther, Ursula (2004 a): "Mohammed Arkoun: Towards a Radical Rethinking of Islamic Thought". In: Taji-Farouki, Suha (ed.), *Modern Muslim Intellectuals and the Qur'ān* (pp. 125–167). New York, Oxford: Oxford University Press.

Günther, Ursula (2004 b): *Mohammed Arkoun. Ein moderner Kritiker der islamischen Vernunft*. Würzburg: Ergon.

Günther, Ursula (2010): "Obituary for Mohammed Arkoun: A Pioneer of Modern Critical Islam Studies", https://en.qantara.de/content/obituary-for-mohammed-arkoun-a-pioneer-of-modern-critical-islam-studies (last accessed: 12 December 2022).

Günther, Ursula (2013): "Mohammed Arkoun: An Intellect in Revolt." In: Middle East – Topics and Arguments (pp. 63–67).

Günther, Ursula (2019): "Mohammed Arkoun's Quest for a Radical Re-Reading of Islamic Tradition". In: Symposium, DFG-Projekt "Diversität, Macht, und Gerechtigkeit. Transkulturelle Perspektiven", unter der Leitung von Franziska Dübgen und Ina Kerner (05.12.–06. 12. 2019). Münster: Universität Münster.

Habermas, Jürgen (2008): "Secularism's Crisis of Faith." In: New Perspective Quarterly (Vol. 25, No. 4, pp. 17–29).

Hall, Kim and Ásta (2021): "What is Feminist Philosophy?" In: The Oxford Book of Feminist Philosophy. Oxford: Oxford University Press.

Hallaq, Wael B. (1984): "Was the Gate of Ijtihad Closed?" In: International Journal of Middle East Studies (Vol. 16, No. 1, pp. 3–41). Cambridge: Cambridge University Press.

Hamblin, Amy (2015): "The Struggle for Political Legitimacy". In: William Zartman (ed.), *Arab Spring Negotiating in the Shadow of the Intifadat* (pp. 183–208). Athens, London: The University of Georgia Press.

Harrison, Olivia C. (2016): "Abrahamic Tongues: Abdelkebir Khatibi, Jacques Hassoun, Jacques Derrida." In *Transcolonial Maghreb: Imagining Palestine in the Era of Decolonization*, 1st ed. (pp. 101–28). Stanford: Stanford University Press, https://doi.org/10.2307/j.ctvqsds4d.10 (last accessed: 17 March 2023).

Hashas, Mohammed (2015): "Mohamed Arkoun: Unveiling Orthodoxy and Hegemony through Spiritual Responsibility", https://www.resetdoc.org/story/mohamed-arkoun-unveiling-orthodoxy-and-hegemony-through-spiritual-responsibility/ (last accessed: 6 January 2022).

Hatem, Mervat (1987): "Class and Patriarchy as Competing Paradigms for the Study of Middle Eastern Women". In: Comparative Studies in Society and History (Vol. 29, No. 4, pp. 811–818). Cambridge: Cambridge University Press.

Hawthorne, Melvill (2007): "The Historical Development of Western Feminism". In: Encyclopedia of Sex and Gender (pp. 539–542). USA: Macmillan Inc.

Hegasy, Sonja (2009): Portrait of the Philosopher Mohammed Abed al-Jabri: Critique of Arab Reason, https://en.qantara.de/content/portrait-of-the-philosopher-mohammed-abed-al-jabri-critique-of-arab-reason-0 (last accessed: 17 March 2023).

Hobuß, Steffi, Lina Khiari-Loch and Moez Maataoui (eds.) (2019): *Tunesische Transformationen. Feminismus – Geschlechterverhältnisse – Kultur. Tunesisch-deutsche Perspektiven*. In: Gender Studies. Bielefeld: transcript.

Huff, Toby E. (1995): "Rethinking Islam and Fundamentalism". In: Sociological Forum (Vol. 10, No. 3, pp. 502–518). Oxford: Plenum Publishing Corporation.

Husain Syed, Muzaffar, Sayed Saud Akhtar and Babuddin Usmani (eds.) (2011): *A Concise History of Islam*. New Delhi: Vij Books.

Ibn Anas, Malik (2010): *Al-Muwatta of Imam Malik ibn Anas: The First Formulation of Islamic Law*, transl. by Aisha Abdurrahman. Bewely, London, New York: Routledge.

International Covenant on Economic, Social and Cultural Rights (ICESCR), adopted and opened for signature, ratification, and accession by General Assembly resolution 2200A (XXI) of 16 December 1966, entry into force 3 January 1976, https://www.ohchr.org/en/professionalinterest/pages/cescr.aspx (last accessed: 2 November 2021).

Ishaque, Nausheen (2019): "Empowerment through Disempowerment: Harem and the Covert Female Resistance in Fatima Mernissi's *Dreams of Trespass: Tales of a Harem Girlhood*". In: Cultural Dynamics (Vol. 30, No. 4, pp. 284–302).

Irving, Sarah. (2016): "Amin, Qasim أمين قاسم (1863–1908)." In: The Routledge Encyclopedia of Modernism. https://www.rem.routledge.com/articles/amin-qasim-1863-1908.

Jebnoun, Noureddine (2014): "Ben Ali' Tunisia: The Authoritarian Path of a Dystopian State". In: Jebnoun, Noureddine, Mehrdad Kia and Mimi Kirk (eds.), *Modern Middle East Autocriticism: Roots, Ramifications, and Crisis* (pp. 103–117). USA, Canada: Routledge.

Jeffery, Kenny T. (2006): *Muslim Rebels: Kharijites and the Politics of Extremism in Egypt*. Oxford: Oxford University Press.

Jules, Tavis D. (2017): "Tunisia: An Overview." In Kirdar (ed.), *Education in the Arab World* (pp. 369–387). London: Bloomsbury Academic.

Kahlil, Unsman and Abida Khan (2013): "Islam and Postmodernity: Mohammed Arkoun's Deconstruction Method". In: Journal of Islamic Thought and Civilization (Vol. 3, No. 2, pp. 79–87), http://admin.umt.edu.pk/Media/Site/UMT/SubSites/jitc/FileManager/JITC%20Spring%202013/2.%20Islam%20and%20Postmodernity.pdf (last accessed: 6 June 2023).

Kamali, Muhammad Hashim (1989): "Sources, Nature, and Objectives of Shari'ah". In: Islamic Quarterly (Vol. 33, No. 4, pp. 216–234). London: The Islamic Cultural Centre.

Karoui, Kaouther (2020): "Relektüren des Klassisch-islamischen Erbes für eine Gerechtigkeitsgrammatik der Gegenwart". In: Transkulturelle Perspektiven auf Gerechtigkeit, Special Issue for: Deutsche Zeitschrift für Philosophie (Vol. 68, No. 6, pp. 915–927) Berlin: De Gruyter.

Karoui, Kaouther (2021): "The Theory of Justice between the Humanism of the Classical Muslim Thinker Miskawayh and the Contemporary Thought Project of Mohammed Arkoun". In: Günther, Sebastian and Yassir El Jamouhi (eds.), *Islamic Ethics as Educational Discourse: Thought and Impact of the Classical Muslim Thinker Miskawayh (d. 1030)* (pp. 321–336). Tübingen: Mohr Siebeck.

Karshenas, Massoud, Valentine Moghadam and Randa Alami (2014): "Social Policy after the Arab Spring: States and Social Rights in the MENA Region". In: World Development (Vol. 64, pp. 726–739). Amsterdam: Elsevier Ltd.

Kersten, Carool (2010): The 'Applied Islamology' of Mohammed Arkoun. Conference: Religion on the Borders: New Challenges in the Academic Studies of Religion. Stockholm 2007, https://www.academia.edu/237854/The_Applied_Islamology_of_Mohammed_Arkoun_2007_ (last accessed: 1 June 2020).

Kersten, Carool (2019): *Contemporary Thought in the Muslim World: Trends, Themes, Issues*. London, New York: Routledge.

Khadduri, Majid (1984): *The Islamic Conception of Justice*. London: Johns Hopkins University Press.

Khatibi, Abdelkebir (2019): *Plural Maghreb: Writings on Postcolonialism*, transl. by P. Burcu Yalim. London: Bloomsbury Academic.

The King James Version of the Holy Bible. Original publish date: March, 2001; revised: January 2004. PDF Bible: Download pdf book of the Bible and free Podcast (holybooks.com) (last accessed: 6 June 2023).

Kleingeld, Pauline and Eric Brown (2006): "Cosmopolitanism". In: Stanford Encyclopedia of Philosophy (Fall 2019 Edition), https://plato.stanford.edu/archives/win2019/entries/cosmopolitanism/ (last accessed: 6 June 2023).

König, Daniel (2016): "Islamic Studies: A Field of Research under Transcultural Crossfire". In: The Journal of Transcultural Studies (Vol. 7, No. 2. pp. 101–135). Heidelberg: The Heidelberg Center for Transcultural Studies (HCTS) at Heidelberg University, https://doi.org/10.17885/heiup.ts.2016.2.23600 (last accessed: 24 May 2023).

Kraemer, Joel L. (1993): *Humanism in the Renaissance of Islam: The Cultural Revival during the Buyid Age*. 2nd rev. ed. Leiden: Brill.

Kurtulmus, Faik and Gürol Irzik (2021): "Distributive Epistemic Justice in Science". In: The British Journal for the Philosophy of Science. Chicago: University of Chicago Press, https://doi.org/10.1086/715351 (last accessed: 2 November 2021).

Kynsilehto, Anitta (ed.) (2008): "Islamic Feminism: Current Perspectives. Introductory Notes." In: *Islamic Feminism: Current Perspectives* (pp. 7–9). Finland: Tampere Peace Research Institute.

Layachi, Azzedine (2005): "The Berber in Algeria: Politicized Ethnicity and Ethnicized Politics". In Shatzmiller, Maya (ed.), Nationalism and Minority Identities in Islamic Societies (pp. 195–228). Montreal, Kingston, London, Ithaca: McGill-Queen's University Press.

Lazreg, Marina (1994): *The Eloquence of Silence: Algerian Women in Question*. London, New York: Routledge.

Lee, Robert D. (1994): "Forwards." In: *Rethinking Islam Common Questions Uncommon Answers* (pp. vii–xiii). Oxford: Westview Press.

Leman, Olivier (2008): "Ibn Miskawayh." In: Leman, Olivier and Seyyed Hossein Nasr (eds.), *History of Islamic Philosophy* (pp. 466–476). London, New York: Routledge.

Mahboub, Samira (2016): "Fatima Mernissi: Moroccan Scholar and Pioneer of Islamic Feminism". In: Soziopolis: Gesellschaft beobachten, https://nbn-resolving.org/urn:nbn:de:0168-ssoar-80363-3 (last accessed: 30 May 2023).

Majid, Anouar (1998): "The Politics of Feminism in Islam." In: Signs: Journal of Women in Culture and Society (Vol. 23, No. 2, pp. 321–361). USA: University of Chicago Press.

Martin, Richard C., Mark. R. Woodward and Dwi S. Atmaja (1997): *Defenders of Reason in Islam: Mu'tazilism from Medieval School to Modern Symbol*. Oxford: Oneworld Publications.

Martin, Richard C., Heather J. Empey, Mohammed Arkoun and Andrew Rippin (2009): "Islamic Studies". In: John L. Esposito (ed.), Oxford Encyclopedia of the Islamic World, https://www.oxfordreference.com/display/10.1093/acref/97801

95305135.001.0001/acref-9780195305135-e-0395#acref-9780195305135-section-16 01 (last accessed: 1 March 2023).

Mas, Ruth (1998): "Qiyas: A Study in Islamic Logic". In: Folia Orientalia (Vol. 34, pp. 113–128), ISSN 0015–5675, http://www.colorado.edu/ReligiousStudies/faculty/mas/LOGIC.pdf (last accessed: 1 June 2020).

Mas, Ruth (2021): "What, to the Modern, is Miskawayh? An Epilogue." In Günther, Sebastian and Yassir El Jamouhi (eds.), *Islamic Ethics as Educational Discourse: Thought and Impact of the Classical Muslim Thinker Miskawayh (d. 1030)* (pp. 338–342). Tübingen: Mohr Siebeck.

Mason, Herbert (1991): *The Death of Al-Hallaj: A Dramatic Narrative*, United States: Notre Dame Press.

Massignon, Louis (1975): *La passion de Hallaj, martyre mystique de l'Islam*, 4 vols., Paris: Gallimard.

Mbembe, Achille (2003): "Necropolitics", transl. by Libby Meintjes. In: Public Culture (Vol. 15, No. 1, pp. 11–40), Durham: Duke University Press.

Mbembe, Achille (2008): "What is Postcolonial Thinking", transl. by John Fletcher (pp. 1–13). Eurozine https://www.eurozine.com: Esprit.

Mernissi, Fatima (1991): *The Veil and the Male Elite: A Feminist Interpretation of Women's Rights in Islam*. Basic Books: New York.

Mernissi, Fatima (1993): *The Forgotten Queens of Islam*. Minneapolis: University of Minnesota Press.

Mernissi, Fatima (1994): *Dreams of Trespass: Tales of a Harem Girlhood*. New York: Basic Books.

Mernissi, Fatima (1996): "Palace Fundamentalism and Liberal Democracy: Oil, Arms and Irrationality". In: Development and Change (Vol. 27, No. 2, pp. 215–256). Oxford: Blackwell Publishers.

Mernissi, Fatima (2001): *Scheherazade Goes West: Different Cultures, Different Harems*. New York: Washington Square Press.

Mernissi, Fatima (2002): *Islam And Democracy: Fear of the Modern World*. New York: Basic Books.

Mernissi, Fatima (2003): *Beyond the Veil: Male-Female Dynamics in Modern Muslim Society*. London: Saqi Books.

Mernissi, Fatima and Francesco Alfonso Leccese (2006): "The New Arab Mass Media: Vehicles Democracy? Interview with Fatima Mernissi." In Oriente Moderno, Nuova Serie (Anno 25 (86), No. 2, pp. 345–356). Rome: Istituto per l'Oriente C.A. Nallino.

Mestiri, Soumaya (2010): "Islam as a Democratic Interlocutor? Towards a Global Concept of Democracy." In SAGE (226, pp. 1–11). Los Angeles, London, New Delhi, Singapore: Diogenes.

Mestiri, Soumaya (2016): *Décoloniser le féminise: Une approche Transculturelle*. France: Vrin.

Micheau, Francoise (1997): "Mécènes et médecins à Bagdad au IIIe/ IX e siècle: Les commentaires des traductions de Galien par Hunayn ibn Ishaq". In: *Les Voies de la Science Grecque: Etude sur la transmission des textes de l'Antiquité au dix-neuvième siècle*. Genève: Librairie Droz.

Mignolo, Walter. D. (2011): *The Darker Side of Western Modernity: Global Futures, Decolonial Options*. Durham, London: Duke University Press.

Mir-Hosseini, Ziba (2006): "Muslim Women's Quest for Equality: Between Islamic Law and Feminism". In: Critical Inquiry (Vol. 32, No. 4, pp. 629–645). Chicago: University of Chicago Press.

Mirsepassi, Ali (2014 a): "Fatima Mernissi: 'Locally' Rooted Cosmopolitanism", in *Islam, Democracy, and Cosmopolitanism* (pp. 178–198). Cambridge: Cambridge University Press.

Mirsepassi, Ali (2014 b): "Arkoun's 'The Unthought in Islamic Thought'". In: *Islam, Democracy, and Cosmopolitanism* (pp. 135–155). Cambridge: Cambridge University Press.

Miskawayh, Ahmad ibn-Muhammad (2002): *The Refinement of Character*, transl. by Constantine K. Zurayk; Seyyed Hosssein Nasr (ed.). USA: KAZI Publications.

Moghadam, Valentine M. (2002): "Islamic Feminism and Its Discontents: Toward a Resolution of the Debate". In: Journal of Women in Culture and Society (Vol. 27, No. 4, pp. 1135–1171), https://doi.org/10.1086/339639 (last accessed: 23 May 2023).

Moghadam, Valentine M. (2005): "Women's Rights in the Middle East and North Africa- Tunisia." In: Freedom House, https://www.refworld.org/docid/47387b702f.html (accessed 6 June 2023).

Moghadam, Valentine. M. (2007): "Qu'est-ce que le féminisme musulman? Pour la promotion d'un changement culturel en faveur de l'égalité des genres" intervention au colloque des 18–19 septembre 2006, organisé par Islam et laïcité. Existe-t-il un féminisme musulman? Paris: Pensamiento Critico.

Moghadam, Valentine M. (2018): "The State and the Women's Movement in Tunisia: Mobilization, Institutionalization, and Inclusion". In: The James A. Baker III Institute for Public Policy (pp. 3–22). Houston, Texas: The James A. Baker III Institute for Public Policy of Rice University.

Moghadam, Valentine M. (2020): "Gender Regimes in the Middle East and North Africa: The Power of Feminist Movements". In: Social Politics (Vol. 27, No. 3, pp. 467–485). Oxford: Oxford University Press.

Mohamed, Yasien (2000): "Greek Thought in Arab Ethics: Miskawayh's Theories of Justice". In: Phronimon (Vol. 2, No. 1, pp. 242–259).

Moura, Jean-Marc (1999): *Littérature francophones et théorie postcoloniale*. Paris: PUF.

Naugle, David K. (2002): *Worldview: The History of a Concept*. Cambridge: Williams B. Eerdmans Publishing Company.

Noram, Richard (2012): *On humanism*. London: Routledge.

Parisi, Laura (2017): "Feminist Perspectives on Human Rights". In: International Studies Associations. Oxford University Press, https://doi.org/10.1093/acrefore/9780190846626.013.48 (last accessed: 2 November 2021).

Pepicelli, Renta (2008): "Islamic Feminism: Identities And Positionalities: Why Keep Asking Me about My Identity? Thoughts of a Non-Muslim." In Anitta Kynsilehto (ed.), *Islamic Feminism Current Perspective* (pp. 91–101). Finland: Tampere Peace Research Institute.

Plato: *The Republic of Plato*, ed. by James Adam (10 vols., vol. i). Cambridge: Cambridge University Press (2009).

Pogge, Tomas (ed.) (2001): *Global Justice*. Oxford: Blackwell Publishing.

Pogge, Tomas (2001): "Priorities of Global Justice". In: *Metaphilosophy* (Vol. 32, No. 1–2, pp. 6–24). Oxford: Blackwell Publishers Ltd.

The Qurʾān. Translated by M.A.S. Abdel Haleem. New York: Oxford University Press Inc (2005).

Rachik, Hassan and Rahma Bouriqa (2011): "La sociologie au Maroc Grandes étapes et Jalons Thématiques", Revue *Sociologies*, Théories et recherches, mis en ligne le 18 octobre 2011, http://sociologies.revues.org/3719 (last accessed: 2 November 2021).

Radez, John Peter (2015): La vie est plus belle que les idées. Existentialist Humanism, Intersubjectivity and Transcendence in the Unified Civic Humanism of Abu ʿAli Ahmad ibn Mohummed ibn Yaqʿub Miskawayh (PhD dissertation; Indiana University Bloomington).

Radi, Abdelaziz (2017): "Protest Movements and Social Media: Morocco's February 20 Movement". In: Africa Development (Vol. XLII, No. 2, pp. 31–55), http://www.jstor.org/stable/90018190 (last accessed: 6 June 2023).

Rawls, John (1971–1999): *A Theory of Justice*. Cambridge: Harvard University Press.

Rhouni, Raja (2005): Secular and Islamic Feminist Critiques in the Work of Fatima Mernissi: Toward a Post-Foundational Islamic Feminism (PhD dissertation; Rabat: University Mohammad V).

Rhouni, Raja (2008): "Rethinking Islamic Feminist Hermeneutics: The Case of Fatima Mernissi". In Anitta Kynsilehto (ed.), *Islamic Feminism Current Perspective* (pp. 103–114). Finland: Tampere Peace Research Institute.

Rhouni, Raja (2010): *Secular and Islamic Feminist Critiques in the Work of Fatima Mernissi*. Leiden: Brill.

Riffat, Hassan (1996): "Rights of Women within Islamic Communities". In: John Witte, Jr. and John D. van der Vyver (eds.), *Religious Human Rights In Global Perspective Religious Perspective* (pp. 361–386). The Hague, Boston, London: Martinus Nijhoff.

Rouibah, Hayette (2021): "Le rôle de la femme Algérienne dans le changement politique". In: Recherches Juridiques et Politiques (Vol. 6, No. 1, pp. 585–601). Algeria: Université de Jijel.

Rouighi, Ramzi (2019 a): "Race on the mind", https://aeon.co/essays/how-the-west-made-arabs-and-berbers-into-races (last accessed: 5 April 2023).

Rouighi, Ramzi (2019 b): Inventing the Berbers: History and Ideology in the Maghrib. Philadelphia: University of Pennsylvania Press.

Roger, Arnaldez (2005): "l'analyse des sept arguments mu'tazilites". In: Les sciences coraniques: Grammaire, droit, théologie et mystique (pp. 130–132). Paris: J. Vrin.

Rowson, Everett K. (2008): Al-'Amiri. In: Leman, Olivier and Seyyed Hossein Nasr (eds.), *History of Islamic Philosophy* (pp. 405–415). London, New York: Routledge Digital Printing.

Royle, Nicolas (2003): *Jacques Derrida*. London, New York: Routledge.

Sadiqi, Fatima (2006): "The Impact of Islamization on Moroccan Feminisms". In: Journal of Women in Culture and Society (Vol 32, No. 1, pp. 32–40): Chicago: University of Chicago Press.

Sadiqi, Fatima and Moha Ennaji (2006): "The Feminization of Public Space: Women's Activism, the Family Law, and Social Change in Morocco". In: Journal of Middle East Women's Studies (Vol. 2, No. 2, pp. 86–114). Durham, North Carolina: Duke University Press.

Sadiqi, Fatima (2009): "Language, Gender and Power in Morocco". In: Herzog, Hanna and Ann Braude (eds.), *Gendering Religion and Politics: Untangling Modernities* (pp. 260–275). New York: Palgrave.

Sadiqi, Fatima (2016): "Introduction: The Centrality of Women's Movements in the Post-revolution Dynamics in North Africa". In: Fatima Sadiqi (ed.), *Women's Movement in Post-"Arab Spring" North Africa* (pp. 1–11). New York, Palgrave.

Said, Edward (1994 a): "From Orientalism". In: Williams, Patrick and Laura Chrisman (eds.), *Colonial Discourse and Postcolonial Theory* (pp. 132–149). New York: Columbia University Press.

Said, Edward (1994 b): The Pen and the Sword. Monroe. Maine: Common Courage Press.

Said, Edward (2003): Orientalism. London: Penguin Classics.

Salem, Chaker (1991): "La question Berbère dans l'Algérie indépendante: La fracture inévitable?". In: *L'Algérie Incertaine* (No. 65, pp. 97–105). Revue du monde musulman et de la Méditerranée. Lyon: Persée.

Samir, Samir Khalil (2013): *Rôle des Chrétiens dans la civilisation arabe*. In: Juan Pedro Monferrer Sala (ed.), *Eastern Crossroads* (pp. 4–30). Gorgias Eastern Christian Studies: Gorgias Press.

Santos, Boaventura de Sousa (2007): "Beyond Abyssal Thinking: From Global Lines to Ecologies of Knowledge". In: Review (Fernand Braudel Center) (Vol. 30, No. 1, pp. 45–89). New York: Research Foundation of State University of New York.

Schimmel, Annemarie (1968): *Al-Halladsch, Martyrer der Gottesliebe; Leben und Legende*. Köln: J. Hegner.

Schimmel, Annemarie (1975): *Mystical Dimensions of Islam*. Chapel Hill: University of North Carolina Press.

Schimmel, Annemarie (1982): "Women in Mystical Islam". In: Women's Studies Int. Forum (Vol. 5, No. 2, pp. 145–151). Oxford: Pergamon Press Ltd.

Schimmel, Annemarie (1995): *Mystische Dimensionen des Islam. Die Geschichte des Sufismus*. Leipzig: Insel.

Schimmel, Annemarie (1996): *Le Soufisme ou les dimensions mystiques de L'Islam*. Paris: Cerf.

Schmidkte, Sabine (2000): *Theologie, Philosophie und Mystik im zwölferschiitischen Islam des 9./15. Jahrhunderts Die Gedankenwelten des Ibn Abī Ǧumhūr al-Aḥsāʾī (um 838/1434/35 – nach 906/1501)*. Brill, Leiden, Boston, Köln.

Schönberger, Thomas (2010): "'Pushing the Limits': Introduction to the Ideas and Methods of Mohammed Arkoun with Special Regard to his Interpretation of Revelation", https://globulous2.files.wordpress.com/2010/02/arkoun-e28093-paper.pdf (last accessed: 1 June 2020).

Seedat, Fatima (2013): "Islam, Feminism, and Islamic Feminism: Between Inadequacy and Inevitability". In: Journal of Feminist Studies in Religion (Vol. 29, No. 2, pp. 25–45). Bloomington: Indiana University Press.

Serequeberhan, Tsenay (1996): "Eurocentrism in Philosophy: The Case of Immanuel Kant". In: Philosophical Forum (Vol. 27, No. 4, pp. 333–356). Boston: Simmons College.

Shaikh, Ameer U. (2002): *The Unthought in Contemporary Islamic Thought: Mohammad Arkoun*. London: Saqi Books, 2002. 352 pages, A Review. In: The American Journal of Islamic Social Sciences (Vol. 21, No. 1, pp. 100–102). Pennsylvania: Temple University School of Law Philadelphia.

Shiyab, Mohammad Khalid (2014): "Mohammed Arkoun's Criticism of 'Religious Mind'". In: Jordan Journal of Social Sciences (Vol. 8, No. 3, pp. 391–405). Jordan: University Sumaya.

Soekarba, Siti Rohmah (2006): "The Critique of Arab Thought: Mohammed Arkoun's Deconstruction Method". In: [MAKARA Seri Sosial Humaniora] MAKARA of Social Sciences and Humanities Series (Vol. 10, No. 2, pp. 79–87). Indonesia: Universitas Indonesia.

Soulié, Charles (1998): "Histoire du département de philosophie de Paris VIII. Le destin d'une institution d'avant-garde." In: Histoire de l'éduction (No. 77, pp. 47–69).

Talahite, Fatiha and Rachida Ennaifer (eds.) (2017): *Fatema Mernissi et la pensée féministe au Maghreb*. Tunis: Editions Journées féministes Maghrébines.

Taher, Haddad (1930–2007): *Muslim Women in Law and Society*, Annotated translation of *al-Tahir al-Haddad's Imra 'tuna fī 'l-sharia wa 'l-mujtama*, with an introduction. London: Routledge.

Tlemçani, Rachid (2016): "The Algerian Woman Issue: Struggles, Islamic Violence,and Co-optation." In: Fatima Sadiqi (ed.), *Women's movements in Post-"Arab*

Spring" North Africa (pp. 236- 249). London, United Kingdom: Palgarve Macmillan.
Tunisia: Pact for Equality, Individual Freedom 2018, https://www.hrw.org/news/2018/07/24/tunisia-pact-equality-individual-freedom. (last accessed: 8 June 2023). https://www.statista.com/statistics/1186480/unemployment-rate-in-algeria-by-gender/ (last accessed: 8 June 2023). https://www.statista.com/statistics/524516/unemployment-rate-in-tunisia/ (last accessed: 8 June 2023). https://www.statista.com/statistics/1266491/quarterly-unemployment-rate-in-morocco/ (last accessed: 8 June 2023). https://www.aljazeera.net/programs/almashaa/2014/7/10/الرباط-فاطمة-والسندباد (last accessed: 16 August 2021).
The United Nations Economic and Social Commission for Western Asia: Social Policy Brief – 8 (2016), Unemployment of Young Women in the Arab Region: Causes and Intervention.
Universal Declaration of Human Rights (UDHR) adopted by the United Nation General Assembly on 10 December 1948, https://www.un.org/en/about-us/universal-declaration-of-human-rights (last accessed: 2 November 2021).
Universal Islamic Declaration of Human Rights (UIDHR) (2008): adopted by the *Islamic Council of Europe* on 19 September 1981. In: Refugee Survey Quarterly Vol. 27, No. 2, pp. 70–80): Oxford: Oxford University Press.
Urbinati, Nadia (2012): "Representative democracy and its critics". In: Alonso, Sonia, John Keane and Wolfgang Merkel with the collaboration of Maria Fotou (eds.), *The Future of Representative Democracy* (pp. 23–49). Cambridge: Cambridge University Press.
Völker, Katharina (2014): "Mohammad Arkoun: The Quran Rethought: Genesis, Significance, and the Study of the Quran". In: Weber, Edmund (ed.), Journal of Religious Culture, https://publikationen.ub.uni-frankfurt.de/opus4/frontdoor/index/index/docId/33656 (last accessed: 22 May 2023). Frankfurt am Main: Goethe University.
Völker, Katharina (2015): "The Humanisti [sic] Heritage of Muhammad Arkoun". In: Philosophical Investigations (Vol. 9, No. 17, pp. 204–227). Otago: The University of Otago Postgraduate Research Scholarship and the UO Publishing Bursary.
Volpi, Frédéric (2013): "Algeria versus the Arab Spring". In: Journal of Democracy (Vol. 24, No. 3, pp. 104–115). Baltimore: Johns Hopkins University Press.
Volpi, Frédéric (2020): Algeria: When Elections Hurt Democracy. In: Journal of Democracy (Vol. 31, No. 2, pp. 152–165). Baltimore: Johns Hopkins University Press.
Von Beyme, Klaus (2012): "Representative democracy and the populist temptation". In: Alonso, Sonia, John Keane and Wolfgang Merkel with the collaboration of Maria Fotou (eds.), *The Future of Representative Democracy* (pp. 50–73). Cambridge: Cambridge University Press.

Wadud, Amina (1999): *Qur'an and Woman: Rereading the Sacred Text from a Woman's Perspective*. New York: Oxford University Press.

Williams, Patrick and Laura Chrisman (1994): "Colonial Discourse and Postcolonial Theory: Introduction". In: *Colonial Discourse and Postcolonial Theory* (pp. 1–20). New York: Columbia University Press.

Wolfs, José-Luis and Samira El-Boudamoussi (2004): "Le concept de 'réflexivité' est-il connoté culturellement ? (Qu'en est-il en particulier dans le monde 'arabo-musulman' ? Ed. Marc Derycke and Jean-Luc Marc Pommier. In: *Le retour réflexif, ses entours, ses détours* (Vol. 25–26, pp. 22–30). France: Presses universitaires de Saint Etienne.

Yacoubi, Youssef (2020): "Redirecting Postcolonial Theory – إعادة توجيه نظرية ما بعد الكولونيالية: Arab-Islamic Reason, Deconstructionism, and the Possibility of Multiple Critique". In: Alif Journal of Comparative Poetics (No. 40, Mapping New Directions in the Humanities / خريطة معرفية: الإنسانية في العلوم جديدة اتجاهات, pp. 85–114). Cairo: American University of Cairo.

Youssef, Olfa (2016): *Sept Controverses En Islam Parlons-En*. Tunis: Éditions elyzad.

Zayzafoon, Lamia Ben Youssef (2005): *The Production of the Muslim Woman: Negotiating Text, History and Ideology*. USA: Lexington Books.

Zeghal, Malika (2012): "Veiling and Unveiling Muslim Women: State Coercion, Islam, and the '"Disciplines of the Heart"'. In: Filali-Ansary, Abdou and Aziz Esmail (eds.), *The Construction of Belief: Reflections on the Thought of Mohammed Arkoun* (pp. 127–149). London: Saqi Books.

Zeghal, Malika (2013): "Competing Ways of Life: Islamism, Secularism, and Public Order in the Tunisian Transition." In: Constellations (Vol. 20, No. 2, pp. 254–274). Oxford: John Wiley and Sons Ltd.

Zemni, Sami (2013): "From Socio-economic Protest to National Revolt: The Labor Origins of the Tunisian Revolution". In: Gana, Nouri (ed.), *The Making of the Tunisian Revolution: Contexts, Architects, Prospects* (pp. 127–146). Edinburgh: Edinburgh University Press.

Zuckert, Catherine (1991): "The Politics of Derridean Deconstruction". In: Polity (Vol. 23, No. 3, pp. 335–356). Chicago: University of Chicago Press on behalf of the Northeastern Political Science Association.

Zurayk, Constantine (2002): Seyyed Hossein Nasr (ed.), *Refinement of Character (Tahdib al-Akhlaq): Ahmad ibn Muhammad Miskawayh*. USA: KAZI Publications.

[transcript]

PUBLISHING.
KNOWLEDGE. TOGETHER.

transcript publishing stands for a multilingual transdisciplinary programme in the social sciences and humanities. Showcasing the latest academic research in various fields and providing cutting-edge diagnoses on current affairs and future perspectives, we pride ourselves in the promotion of modern educational media beyond traditional print and e-publishing. We facilitate digital and open publication formats that can be tailored to the specific needs of our publication partners.

OUR SERVICES INCLUDE

- partnership-based publishing models
- Open Access publishing
- innovative digital formats: HTML, Living Handbooks, and more
- sustainable digital publishing with XML
- digital educational media
- diverse social media linking of all our publications

Visit us online: www.transcript-publishing.com

Find our latest catalogue at www.transcript-publishing.com/newbookspdf